A GUIDE
TO THE
ARCHAEOLOGICAL
SITES OF
ISRAEL, EGYPT
AND
NORTH AFRICA

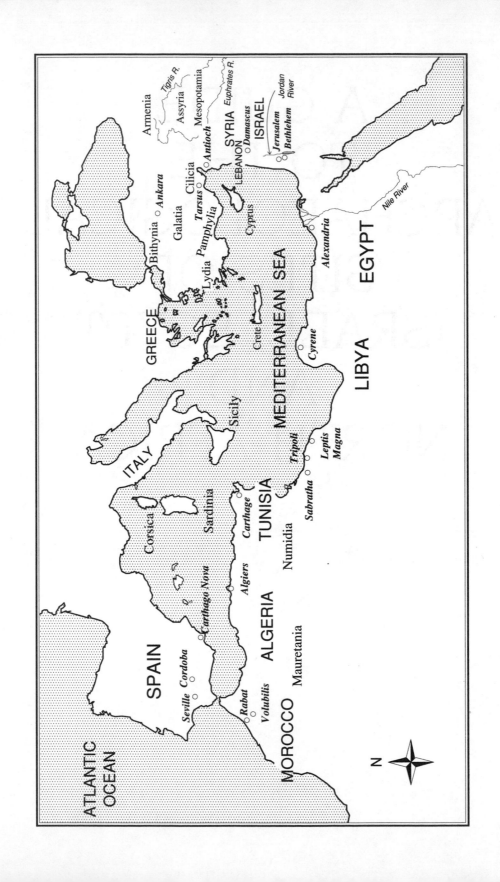

A GUIDE
TO THE
ARCHAEOLOGICAL
SITES OF
ISRAEL, EGYPT
AND
NORTH AFRICA

Courtlandt Canby

with
Arcadia Kocybala

A HUDSON GROUP BOOK

Facts On File
New York • Oxford • Sydney

A Guide to the Archaeological Sites of Israel, Egypt and North Africa

Facts On File, Inc.	Facts On File Limited	Facts On File Pty Ltd
460 Park Avenue South	Collins Street	Talavera & Khartoum Rds
New York NY 10016	Oxford OX4 1XJ	North Ryde NSW 2113
USA	United Kingdom	Australia

Library of Congress Cataloging-in-Publication Data

Canby, Courtlandt.
    A guide to the archaeological sites of Israel, Egypt, and North
Africa / Courtlandt Canby with Arcadia Kocybala.

      p.   cm.
    "A Hudson Group book."
    Bibliography: p.
    Includes index.
    ISBN 0-8160-1054-4
    1. Palestine—Antiquities—Guide-books.   2. Egypt—Antiquities—
Guide-books.   3. Africa, North—Antiquities—Guide-books.
I. Kocybala, Arcadia Xenia.   II. Title.
DS111.C36   1990
916.1—dc20   89-11810

British and Australian CIP data available on request from Facts On File.

Facts On File books are available at special discounts when purchased in bulk quantities for businesses, associations, institutions, or sales promotion. Please contact the Special Sales Department of our New York office at 212/683-2244 (dial 800/322-8755 except in NY, AK or HI).

Composition by Maple-Vail Book Manufacturing Group
Manufactured by R. R. Donnelley & Sons Company
Printed in the United States of America

10 9 8 7 6 5 4 3 2 1

This book is printed on acid-free paper.

Contents

Introduction

This Guide covers the archaeological sites of three contiguous areas of the ancient world, not often brought together in one volume—Israel, Egypt and North Africa. Geographically, their territories sweep in a single stretch around the eastern and southern shores of the Mediterranean from the borders of Syria in the east to the shores of the Atlantic Ocean in the west. Though there has always been much cultural and political interaction between them, especially between Israel and Egypt, and they have for the most part been subject to invasions by the same great powers, each one of these territories has always been a cultural unity in its own right. And how different they were from each other, each with its own rich and special history! There is an added bonus in including them all in one volume, for the contrasts and occasional similarities between the three inevitably lead one to interesting thoughts about the marvellous complexity of human culture, which can take so many different forms and yet remain a part of the history of mankind.

The known early history of these three areas would be meager indeed were it not for the industrious activities of generations of archaeologists, especially during the last century. Archaeology is all we have to investigate the earliest periods, and it is to the credit of the archaeologists that they have been able to open up entirely new and exciting pages in the history of the most ancient times. Even as we move up into the historic periods archaeology continues to play a significant role in supplementing and enriching the written records.

As an aid in understanding the long and fruitful early histories of these three seminal regions, this Guide offers an up-to-date and comprehensive description of the most important archaeological sites and monuments in all three, both prehistoric and early historic—and many lesser sites as well. The listing is alphabetical under countries, for the Guide is twofold in its purpose: It is intended as a reference book for the stay-at-home, but it can be equally useful as a field manual for the interested traveler, supplementing the usual tourist guides. The student, no doubt, will also find it invaluable and so will even the occasional scholar or archaeologist seeking information outside of his or her chosen field.

Every attempt has been made to make the Guide as accurate as possible, but it is written primarily for the layman and thus, where possible, avoids most scholarly terminology.

The time limits of the Guide run from the Paleolithic up through the Byzantine, with an added excursion into the earliest Islamic monuments after the Arab invasion which engulfed all three districts. I have made no attempt to include every archaeological site or monument in the three regions. The choice of what to include has been difficult, and some will quarrel with my decisions, but in general I have tried to include most sites or monuments of any importance, or at least representative examples of every type of field monument or site in the three regions. The emphasis is on those sites that seem to me to be interesting or important and/or worth visiting because there is something to see there. Now and then, however, I have included a site where there is little or nothing to see, because of its importance in the archaeological record.

The unusual alphabetical rather than chronological or geographic listing of sites within countries in this Guide makes it easy for the stay-at-home or student to look up any given entry by name—as in an encyclopedia. However the method does throw together a variety of sites from many different periods and places—in Israel a Jewish synagogue next to an Early Bronze Age city, in Egypt an ancient temple next to an Islamic mosque, in North Africa a Punic mausoleum next to a Roman bath complex. Various aids have been provided to minimize this difficulty. The prefaces provide an historical and chronological framework; the sites themselves are extensively cross-referenced, by type, by location, by period. And each site is located with reasonable precision, usually by naming the nearest town or other geographical indication.

The term "archaeology" is used in its widest and loosest context in the Guide. Thus an archaeological site or monument may be defined as one where excavation or analysis has made a significant contribution to the elucidation of the site's plan, purpose and place in the history of ancient cultures. The archaeological contribution in this sense can be important all the way up to the early historic period—the investigation and restoration, for instance, of an Islamic mosque. Because modern archaeology has immensely broadened its scope and refined its techniques in recent years, today's excavation for example may embrace a wider range of disciplines than mere digging. There has been a healthy infusion into modern archaeology of methods and ideas borrowed from many related disciplines—anthropology, sociology, economics, architecture, geography and geology and environmental studies. More attention is now paid in a dig today not only to the usual material remains excavated but also to pollen analysis, animal and human bones, evidences of agricultural practices and settlement patterns in order to reconstruct the original environment of a site, thus placing it more securely in its wider historical context.

Today's excavations, fortunately, are no longer the treasure hunts of old, more truthfully called looting—digging one's way carelessly into an Egyptian tomb to rob it of its burial goods—but are generally larger and more inclusive in order to analyze a site in all its aspects. This applies even to the typical standing monument where the excavation and analysis calls upon different disciplines to elucidate its date and structural history. The largest projects today are often urban excavations—Jerusalem is an admirable example—a series of sites of opportunity in a living city involving enormous difficulties but also great rewards. New methods of dating, in particular radiocarbon dating, have joined the old determinants of age and culture—stratigraphy, the evidence from the finds, including styles and motifs in pottery and other objects—to bring greater precision into the interpretive process.

But we are dealing here with vast reaches of time, and even the new dating methods are often only approximate at best. Therefore since this Guide is written for the layman, I have used dates only to give the reader a general idea of comparative chronology. I have tried to use those dates that seem to me to be most reliable, chosen by comparing a number of sources for each entry—whether radiocarbon dates or, for example, accepted dates from the Egyptian chronology, and have generally employed the old terms for the earlier periods—the Paleolithic, Neolithic, Bronze Ages, Iron Ages and so forth.

My sources are so various, and for the most part easily available, that I do not feel it necessary to list them all here. They include tourist guidebooks, other archaeological guides for particular areas, magazine articles, newspaper clips, as well as the occasional scholarly book for certain sites and for background, and a culling of archaeological periodicals and reports. For this Guide is above all a synthesis of easily available materials in one overall volume. It breaks no new ground; and in this, I suggest, lies its real value for the average reader. In the case of North Africa, however, where the sources are far less abundant than for Israel or Egypt, I must acknowledge the exceptional usefulness of Paul Mac-Kendrick's *The North African Stones Speak* (1980), one of the few overall treatments of the early archaeological history of the entire area.

I have mentioned the names of the archaeologists involved in various sites only if they already have some general reputation. The names of the others, no matter how worthy they may be, would mean little to the average reader.

Finally, I must salute the devoted work of Arcadia Kocybala, a trained archaeologist and an indispensable colleague, who did much of the spade work in the more scholarly sources and put together the original listing and analyses of many of the sites for all three regions, as well as the meticulous reading and emendations of the Israel section by Yonathan Mizrachi. And without the help and encouragement of Kate Kelly, best of editors, the task of getting this book off the ground would have been immeasurably more difficult.

ISRAEL

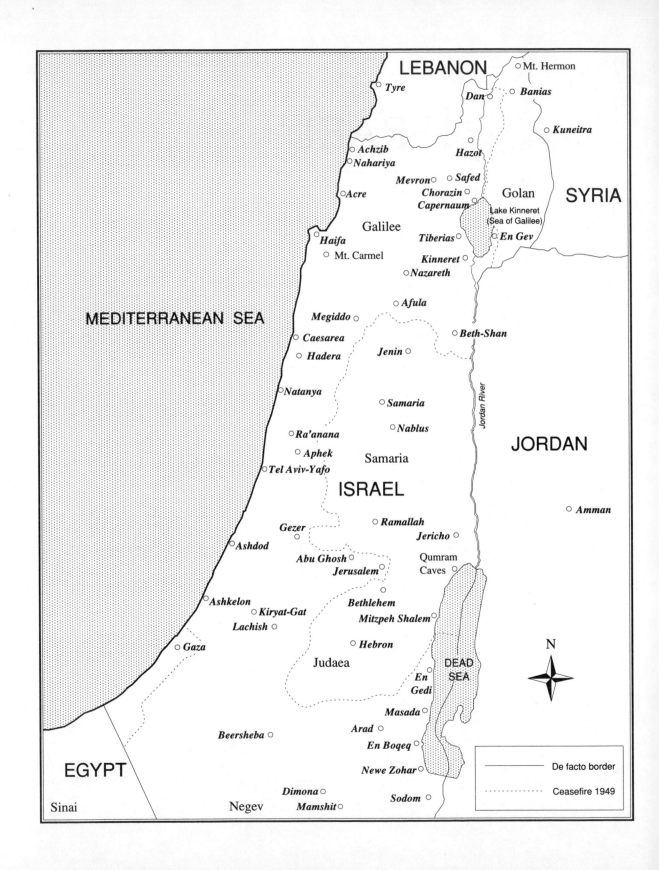

The Archaeology of Israel

The modern state of Israel is a small country set into the midst of a far larger area commonly called The Holy Land, a vaguely defined region centered on Palestine but reaching into Jordan, Iraq, Syria and Lebanon, and even further into Turkey and Egypt—the geographic spread of the Bible stories. It is the Bible that defines the Holy Land, and in biblical times it was a very different area than it is today with the "westernized" state of Israel surrounded on three sides by Muslim "Arab" countries. In those earlier times it was an area of many diverse peoples and cultures, a crossroads of influences and invasions from the more powerful civilizations to its east and south—and in New Testament times from Greece and Rome to the west.

Looking back on this earlier "biblical" period, especially Old Testament times, what do we find in the Bible, starkly corroborated in the many archaeological excavations in the area? A tumultuous crossroads indeed, an ever-changing scene of constant warfare, of the besieging, burning and leveling of one city after another by jealous neighbors or foreign invaders, with cruel massacres, butchering of prisoners, the deporting of whole populations—the excavated walls of a Canaanite palace at *Tell Aphek* peppered with embedded arrowheads from its last desperate stand, or on the slopes of doomed *Lachish* deep beds of ashes mixed with slingshots and arrowheads from the Assyrian siege, and here and there pits filled with the discarded bodies of the defenders.

And from the earliest years of civilization in the area these first cities were surrounded by massive walls with towers to deter the enemy. Even the earliest known city, Neolithic *Jericho*, was a walled town. And as time went on increasingly sophisticated systems of defense were developed, and cisterns and tunnels dug out of the rock to capture precious water—all of this a feast for the student of military architecture but a portent of dangerous times for the people concerned. Lucky was the rare city, like *Tell Kisan* or *Beth-Shan*, that managed to survive for many thousands of years with relatively few or any catastrophic interruptions. The excavators of Beth Shan uncovered 18 levels of superimposed cities. Not until perhaps the Persian period, during and after which a succession of major powers controlled Palestine, did things begin to calm down. Indeed the early history of the Holy Land is a tale above all of cities, of powerful city-states in constant angry contention and always in danger from foreign invaders. A crossroads region indeed!

Geographically the Bible stories cover the whole area of the Holy Land; but this Guide, necessarily based on modern boundaries as are all the other guides in the series, cannot cover the larger area of the Holy Land. Fortunately for our purposes, however, Jerusalem was and is the focus of both this larger Holy Land and of modern Israel; and though biblical sites (and a majority of the sites covered here can be so described) are of course scattered all over the Holy Land with no regard to modern borders, a great many of those that have been excavated can be found within Israel's present borders, including the West Bank. Moreover much of the important "digging" has actually taken place within Israel, since the modern Israelis, often working with colleagues from overseas, are superbly industrious archaeologists.

This brings up an important question: should these archaeological sites that pertain to the Bible, whether in Israel or elsewhere, be considered primarily "biblical" sites, excavated for the express purpose of corroborating the Bible and elucidating its background, or should they be considered as purely "archaeological" sites devoted above all to increasing our knowledge of the ancient peoples and cultures of the early Middle East? In the latter case the Bible becomes merely one source among many others to help in interpreting the evidence from the ground. And if certain biblical references are confirmed in the course of the excavation, so much the better. (Actually of course not all the sites covered in this Guide are "biblical"; many, especially the earlier sites, are "archaeological" in the sense above, and here Israel is as rich as anywhere else.)

The point, however, is important: for the archaeologist must interpret as well as dig. Too much emphasis on the biblical aspects of a site can warp the judgment of the archaeologist. If he is seeking only to confirm "the truth of the Bible" he is apt to concentrate in his dig on corroborative and descriptive details, while neglecting the true aim of any modern archaeologist: the elucidation of the processes of cultural and social change in history.

In fact the archaeologist can never hope to confirm the truth of the Bible, simply because the Bible is the story of a religion. The purpose of the Bible was to reveal how the acts of God redeemed man in his earthly existence, never to recount the history of man in any secular sense. The authors of the Bible were not historians; they were interested only in the religious meaning of their stories in terms of their faith. So archaeology can never hope to confirm or to deny this essentially spiritual faith; all it can do is confirm here and there the actuality of certain places, people and acts mentioned in the Bible stories.

Therefore the answer to the question above, in actual practice, is something of both—the earlier excavations in the Holy Land were far more "biblical," seeking to confirm the Bible, while the more recent digs have been decidedly more "archaeological," but still with a mix of both attitudes. Within these limits, however, archaeology has made enormous contributions to biblical studies—as well as to history. It has excavated and identified many sites of importance in the Bible—though many vexing questions still remain—and it has confirmed many facts and substantiated many of the deeds of biblical characters. Two examples come to mind: the actual crude fortress-headquarters of Saul, that shadowy first king of Israel—he of the David and Jonathan stories—has been excavated and identified at *Gibeah*, while on the other hand the site of Solomon's port on the Red Sea, *Ezion-Geber*, despite numerous searches, has so far not been identified.

Then there is the quite recent find in *Jerusalem* of two tiny silver scrolls in a burial of the 7th cent. BC, one inscribed with a very familiar prayer from Numbers, the oldest biblical verse ever found, 400 years earlier than the Dead Sea Scrolls. It was written 2,600 years ago, at a time when the scholars think the earliest parts of the Old Testament were first being formed.

Above all, archaeology has brought the Bible down to earth, it has filled in the cultural background out of which it sprang. It has placed the Bible squarely within the framework of known history, presenting to us things that we can actually see, touch and feel—the walls of their cities, the city gates within which the elders sat, the houses and temples of the time, the pots and pans, the coins and personal belongings of those ancient people who were actually living the Bible. Archaeology has revealed nothing about the spiritual truths of the Bible, but it has helped enormously to make it palpably real and alive.

The Early Stone Ages (about 700,000—8000 BC)

That ancient man had already reached Israel at least as far back as 1.2 million years ago is proved by the finding of his stone tools in profusion at *Ubeidiya*, a site in the Jordan valley. The earliest tools here resembled the crude choppers found at Olduvai Gorge, Leakey's famous site in East Africa. In fact Ubeidiya is one of the earliest human sites found outside Africa, the homeland of mankind. There have been many fascinating discoveries of later Paleolithic man in the various caves in Israel, notably on Mt. *Carmel* where a number of caves have yielded remains dating from 150,000 BC down to the Mesolithic period of about 10,000 BC. The finest cave, et-Tabun, with some 60 ft. of strata from the earlier periods, yielded a skeleton of a female Neanderthal, those immediate precursors of modern man. Other Neanderthal remains have been found in the Mt. Carmel area—one fossil in the *Kebara* cave was about 60,000 years old. But there is also much evidence of early modern man both earlier and later than the Neanderthals (one dated as early as 92,000 BC!) that suggests that the Neanderthals were late visitors, fleeing from ice age conditions in western Europe. Finally, es-Skhul cave on Mt. Carmel yielded ten burials with largely *Homo sapiens* features but also with certain Neanderthal characteristics, a puzzle for the archaeologists! Intermarriage? In the Judean desert the first evidence for the use of fire in Israel was uncovered at *Wadi Khareitun*.

Human remains become abundant by the mid-Paleolithic (see *Amud Caves*). By the late Paleolithic period early man was beginning to exploit his environment more efficiently. For instance a Kebaran man was found buried with his stone mortars used to grind wild grain, a first step towards agriculture (see *Kebara*). By the Mesolithic (Middle Stone Age) period, 10,000 to 8000 BC, the Natufians, semisedentary hunter-gatherers (named for a local site), were building round huts on terraces outside their caves, burying their dead with ornaments, gathering wild plants, producing the first carved stone art and engaging in limited trade (see *Carmel, Mount, Kebara, Nahal Oren*). A remarkably early Natufian village of some 50 crude huts has been excavated at *Eynan*.

The Neolithic

By about 8000 BC the local people were ready for that great social watershed, the Neolithic revolution—the beginning of a settled farming life. While still relying on hunting, and possibly herding, of animals, certain grains (emmer wheat and barley) were domesticated and cultivated, though pottery was still unknown. The best example of this early "Pre-Pottery Neolithic A" period is the remarkable and unique site of Jericho, the world's earliest walled town, magnificently excavated by Dame Kathleen Kenyon in 1952–58. Based on a Natufian settlement, this highly organized 10-acre "city" with its rounded houses, defensive walls and elaborate irrigation works, sprang into existence about 8500–8300 BC. It may have based its rich economy in part on trade in Dead Sea products: salt, bitumen and sulfur. The PPNA is also represented at Nahal Oren with its round stone houses.

Jericho's walls fell for the first time about 7500 BC, bringing in a new people from the north and a new phase, the Pre-Pottery Neolithic B. From burials at Jericho came those lifelike heads modeled on skulls so often pictured. Houses became larger and more sophisticated and the goat may have been domesticated. Other PPNB sites include Munhata, Nahal Oren again, and the submerged village of Atlit-Yam, being excavated under 40 ft. of water off the Haifa coast. Even more interesting is the cache of early PPNB materials recently discovered in the Nahal Hemer cave in the Judean desert: textiles, baskets and the like, well-preserved in the dry conditions, probably the earliest known.

That great and useful innovation, pottery, was introduced about 6000 BC. The Yarmukian culture, flourishing at Munhata and Sha'ar Ha-Golan, is known for its remarkable early art—fertility figurines made of pebbles and tall clay figurines with peaked heads and "coffee-bean" eyes. Just before the "Dawn of Civilization" around 3000 BC we reach the Chalcolithic or Copper Age. Among numerous sites, the underground "troglodyte" houses of many desert villages around Beersheba in the Negev are outstanding. The people fashioned figurines of ivory. At En-Gedi on the Dead Sea a Copper Age "temple" has been found and nearby in a cave at Nahal Mishmar a hidden cache of beautiful copper objects, possibly hidden by the temple people. At Timna near the Red Sea, Copper Age mining operations were also discovered.

The Bronze Ages

The world's earliest civilization, arising in nearby Mesopotamia shortly before 3000 BC, was reflected in our area at about the same time by the sudden and widespread appearance of large walled cities with monumental buildings—city-states such as Ai, Arad or Megiddo. Perhaps this sudden spurt forward was too rapid for the fragile fledgling urban society, for around 2500–2300 BC there was a faltering of urbanization, a mysterious collapse of civilized life, bringing the Early Bronze Age to an end. It was caused in part at least by the assaults of the nomadic Amorite tribes as indicated by destruction levels in many of the cities. Others, like Arad, were abandoned, never again to be occupied. Tell Halif, Lachish and Taanach disappeared, only to be reoccupied many years later. A good example is Tell Yarmuth, now being excavated, a huge city for the times, a mighty fortress covering some 40 acres with an acropolis and a large lower town and the most extensive and complex fortifications of the period so far discovered in Israel. While the small acropolis was reoccupied, the lower town was never revived.

After a slow recovery new cities arose and old ones were rebuilt to usher in the Middle Bronze Age around 2200 BC. The Syrian-Palestine area was now occupied by those West Semites known as the Canaanites, who were eventually to be overwhelmed in Palestine by the early Israelites. The Canaanites were middlemen in trade and culture between the two great powers of the day, centered in Egypt and Mesopotamia, and they invented the alphabet (see the early pictographs discovered at *Gezer*), a step forward with enormous consequences. Gezer is also known for its High Place or outdoor shrine. Another High Place and a temple were discovered at *Nahariya*

Again there were powerful contending city-states such as *Tell Ajjul*, *Tell Aphek*, *Tell el-Farah South*, *Hazor*, *Jericho*, *Megiddo*, Shechem (see *Nablus*) and *Tirzah*. From time to time Egypt was in control of parts of Palestine. From 1650 to 1550 BC those chariot-riding warrior tribes, the Hyksos, overran and controlled both Egypt and Palestine. They introduced the horse and two-wheeled chariot and a distinctive type of fortification called the glacis, a plastered sloping scarp of earth. The end of the period was marked by the expulsion of the Hyksos from Egypt and Palestine by 'Ahmose, founder of Egypt's powerful Eighteenth Dynasty.

By about 1550 BC (the Late Bronze Age) a resurgent Egypt brought Canaan under its control in the reign of Tuthmosis III (1504–1470 BC). Egyptian governors were placed in the major city-states while vassal rulers or client kings ruled under Egyptian supervision. An important source of information on Egyptian-ruled Canaan at this time are the Amarna letters, which also mention the Habiru, roving armed bands identified by some as the early Hebrews. For this was the period of the Exodus, the gradual infiltration (as most scholars now think) of the Israelite tribes into Canaan, the biblical "promised land," from the deserts and hilly fringes of the land.

The Israelites were at this time seminomadic patriarchal tribes united only by their common worship of Jehovah (Yaweh). A remarkable recent discovery is the probable altar on *Mt. Ebal* erected by Joshua at Moses' command, as told in the Bible. Joshua again, who according to the Bible razed *Lachish*, largest of Canaanite cities, was probably responsible for the widespread destruction layer found in the excavations of that city. For more light on the period, see the Canaanite-Israelite cult centers of *Bethel* and Shechem (see *Nablus*). For typical Canaanite cities, see *Ashdod*, *Beth-Shan* and the mighty fortress-city of *Megiddo*. Extensive Egyptian mining operations in this period have been discovered at *Timna* on the Gulf of Aqaba.

The Iron Ages

Around 1200 BC the Israelite tribes, well-established in the hill country, had occupied some of the Canaanite cities, but others, especially along the coast, were still independent. As a result of a widespread time of troubles in the eastern Mediterranean, fierce hordes of warriors called the Sea Peoples moved down through Syria and Palestine by sea and by land, burning and destroying everything in their path. Driven from their homelands in the Aegean area or Anatolia by famine, they carried with them elements of the old Aegean civilizations, including now the use of iron. Moving on to Egypt, they were turned back in a great sea battle by Ramesses III, recorded in detail in the huge battle relief at his temple at *Medinet Habu* in EGYPT. One tribe of Sea Peoples, the biblical Philistines—called the Peleset by the Egyptians—sailed back to Palestine (ironically, they gave their name to the country) and conquered and settled the Canaanite cities of the coast. They may at first have been Egyptian vassals, but as Egyptian power waned their cities became independent.

According to the Bible the Philistines were organized in a league of five major cities: *Ashkelon*, *Ashdod* (their religious center), Ekron (see *Tell Miqneh*), *Gaza* and Gath—only the latter has not been located. The Bible gave the Philistines a bad press. Actually their economy was strong, based on commerce and the coastal trade routes, their armies, led by warrior aristocrats, were powerful, and they possessed a far higher standard of culture than the Israelites, jealously holding on to their monopoly of ironworking. In 1971 the only known example of a Philistine temple was discovered at Tell Qasile (see *Tel Aviv-Jaffa*).

By the 11th cent. BC the Philistines, at the height of their power, were pushing inland, leading to inevitable border clashes with the Israelites in the hills, now organized under leaders called Judges. One of these Judges was Samson, the mighty warrior, whose stories in the Bible reflect the situation at the time. About 1050 the armies clashed for the first time, the Philistines issuing from *Tell Aphek* to battle the ill-armed Israelite tribes on the plain of Eben-ezer. In recent years archaeologists have identified and excavated the probable site of Eben-ezer at *Izbet Sartah*, a small Israelite settlement of the time in the hills a few miles behind Tell Aphek. Abandoned about 1000 BC when David had opened the plains to Israelite expansion, it was a typical town of the time when the Israelite tribes were just settling down. Meantime the Philistines, routing the tribes in the battle, had overrun and now dominated the whole of the hill country. They even captured the Israelites' sacred Ark of the Covenant at the battle, hastily brought from its traditional resting place at the cult center of *Shiloh* to encourage the tribes in their fruitless struggle. Hard-pressed by the Philistines, the Israelites finally abandoned the ineffective system of Judges and elected their ill-fated first king, Saul, around 1020 BC, at whose court the young David began his meteoric career. Saul's small fortress-capital has been identified and excavated at *Gibeah*.

With David as king began the so-called Iron Age II period, around 1000 BC. The Israelites were learning fast, absorbing the way of life and cultures of the Canaanites and Philistines. For instance David, as a former Philistine mercenary, now put to good use the Philistine military skills, defeating and humbling those mighty warriors. The plains were now open to the Israelites and as his capital David seized *Jerusalem* from the Jebusites, a Canaanite tribe. The Philistines, their power broken, were gradually absorbed into Israel.

Under David's son and successor Solomon (965–28) Israel briefly became a great power, filling a power vacuum in the Middle East. Solomon was a master builder. Calling upon his ally Hiram of Phoenicia (Lebanon) for materials and craftsmen, he instituted a system of taxation to pay for his creations. In Jerusalem he built his famed temple, based on Canaanite prototypes (see *Hazor*). An actual small temple of his time was discovered in *Arad*, throwing much light on that in Jerusalem. In his royal cities—*Hazor*, *Jerusalem*, *Gezer* and *Megiddo*—Solomon rebuilt the fortifications with characteristic casemate (compartmented) walls and "Solomonic" triple gates with three chambers on each side. Elaborate water supply systems were also dug, such as those in Hazor, Jerusalem and Megiddo.

At Solomon's death in 928 the United Monarchy collapsed, breaking into two Hebrew states, Judah in the south with Jerusalem as its capital, and Israel in the north. Shortly thereafter the military state of Assyria began its long series of incursions into the west. Israel and Judah were again but two small states among others, though as time went on both experienced periods of power and prosperity. Shechem (see *Nablus*) and *Tirzah* briefly became the capital of Israel, then *Samaria*, where kings Omri and Ahab built their luxurious palaces. A later (7th cent.) Judean palace has been excavated at *Ramat Rahel*, as well as a typical Judean city of the times called Debir (see *Khirbet er-Rabud*). Other major cities of the Israelite period include *Ashdod*, Tell *Beersheba*, *Tell Dan*, *Gibeon* and *Lachish*.

The Assyrians, now in the ascendant, menaced the entire west, and in 722 Israel fell to their armies, many of the inhabitants being deported en masse (the "lost tribes"). In 701 Jerusalem was besieged by Sennacherib, but unsuccessfully, though thereafter Judah became a vassal state of Assyria. The Assyrians then extended their conquests to Egypt in the 7th cent., using the fortress of *Tell Jemmeh* as a springboard. Jerusalem was finally destroyed by Nebuchadnezzar of Babylon, successor to the Assyrians, in 586 BC and its inhabitants deported.

As a postscript, the "Babylonian Captivity" ended for these exiles when Cyrus, founder of the great Persian Empire, allowed some of the exiles to return to a wrecked Jerusalem in 539, though Palestine was now under Persian rule. Excavations have uncovered the new walls of a shrunken *Jerusalem* built by the fanatic Nehemiah in 440 BC, as well as a major Persian-period industrial site at Tell Michal (see *Tel Aviv-Jaffa*), while traces of a Persian governor's palace were uncovered at *Lachish*.

The Hellenistic Period (332–37 BC)

With Alexander the Great's destruction of the Persian Empire in 332 BC Palestine fell under Macedonian rule. After Alexander's death in Babylon in 323 BC, his quarrelling generals divided his kingdom. Ptolemy of Egypt dominated Palestine from 301 to 198 BC when the Seleucid Empire, based in Syria, took over. Religious persecution of the Jews in 165 BC by a Seleucid ruler led to a rebellion under Judas Maccabeus. He seized control of Judah and his successors ruled a Jewish state for 100 years. The Maccabean (or Hasmonaean) dynasty finally fell to the armies of Rome under Pompey in 64–63 BC.

Comparatively few sites in Israel date from this period. Examples of Hellenized cities are to be found at *Tell Anafa* in Galilee and Marissa (*Mareshah*), though nothing is now to be seen at the latter. Remnants of a luxurious Hasmonaean palace (under a later palace of Herod) have been found at Khirbet el-Mafjar near Jericho. Of more interest is the rise of the Nabataeans, desert Arabs who grew rich on the caravan routes to the coast, with their capital at the magnificent site of Petra in Jordan. They first emerged into history in the 3rd-2nd cents. BC and their state lasted, with periods of widespread power, to 106 AD when it was incorporated into the Roman Empire. However they were in effect vassals of Rome from the time of Pompey on. In Israel's Negev there are a series of desert cities founded by the Nabataeans—*Avdat*, *Elusa*, *Mamshit*, *Nitzana*, *Rehovot* and *Shivta*. Though the extensive ruins of these cities one sees today are mostly Byzantine, one finds remnants of their Nabataean origin in the architecture and water-conservation methods of these sites, especially at *Elusa*.

Roman Palestine (37 BC–324 AD)

Rome now dominated the eastern Mediterranean, ruling a patchwork of Roman provinces and client states in Syria-Palestine. In time Herod the Great (37–

4 BC) emerged as king of Judea under Roman protection. He was an Arab (Idu-maean) of ferocious temperament, but he was also one of the world's great builders. His magnificent Jewish temple in Jerusalem is well known; he also built a sumptuous palace there of which little remains. He created the opulent city of Caesarea out of a small village; its huge artificial port was, at the time, a miracle of advanced engineering. He rebuilt Samaria, renaming it Sebaste, and was responsible for two extraordinary fortress-palaces, the dramatic "hanging palace" at Masada in the Dead Sea desert and the Herodion on its artificial conical hill, as well as a huge pleasure-ground palace with a theater and hippodrome near Jericho.

The Romans had a hard time holding down the Jews, always a special people with a special religion. Hatred of Roman rule brought about the first revolt of 66–73 AD, which the Romans put down with calculated and methodical ferocity, destroying Jerusalem in 70 AD and besieging the rebels in Gamla, Masada and Yodefat, as described by Josephus, the historian. It was at this time that the famous Dead Sea Scrolls were hidden in caves by the religious community of Qumran. The Jews revolted again in 132–35 AD under Simon Bar Kochba (see Nahal Hever), were again defeated, and this time banished altogether from Jerusalem, renamed Aelia Capitolina by Hadrian. Orthodox Jews, fleeing north to Galilee, took refuge in Beth Shearim (under the famous Rabbi Judah ha-Nasi) and in Tiberias and Zippori, and thereafter built numerous beautiful synagogues in Galilee (see Capernaum, Meiron).

Among Roman-style cities, Beth-Shan, with its fine theater and recently excavated amphitheater, is outstanding. In Tell Aphek there are Herodian Roman remains, and Susita offers a mountain setting. Remnants of Roman Ashkelon still survive, and the huge bath complex in Hammat Gader was reputed to be the second largest in the Roman empire. Roman forts have been investigated at Mesad Tamar near the Dead Sea, En-Boqeq on the Sea, where there was also a Herodian "factory" for processing herbs, and at Tell Beth Yerah. Remains of a temple on Mt. Gerizim at Tell er-Ras (see Nablus) have also been excavated.

Byzantine and Early Arab (324–750 AD)

After the Roman Empire had become Christian under Constantine the Great around 325 AD, pilgrims flocked to Palestine and to the holy places of Jerusalem, where numerous churches and monasteries appeared in the following years—as well as in the rest of the country. Remnants of Constantine's great basilica, dedicated by him in 335 AD, can still be seen in the Church of the Holy Sepulcher in Jerusalem. The following centuries (5th and 6th) were times of great prosperity in Palestine and the whole eastern Mediterranean, especially during the reign of Justinian the Great (483–565 AD). In Jerusalem numerous Byzantine remains have been excavated—various buildings to the south of the Temple Mount, and most evocatively, the excavation and reconstruction of the Byzantine cardo or main street, an extension south of the Roman cardo, which visitors can now walk through.

The Church of the Nativity at Bethlehem is largely Byzantine, while inside the modern Basilica of the Anunciation at Nazareth one can glimpse through an opening the excavated remnants of the earlier churches on the site (4th and 5th cents. AD). At Tabgha is an appealing mosaic depicting the miracle of the loaves and fishes (see *Heptapegon*). More fine mosaics, and Byzantine churches, houses and monasteries, were uncovered at the ancient city of *Beth-Shan*, and another essentially Byzantine excavated town is at Shikmona (see *Haifa*). Monasteries in fact proliferated in Byzantine times, especially in the lonely Judean desert where 130 monastic communities once flourished. Examples are at *Khan el-Ahmar* and *Khirbet ed-Deir*. In the general prosperity many fine synagogues were also built, for example at *Beth Alpha* (6th cent.), with its charmingly primitive mosaics, and at *Khirbet Suseya*. The former Nabataean cities in the Negev, mentioned earlier, also flourished as wealthy and beautiful cities, adorned with many a fine church. Consequently the ruins we see today are mostly Byzantine. Among the most charming of these towns, excavated and well-restored, are *Mamshit* and *Shivta*.

During the earliest Islamic period after the Arab conquest, the Umayyad dynasty, based in Damascus, closely carried on in its building and arts the recent Byzantine traditions, occasionally mixed with Persian influences, as for instance in the luxurious Umayyad palace at Khirbet al Mafjar (see *Jericho*), thought to have been built by the eccentric Caliph Walid ibn Yazid (743–44). It was never finished, for the caliph was shortly assassinated. Another smaller Umayyad palace has been partially excavated at *Khirbet el-Minya* on the Sea of Galilee. The lovely octagonal mosque, the Dome of the Rock, on the Temple Mount in *Jerusalem*, built in 691 AD with mosaics crafted by Christian artisans, is one of the earliest Islamic monuments in the whole Arabic empire.

ABU MATAR   See *Beersheba*.

ACHZIB   Ancient site on the coast, 17 mi. N. of Haifa, close to the Lebanese border, inhabited from the Middle Bronze Age to Crusader times, though its most prosperous period was from the 10th to the 6th cent. BC when it covered 20 acres. Its twin mounds, excavated from the 1940s into the 1960s, are now preserved by the National Parks Department and are open to the public. On the southern mound, remains of Hellenistic buildings may be seen; the older north mound was encircled by ramparts from the Middle Bronze Age (about mid-18th cent. BC) and on the mound itself excavations uncovered public buildings and numerous storerooms from later periods up to the Hellenistic. The richest finds came from two cemeteries nearby, both with rock-cut tombs. Large family vaults with up to 400 burials, dating from the 10th to 8th cents. BC, were found in the east cemetery. That to the south was a Phoenician necropolis. Its tombs, dating down to the 6th cent. BC, contained many artifacts such as Phoenician pottery, ritual vessels, incense burners, figurines and masks, and clay models. The finds are on view in Jerusalem's Israel and Rockefeller museums and in the nearby Nahariya museum.

ACRE   The ancient port city of Akko on a fortified peninsula jutting into the Bay of Acre 9 mi. N. of Haifa. With its once famous harbor silted up, it is now a backwater, a crowded, picturesque little city beloved of tourists and vacationers, with 18th-cent. Turkish buildings overlying and mixed in with the massively built remains of the Crusader capital of St. Jean d'Acre. Seized by Baldwin in 1104 during the First Crusade, Acre was lost to Saladin in 1187, then recaptured by Richard the Lion-Hearted of England and his ally, King Philip of France, in 1191. For exactly 100 years thereafter it was the capital of the truncated Latin Kingdom of Jerusalem and was three times as large as the present city, until it fell

Acre, the very ancient city of Akko, now a picturesque backwater with its old harbor silted up. It was a Canaanite city, a flourishing Phoenician port, a Crusader fortress, again an important port under the Turks, and besieged by Napoleon in 1799. Today it displays an attractive jumble of old Crusader and Turkish buildings dominated by the 18th-century mosque of the "butcher" Ahmed el-Jazzar. (Courtesy: Israel Ministry of Tourism.)

to the Muslim Mamluks of Egypt. It then lay derelict until revived as a port by various Turkish and local rulers in the 18th cent. Its rebuilt fortifications successfully resisted a siege by Napoleon in 1799, a siege that was but one of an estimated 17 known sieges suffered by the city during its very long history, beginning with Ramesses the Great in the late 13th cent. BC.

Excavations on a small scale, intensified after 1973, both inside and outside the city, have revealed a good deal about Acre's earliest history. The original Canaanite agricultural and market town, founded as early as about 3000 BC, was centered on an inland mound slightly northeast of the present walls where a gate complex (with a mud brick bench and guard chamber, and an early type glacis) in the massive earthen Middle Bronze Age ramparts has been excavated. A sloping glacis of the 18th-cent. Hyksos type overlays the whole. The city came under Egyptian control after its capture by Ramesses II, and when the Egyptian empire weakened it may have been occupied by a group of Sea Peoples, as suggested by finds of Mycenaean-type pottery. Under the Assyrians and Persians it became a major Phoenician port, eventually overshadowing Tyre and Sidon. The remnants of a Phoenician temple and public building have been discovered, yielding an important sherd with the longest Phoenician inscription known from the Persian period, concerned with the affairs of the temple. There was also a strong Greek mercantile quarter.

Acre was taken by Alexander the Great, who endowed it with a mint, and after his death it fell to the Ptolemies of Egypt, was renamed Ptolemais and grew far outside the present walls. Later it came under the Seleucids and eventually, by 63 BC, under Rome. Traces of a small Hellenistic temple have been found, and of a large round tower in the fortifications. The building of Herod the Great's massive artificial harbor at *Caesarea* to the south, however, was a blow to Acre, which languished until Arab times, when its maritime importance was again reestablished. Once more a flourishing port, it became under the Crusaders even more important as a vital link between Europe and Asia, between East and West.

The Acre the tourist sees today is wholly Turkish-Crusader in appearance. Its streets are lined with heavy stone-built Crusader houses, and numerous Turkish khans or caravanserais are built into and over earlier Christian churches and monasteries that belonged to the various quarters of the Templars, the Knights Hospitallers and the Italian city-states—Genoa, Venice, Pisa—whose fleets made the Crusader conquest possible. The great mosque of the cruel 18th-century Ahmed-el-Jazzar, "the Butcher," includes columns stolen from Roman Caesarea; the Municipal Museum is housed in his Turkish baths. Most interesting is the so-called underground city of Crusader crypts and passages, and the most impressive site here is the so-called Crypt of St. John, once the refectory of the Knights Hospitallers, a huge double-knaved hall with heavy piers and fan vaulting, one of the earliest examples of pure Gothic in East or West. Here the kings of France and England met to lay their battle plans. The Akko Museum displays local finds.

AFULA

A modern market town 6 mi. S. of Nazareth. A high mound in the city covers what remains of an ancient site dating back to the late Chalcolithic or Copper Age but more fully developed during the Bronze Age and later. From the earliest period a brick wall, oven and burnished gray pottery have been found. Other scattered finds in the mound and around it include indications of Iron Age occupation, a Byzantine oil press and a medieval fort (11th–13th cent. AD); its walls still stand some 17 ft. high.

AI

A large Canaanite city, identified with the mound of et-Tell 15 mi. N. of Jerusalem, thoroughly excavated in the 1930s, and again from 1964 to 1974 by a major consortium of 20 institutions. There was an early, unwalled settlement here as early as 3200–3100 BC; then about 3000 BC, at the time of the "dawn of civilization" in nearby Mesopotamia, Ai, remarkably, became a large walled city covering some 27 acres. Destroyed and rebuilt several times in that parlous age, it came under Egyptian influence and finally suffered a major destruction about 2400 BC and was abandoned. It lay derelict until about 1200 BC when a small (2½ acre) settlement of squatters, presumably the seminomadic Israelite invaders, occupied the terraces below the ruins of the great Bronze Age citadel until about 1050 BC, when the site was again abandoned.

Ai poses a mystery. According to the Bible Joshua took Ai and burned it, slaughtering the inhabitants and hanging its king on a tree (Joshua 8:25–29). But as we have seen archaeological evidence indicates that Ai had been deserted for over 1,000 years at the time of the Israelite invasion (1250–25 BC). One of several explanations offered is that in the biblical traditions the destruction of Ai had become confused with that of Bethel, only a mile or two west of Ai, where evidences of destruction by fire at the right time were abundant.

At Ai the excavators uncovered impressive remains of the Early Bronze Age city: stretches of the triple circle of walls with four city gates, a sanctuary just inside the walls, an acropolis, residential and industrial areas, the remains of a lower city, many tombs, and a large reservoir. On the acropolis was one of the finest temples discovered in Palestine, fully 110 ft. long with a row of columns down the center. It was rebuilt at one time, possibly with the help of Egyptian craftsmen. Next to it was a large walled structure that may have been the king's palace. If a palace, it is the earliest known in Palestine. The reservoir, with a capacity of 1,800 cubic meters of water, was paved with stone and plastered.

AIN MALLAHA

See *Eynan.*

AJJUL, TELL EL-

One of the major Canaanite Bronze Age cities, about 4 mi. SW of Gaza on the southern Mediterranean coast. The mound, excavated by Sir Flinders Petrie in the 1930s, covers about 30 acres. Evidence for settlement in the area during the Chalcolithic or Copper Age has been turned up, and two large Early Bronze Age cemeteries were excavated east and west of the mound, but the site itself was apparently not settled until the Middle Bronze Age (around 2000 BC). At its height the city was protected by walls, a plastered glacis of the Hyksos type, and a ditch about 20 ft. deep on three sides, with a ring road flanked by buildings encircling it within the ditch. Five successive palaces have been excavated within the walls, the first resting on foundations of carefully dressed stone, the last dating from the Iron Age.

Tell el-Ajjul is well known for its Middle Bronze Age pottery, first defined here by Petrie—red on black with panels on the shoulders showing animals, fish, birds and geometric designs—which has been found well up into Syria. Several hoards of jewelry from the Late Bronze Age, the finest and most varied discovered in Israel, have also turned up here. These include earrings, rings, bracelets, pendants etc. of gold and electrum, dated from about 1550 to 1480 BC.

AKKO

See *Acre.*

AMWAS

See *Imwas.*

AMUD CAVES

Paleolithic caves above the Wadi Nahal Amud, NW of the Sea of Galilee and W. of Chorazin, excavated by different hands in the 1920s, '30s and '60s. They yielded human remains from the Middle Paleolithic period (80,000–30,000 BC), and Mousterian tool assemblages. From the Cave of the Gypsy Woman came skull fragments in 1925 dubbed Galilee Man (though it was possibly a woman) as well as animal bones, including those of a bear and a hippopotamus. The Cave of the Column yielded the intact skeleton of a young man (about 25), and fragments of another male skeleton and of two young children.

ANAFA, TELL

Hellenistic and Roman site in the Upper Galilee, a few mi. SE of Qiryat Shemona. Surface surveys also indicated occupation in the Copper, Bronze, Iron Ages and the Persian period. It lies at the base of the Golan Heights between Kibbutz Shamir and Kefar Szold. The ancient city, name unknown, is covered by a 30-ft.-high mound on the plain, 44 acres in all. American excavations since 1968 have determined that the Classical city was founded about 200 BC under the Seleucids and was abandoned about 75 BC. Stretches of city wall with an acropolis and lower town, a large late Hellenistic building with stuccoed stone walls, clay floors and a colonnade, another courtyard house with ovens, and a large stone-built structure whose walls still stand about 9 ft. high have been uncovered. It contained a heated three-room bath. That the town was a prosperous one is attested by finds of stucco moldings decorated with paint and gold leaf, bits of early stone and glass mosaics from this building, many vessels of red-glazed pottery, bronze and glass, many coins, and iron implements. There is a small museum at Kibbutz Shamir.

ANTIPATRIS

See *Aphek*.

APHEK

A 5,000 year-old city by the springs of the Yarkon River, sited at a strategic gap leading inland, about 10 mi. NE of Tel Aviv, now in an attractive national park. The mound of Rosh Ha'ayin above Aphek, covering the ancient site, is dominated by the enclosing walls of a ruined 16th-cent. Turkish fort of considerable size. In ancient times the city was on the border between Philistia and Israel. Won by Joshua, later lost to the Philistines, it was near here, about 1050 BC, that the antagonists met in battle for the first time, the disciplined Philistine army routing the Israelites and capturing the Ark of the Covenant. This was but one minor episode in Aphek's long history. It was a walled city by 3000 BC, at the dawn of history, and thereafter became an important Canaanite city, often subject to Egypt, until the Israelite conquest, which was shortly followed by Philistine occupation. Later, as the Hellenistic city of Pegae ("the springs"), it was rebuilt by Herod the Great (37–4 BC), renamed Antipatris after his father, and continued to flourish during the Roman period. The mound was excavated in the 1930s and again by an Israeli and American group from 1974 to 1984.

The foundations of a large building exposed within the walls of the Turkish fort have been identified as those of the last Canaanite palace on the mound, destroyed in a conflagration of about 1200 BC, with evidences of a bitter battle (arrowheads stuck in the walls), possibly dating from the Israelite, or Philistine, conquest. A cuneiform tablet found in the palace was identified as a letter from an official of Ugarit in the 13th cent. to the Egyptian governor of Aphek. On the site the remains of six superimposed palaces have been found, the first (20th cent. BC) with mud brick plastered walls on stone foundations, the largest (18th–17th cent. BC) built of coursed boulders, one of the finest examples of Bronze Age palace architecture in Israel. From the Roman period a Herodian flagstoned street, lined with shops, leads from outside the fort east to the remains of a large house of the imperial period. The forum, the theater, a small odeon, the foundation arches of a public building and of a mausoleum have also been investigated. The finds are attractively displayed in a site museum at nearby Petah Tikvah. Another site with Early Bronze Age fortifications, difficult of access, is at nearby Tell Dalit.

ARAD, TELL

Ancient Canaanite city some 18 mi. E. of *Beersheba*, and SW of *Masada* and the Dead Sea. Its name has been given to a modern Israeli city about 7 mi to the SE. The horseshoe-shaped site of 22 acres, bordered by hills and lower in the center (thus catching the rains), was sparsely settled in the early years of the Bronze Age, but by the 29th cent. BC it had become a large city enclosed within heavy walls, with semicircular towers, running around the rim of the encircling hills. The public buildings were grouped in the low center near the reservoir, and were surrounded by well-planned houses separated by streets and squares. This city was destroyed about 2600 BC and never reoccupied. Excavated by Ruth Amiran and Yohanan Aharoni in the 1960s, and again from 1971 into the 1980s, the site has been judiciously restored and signposted to give the visitor a vivid impression of a complete Early Bronze Age city. It lived on agriculture and on trade (Egyptian imports were found at all levels). In the center was a large temple with two halls and other public buildings, one possibly a palace. The houses consisted uniformly of one large room with benches on all four sides, usually a storeroom or kitchen, and courtyard. There were no windows, and the roof was supported by a wooden pillar.

After the destruction the site lay abandoned for 1,500 years; then in the late 10th cent. BC the Israelites built a fortress on a small hill on the northeast part of the site, the Upper Citadel, as an outpost against the Edomites. Altogether, six Israelite fortresses were built there, each destroyed by some enemy, until the 7th cent. BC. The ruins of the latest are still visible. Later the citadel held a small settlement in Persian times, a tower and settlement in the Hellenistic period, a Roman fortress (70–106 AD) and finally an Islamic inn (7th–8th cent. AD).

The earliest Israelite fortress, with casemate walls and towers, is of particular interest because, aside from storerooms, industrial areas and houses, it enclosed a large sanctuary, the earliest Israelite temple yet discovered, the whole dating from Solomonic times (10th cent. BC). In the temple courtyard was a large altar for burnt offerings, and off a large inside room a small holy of holies or inner sanctuary, consisting of a raised platform (a *bamah*) reached by three steps, on which once stood a stone stela (*massebah*) about 3 ft. high and painted red. On the steps were found two incense altars of different sizes. The parallel with the biblical description of Solomon's Temple is close (the whole has been reassembled in Jerusalem's Israel Museum). The temple was deliberately destroyed in the 7th cent. BC, perhaps during King Josiah's reforms, and never reused. Some 200 *ostraca* (pottery sherds inscribed in ink), written in Hebrew, Phoenician and Aramaic and dating from the 10th to 7th cents. BC, were found at Arad. Some throw light on the last days of the Kingdom of Judah; one identifies a temple as "the house of God," possibly refering to the Temple in Jerusalem.

ASHDOD

One of the five principal cities of the Philistines, which included *Ashkelon* 9 mi. to the S. Earlier it was a Canaanite city, first fortified in the Middle Bronze Age (before 1600 BC) with a long history of later occupation into the Byzantine era (7th cent. AD). It lies a few miles back from the sea, 3½ miles south of the bustling modern city of Ashdod, Israel's largest port. The mound, Tell Mor, excavated by an American-Israeli team headed by Dr. Moshe Dothan in the 1960s and early 1970s, consists of a 20-acre acropolis and a lower city of 70 acres. Altogether, 20 levels of occupation were uncovered. From the Canaanite city came the foundations of a large building with rooms grouped around a central courtyard, other buildings of brick, stone pavements and much imported Mycenaean and Cypriot pottery—for Ashdod was a prosperous trading city. It was burned and utterly destroyed in the late 13th cent. BC, probably by the Sea Peoples as they ravaged their way south from the Aegaen area.

Shortly afterwards the Philistines (Pulesti), a tribe of the Sea Peoples, settled on the site after their defeat in Egypt by Ramesses III, building a fortress of brick whose walls still stand in places to a height of 7 ft. As the city grew it expanded outside the acropolis into the lower area, which was eventually walled. There is evidence for extensive ironworking, a Philistine speciality, as well as a potter's quarter, and (according to the Bible) the city held the chief shrine of their god, Dagon. From the Philistine period, streets, houses, a small temple

The harp player from Ashdod, a large Canaanite trading city, then one of the five main cities of the Philistines. The harp player, dating from the Iron Age, was found in the excavations. Perhaps this was the kind of harp played by young David at the court of Saul to calm the king's troubled spirits. (Courtesy: Israel Department of Antiquities and Museums.)

and quantities of handsome Philistine pottery have been excavated. A particularly impressive gate of the Solomonic type in the lower city and stretches of mud brick wall have now been preserved under a roof. Ashdod remained a center of Philistia until the late 8th cent. BC, when it was sacked by the Assyrians—mass graves of some 3,000 victims were found. Then it came under Babylonian rule, and later was the capital of a province of the Persian Empire. From this period date the stone foundations of a large public building. It became a Hellenistic and Roman city, and was apparently destroyed at the time of the Jewish revolt of 67 AD, thereafter declining.

On the coast, just beyond modern Ashdod, is the site of the port for ancient Ashdod. Excavations in 1959–60 show that it was inhabited, with interruptions, from the Middle Bronze Age into the Hellenistic period.

ASHKELON

The site of ancient Ashkelon lies about 1 mi. S. of the modern city of the same name on Israel's coast. As a Canaanite settlement, founded about 2000 BC with earlier antecedents back to the Neolithic, it had the only good harbor on the southern coast (long ago washed away by the sea), and lay moreover on the important trade route, the Way of the Sea, which led up from Egypt along the coast and then through upper Palestine and on to Mesopotamia. There is evidence for Hyksos occupation; then Ashkelon became a vassal state of Egypt, though often rebelling. Ramesses II subdued it after one such rebellion and celebrated the bloody capture in a vivid relief at *Karnak* (see EGYPT). Shortly thereafter it was destroyed by the Sea Peoples as they moved south, then occupied by the Philistines after they had been driven from Egypt. It became one of the five principal Philistine cities of the Bible, which included Ekron (*Tell Miqneh*), *Gaza* to the south and *Ashdod* to the north. It is familiar to us from the biblical story of Samson, who stormed into Ashkelon and slew 30 men. Occupation by the Assyrians, Babylonians and Persians followed, and under the Ptolemies it became a Hellenistic city. Putting itself under the protection of Rome in 104 BC, it became a "free allied city" and later was much embellished by Herod the Great, possibly a native of the city. Ashkelon's onions, "caefsa Ascalonia," were much prized in the Roman period, giving rise to our words "scallion" and "shallot." It flourished as a cosmopolitan commercial port during the Roman and Byzantine periods. The surviving city was utterly destroyed by the Mamluk Baybars in 1270 AD.

The remains of the ancient city lie within a charming national park behind a popular bathing beach. The 160 acres of the park are outlined by the foundations of a medieval wall and towers—Byzantine or Crusader—forming a great semi-circle, embellished with Roman statues and dotted with picnic tables among the trees. A mound at the center marks the oldest part of the site.

Early excavation was limited, the major effort being in 1920–21, which uncovered levels in the mound dating from the Canaanite and Philistine cities, separated by a level of burning, probably from the Sea Peoples' assault. Roman remains in the park, now mostly covered over again, include a 335-ft.-long council house, which had a theater-like semicircular hall and a porticoed quadrangle. There are also badly ruined churches and a synagogue from the Byzantine period. Roman columns, used for reinforcement, stick out of a stretch of seawall, Byzantine or Crusader, along the beach, once built in a vain attempt to hold back the sea. North of the park a 3rd cent. AD Roman tomb displays exquisite frescoes of painted stucco, and in the modern town itself one can see two Roman sarcophagi with interesting reliefs, the mosaic floor of a Byzantine church, and Crusader remains.

A major new excavation at Ashkelon under the American Lawrence Stager began in 1985 and has so far uncovered Canaanite and Philistine courtyard houses and public buildings, a Roman forum, Persian-period warehouses, an extremely odd dog cemetery, and a Roman-Byzantine bath with attached bordello. Work has also begun on the Philistine harbor area.

ATLIT-YAM

A submerged Neolithic village, about 8,000 years old, off the Carmel coast about 9 mi. S. of *Haifa*. Discovered by a survey team from Haifa University's Center for Maritime Studies, after a violent storm in 1984 had uncovered part of it, the site lies some 30 to 40 ft. under the sea and about 1,300 ft. off the shore from the present village of Atlit. It is the largest, deepest, and earliest such site discovered so far. Underwater excavation, an ongoing project, continues to date (1989). The village, in its day 1,000 ft. inland on the southern bank of the *Nahal Oren* stream, dates from the Pre-Pottery Neolithic B period (see *Jericho*) and was abandoned when the sea level slowly rose and engulfed it.

So far only a small part of the village has been explored, but considering the difficulties of underwater excavation a remarkable amount of information has been gleaned from the site. Four houses have been exposed, as well as many enigmatic walls—one of brick over 65 ft. long—and other structures. One house, exposed in its entirety, measures 30 by 17 ft., is rectangular and built of large undressed stones, and may have had additional rooms and courtyards off it. The recovery of hoes, axes, adzes, mortars and pestles, and sickle blades, as well as some domesticated emmer wheat and lentils, points to a major dependence on farming, while arrowheads and wild animal bones suggest hunting. The bones of cattle and goats probably belonged to the earliest domesticated animals, not yet genetically changed after generations of breeding in captivity.

Burials were in and near the houses. Five skeletons have so far been recovered and carefully studied: a 17-year-old girl, a double burial of an adult and a child, an individual with auditory exostosis in one ear, common among free divers—in this case possibly from diving for fish—and another with an elbow abrasion known from primitives who paddle dugout canoes. Teeth were generally extremely eroded, for what reason is not known. As would be expected, there were also many health problems in evidence. See also *Carmel, Mount*.

AUJA EL-KHAFIR

See *Nitzana*.

AVDAT

Dramatic fortress-town in the Negev desert, on a high spur of a mountain ridge overlooking the ancient Wilderness of Zin. It was established in the 3rd cent. BC by Nabataean traders and became one of the most important of the Nabataean cities in the desert (see also *Mamshit, Shivta*) since it commanded the trade routes from the Nabataean capital, Petra, in Jordon, to *Gaza* on the coast and to Egypt. When the deified Nabataean king Obodas II (30–9 BC) was buried there, the town was renamed Oboda (Avdat is its Hebrew equivalent). Shifts in the trade routes and increasingly hostile incursions of nomads in the early Christian centuries turned the Nabataeans increasingly towards intensive dry farming in the desert for support, and their sophisticated water-supply systems (dams, cisterns and the canalizing of rain runoff in the wadis) are still being studied by agronomists from the desert kibbutzim today. They also produced lovely egg-shell pottery; the only Nabataean pottery workshop known, with three kilns (1st cent. AD), may be seen on top of the acropolis.

Eventually (106 AD) the Romans moved in and settled veterans at Avdat to protect it, and the city again prospered. In the 3rd cent. AD Diocletian built a garrison camp northeast of the city whose remains today indicate double stone walls, square towers and eight barracks. Avdat's most prosperous period was the Byzantine, when it became a town of 2 to 3,000 inhabitants, and most of the visible ruins date from this time. Still relying heavily on controlled agriculture, it specialized in vine growing. Several large Byzantine winepress installations are shown to the visitor to the acropolis. The town was sacked by the Sassanian Persians in 620 AD. Shortly thereafter came the Arabs; and that was the end.

Excavations on the acropolis (1958–1960) have uncovered much Nabataean work among later fortifications—retaining walls, arched portals, evidence of a temple—and the pottery workshop. Two towers survive from the Roman period, one, reconstructed and dated 294 AD, was incorporated into the Byzantine fort. Near the upper parking lot, rock-cut burial chambers are also on view, notably

Ruins of the Byzantine North Church on the citadel of Avdat, once a prosperous Nabataean trading town in the central Negev. The dramatic ruins seen today, however, are mostly Byzantine, when Avdat flourished again before its destruction by the Arabs in 636 AD. (Courtesy: Israel Ministry of Tourism.)

a large one that held 22 burials; there is also a street of the residential quarter. The massive Byzantine fortress consists of a rectangle of heavy walls with nine towers, an arched gate, and cisterns and a few buildings within it. To its west is an ecclesiastical area with two basilicas: the north church (4th cent. AD) with baptismal font, and St. Theodore to the south, roofless but well preserved and surrounded by monastic cells. In the interior are a number of tombstones of the 6th and 7th cents. Down the western slope of the hill, extensive remains of Byzantine and Nabataean houses have been found. One has been reconstructed. The rooms and courtyards of these houses were built out from caves used for storage and other purposes. At the bottom of the acropolis hill is a Byzantine bath establishment on Roman foundations, very well preserved and now roofed. There is a local museum. See also *Elusa, Nitzana, Rehovat*.

The deep canyon of En Avdat, now a nature reserve, cuts into the plain near the city. Along the rims of the canyon, heavy concentrations of flint tools indicate continuous early habitation from Paleolithic to Mesolithic times (80,000 to 15,000 BC).

BALATA, TELL   See *Nablus*.

BARAM   See Kefar Baram in *Meiron*.

BATASH, TELL   See *Timnah*.

BEERSHEBA   A biblical city associated with the Patriarchs and the story of the well dug in the desert by Abraham. The site of the ancient city lies at Tell Beersheba, or Tell es-Saba, 3 mi. E. of the large city of Beersheba, present capital of the Negev, 45 mi. SW of Jerusalem. The latter was not settled until late Roman-Byzantine times, and scattered Byzantine remains and a church mosaic floor in the Municipal Museum may be seen, but little else. However, excavations by the French under Jean Perrot in 1954–61 have located up to 50 remarkable Chalcolithic or Copper Age sites near the modern city, on both banks of the Wadi es-Saba, dating from about 4000 to 3000 BC. Of these a few have been intensively excavated, notably at Abu Matar, Bir Safadi and Bir Ibrahim. This Copper Age culture, with variants in Jordan and the coastal plain, is now called the Beersheba culture. It was highly sophisticated for the period, but it disappeared as quickly as it had come.

In these "troglodyte" villages, an early example of attempted adaptation to a harsh climate, three phases of occupation have been proposed. The earliest settlers cut their rectangular houses deep into the sandy loam of the valley slopes to avoid the desert heat. Entered by a shaft, they had rectangular rooms. But in the soft soil they soon collapsed. The next group tried a series of small, underground oval-shaped rooms connected by tunnels, again with access by shafts. Another type had a large, sunken open courtyard with rooms off it. After a long gap, the latest settlers built rectangular houses above ground, of mud brick on pebble foundations. These people buried infants under the floors; adults were exposed and their bones, sewed into hides, were buried in special underground rooms or pits. Bowl-lamps, to light the rooms, were found.

At Abu Matar evidence of copper smelting and manufacture was found, and at Bir Safadi an ivory carver's workshop, complete with workbench, tools and an elephant tusk, the ivory imported from Africa or Asia. A truly remarkable find was a group of sophisticated ivory figurines—several male figures and a fertility goddess. The sites also yielded basalt vessels, painted pottery, stone and ivory bracelets, beads of fruit and shell, and pendants of mother-of-pearl, bone and turquoise.

Another Copper Age site lies at Shiqmim, on the north bank of the Wadi Beersheba, about 15 miles west of Beersheba. Here one of the largest Copper Age village sites in Israel is being excavated, occupied from 4500 to 3200 BC, revealing again early house types and extensive burial fields. Five lesser Copper Age sites are nearby.

At biblical Tell Beersheba, a mound rising dramatically from the desert, extensive and continuing excavations, begun by Prof. Aharoni in 1969, have uncovered a complete Israelite fortified city, the southernmost outpost of the ancient kingdom of Judah. There is even evidence of earlier occupation in the Patriarchal period (12th–11th cents. BC), notably a deep well just outside the outer gate. It could have been the original of Abraham's well. But the first real city, founded by King David late in his reign, is dated to the 10th cent. BC. Encircled by a mud brick wall on stone foundations, with a glacis and moat, it was nevertheless destroyed, perhaps in 925 BC by Pharaoh Shoshenq (Shishak) I of Egypt. Rebuilt, it once again prospered in the 9th and 8th cents., and this time was fortified with a new casemate type of wall, typical of Solomonic times. The old outer gate was abandoned and the inner gate, now with three piers and guardrooms, was strengthened. The ruins, visible today and somewhat reconstructed, are of this second city. Roads radiate from a small square inside the gate, especially a circular road following the line of the walls, with houses on both sides. Three four-roomed houses in the western quarter have been reconstructed, and the elaborate drainage system with a central cistern has been traced.

A number of public buildings are also visible, one perhaps the governor's residence, another containing cult objects, mostly Egyptian. Just inside the wall by the gate is a complex of three long storehouses of the type established by Solomon and similar to the "stables" at Hazor and Megiddo. In a later repairing of this complex, a large four-horned altar was found, broken up and used as building material in a rebuilt wall. It was probably deliberately destroyed during the wrecking of local cult sites (in favor of the Temple at Jerusalem) by the reforming King Hezekiah, or during the later 7th-cent. reforms of Josiah. This second city was burned, probably by Sennacherib the Assyrian in 701 BC, and came to an end—fortunately for the archaeologists, for thereafter only forts were built on the site, first Persian then Roman with service buildings, including a bath. Finds from the Beersheba region are in the Begen Museum, Beersheba, and some of the Copper Age finds are in Jerusalem's Israel Museum.

BEIT MIRSIM, TELL

Ancient Bronze Age and Israelite city in the hill country S. of the Judean mtns., SW of Hebron and 8 mi. SE of Lachish. It was excavated between 1926 and 1932 by W. F. Albright, who identified it erroneously with the biblical Debir, also called Kirjathsefer (see Khirbet Rabud). Its ruins date back to the Early Bronze Age (about 2300 BC), and occupation continued through Philistine and Hyksos periods, with a gap after the end of the Middle Bronze Age, until its destruction by the Babylonians in 588 BC. Indeed the finds, especially pottery, helped greatly in establishing a chronology for the Levant. Middle Bronze Age fortifications and houses have been uncovered, and Mycenaean pottery from Late Bronze Age levels suggests extensive trade; other finds indicate a flourishing textile industry. Before the Israelite period began, a layer of ashes 3 ft. thick in places shows that the Bronze Age town was burned. From the Israelite period a gate and tower and four-room houses with internal pillars have been excavated.

BETH ALPHA

Ruins of a 6th cent. AD synagogue, famous for its charming mosaics, perhaps the best preserved in Israel, executed in a delightfully primitive style breathing both sincerity and naïveté, are found here. It lies some 5 mi. NW of Beth-Shan on the slopes of Mt. Gilboa in the Jezreel valley. Excavated in 1929, the building's walls now stand a few feet high, outlining a courtyard and vestibule paved with geometric mosaics, and the basilican hall with the principal mosaics, carefully restored. As one enters the basilica the mosaics begin with an inscription, flanked by a lion and a bull, giving the names of the craftsmen who laid the mosaic (in Greek) and the date (in Aramaic)—during the reign of Justinian the Great. Next comes a panel showing Abraham about to sacrifice Isaac and a crude hand of God issuing from a cloud above. The label (in Hebrew) says in effect: "Stop!" The middle panel further into the basilica is circular, outlined in borders of twisted cord, with a center showing the sun god Helios (the iconography here is thoroughly Classical) in his chariot. Radiating from this are 12 segments (labeled again in Hebrew) depicting the four seasons as winged women, along with the signs of the zodiac. The final panel at the end of the hall invites one to contemplate (revealed by a drawn curtain) the Ark of the Covenant or the Law, richly ornamented and surrounded by symbols of the long-lost temple such as two menorahs (seven-branched candelabrum) and two shofars (ram's-horn trumpets) as well as birds and animals.

BETHANY

See Jerusalem.

BETHEL

Or Beth-El, an important Canaanite and Israelite town, 10½ mi. N. of Jerusalem, situated almost 4,000 ft. above sea level in the mountains of Ephraim. It was here that Jacob dreamed of a ladder reaching up to heaven. Now largely covered by the village of Beitin, the site was excavated from time to time between 1934 and 1960, revealing remains dating from Early Bronze Age times into the Byzantine. From the Middle Bronze Age period parts of the town wall, gates and a sanctuary belonging to a substantial town were discovered, a town destroyed by the Egyptians about 1550 BC when they were chasing the Hyksos out of Egypt. The city lay in ruins until revived in the Late Bronze Age during the 14th cent. in even greater splendor. Many houses, pavements, an oil press and a drainage-sewer system were recovered from this flourishing Canaanite city. Once again it was destroyed, undoubtedly by the invading Israelites, whose ramshackle huts were built on the ruins.

Long a Canaanite cult center, Bethel continued as such under the Israelites. Under the Divided Monarchy, as the southernmost city of the state of Israel, its temple, with that of *Dan* to the north, was endowed with a golden calf by Israel's first king, Jeroboam, to help offset the influence of Jerusalem's Temple, now in rival Judah. In Roman times the city grew larger; the Byzantine city was even more extensive. East of the mound, a principal Byzantine street is still in use today.

BETH GUVRIN

See *Mareshah.*

BETHLEHEM

Holy city of Christendom, 5½ mi. S. of Jerusalem, the traditional site of the birth of Jesus. The city was first mentioned in Egyptian records of the 14th cent. BC, and if there was a Canaanite town here it was probably centered on a mound east of the Church of the Nativity, where Bronze Age and Iron Age sherds have been found. The presumed tomb of Rachel, wife of the Patriarch Jacob, sacred to both Jews and Muslims, lies under a 19th-cent. mausoleum on the outskirts of Bethlehem. Frequently mentioned in the Bible, Bethlehem was the setting for the story of Ruth, and it was the birthplace of King David, who later seized it from the Philistines. The limestone cave or grotto, now under the Church of the Nativity, was first mentioned as the traditional site of the birth of Jesus in the 2nd cent. AD, and in 135 AD Hadrian, after expelling the Jews from the city, set up a sacred grove of Thammuz-Adonis at Bethlehem in order to counteract the growing Christian veneration of the site.

Constantine the Great built the original Church of the Nativity. It was begun in 326 AD and was dedicated by Queen Helena in 339. At one end of the square basilica an octagonal apse was sited directly over the cave. In 384 AD St. Jerome came to Bethlehem to live and made it a famous monastic center. Here he wrote his great translation of the Old and New Testaments, the Vulgate, until very recently the Catholic authorized version of the Bible. The Constantinian church of his time was destroyed in the Samaritan uprising of 529 AD, and was entirely rebuilt by Justinian, who lengthened it, enlarged the apse over the grotto and added a vestibule, but retained the columns from the earlier church. In the 12th cent., in a most unusual collaboration, Crusaders and Byzantines together renovated the church. The Crusader kings were crowned here. The church fell on hard times in the succeeding centuries, but the fabric we see today is essentially that of Justinian. The grotto area, reached by stairs, has by now been much enlarged. Parts of the Constantinian church have been excavated. For instance it is possible to see under trap doors in the nave and the apse the remains of its mosaic floors.

BETH-SHAN

Often Beth-Shean, an imposing mound (Tell el-Husn), the site of ancient Beth-Shan, 19 mi. SE of Nazareth. Continuously inhabited for over 5,000 years (the modern town is just south of the tell), Beth-Shan lies on a strategic crossroads in a well-watered spot where the Jezreel and Harod valleys form a natural east-west route from the Jordan valley to the coast. As Scythopolis, the Roman-Byzantine city was a major metropolis. Visited today for its almost perfect Roman theater and other ruins and its Byzantine mosaics, the site is best remembered for the biblical story of King Saul. After his defeat and suicide at the Battle of Gilboa, his body was taken by the Philistines to their fortress of Beth-Shan nearby, beheaded, and the corpse hung on the walls of the city, while his armor was placed in the temple of Astarte (Astaroth).

Excavations in the mound between 1921 and 1933 by an American team uncovered the remains of 18 superimposed cities dating from the Copper Age (4th millennium BC) to Crusader times. There were traces of late Copper or Early Bronze Age houses, rectangular, of mud brick with apsidal ends. The later Canaanite city (14th to 12th cents. BC) was a powerful stronghold of the Egyptians in their attempt to hold down Palestine. Heavy fortifications included an inner tower or keep (a *migdol*) that also functioned as the Egyptian governors' residence. There was a large, round public granary of the 13th cent. and two temples, four times rebuilt over a long period, each with antechamber, central hall, and holy of holies or sanctuary. Relics of the Egyptian occupation included a victory stela of Seti I and a statue of Ramesses III.

The Philistines, formerly Sea Peoples subdued by Egypt, may have first appeared here as a mercenary garrison for the Egyptians, then perhaps took over the city when Egyptian control weakened, for it is hard to distinguish Canaanite from Philistine in the early Iron Age levels. Indeed, the Philistine temples were similar to the earlier ones, and the north temple, confirming the biblical account, was dedicated to Astaroth, the fertility goddess. Though no Philistine pottery was found, the extensive necropolis north of the mound did yield so-called Philistine anthropoid coffins of clay (with human faces) from the time of Saul. Later, as an Israelite city, a monumental gateway was built south of the temples, and storerooms were also found.

From the Hellenistic period, when the city was known as Nysa, or Scythopolis, a few remains have been found. After 63 BC, when the Romans took over, the city became one of the Decapolis (league of 10 Roman-Hellenized cities) and flourished, becoming famous during imperial times for its linen cloth. The theater, south of the mound, was built about 200 AD and is remarkably preserved except for the top seats. It could hold 5,000 spectators. Between it and the mound was a colonnaded street and bridge. On the mound itself the remains of a temple were found, and at its foot a Roman villa (2nd-3rd cents. AD) with mosaic floors and a bath with heating hypocausts. Byzantine relics are also numerous. On the mound a house and a circular church were found, and off it a large Byzantine house (5th-6th cents. AD) with 22 rooms. Part of a monastery of the same period, including living quarters, public lavatory, hall and colorful mosaic floors, can be found at Housing Project A: "Imhoff." There are also sections of the city wall, a potter's workshop, and across the Harod River the well-known 6th-cent. monastery of Lady Mary (its donor) with exceptionally fine mosaic floors. In the main hall a circular calendrical mosaic surrounds a personification of the sun and moon, with 12 panels showing the activities of the seasons. In another room 12 medallions depict country scenes of daily life, and other medallions in the chapel depict small birds and peacocks. Other rooms are paved with geometric mosaics.

Two Jewish synagogues outside the mound have also been excavated. At Tell Mastaba a 6th-cent. basilican type of building contains mosaics showing ritual objects and the Ark of the Law, as well as other mosaics. The other synagogue is across a courtyard from the excavated House of Leontius (with mosaic floors). Its floors include nine medallions.

Further large-scale excavations in the 1980s have revealed more of the impressively splendid Roman-Byzantine city. The stage building of the theater, already excavated, is being investigated as well as a Roman-Byzantine bathhouse nearby. Also near the theater the city's large amphitheater of the 2nd city AD has been discovered, and one-half of it excavated and restored. Originally outside the ancient city's walls, the amphitheater, oval in shape, measures about 335 ft. across at its widest. Its lower seats, of limestone from Mt. Gilboa, rose up behind a 9-ft.-high stone wall to protect the spectators from the wild beasts. The upper seats, long disappeared, were built of wood over basalt vaults. After the amphitheater fell out of use in Byzantine times, these vaults and the arena itself were occupied by houses until very recent times.

Some of the Byzantine road, paved with basalt blocks, that ran from the amphitheater to the city center has been uncovered, and in the city center itself another part of it has been found. The center has yielded a wealth of inscriptions in Greek (the official language) as well as statues, altars with bas-reliefs on their sides and many huge toppled columns. Some of these appear to have bordered the forum as well as the basalt-paved road which, in 5th-6th cent. Byzantine times, was lined with columns topped by arcades with shops behind them. It was at this time that Scythopolis attained its greatest size with a population of some 30,000. This magnificent city was apparently dealt its death blow by an earthquake in 747 AD that toppled most of the columns and arcades, all in one direction.

The finds from Beth-Shan are divided between the Municipal Museum in the town, the University Museum, Philadelphia, and the Rockefeller Museum, Jerusalem.

BETH SHEARIM

Remarkable Jewish catacombs and important religious center during the late Roman period, in the Jezreel valley, 12 mi. SE of Haifa. Beth Shearim itself, once a thriving center of Jewish learning, is now a ghost town on top of a hill (the new Beth Shearim lies a few miles to the east). The extensive necropolis is lower down around the slopes of the hill. When Romanized Jerusalem was all but denied to the Jews by the Roman occupiers after the second Jewish revolt of 138 AD, they also lost their traditional burying ground on the Mount of Olives. Their recognized leader, the saintly teacher Rabbi Judah (Yehuda) ha-Nasi (about 135–220 AD), probably through the intercession of his friend the emperor Marcus Aurelius, was allowed to move to Beth Shearim and brought with him the Jewish Sanhedrin, or supreme court (later moved to *Tiberias*). Rabbi Judah was famous as the compiler of the influential Mishnah, or codification of the Jewish laws, and under him Beth Shearim became a center of liberal Jewish learning, with a strong emphasis on the Greek Classical tradition. So venerated was this teacher that Jews hoped to be buried near him in Beth Shearim, and for over a hundred years the dead were brought not only from Palestine but from other lands of the widespread Diaspora to be interred here. In 351 AD Beth Shearim was destroyed during a Jewish revolt against the East Roman policies of Gallus Caesar. It limped on through the Byzantine period, but in the Arab period its rich necropolis was given over to tomb robbers.

Excavations in the old town, begun in 1936, have revealed the foundations of some of the large public buildings that adorned it in its prime, notably one of the largest synagogues in Israel (3rd cent. AD), and a basilica for public meetings and business (probably 2nd cent.), both with a double row of interior columns. Houses, a glass factory and a heavy olive press have also been found. There are 31 rock-cut catacombs in the necropolis, all robbed, but nevertheless yielding an abundance of inscriptions—about 80 percent in Greek—carvings, reliefs and sculptured sarcophagi. Usually a courtyard fronts the burial chambers, sometimes at the end of corridors, which are closed by stone doors (most still turn on their hinges), and they lead from one to the other through arched openings. The chambers have burial recesses, pit graves in the floor, or sarcophagi placed where feasible. The largest, Catacomb 20, a public cemetery with a triple entranceway, was built in Rabbi Judah's lifetime; No. 14, also with a triple arch, seems to have been a family tomb for the rabbi's two sons and a companion—and probably for Rabbi Judah himself. Both had above them open-air walled sanctuaries with benches for prayer. The later catacombs were simpler, with fewer sarcophagi. Some were crowded, others more spacious, depending on the status and wealth of the clients—for the town's industry was the cutting and furnishing of these tombs. Catacomb 13 has 12 chambers on four levels, with 192 burial places! The carvings on the sarcophagi are eclectic—Zeus, Aphrodite, the Amazons, oxen, the Roman eagle, as well as Jewish symbols. A museum in an old water tank displays the best of the glass and earthenware found in 1960 excavations. See also *Zippori*.

BETH-SHEMESH

Ancient city under Tell Rumeilah, about 1 mi. W. of the modern city of the same name, about 19 mi. W. of Jerusalem in the Judean hills, excavated 1911–12 and 1928–33. A walled Canaanite-Hyksos city in the Middle Bronze Age probably destroyed by the Egyptians, its most prosperous period came in the Late Bronze Age. A large building, two smelting furnaces and cisterns were uncovered from this period, and the more interesting finds included a tablet incised in the Ugaritic cuneiform, and a sherd with early Canaanite script (the remote ancestor of our alphabet). This city was destroyed, as were so many others, roughly around 1200 BC, probably by the Sea Peoples, for it was then occupied by the Philistines and prospered anew until the Israelites finally conquered it in the early 10th cent. They apparently built it up as a provincial capital under the United Monarchy of David and Solomon. From this period came parts of a governor's residence, a large public granary with three long parallel rooms, and a stone-lined silo about 25 ft. deep. Again the city was burned, probably by Pharaoh Shosenq of Egypt in 924 BC or the Babylonians in 586, and was succeeded by an unwalled village, though the copper industry and a dyeing industry continued and olive oil and grape vats were found. Light settlement continued into the Byzantine period.

BETH YERAH, TELL

Khirbet Kerak in Arabic, it is a 50-acre mound near the lower end of the Sea of Galilee, on its western side, just north of the Jordan River where it runs briefly west out of the lake. Its history is interesting, though there is little to see except a few late Roman-Byzantine remains. There was an early settlement here, dating perhaps to about 3000 BC, which was abandoned in the Middle Bronze Age, about 2000 BC. Centuries later in the Persian period another small settlement was founded that later formed the basis for a larger Hellenistic town, probably that Philoteria known to have been founded by Ptolemy II Philadelphus (285–246 BC). This town flourished through the Roman and into the Byzantine period.

Excavations begun in 1944 uncovered the prehistoric settlement, which was protected only on its southerly sides by a 25 ft.-thick mud brick wall—for at the time and up until the Middle Ages the Jordan flowed north of the mound, not to its south as it does now. There were two finds of interest from the early settlement. One was the first discovery of the distinctive Khirbet Kerak ware, subsequently found elsewhere in Palestine and in northern Syria. It may have originated in Anatolia. The other was a large rectangular structure of about 2500 BC with a central hall and paved courtyard, and on the courtyard a series of ovens and nine circular foundations (each some 30 ft. in diameter). These seem to have been grain silos, and the whole a large public granary, suggesting large-scale farming here at an early date. Excavations also uncovered some houses of the Hellenistic town and found that it had been fortified. The Romans built a square fort at the northern edge of the mound, close to the lake (3rd cent. AD). It has corner towers and two more flanking the gate. Later a bathhouse was built against its southeast corner, and in the Byzantine period a large synagogue, one of the largest in Israel, was erected inside it. Only part of its mosaic floor can now be seen. Further south was a Christian Byzantine church of the 5th cent., often modified and finally destroyed in the early 7th cent. AD.

BIR IBRAHIM	See *Beersheba*.
BIR SAFADI	See *Beersheba*.
CAESAREA	Herod the Great's metropolis of Caesarea Maritima with its artificial port, 22 mi.

Herod the Great's metropolis of Caesarea Maritima with its artificial port, 22 mi. S. of Haifa, the capital of Roman Palestine for almost 600 years. Its extensive ruins, tastefully displayed and partly reconstructed, are spread over a large area centering on the small Crusader city. Caesarea is now a popular resort with a famous golf course and swimming and boating off the Roman harbor. In ancient times it was originally a small Phoenician naval port called Strato's Tower (Strato was the Hellenized name for certain kings of Sidon). Remnants of Phoenician houses and of the port works of this small fortified town have been found in the excavations. In 30 BC Augustus in gratitude gave it to his favorite client king, Herod, one of the greatest builders of antiquity, who turned it into a major commercial port by constructing massive harbor works on a scale hitherto unheard of. Herod's vast new city, designed to funnel the goods of the east towards Rome, was a planned metropolis, like Brasilia today, laid out with a regular grid of broad streets, an elaborate sewer system, splendid public buildings, a forum, baths and luxurious villas. Built between 22 and 10 BC, it was, it has been estimated, at least three times larger than the small Crusader city on the shore one sees today, and by Byzantine times it had grown nearly eight times larger. With the gradual submergence of the coastline and with the coming of the Arabs, this great city fell on evil times and its harbor silted up. The Crusaders took it in 1101, using part of the port, then lost it again. It was King Louis IX of France, recapturing the city in 1251, who built the fortifications, castle and ca-

Caesarea, the great city and port built by Herod the Great, a planned metropolis. It was the capital of Roman Palestine for nearly six centuries. The remains of the massive southern breakwater of Herod's artificial harbor may be seen—one of the greatest engineering feats of the Roman world—and beyond some of the excavated parts of the vast Roman city, overlain near the harbor by the far smaller, heavily fortified Crusader city. (Courtesy: Israel Government Press Office.)

thedral whose ruins, cleaned up and restored, may be seen today. Years later, Baybars, the Mamluk ruler of Egypt, took the city in 1291 and leveled it, and thereafter its precious statues, beautifully cut stones, carvings and columns have been freely looted and are to be found scattered about or built into many a village and city around the Mediterranean.

Caesarea became the Roman capital of Palestine in 6 AD, seat of the Roman prefect (later procurator), including Pontius Pilate. A recent and dramatic find in the theater is an inscription on a reused block from a temple bearing his name, known only from the Gospels and Josephus' histories. Peter made his first Gentile convert here, the centurion Cornelius, and St. Paul knew the city well. He was imprisoned here for two years before his final journey to Rome. During the Jewish revolt of 66–70 AD, Vespasian, the Roman commander, was proclaimed emperor here. In the 3rd cent. AD Caesarea became a leading intellectual center with a famous rabbinical academy; about the same time it became the home of the brilliant Christian teacher and scholar, Origen, who founded a library in the city second only to that of Alexandria. In the 4th cent., Eusebius, the church historian, was its bishop.

It has been estimated that the ancient city covered 8,000 acres or 12 sq. mi., and to date only a small part of the city has been excavated, beginning in earnest in 1959. Since then two large international projects have been set up—the Joint Expedition to Caesarea Maritima (JECM) and the Caesarea Ancient Harbour Excavation Project (CAHEP). The latter, organized in 1979–80, became one of the largest international underwater projects in the world. Since 1971 the two projects have attracted and employed over 3,500 volunteers from many lands: diggers, divers, and supervisory personnel. On land, aside from the small Crusader city and its massive fortifications, now cleared, the most prominent feature is the restored theater, the first Roman theater in Judaea and one of Herod's innovations, though frequently modified in later years. It is about the same size as that at *Beth-Shan* and is now used for concerts. Of the pre-Herodian Hellenistic town some house foundations have been recovered and part of the city wall, with two towers, later incorporated into the Herodian city.

Other finds from the Roman city include a vast artificial podium, partly vaulted, on which stood Herod's columned temple of Augustus dominating the harbor, as well as two aqueducts. The earlier one is partly Herod's, partly Hadrianic, with a length of well-preserved arches along the shore. It brought water from the slopes of Mt. Carmel, 9 mi. away, part of it tunneled by Herod's workers through over 4 mi. of solid rock. The other aqueduct, built in the 4th cent. as the city grew, is low-level and roofed. The Arabs crept through it in 639 to enter the besieged city. In the 1970s a magnificent Byzantine concourse was uncovered. It was 54 ft. wide, paved with marble slabs and white mosaics robbed from the old city and with a triple gateway and statues. The hippodrome, once famed for its races, is now much ruined. Seating 20,000, it was one of the largest in the Roman world. It can be discerned inland with its obelisk and stone turning points tumbled about in what is now a field.

An oval depression to the east of the city marks the site of the amphitheater where 2,500 survivors of the Jewish revolt of 70 AD were fed to the beasts. Some of the mosaic floors unearthed in the city may have belonged to Origen's library, while the Jewish quarter just north of the Crusader city, built on the site of the pre-Herodian town, has yielded a series of superimposed synagogues of the 3rd to 5th cents. AD, rebuilt again in Byzantine times. From the Byzantine period, when the city reached its maximum size, a number of grand public buildings have been identified, remnants of the walls have been cleared, a bath discovered, and a church with a mosaic floors—the huge Great Bird mosaic, 46 by 52 ft., now restored. Several streets have also been recovered, including the aforementioned principal "Street of the Statues." Just off it lies a large square paved in marble.

Maritime archaeologists have been particularly interested in the huge artificial harbor, originally built by Herod and completed in less than 10 years. Herod called it, grandly, Sebastos (Augusutus in Greek). It was in constant use for seven centuries. One of the largest and earliest of such engineering feats in the Roman world, it was begun about 50 years before the famous Portus harbor at Ostia, the port of Rome. It consisted of a large round harbor enclosed, except for a narrow north-facing entrance, by a massive curving breakwater to the south and a shorter one jutting out on the north side, with a small safe harbor off it inland, used by Herod's warships. Another bay, almost as large and later the main Byzantine harbor, adjoined it to the south, and a smaller harbor—the older Hellenistic and probably Phoenician harbor—to the north. In all, the main harbors enclosed 200,000 sq. yds. and could shelter up to 300 ships. Around the principal harbor ran a seawall with square towers and warehouses along the inside as well as a wide promenade along the quays and breakwaters for the use of Caesarea's citizens. A tall lighthouse stood by the entrance and outside it six huge statues on wide bases, three on each side. The great volume of trade passing through Caesarea is suggested by the discovery of five city blocks of long, barrel-vaulted warehouses (*horrea*), 20 to a block, along the southern shore, each 90 ft. long and 15 ft. high. They were in use from the 1st cent. to the 7th. In one, a late Roman shrine to Mithras, the soldiers' god, with an altar and frescoes on the walls, was discovered in 1972.

The harbor works of Herod, a magnificent and innovative feat of engineering executed under water and in the open sea—and a treacherous sea at that—included dressed stones, some nearly 50 ft. long, to build up the main break-waters, and enormous blocks of concrete weighing up to 50 tons, lowered into the sea in double-walled wooden forms and filled with hydraulic cement, one of its earliest uses. The bases of the breakwaters were protected by more courses of stone blocks on the outside. There was also a sluicing system to clear the harbor of accumulated sand-silt periodically, a secondary breakwater along the vulnerable south side to slow the incoming waves, and loading jetties. In 1973 the hull of a large Roman merchant ship of the late 1st cent. BC was found in the bottom and is now being studied. The southern, or Byzantine harbor has recently been given attention. On a promontory enclosing it to the south, a pool, or fish farm, has been found, probably part of a Herodian palace. The earlier northern harbor has also been surveyed, and the base of a pre-Herodian tower, similar to the two located on land, has been identified under water. This earlier harbor and associated fortifications may have been incorporated directly into Herod's grand plan. There is a small museum in the nearby kibbutz of Sedot Yam.

CAPERNAUM

Or Kfar Nahum, on the NW shore of the Sea of Galilee, 6 mi. N. of Tiberias. Jesus chose this small, poverty-ridden lakeside fishing village as the base for his Galilean ministry, probably because he made his first converts here, Andrew and Simon Peter, the fishermen. The town later prospered and grew towards the hills; the old synagogue of Jesus' time, in which he had undoubtedly preached, was pulled down and a magnificent and ornate new one built on the same site, as was the custom, whose ruins, partially restored, are now a major attraction. Most famous of the numerous Galilean synagogues, and the finest found in Israel, it was a basilica of the Classical type, with richly ornamented friezes and lintels and rows of Corinthian columns. The menorah and shofar appear in some of the capitals. On the eastern side was the traditional colonnaded courtyard. Excavated in the 19th cent., 1905 and 1969 on—largely by the Franciscans—the synagogue has been dated anywhere from the 2nd to the 4th cents. AD. Below it a few basalt stones of the synagogue of Jesus' time have been found.

Close to the synagogue is the traditional site of St. Peter's house, in which Jesus lodged and taught. It lies amidst the remains of the ancient town of Jesus' day, small crude houses of black basalt contrasting with the white limestone of the synagogue. Franciscan friars have excavated five blocks, or insulae, of these houses, which date from the 1st to the 6th cent. AD when the town was de-stroyed by the Arabs. An early Roman bathhouse can be seen, and the town plan is now clear. Among the houses was a single-room house of the 1st cent. (Peter's time) that had been venerated as a shrine over a very long period. Early in the 4th cent. the room had been closed off within an enclosure and refloored and reroofed, the whole complex making a house church as described by a traveling nun, Egeria, in the 380s AD. Peter's house, she reported, "has been made into a church, with its original walls still standing . . . There also is the synagogue." In the 5th cent. the site was further honored with an octagonal basilica enclosing the room, which was given a mosaic floor, and there was an apse to the east. This church was destroyed by the Arabs.

The ancient Chorazin, or Korazin, now Khirbet Kerazeh, lies in the hills 2½ mi. N. of Capernaum. The Jewish town of the Roman period, occupied from the 4th to 7th cents. AD and now in ruins, was built on terraces, with another ornate synagogue of the basilica type on the highest terrace. Probably 3rd or 4th cent. AD, it is very similar to that of Capernaum, but is built in black basalt. It has the same columns and profusion of carvings. Excavations around it have uncovered the remains of a large building with its own cistern, ritual bath and storeroom. An octagonal building discovered south of the synagogue was probably a church, for here, as in Capernaum, Christians and Jews lived in harmony. In the synagogue a notable find was a stone armchair of black basalt, decorated with rosettes, of the kind reserved in synagogues for important teachers of the Law, "The Throne of Moses." The donor of the chair is named in an Aramaic inscription. The chair is now in Jerusalem's Israel Museum. Just outside Chorazin is a field of some 300 megalithic dolmens, or burial chambers, dating to the Neolithic period. (See also *Meiron.*)

CARMEL

See *Khirbet Suseya.*

CARMEL, MOUNT

Well known from biblical references, Mt. Carmel today is even better known for its prehistoric caves. Easily visited, these flank the Valley of the Caves on the western slopes of the mountain range, about 8 mi. S. of Haifa. Excavations between 1929 and 1972 in four caves here have yielded an astonishing sequence of various finds, including almost 100 skeletons, dating from the early Paleolithic (after 300,00 BC) to the Natufian (about 10,000–7500 BC). The earliest site, the Cave of the Oven (et-Tabun), was occupied through most of the Paleolithic (from about 150,000 BC) into the period of Neanderthal man (about 40,000–30,000 BC), yielding crude flake tools from the early Tayacian industry. A female Neanderthal skeleton (the Woman of Tabun) was found here and the jaw of a male. The Cave of the Valley (el-Wad) was occupied from the Middle Paleolithic to Natufian times, and was especially rich in remains of the latter, including about 70 burials. These were found mostly on the terrace outside the cave, partly paved with flat stones. Some of the dead were wearing ornaments. Over 12,000 implements were found, including sophisticated sickles of flint set in bone hafts. One such haft was carved with the head of a fawn, for the Natufians were among the earliest prehistoric people in Palestine to produce art. A human head in limestone was also found, and there were bowls and grinding tools of stone and other artifacts. The best-known and most puzzling of the caves, the Cave of the Kid (es-Skhul), yielded amongst Mousterian (Neanderthal) implements about 10 burials with curious evolutionary features—definitely of the *Homo sapiens* type but with certain Neanderthal characteristics as well. Their meaning is still being debated. They were not, however, the descendants of the people who lived in the el-Wad cave, being dated 10 to 20,000 years later. The Geula cave yielded many tools and animal bones, starting with the Mousterian period. The finds are in the Museum of Prehistory, Haifa. See also *Eynan, Kebara, Nahal Oren.*

CHORAZIN, or Korazin.

See *Capernaum.*

CORAL ISLAND	See *Ezion-Geber*.
DALIT, TELL	See *Aphek, Tell*.
DAN, TELL	A 50-acre mound (Tell el-Qadi) in the midst of a luxuriant nature reserve at the SW foot of Mt. Hermon, 20 mi. NE of Safad and close to the Golan Heights and the Syrian Border. It is the site of the ancient Israelite city of Dan, the northern-most city of the land of Israel, as *Beersheba* was the furthest south (as in the Old Testament: "from Dan to Beersheba"). Before the Israelites took it, it was the Canaanite city-state of Laish, referred to in Egyptian texts of the 19th and 15th cents. and in the archives of Mari in Syria. Laish was captured by the tribe of Dan in the 11th cent. BC (a destruction layer of ashes was found in the excavations, begun by the Israeli archaeologist Biran in 1966). At first the Danites, as the excavations showed, merely camped on the ruins within the massive Canaanite wall, but later they settled down and rebuilt the fortifications. The city came into prominence under Jeroboam of the 10th cent., the first king of Israel after the separation of the two kingdoms, who made it into a northern bastion of his kingdom, heavily fortified, by encircling the old walls with a new wall and gate. He also set up two cult centers, at Dan and *Bethel*, to counteract the influence of the temple at Jerusalem, and placed a golden calf in each. For this political idolatry the priests at Jerusalem never forgave him. In 732 BC Dan was destroyed by the Assyrians and its inhabitants presumably marched into exile with the other "lost tribes of Israel."

The site was first occupied in the Early Bronze Age. In the Middle Bronze Age (18th cent.) it was fortified with a massive rampart 30 ft. high, a stone core piled with steeply sloping banks of earth and smoothed with clay on the outside to form a glacis. Recently a northern gate in this wall has come to light, of mud brick with a three-arched passageway flanked by two guard chambers on each side, the only fully preserved Bronze Age gate found so far. Steps led down to a pebbled street within the city. From the prosperous Late Bronze Age period comes a mass grave (45 burials) dug into the inner rampart, with imported Mycenaean pottery. From the period of King Jeroboam an even more impressive southern gate complex was excavated, linking the new outer and the old inner walls. The outer gate had two towers and four guardrooms and a long bench for the elders, who usually "sat in the gate." A paved processional way led through it and the inner gate up to the town. In a paved square fronting the main gate a dais and four pillar bases were found, probably once supporting a canopy to shelter the king when he received at the gate; or perhaps it was for a statue. Much of this, particularly the Canaanite triple gate, can still be seen, as well as a Roman fountain house.

The gates and fortifications were destroyed in the 9th cent. by King Hadad of Syria, leagued with Judah to the south against Israel. Again the city was rebuilt and reached new heights of splendor under King Omri and his son Ahab (he who married Jezebel). Excavations have uncovered a large open platform, largely from this period, in the northern part of the mound. It was approached by steps and was enclosed with low walls. It is thought to be a *bamah*, a High Place or cult sanctuary, probably begun under Jeroboam and long in use. A large horned altar of limestone for sacrifices was found near it in 1974, but so far no golden calf! Excavations continue. There is a museum at Kibbutz Dan.

DEAD SEA SCROLLS	See *Nahal Hever, Qumran.*
DEBIR	See *Khirbet er-Rabud.*
DEIR EL-BALAH	In the Gaza Strip about 8 mi. S. of Gaza. An Israeli excavation by Trude Dothan, begun in 1972, resumed in 1977, has uncovered, under the sand dune (from the bottom up): an Egyptian town of the late 14th cent. BC, an Egyptian fortress of the early 13th cent., evidence of Philistine settlement in the 12th and 11th cents., Israelite campsites in the succeeding two centuries, and finally Byzantine remains. For the site was obviously an important coastal way station on the route from Egypt up into Palestine. Thus the earliest levels represented an important Egyptian outpost at the time of the empire, yielding many fine ornaments and artifacts of Egyptian origin or type. But there were also quantities of Mycenaean, Cypriot and Palestinian pottery, indicating intensive trade by an internationalized settlement probably including Egyptianized Canaanites and others, with a hybrid culture of their own.

The first find at the site was of a 14th–13th cent. BC cemetery buried under the dunes from which came four anthropoid coffins, one surrounded by rich grave goods, of a type imitating the Egyptian, which the Philistines later adopted as their own (see *Beth-Shan*). Some 60 others are known to have come from this site earlier. Searching for the settlement of the cemetery, the lowest level, partly excavated as of 1982, yielded a town and sumptuous small palace of over 15 rooms of the type built in the *Amarna* Egyptian period under Akhenaten (see EGYPT). Above it was the 13th-cent. Egyptian fortress with corner towers, obviously one of the string of strongholds along the coast guarding the imperial route as depicted on a relief of Seti I at Karnak (see *Thebes* under EGYPT). It flourished as well in the reign of Ramesses II, his son, the period determined for the cemetery. It also had a large lake or reservoir (as shown for all the fortresses on the relief), as well as attendant buildings. These fortresses may have forced the Israelites of the Exodus to take the inland desert route on their way to Canaan. The lake was later filled in and became the site of an artisan's village (kilns, etc.) in the next period. As the empire waned, Philistines, perhaps brought in by the Egyptians as a mercenary garrison, lived on here in an undefended settlement, their presence marked by pits filled with sherds of their typical pottery. More pits indicated a later Israelite encampment.

DIOCAESAREA	See *Zippori.*
DOR, TELL	Once-important coastal town and harbor on a promontory about 10 mi. N. of *Caesarea* (whose massive artificial harbor posed a threat to that of Dor during the Roman period), and about 15 mi. S. of Haifa. It was most prosperous during the Phoenician-Persian, Hellenistic and Roman periods. Sporadic explorations in the 75-acre site since the 1920s were intensified after 1979 when a double excavation was begun, one of the tell on the promontory, north of a public beach and Crusader castle and the deserted Arab village of Tantura, the other of the harbor works south of the tell. They continue. From ancient times the town produced the famous Phoenician dyes extracted from the murex shellfish. A Persian-period dye installation has been found in the harbor area. The site

dates at least from the Middle Bronze Age (16th cent. BC)—from which a house foundation has recently been discovered—and is mentioned in Egyptian texts. In the 12th cent. BC it was taken over by a group of Sea Peoples associated with the Philistines. Eventually it became an important Phoenician port. In the Hellenistic period, after a century of Ptolemaic rule from Egypt, it fell to the Seleucids in 201 BC, and finally to the Romans in 63 BC. It remained a viable town until at least the 3rd cent. AD, and in the 5th cent. had a bishop.

From the Iron Age period a massive limestone gatehouse has recently come to light, but the most visible features of the site are Hellenistic, including ashlar masonry stretches of the city wall, and a glacis, gate and square towers built by the Ptolemies in the 3rd cent. BC. A residential quarter has been uncovered and a Hellenistic-Roman industrial area with silos, winepresses, ovens, cisterns and dye works. A complex of basins and channels on the north was probably used for the dye industry. Next to the old acropolis on the tell is the large podium of a temple, now being explored, and outside of it the vestiges of a Roman theater, as well as a Roman aqueduct and street and the agora areas. The artificial port works, though not as sizeable as those of Caesarea, offer a wider variety of remains—quays built by the Sea Peoples, Phoenician shipyards, and Hellenistic harbor works, including three large boat slips cut into the rocky sides of one of the harbors.

A large Christian basilica complex, located on the landward slopes of the tell, was built in the 4th cent. AD and was in use until the 8th. With three aisles and mosaic pavements, it has the tomb of a saint in the southern aisle. There is an on-site museum (opened on request), and a Museum for Marine and Regional Archaeology is at nearby Kibbutz Nahsholim.

DUWEIR, TELL, ED-   See *Lachish*.

EBAL, MOUNT   The remarkable discovery of a large early Israelite site, most likely an altar, very well preserved, in an open-air cult site on Mt. Ebal, now dated, after excavations, to the presumed time of the Exodus. Mt. Ebal, 1,900 ft. high and bare and rocky, rises north of *Nablus* with Mt. Gerizim, the sacred mountain of the Samaritans, to its south. The Samaritans consider Ebal an accursed mountain. The existence of the altar is actually corroborated by the Bible (Deuteronomy 27, Joshua 8). According to these passages Joshua, commanded by Moses, built an altar of unhewn stones on the summit of Mt. Ebal. The tribes of Israel then assembled on the slopes of the two mountains to hear the Law and its commandments. The excavations, currently (1989) still in progress, have uncovered an Egyptian scarab on the site that can be dated to 1525 to 1220 BC in the latter part of the reign of the great pharaoh Ramesses II, a period that corresponds, according to many experts, to the time of the Exodus of the Israelites from Egypt.

EBEN-EZER   See *Izbet-Sartah*.

EFSHAR, TELL EL-   Ancient site a few mi. N. of Netanya and somewhat inland near Kibbutz Ma'abarot, overlooking the Alexander River valley in the northern Sharon plain. Joint Israeli-American excavations, begun in 1979, have indicated occupation from about 3000 BC to the Byzantine period (7th cent. AD). On the property of the kibbutz a Chalcolithic or Copper Age burial cave has been found with human bones in house-shaped ossuaries. A Middle Bronze Age palace with plastered walls, as well as Early Bronze Age, Late Bronze age and Iron Age remains have been found in the tell, and from the late Roman-Byzantine period remains of stone-built architecture, including a stone-floored villa. Nearby Michmoret on the coast was the city's port. Excavations here have revealed Persian period buildings and evidence of trade in obsidian from Anatolia as early as the 7th millennium BC, and pottery from the Late Iron Age into the Byzantine period, as well as Phoenician-style shaft tombs. Finds can be seen at the Kibbutz Ma'abarot and the Rupin Institute museums nearby.

EGLON	See *Tell el-Hesi*.
EIN YAEL	See *Jerusalem*.
EKRON	See *Tell Miqne*.

ELUSA

Nabataean-Byzantine town in the Negev, the modern Haluza or Halutza, in Arabic el-Khalasa, about 13 mi. SW of *Beersheba*. In the late Roman period Elusa was the largest and most important town in the central Negev. However since its ruins were extensively robbed and the rest covered in shifting sand, little was to be seen on the surface. Assuming nevertheless that much was left under the sand, Israeli archaeologists excavated the site in 1973 and 1979, and again in 1980, joined by an American team. One late Nabataean house, for example, proved to have been preserved up to a height of 7 ft. Elusa was an early Nabataean creation, founded in the late 4th or early 3rd cent. BC as one of the important way stations on the road from Petra, the Nabataean capital in Jordan, to *Gaza* on the coast. At its height in the Roman period, Elusa was the home of the famous rhetorician Libanius and was the earliest of the towns of the central Negev to harbor a Christian community.

Excavations uncovered a tower, part of the city's defenses, still standing up to the second story, a late Nabataean residential quarter, a large reservoir, and a theater dating back to the Middle Nabataean period whose stone-paved orchestra, donor's box and stage building were uncovered. The theater was in use for a long time as a Greek inscription of the 5th cent. AD proved. Much evidence of the Nabataean presence and traditions were revealed on the site, including examples of the typical classic Nabataean capitals. The cathedral, 90 by 210 ft., proved to be the largest church known in the Negev. Originally it was built with one apse, but was later rebuilt with three apses. Its floor, columns and capitals were of marble and there were gold-plated glass mosaics on the walls. The church was entered up monumental stairs from a huge atrium with four porticos that may once have belonged to an earlier Nabataean temple. Another large church and two smaller ones were also identified. Cemeteries of the three principal periods of the town's history were also investigated. In the Middle Nabataean cemetery, as at Mampsis (*Mamshit*), there were tables and a kitchen for the preparation and eating of funeral feasts. See also *Avdat*, *Nitzana*, *Rehovot*, *Shivta*.

EMMAUS,	See *Imwas*.
EN AVDAT	See *Avdat*.

EN BOQEQ

On the SW shore of the Dead Sea about 15 mi. SE of *Arad*, now an oasis of greenery in the dry, desolate desert, and a beach resort. It was first occupied in the time of Herod the Great (he of the Massacre of the Innocents), when pharmaceutical herbs were intensively cultivated and processed here. A "factory" for the purpose was excavated on the site between 1967 and 1972, a large square building with rooms around an inner court where leaves, buds, petals and resins were processed. It was destroyed in the bloody revolt against the Romans (66–70 AD) and the site lay desolate until the late 4th cent. when another square building, this time a fort or *castellum*, was constructed nearby as part of the *limes*, or frontier defense line of Palestine. The fort, occupied from 360 to 635 AD, with corner towers, is still visible, for the walls stand in places 20 ft. high, though there is not much else to see at the site. An aqueduct brought water from the En Boqeq spring, and the frontier militia stationed here established an agricultural settlement that was destroyed by the Sassanian Persians in 614 in their war against Byzantium. Remains of a nymphaeum and cistern at the En Noith spring have also been found, as well as a cemetery. There may also have been a bathhouse (apparently not excavated).

EN-GEDI

Or Ein-Gedi, a luxuriant oasis and watering spa on the shores of the Dead Sea, 11 mi. N. of *Masada* (and 20 mi. N. of *En Boqeq* above), famous in antiquity for its aromatic herbs, perfumes, wine and dates. The spring in En-Gedi's nature park, called David's Fountain, issuing in a lovely waterfall and sparkling pool, is associated with the young David, who took refuge from the wrath of King Saul in the wilderness of En-Gedi. Today a kibbutz of modern settlers here raises vegetables, fruit and flowers for the market. Archaeologists investigating the area after 1949, but chiefly in the 1960s, discovered on a terrace above the spring a remarkable Copper Age temple or sanctuary, in use from about 3600 BC to about 3200 then abandoned. The stone foundations of the mud brick walls indicate an irregular walled enclosure with two entrances (one with a gatehouse), a small round structure (an altar or basin) at its center, and a long building, about 65 ft. long, at the north that was obviously a cult center with a sacrifice place in the middle and benches around the walls, and a small building to the east—a storeroom? For more on the Copper Age remains around En-Gedi, see *Nahal Mishmar* ahead.

There was an Israelite settlement at En-Gedi, but long after David's time. Excavations at the mound of Tell Goren (or Tell el-Jurn) in the southern part of the oasis have revealed remains of a settlement from the late 7th cent. BC that flourished on the mound and its slopes in the time of the Divided Monarchy. Buildings with courtyards were found, some with pithoi, storage jars, in the courtyards, probably used in the perfume business, especially from the balsam. This settlement was destroyed, undoubtedly at the time of the Babylonian exile. Next from the Persian period (5th–4th cents. BC) several buildings appeared—of course the excavators found these in reverse order as they went down into the mound—one with courtyards and 23 rooms and storerooms. In the Hellenistic period (3rd–2nd cent. BC) a trapezoidal fortress was built on top of the mound, then as business boomed in the 2nd cent. the site became a royal Hasmonaean estate specializing in agriculture and salt and bitumen from the Dead Sea. It was also an Idumaean center. Decline set in, and finally complete destruction during the first Jewish revolt (66–70 AD).

In the late 1st and 2nd cent. AD a new citadel and houses appeared and the

David's Fountain in the luxuriant oasis of En Gedi on the Dead Sea, known in antiquity for its herbs, perfumes, wines and dates and today for its vegetables, flowers and fruit. David's Fountain commemorates the biblical story of David and Saul when young David fled to the Wilderness of En Gedi to escape the king's wrath. (Courtesy: Israel Government Press Office.)

town became a Roman imperial estate. A long narrow bathhouse has been discovered northeast of the mound. During the second Jewish revolt (132–135 AD), its leader, Bar Kochba, used the town and its baths as a headquarters until driven to take refuge, like David, in the caves over the Dead Sea. Finally, when there was a large Jewish town here in the 2nd and 3rd cents. AD, a synagogue turned up, much rebuilt in the 5th and 6th cents. Its mosaics feature birds, inscriptions and the signs of the zodiac. After the Arab conquest the town was abandoned. There is an interesting museum at the nearby En-Gedi Nature School in the park.

ER-RAS (MANAHAT)	See *Jerusalem*.
ER-RAS, TELL	See *Nablus*.
ESHTEMOA	See *Khirbet Suseya*.
ET-TELL	See *Ai*.

EUTHEMIUS MONASTERY	See *Khan el Ahmar*.

EYNAN

Or Ain Mallaha, one of the earliest settled villages known. A Natufian settlement (about 10,000—7500 BC), the site overlooks Lake Huleh about 5 mi. NE of *Hazor* and was discovered during the draining of the Huleh swamps in 1954. It was then excavated by the French under Jean Perrot from 1955 to 1961. Only a part of the village was uncovered, but it is estimated that, over three occupation periods, there were around 50 houses here and a population of some 200 to 300. The settlement seemed to be a permanent one—most unusual in those times of seminomadic hunter-gatherers—and the inhabitants lived by hunting large animals (including the possible herding of gazelles), fishing, and gathering wild cereals. The houses, larger in the first period, were pits in the ground, often floored with stone and with a lining of rubble. The roofs were probably of reeds or matting. One early house, about 15 ft. across, with a paved floor and red painted plastered walls (earliest example known), was later used as a tomb for an important couple. The woman was buried with a shell headdress. Open spaces in the village held storage pits, and some 82 burials, single and collective, were found, mostly outside the houses. Some were skull burials; funerary goods were rare. One burial was marked by a circle of stones, others with vertical markers, one of the earliest known examples of stone grave monuments. The finds included bone implements, basalt artifacts, and two pebbles with possible human faces incised on them.

EZION-GEBER

According to the Bible, "King Solomon built a fleet of ships at Ezion-Geber, which is near Eloth on the shore of the Red Sea . . ." King Hiram of Tyre sent experienced seamen to help with the ships in a deal that was supposed to funnel the spices and exotic goods of "Ophir" directly up through Palestine to his Phoenicia, while Solomon benefited from the trade. Where was Ezion-Geber? The search has intensified. In 1938–40 the late Dr. Nelson Glueck excavated the mound of Tell el-Kheleifah near Eilat (the ancient Eloth) at the head of the Gulf of Aqaba, and claimed it was Ezion-Geber. He later retracted, and recently, following a suggestion as early as 1833, marine soundings were made from 1968 to 1970 at Coral Island (Jezirat-Far'un), a tiny island with a natural anchorage further down the gulf. Nothing conclusive has been found. The search continues. See also *Timna*.

FARAH, TELL EL-, NORTH	See *Tirzah*.
FARAH, TELL EL-, SOUTH	See *Tell el-Farah South*.
FUL, TELL EL-	See *Gibeah of Saul*.

GAMLA

Or Khirbet es-Salam, a dramatic rocky promontory obtruding off the Golan Heights plateau, about 4–5 mi. due E. of the head of the Lake of Galilee. Here are the ruins of a Jewish fortress-town captured by the Romans in 67 AD during the first Jewish revolt, its slopes still strewn with the catapult stones used in the siege. It is generally identified with the ancient Gamla, besieged by Vespasian with three legions. According to the historian Josephus, "the houses were built against the steep mountain flank and astonishingly huddled together, one on top of the other." Breaking through the walls, the Roman met defeat in the steep narrow streets, then regrouped and attacked the inhabitants, now huddled in the citadel. They killed 4,000 and 5,000 more threw themselves over the cliffs to their deaths. Khirbet es-Salam is rightly called the *Masada* of the north. Continuing excavations have uncovered a large public building and other parts of the town, olive oil presses and ritual baths, as well as the earliest synagogue—if it was a synagogue—found in Israel. Under these levels a large Early Bronze Age settlement has been detected in recent years. Finds from the town are in the Golan Archaeological Museum at nearby Kazrin in the Golan Heights.

GAZA

Renowned ancient city, now Azza on the southern coast, the last stop on the way to Egypt before entering the desert. Apparently the modern city, about 3 mi. inland from the coast, lies over the ancient city (though the Roman city extended to the coast), so that virtually nothing is visible except its Byzantine churches, which attest to the importance of Gaza as an early Christian center. Gaza, however, is remembered as one of the five Philistine coastal cities, which included *Ashkelon*, *Ashdod*, Ekron (see *Miqne, Tell*) and Gath, though its long history extends far earlier and later than that brief period. As a strategically important city and a caravan center it was involved in numerous campaigns of Egyptians, Canaanites, Syrians and the Mesopotamian powers from early times, and was under Egyptian, Philistine, Israelite, Assyrian and Persian rule. The anthropoid coffins found at *Deir el-Balah* near Gaza attest to the Egyptian and Philistine occupations of the city.

Alexander the Great conquered Gaza in 332 BC and thereafter it was controlled first by the Ptolemies, then the Seleucids, then became a port for the Nabataeans, the property of Herod, and finally a prosperous Roman period city that became in Byzantine times a renowned Christian center, known for the rhetorician Procopius of Gaza. It is to be hoped that some day the archaeologists may be able to get at some of this rich buried history.

GERGESA

See *Kursi*.

GERISA, TELL

See *Tel Aviv-Jaffa*.

GERIZIM, MOUNT

See *Nablus*.

GEULA CAVE

See *Carmel, Mount*.

GEZER

Site of one of the most important Canaanite and Israelite cities of Palestine, a mound of some 30 acres overlooking the coastal plain 7 mi. SE of Ramla and just S. of the older road from Tel Aviv to Jerusalem. In antiquity it stood at a strategic crossroads between this ancient route and the Way of the Sea from Egypt into Mesopotamia. The mound, almost continuously occupied from the Copper Age into Roman-Byzantine times, was excavated, quite inexpertly, by Macalister from 1902 to 1909, the earliest large-scale excavation in Palestine, and then more carefully between 1964 and 1973, and in 1984.

Occupied by Neolithic peoples from the 4th millennium and into the Early Bronze Age, it was resettled in the Middle Bronze Age after a gap, then shortly (about 1650 BC) was fortified with a massive double wall of stone and mud brick 50 ft. wide (parts still stand about 15 ft. high), and a glacis. This town was destroyed by Tuthmosis III of Egypt, and he boasted about it on his temple wall at Karnak (see *Thebes* in EGYPT). From this early Canaanite town dates the famous High Place, three rows of monolithic stones up to 10 ft. high, and an altar or basin. It is still in situ. Also uncovered was a sherd with an interesting bit of early writing (early 2nd millennium BC) in a "proto-Sinaitic" script (pictographs). In the Late Bronze Age, after a slow recovery, the town revived, now very much under Egyptian domination, and a new wall (again surviving up to 15 ft. high) with rectangular towers was built. Gezer of this period is often mentioned in the *Amarna* letters (see EGYPT), which include 10 letters from its various kings, and later on the 13th-cent. "Merneptah Stela." The Philistines seem to have taken over Gezer in the early 12th cent., perhaps at a time when it was deserted (no destruction is evident).

Too strong for the early Israelites to conquer, the town, according to the Bible, was given to Solomon as a dowry when he married the pharaoh's daughter. In any case, Solomon fortified it, for at the site an elaborate "Solomonic gateway" with four passages, similar to those found at *Megiddo* and *Hazor* was uncovered—two heavy towers guarding the entrance and three guardrooms on each side of the main passageway—as well as parts of a typical casemate wall. Gezer, again like the two other major cities, had an elaborate water system, a shaft and tunnel with steps leading down through the rock to a cavern and spring 100 ft. underground. It could date from either the Bronze Age or Israelite periods. From the latter came the famous 10th-cent. limestone "Gezer calendar," one of the earliest examples of Hebrew script known, apparently a schoolboy exercise listing the months of the year in terms of agricultural activities. The city was destroyed by Tiglath-Pileser III of Assyria in 734–33 BC and again by the Babylonians in the 6th cent. and thereafter lost all importance, though it briefly became a Maccabaean headquarters in the 2nd cent. BC, and there are late Hellenistic and Roman remains. The finds are in the Rockefeller Museum, Jerusalem.

GIBEAH OF SAUL

A large mound, Tell el-Ful, only 3 mi. N. of Jerusalem on the main Jerusalem-Nablus road, identified as the fortress, headquarters and native town of Saul, the first king of Israel. It was excavated by W. F. Albright in 1922–23 and 1933, and again in 1964 just before King Hussein of Jordan began to build a large palace on the summit. Overtaken by the 1967 war, the palace was never finished. Saul's fortress proved to have been a fairly small rectangular structure (100 by 160 ft.). What was left of it consisted of a square tower with remnants of a casemate wall indicating the original size of the fortress. The tower, first built of rough stones, had been burnt in the 11th cent. BC, then rebuilt later in the century in much finer masonry. Either the fortress had been erected by the Philistines as one of a chain of their fortresses to hold down the Judean hills, then recaptured and rebuilt by Saul, as the Bible seems to indicate—or more likely it had been built by Saul, captured and burned by the Philistines, then later rebuilt by David. The excavators also found that a later small Israelite fortress had been built on the site, also with casemate walls and a glacis, for the protection of Jerusalem. It was dated either in the 7th–6th cent. BC, or possibly was built in the 8th cent. by King Hezekiah to defend the approaches to Jerusalem when it was about to be invested by Sennacherib the Assyrian.

GIBEON

Ancient site next to the Arab village of el-Jib, about 7 mi. N. of Jerusalem. Excavations at the mound from 1957 to 1962 by Dr. James Pritchard of the University of Pennsylvania uncovered no less than 56 handles from broken wine jars inscribed with the name of Gibeon, thus dramatically proving that this was indeed the site where Joshua commanded the sun to stand still, where Abner and Joab had their bloody encounter by the Pool of Gibeon, where Solomon offered up his burnt sacrifices. In fact the Bible mentions Gibeon 45 times, very often in connection with water. The pool itself (there can be little doubt about it) was discovered early on by Dr. Pritchard. It proved to be part of a massive Canaanite water system, a great round pit 37 ft. across and 35 ft. deep, excavated out of the solid rock, probably in the 12th-11th cents. BC.

Habitation began at Gibeon in the Early Bronze Age (pottery and houses recovered) and continued right through into the Iron Age. Apparently Gibeon was one of those Canaanite cities that submitted to the invading Israelites and was not destroyed. It was finally crushed by the Babylonians in 587 BC and never fully recovered. Many centuries before its capture a second water system was constructed, the Great Pool system having proved inadequate. The intention apparently was to take this Great Pool down to the water table. Some 3,000 tons of limestone were removed in this mammoth undertaking, leaving a spiral descending staircase of 40 rock-cut steps around its outside. At 35 ft. the excavation, proving too arduous, was narrowed to a tunnel which, with 39 more steps, finally reached the water table 82 ft. down, where a water chamber was excavated. This brave undertaking was not long in use, and perhaps in the 10th cent. a new tunnel, 150 ft. long with 93 steps, was excavated down under the walls to a covered cistern fed by another tunnel from a spring inside the hill. Another entrance to the cistern from the outside (it can now be visited) could be closed in times of siege by massive stone blocks slid into place.

After its disuse the Great Pool was gradually filled up with debris to the top (it took two years to clear it). It was here that the 56 jar handles were found, all of the 7th cent. BC, for Gibeon in this most prosperous period had been an active center for the production and export of wine on a very large scale—for the day. On both sides of the Great Pool 63 bottle-shaped wine cellars carved out of the rock were found, with narrow openings at the top. In one a large wine storage jar was found. These cellars, always an optimum 65° F. inside when capped, could hold over 25,000 gallons of wine in storage. From them the wine was transferred to smaller jars, their handles inscribed with the name and city of the maker, for export. A large winepress for treading out the grapes, with settling basins, was also discovered here, as well as some of the house foundations of this prosperous wine center.

Settlement continued through the Persian into the Roman period, from which a plastered pool with steps, two reservoirs and conduits were uncovered, as well as a communal tomb or columbarium with 200 niches for the ashes, decorated with stucco and a mural. The finds from Gibeon are in the National Museum in Amman, Jordan, and the University Museum, Philadelphia.

GILGAL REPHAIM	See *Rujm el-Hiri*.
GUSH HALAV	See *Meiron*.
HADAR, TELL	Important fortress town on the NE shore of the Sea of Galilee, W. of Ramot. Under excavation by Tel Aviv University and the Americans, the small mound of about 4 acres has disclosed two concentric walls of basalt boulders still standing in parts nearly 10 ft. high. This seems to have been a fortress-town of the Geshurites, part of the Aramaean kingdom of Damascus, which came to a fiery

end in the 11th cent. BC—probably at the hands of the expanding Israelites. Above the remains of this fortified town (strata II), a final level (strata I) belonged to an unwalled small village that flourished during the prosperous years of the Israelite monarchies (9th–8th cents. BC).

The most substantial building activity dated from the earlier Geshurite period, notably a monumental structure defended by two unusually wide walls with a gate. The building's interior included a number of storage rooms containing storage vessels and a quantity of burned wheat seeds. The architectural tradition of strata II was totally unlike that of any other site of the same period excavated in Israel, indicating a different material culture—undoubtedly that of the Aramaeans whose center lay to the north. The excavators have suggested that this walled town may have been an administrative center of Aramaean Geshur, the Land of Geshur, which is mentioned in the *Amarna* tablets from EGYPT.

HAIFA

Israel's principal seaport, on the slopes of Mt. Carmel, 55 mi. N. of Tel Aviv. A large and attractive modern city, it offers nothing of archaeological interest except its museums and the site of the ancient settlement at Tell Shikmona. The museums include the Museum of Ancient Art in the Haifa Museum Center, the Maritime Museum with models and other displays concerned with the maritime history of the Middle East since prehistoric times, an interesting museum in the tall Dagon silo on the edge of the harbor concerned with the history of grains and cereals in the region, the Museum of Prehistory with the finds from the *Mt. Carmel* caves, and the Stella Maris Museum at the Carmelite monastery with a small antiquarian display. Near the latter is Elijah's Cave, sacred to Jews, Christians and Muslims, traditionally the refuge for the prophet when he fled from the anger of Ahab and Jezebel. The Reuven and Edith Hecht archaeological museum at the University of Haifa opened in 1984.

Tell Shikmona, the Sycaminos of the Greco-Roman period, lies just south of Haifa on the Tel Aviv road. The most visible remains, on and around the mound, excavated since 1963, are those of the Byzantine period. Though there may have been a Middle and Late Bronze Age presence here, settlement really began in the Iron Age, when there were five successive towns, each destroyed in turn. The earliest, destroyed in the 10th cent. BC, had a casemate wall. Two streets, four houses and a palace have been uncovered in the interior, the latter with rooms on two sides of an inner courtyard. In the 6th cent. the site was resettled as a Phoenician town under the Persians. Houses were built on a ridge and on a series of terraces on the mound's slopes. Two intersecting streets with houses, quite regularly laid out, have been recovered. A fortress, Tyrian or Persian, was built here in the mid-4th cent. BC and several later ones in the Hellenistic and Roman periods. In the Byzantine period the town reached quite a size. The summit of the mound was adorned with a large 6th cent. AD villa, and substantial houses were built on its slopes and spilled down into a residential quarter south of the mound, with shops and workshops to its northeast. There is an on-site museum here, and a mosaic pavement and other finds are in the Haifa Museum of Ancient Art.

HALIF, TELL

Site of a very ancient fortress-city, about 10 mi. N. of Beersheba at Kibbutz Lahav. The mound lies at the head of a strategic pass leading from Egypt and the coast near Gaza into the southern hill region of Judah. Excavated since 1977, it has yielded the remains of four major cities, widely separated in time. As early as 3000 BC there was an Early Bronze Age city here, well-fortified, from which the excavators recovered a 25-ft.-high tower flanked by parts of the wall with an unusual sloping glacis outside the wall (generally thought to have been imported into Palestine in the Middle Bronze Age). A great fire, leaving a foot of ashy debris, utterly destroyed this early city about 2600–2500 BC. No major settlement followed for about 1,000 years, until another large city arose in the Late Bronze Age (1550–1200 BC). An enigmatic find from this city was a large clay platform, 33 ft. wide, covered with the remains of walls and bins.

The third city, in the Israelite period (about 1000–700 BC), may have been the Bible's Ziklag, or Rimmon. It was one of Judah's fortress-cities protecting the southern approach, along with *Beersheba* to the South, *Arad* to the east, *Tell Beit Mirsim* to the northeast, *Lachish* to the north and *Tell el-Hesi* to the northwest. A casemate wall, a glacis surfaced in cobblestones, house foundations and tombs have been excavated from this period. After this city was abandoned there was only sparse habitation here until the late Roman-Byzantine period, when the fourth city arose, probably called Tilla. Some tombs from the city are on view. There is an on-site museum at Kibbutz Lahav, and in the vicinity some caves, formerly inhabited by the bedouin who live in this arid area have been excavated and reconstructed. An interesting new Bedouin Museum, with the Joe Allon center for regional and folklore studies, lies south of the tell. At Khirbet er-Rammamin further south, a Byzantine-period synagogue has been excavated.

HALUZA

See *Elusa*.

HAMMAT-GADER

Ancient mound and Roman baths in the Yarmuk River valley, about 8 mi. E. of the lower end of the Sea of Galilee and about 18 mi. from *Tiberias*. The modern spa of Hammat-Gader has become one of the most popular resorts in Israel, and the Roman mineral baths here, built over two hot springs in the 2nd cent. AD and in use until the 9th cent. into the Muslim Umayyad period, are one of its principal attractions—along with an alligator farm! According to a late Roman writer the baths were the second largest in the Roman Empire, after those of Baiae in Italy, and the continuing excavations (since 1979) have uncovered the huge complex in a remarkable state of preservation—pools, marble fountains, pipes of lead and stone—as well as quantities of fine glass bottles, pottery jars and marble inscriptions. The baths belonged to the nearby resort city of Gadara, one of the Roman Decapolis, whose ruins lie high on top of a steep hill about 3 mi. away across the Yarmuk at Umm Qais in Jordan. At the baths there is also a Roman theater (2,000 seats) and the remains of a 5th cent. AD synagogue on top of the mound. Brief soundings in the mound itself have indicated settlements dating from the Early Bronze Age.

HAMMAT TIBERIAS

See *Tiberias*.

HASSAN, TELL

See *Jericho*.

HAZOR

Major archaeological site, excavated by the celebrated Yigael Yadin in 1955–58 and again in 1968–70. Hazor was one of the largest and most important of Canaanite and Israelite cities, commanding a strategic site in northern Israel at the intersection of several ancient trade routes. It lies 9 mi. straight N. of the

The ruins of Hazor as they look today, after the extensive excavations in the 1950s and 1960s. First occupied in the Early Bronze Age (about 2500 BC), Hazor grew to become the largest city in Canaan, covering some 200 acres and with a population of well over 30,000. The evidence strongly suggests that this magnificent city was indeed utterly destroyed by Joshua, the Hebrew war leader, about 1225 BC, as recounted in the Bible. After a renewal in Solomonic times, Hazor met its end at the hands of the Assyrians in 732 BC. (Courtesy: Israel Government Press Office.)

Sea of Galilee, 6 mi. NE of Safad. At its largest in the Late Bronze Age the city covered over 200 acres and may have had a population of up to 40,000 people. The original acropolis, Tell el-Qedah, is a huge bottle-shaped mound of 32 acres. The lower city, on a rectangular plateau to the north, first settled in the Middle Bronze Age, covered an additional 175 acres protected by a massive rampart and ditch on the north and west, and a steep glacis on the east. This was the city, the leader of a coalition of northern Canaanite kings, that Joshua destroyed about 1250–25 BC, after defeating its king in battle—"and he burned Hazor with fire," the only one of the cities, according to the Bible, that he did burn.

The city—or cities, for 21 levels were uncovered on the mound—was already an ancient one. First inhabited in the Early Bronze Age (2600–2300 BC), it is mentioned in the recently discovered tablets of Ebla in Syria (around 2300 BC), in the *Amarna* letters (see EGYPT) and other inscriptions, as well as in the later Egyptian Execration Texts of the 19th cent. BC and in the archives of Mari, also in Syria, of the 18th cent. BC. In the Middle Bronze period a new people settled in Hazor. Their walls, part of a palace and a temple have been uncovered on the acropolis. They also spilled down into the lower city and fortified it. By the Late Bronze period, before it was burned by the Israelites, this city—destroyed and rebuilt several times—had become by all odds the largest in Canaan. Among the abundant remains excavated in the lower city of this virtual Bronze Age metropolis were rock-cut tombs with an elaborate network of connecting tunnels. There were also well-built houses, fragmentary remains of a double temple or palace, and another site with four superimposed temples, perhaps dedicated to Baal-Hadad. The latest of these, with a porch fronted by two basalt pillar bases, a main hall and a holy of holies, was almost a pagan prototype of Solomon's temple as described in the Bible. A dado of well-dressed basalt orthostats lined the lower walls of the porch and the holy of holies or sanctuary, one showing a lion in relief. Found in the holy of holies were offering tables and an altar of basalt, libation tables, a basin, and the seated statuette of a god. Another temple, the famous "stelae temple," a small shrine, contained a row of upright stelae (one carved with hands raised in prayer to the crescent moon), a seated deity, and an offering table. This has now been reerected in the museum at nearby Kibbutz Ayelet Hashachar. Near it the foundations of large houses were found, and a potter's shop with a cult mask and the potter's wheel in situ.

The fury of the onslaught, presumably by the Israelites under Joshua, was indicated in the destruction layer found in the excavations. The statues in the temples were beheaded, the stelae thrown down, and the entire city razed. The lower city was never again occupied. Later the crude encampments of a semi-nomadic people appeared on the acropolis alone—undoubtedly those of the early Hebrews. Not until the 10th cent. was the upper city on the acropolis refortified, probably by Solomon as stated in the Bible, because the principal find here was a triple gate of the kind he built at M*egiddo* and *Gezer*, associated with the usual stretches of casemate wall.

The acropolis city was destroyed by the Aramaeans (Syrians) in 885 BC but was rebuilt on a larger scale thereafter by Omri and especially by his son, Ahab, of the northern kingdom of Israel. Ahab's "pillared building" was obviously a storehouse, with two long rows of pillars down its middle. He also built an elaborate citadel at the western edge of the mound; from its formal entranceway came two elegant "proto-Aeolic" columns. In later years, as the Assyrian menace loomed, the fortifications were strengthened and a sophisticated water system excavated, similar to but larger than that at Megiddo from the same time. A wide shaft with steps was cut down 100 ft. into the rock to meet a sloping tunnel, which led down another 50 ft. to an underground reservoir at the water table. But to no avail. In 732 the Assyrian monarch Tiglath-Pileser III struck with fury, leveling and burning the city—the evidence was all too clear in the excavations. Hazor was finished. Only Assyrian, Persian and Hellenistic forts appeared on the site thereafter. A large museum at the kibbutz of Ayelet Hashachar, with its guesthouse close to the mound, displays models, remains of temples and other finds. The Israel Museum, Jerusalem, has more. .

HEBRON

One of the four holy cities of Israel, situated at over 3,000 ft. in a richly fertile area, 18 mi. S. of Jerusalem on the road to Beersheba. Here Abraham pitched his tents and bargained with the men of Hebron for the cave of Machpelah, which he brought for a family tomb. The cave, the traditional burial place of Abraham, Jacob and Isaac and their wives, is supposed to lie beneath the venerable mosque of Haram el-Khalil in Hebron, sacred to Jews, Muslims and Christians alike, for Abraham is accounted a prophet of Islam. It was in Hebron, too, that David was anointed king and reigned here for a number of years before capturing Jerusalem as his capital. Actually the site of ancient Hebron, or Kiryat Arba as it was called in Hebrew, lies across the valley on Jebel er-Rumeidah. It has been excavated, indicating occupation from about 2000 BC, and again recently by Tel Aviv University with the finding there of a Middle Bronze Age cuneiform tablet, one of the earliest ever found in Israel.

The cave, deep in a hill under the mosque, cannot be entered, though it was investigated in the 12th cent. by Christian clerics of Crusader times, who left a detailed record. It may well be the tomb of the Patriarchs, though some think it merely an ancient cistern. Certainly veneration of the spot dates from antiquity, and the lower part of the present monumental walls of the mosque were built by Herod the Great. The masonry, including the flat pilasters, is typically well-fashioned, and some of the larger dressed stones are up to 23 ft. long. The floor of the mosque is also Herodian; apparently in Herod's day this magnificent structure enclosed a courtyard open to the sky. Later there was a Byzantine church here (only fragments remain), and the structure was constantly built, rebuilt and decorated by Arabs and Crusaders up through the Mamluks. Saladin donated the superb *minbar* (pulpit) of carved wood in 1191 AD. The mosque features on its floor six ornate cenotaphs from various periods, of the three Patriarchs and their wives, and a little mosque of Joseph of the 14th cent. AD (traditionally also buried here) is attached to the main building. Another mosque lies behind it. Hebron's Municipal Museum displays the archaeological finds.

About 2 mi. north of Hebron, at Ramat el-Khalil on a mountaintop, is an ancient walled enclosure on the plain of Mamre where Abraham is supposed to have pitched his tents beside a large oak, dug a well and erected an altar. It was long a popular cult site for Christians, Jews and pagans and was known for its annual pagan festival, which was carried on until the 7th cent. AD—though in an attempt to Christianize the site the mother-in-law of Constantine the Great built a church here, crammed into one side of the enclosure, one of the earliest of the basilican type. Under Hadrian the captured Jews from the second revolt against Rome (132–135 AD) were sold into slavery on the site, then a market. There is actually a well inside the enclosure, pointed out as Abraham's, though excavations in 1926–28 showed that the site originally dated from the 9th to 7th cent. BC (long after Abraham), when there was a long paved way leading to the center of the western side of the enclosure. A pagan altar stood at its middle, and the foundations of the Constantinian church, a much-narrowed basilica type, were uncovered, squeezed in at the western end. The whole structure was rebuilt in Herodian times and again under Hadrian, and became a marketplace/cum/shrine. The presumed site of Abraham's terebinth (altar) could have been in the atrium of the church.

HEPTAPEGON

Greek, for seven springs, the ancient name for Tabgha, now called Ein Shova, on the northwestern shore of the Sea of Galilee, 6 mi. N. of *Tiberias* and not far from *Capernaum*; it was excavated in 1932 and 1936. Though there are indeed seven powerful springs here, this is traditionally the site of Jesus' miracle of the Feeding of the Multitude (although the Gospels firmly place the miracle on the other side of the lake). The 5th cent. AD Church of the Multiplication of the Loaves and Fishes once stood here, as part of a complex with courtyard and hospice. It was rebuilt in 1982. Today all that remains of the earlier period are the superb mosaics in the new church, now protected by a roof and flanked by the two wings of a Benedictine monastery. The miracle is commemorated by a mosaic in front of the altar depicting a basket of loaves of bread flanked by two fishes; two rectangular panels, beautifully designed and strongly reminiscent of the Nile scenes so popular among earlier Romans, show birds and plants, notably a lotus-like flower.

Beneath the floor of the 5th-cent. church were found the remains of a much smaller 4th-cent. chapel, probably the one mentioned by a traveler in the 4th cent.—the earliest association of the site with the miracle. Two other 4th-cent. churches stood here; the ruins of the Church of the Sermon on the Mount (the

The miracle of Jesus' Feeding of the Multitude, touchingly pictured in a mosaic from a 5th century AD church at Heptapegon (Taghba). It depicts a basket of bread flanked by two fish. The church's mosaics are all that is left of the old church, now incorporated inside a new church of the 1980s. Traditionally, this was the site of the miracle; actually the Gospels place it on the other side of the Sea of Galilee. (Courtesy: Israel Ministry of Tourism.)

Mount of Beatitudes is close by) are still visible. The walls of the other church are built into a modern Franciscan chapel by the lake. There are also two Byzantine water towers and a small Crusader building.

HERODION

Fortress-palace rising dramatically on a conical artificial hill in the Judean desert 8 mi. S. of Jerusalem and about 3 mi. SE of Bethlehem, built by Herod the Great between 24 and 15 BC, in part as his own tomb. The heavy circular double walls rise 70 ft. high, the whole soared 200 ft. above the surrounding countryside. An additional rampart of earth and stone encircled the top of the mound, pierced by an imposing entrance on the east. The four towers were regularly spaced—three half-towers and one round keep where Herod was probably buried. The luxurious palace-fortress area inside included a rectangular garden court bordered by columns in front of the keep or citadel, with baths, living quarters and a large dining hall filling the rest of the space. The baths were adorned with mosaics and the walls of all the buildings were plastered and painted.

Much of this was revealed in the excavations in the 1960s and 1970s, which confirmed the contemporary account by the historian Josephus. Another sumptuous palace at the base of the hill faced onto a long hippodrome (Herod loved the races). On an artificial platform to its west was a large rectangular pool, aqueduct-fed, used to supply huge cisterns inside the hill, reached from the palace-fortress above. A colonnaded pavilion, formal gardens, other buildings and a long storeroom have been traced around the pool. In the first Jewish revolt against Rome the fortress was held by the Zealots, and like *Masada* to the south was one of the last to fall to the enemy. In the second revolt it was again a headquarters of the insurgents, who used the dining hall as a synagogue. During the 5th to 7th cents. AD a Byzantine monastery occupied the bath area.

The dramatic fortress-tomb-palace called the Herodian, another example of the building mania of the odious and tyrannical Herod the Great. The huge mound, encircled by heavy walls at the top and bottom, was wholly artificial. Of the four towers, the largest probably held Herod's tomb. Inside the fortress was a luxurious palace, gardens and a bath suite. Below the hill (rear) was another palace complex. The fortress was held by the rebels during both Jewish revolts against Rome. (Courtesy: Israel Government Press Office.)

HESI, TELL EL-,

Large mound, site of an ancient city, presumably Eglon, with a long history of occupation from the Copper Age through the Islamic period, about 15 mi. NE of Gaza. The site was the first in the area to be excavated on scientific principles, by the great W. M. F. Petrie followed by F. J. Bliss, from 1891 to 1893, paying careful attention to an overall correlation between pottery finds, the stratigraphy of building levels, and datable imports, mostly Egyptian. This early dig set the pattern for all subsequent Near Eastern excavations. The site has again been excavated since 1970 by an American team. In the prosperous Early Bronze Age period (after about 2600 BC) the acropolis (11 acres) and also a far larger lower town (23 acres) was occupied; after the destruction of the city in about 2350 BC the lower town was permanently abandoned. Excavations from this early period uncovered a mud brick wall with associated houses, and outside the wall a sloping glacis of an early type (usually associated only with the Middle Bronze Age) covered with water-impervious crushed limestone. In the much later Israelite period (about 1000–586 BC) another novel method of fortification was developed. Utilizing the earlier walls, a system of double and triple walls, with cross-walls, was constructed, the resulting compartments filled with earth, which raised and enlarged the area of the acropolis.

HORVAT EQED

See *Imwas.*

IFSHAR, TELL

See *Tell el-Efshar.*

IMWAS

Or Amwas, village on the western slopes of the Judean hills, 15 mi. NW of Jerusalem, now called Canada Park. A site south of the town is the most likely contender for the location of ancient Emmaus, the Nicopolis of the Romans, home of the 3rd cent. AD Christian scholar Julius Africanus. It was so identified by the early church historian Eusebius. It was on the road to Emmaus that the risen Christ first appeared to some of the Apostles (Luke 24:13). Near the village are the well-preserved though overgrown remains of a Crusader castle, and excavations on the site itself since 1873 have uncovered early walls, tombs, a 2nd cent. AD Roman villa with mosaics, Byzantine winepresses, a Roman-Byzantine bath (3rd cent. AD), Roman aqueducts, and the foundations of a 6th cent. AD basilica under a small Crusader church, with baptistery. Beneath that again was a smaller 3rd-cent. Christian basilica, both with mosaics. Nearby at Horvat Eqed a hill fortress of the Second Temple period has been excavated, and the caves used as secret bases by the rebels of the 2nd cent. AD under Bar Kochba are on view. Both sites are in the Canada National Park, in which is a small museum of prehistoric tools, open on request.

IRQ EL-AHMAR CAVE

See *Wadi Khareitun*.

IZBET SARTAH

The ancient Eben-ezer, an early Israelite settlement of the period of the Judges (about 1250–1050 BC), when the previously nomadic tribes were just settling down, absorbing Canaanite culture, and contending for the land with them and the Philistines. Sited at the very western edge of the Judean hills, about 15 mi. E. of Tel Aviv, overlooking the coastal plain and *Aphek*, it was briefly occupied when the Israelites were still confined to the hills by the Philistines in Aphek and elsewhere. Excavations revealed a walled oval with houses surrounding a central open space, the latter first occupied only by grain silos, later by a large house with four rooms, now restored. A sherd from this house was inscribed in the early Canaanite-Hebrew alphabet, the oldest yet found. The disastrous defeat of the Israelites by the Philistines, in which the Ark of the Covenant was captured, took place on the plain below. The town was abandoned after David had subdued the Philistines about 1000 BC and opened the plain to Israelite settlement.

JAFFA

See *Tel Aviv-Jaffa*.

JARISHA, TELL

See *Tel Aviv-Jaffa* (Tell Gerisa).

JEMMEH, TELL

Or Jamma, the Canaanite Yurza and Assyrian Arsa, an important excavation by the Smithsonian Institution (1970–79) of a trading town and frontier post in the Negev, 6 mi. S. of Gaza and 6½ mi. from the sea. The 12-acre mound lies on a bend of the Besor River, which has partly eroded the site. Earlier, Sir Flinders Petrie excavated a small section in 1927. A Copper Age or Chalcolithic settlement here lasted only 200 years (3200–3000 BC). Over 1,000 years later the Canaanites established a town on the site (in about 1800 BC), which after about 1550 BC became an important market for goods imported from Cyprus and the Aegean. Egyptian traders, and incense caravans bound from Arabia to Gaza, also made it a stop. The town expanded over the entire mound and was heavily fortified. Nevertheless it was several times destroyed and rebuilt. From the end of this period a large cobblestone court and rooms (13th cent.), possibly a palace, was uncovered, as well as evidence of much industrial activity—kilns, blacksmith shops, a furnace. Under the Philistines, who took the town in the 12th cent, it flourished again as an industrial center and regional market. On the mound one of the largest kilns found in the Near East came to light, more evidence that the Philistines were sophisticated potters.

In the 7th cent. BC the town became a forward base for the Assyrians in their conquest of Egypt, and was again heavily fortified, with a double wall, cross-walls and compartments. From the period came a large six-room house, probably that of the governor. Its barrel-vaulted basements, made of keystone-shaped mud bricks, are unique in Palestine and one of the earliest in the Near East. They have been preserved. The Babylonians soon replaced the Assyrians, then came the Persians. Under the Ptolemies of Egypt (about 310–200 BC), before the mound was abandoned, huge round grain silos were erected on it. One example, thoroughly excavated and reconstructed, yielded quantities of pottery.

JERICHO

Famous town 6 mi. N. of the Dead Sea; at 820 ft. below sea level it is the lowest town on earth. It lies in a huge oasis, lush green amidst the arid Jordan valley, well-watered as it has been for millennia by the copious spring of Ein es-Sultan. This still issues at the base of the mound of Tell es-Sultan under which excavators discovered "the oldest walled town in the world," first of a long sequence of prehistoric towns, of which one of the latest was the city whose "walls came tumbling down" at the sound of Joshua's trumpets. The oasis as a whole has a long history. Here were Hasmonaean and Herodian palaces; near here Jesus was baptized by John in the Jordan, and was tempted by the devil on a small mountain to the west, now topped by a monastery. Much later an Umayyad prince built another palace here, one of the most attractive sites in the oasis.

But the important site here is Tell es-Sultan, though now pitted by numerous excavations and disfigured by erosion. It was excavated by Charles Warren in 1868 and by John Garstang in the 1930s, who thought that he had found Joshua's collapsed walls, but by all odds the most significant dig was that of Dame Kathleen Kenyon from 1952 to 1958, who not only decisively refuted Garstang, but established a complete sequence of occupations from the Mesolithic to the end of the Middle Bronze Age—when a violent destruction ended Jericho's glorious period. Kenyon's sequence also documented in great detail the "Neolithic Revolution" from nomadism to a settled urban civilization.

The earliest remains belonged to the Mesolithic (Natufian here) of about 9000 BC or earlier. These nomadic people honored the spring by which they camped with what appears to be a sanctuary, a small rectangle of clay bounded by crude stone walls. Their descendants, generation after generation, began to settle down, leaving innumerable surfaces of tramped earth marking their flimsy, seminomadic shelters. In time these became more permanent round huts built of loaf-shaped mud bricks—and here we enter the so-called Pre-Pottery Neolithic A (PPNA), beginning about 8500–8300 BC, a period of remarkably early, fully sedentary urban existence.

Lasting until 7600–7500 BC (calibrated radiocarbon dates), this highly organized community had no parallel elsewhere in the world. Crops were grown (wheat, barley and legumes) and tools and utensils of flint, limestone, wood and bone were used, though they had no pottery. As their houses spread all across the mound they proved themselves capable of organizing the massive field and irrigation works needed to feed a town of perhaps 2,000. Even more astonishing, they were able to build a stone rampart around the 10 acres of their town, which survives in one place to a height of 17 ft., protected on the outside by a rock-cut ditch 27 ft. wide and 9 ft. deep. Just inside the wall Kenyon found the famous round stone tower, still standing 23 ft. high in its trench. Built into it is a staircase of 22 steps giving access to the tower's top from the town below. See also *Sha'ar Ha-Golan*.

This period lasted about 1,000 years, involving 25 building levels and many reconstructions of the wall, and ended in a catastrophic destruction. A new people moved in, ushering in the Pre-Pottery Neolithic B (PPNB), a period which lasted over 1,500 years (dates range from 7600–7500 to 6000 BC). The town prospered again, growing larger than the earlier one, with a succession of town walls, and far more sophisticated houses. These had large rectangular rooms with plastered floors and walls, grouped around courtyards. Two of the houses may have had religious functions. Among the burials beneath the floors were found 10 skulls with ears, noses and eyebrows delicately modeled on to them in plaster and tinted to give a startling lifelike appearance—perhaps some form of ancestor worship. These famous skulls are now on view in the Rockefeller Museum, Jerusalem. See also *Nahal Hemer*.

The PPNB also came to an abrupt end. The site lay fallow for a time, then about 4500 BC was resettled as a mere village by people who lived in simple pit houses and made crude pottery, among the earliest Neolithic pottery known. Later their houses improved and their pottery began to be painted. This Pottery Neolithic stage merges indistinctly into Kenyon's Proto-Urban phase about 3200 BC, which ushered in the Early Bronze Age. Once again Jericho became a city surrounded, for centuries, by a succession of town walls, and a long line of rock-cut tombs appear in the surrounding slopes. One tomb, for instance, contained 113 skulls around the cremated bones in the center. This large city was again destroyed about 2300 BC, possibly by the nomadic Amorites, who merely camped on the site until about 1900 BC, when a full-scale Middle Bronze Age city arose, once again walled and closely linked with the other Canaanite cities on the coast. Erosion has destroyed most of this flourishing city, except evidence that the old wall was replaced in the 18th cent. by a new wall topping a formidable sloping plastered glacis of the kind usually associated with the Hyksos, who dominated Egypt and Syria at this time.

What we know about these Middle Bronze Age people comes mostly from the large, rock-cut family tombs furnished with everything the deceased might need in the hereafter—beds, tables, stools, food and drink on the tables, in wooden bowls and in jugs, gifts, jewelry, reed mats and baskets—much of it happily preserved in the dry climate. One such communal tomb has been re-constructed in the Rockefeller Museum, Jerusalem. This great city was again destroyed about 1580–60 BC, probably by the avenging Egyptians after they drove the Hyksos out of Egypt. This was the virtual end of ancient Jericho. There is some evidence for a resettlement about 1400 BC and in the Late Bronze Age, and this would be the city presumably destroyed by Joshua; but we are now near the top of the mound where erosion had washed away the upper layers, including any evidence whatsoever for Joshua's tumbled walls. Faint traces indicate occupation in the 7th cent. BC, just before the Babylonian Captivity. After it, settlement at Jericho moved off the mound entirely.

There was a Persian post at Jericho, but in the Hellenistic period after Alexander the oasis became a royal preserve because of its mild winter climate, a resort for Jewish kings and their courtiers. On either side of the Wadi Qelt, well south of Tell es-Sultan, two mounds at Tulul Abu el-Alaiq mark the sites of a palace of the Hasmonaean kings (possibly Alexander Jannaeus, 103–76 BC) and the later palaces of that insatiable builder Herod the Great (37–4 BC), both extensively excavated in 1950–51, and later in 1973–83. The Hasmonaean palace consisted of a large mud brick main building, ritual baths, a peristyle, gardens and long storerooms, and a Doric pavilion, as well as two villas with courts and pools. Herod, who leased the area from Cleopatra of Egypt (who got it from Mark Antony) built a first palace here (traces have been found). Later he filled in the now ruined Hasmonaean building, creating a raised mound to catch the breezes (the present northern mound), on which he erected his own elevated central building. The rest of the area he turned into gardens with a pavilion and terraces, a peristyle court, a pool and Roman baths. Still later he erected a third and new palace complex, a vast pleasure domain on both sides of the wadi with a long sunken garden and huge pool on the south and another sumptuous palace across the wadi to the north. Columned porches at each end of the sunken garden were linked by a monumental facade in Roman *opus reticulatum* (a net-like masonry surface). The garden was overlooked by another artificial mound (the southern mound) topped by a building. The northern palace across the wadi contained a large columned reception hall, courtyards, a bath suite and dining rooms—all decorated with frescoes and stucco moldings. A number of aqueducts were built or refurbished to supply the needed water.

Herod also refortified a peak over his new palace and named it Kypros for his mother. In the nearby cliffs are over 120 rock-cut tombs in use from about 100 BC to 68 AD. They yielded wooden coffins and stone ossuaries. To entertain his guests Herod also built a theater and hippodrome at Tell es-Samrat to the north, just south of the old mound, excavated 1975–76. The theater, seating perhaps 3,000–4,000, was backed by a reception hall and courtyard. In 4 BC the paranoid Herod, a dying man, rounded up the most eminent men of Israel inside the hippodrome with orders to kill them all at the moment of his death. Fortunately, when he died his sister Salome countermanded the order.

The oasis supported a heavy population in the Byzantine period. The mosaics of a Byzantine basilica may be seen in the modern town, and among synagogues, one with elaborate mosaic floors may be seen 2½ mi. northeast of modern Jericho. There were many monasteries too, notably that of St. George of Koziba dramatically sited on the cliffs over the Wadi Qelt. Built around the 4th–5th cents. AD, it has often been reconstructed. The latest glorious site of Jericho, built before the oasis fell into neglect until recent times, are the ruins of the fabulous Umayyad palace and hunting park at Khirbet al-Mafjar about 1 mi. north of modern Jericho, erected 739–744 AD, probably by the eccentric and brilliant Caliph Walid—and never finished when he was assassinated. An earthquake destroyed it in 747. Locally called "Hisham's Palace," it was excavated 1937–48.

Its sheer luxury reflects a dynasty that ruled from the Pyrenees to India and had inherited all the artistry of previous civilizations in this area, for it is more Classical than Islamic. A columned forecourt led through a vaulted entrance gate into a two-storied palace with rooms around a court and a large banqueting hall; the floors and enough of the walls were revealed by the excavations to envisage what it was like. The whole palace, in an early example of Persian influence, was enlivened with patterned reliefs, busts, and even almost lifesize

The ornamental enclosure around the bath pool in the Arab Umayyad palace, "Hisham's Palace," at Jericho, probably built by the eccentric Caliph Walid in the 8th century AD. Walid is reputed to have filled the pool for his delight with rosewater, musk and turmeric. The palace is one of the most attractive sites in the large oasis of Jericho, better known for the "oldest walled city in the world," excavated by Dame Kathleen Kenyon in the 1950s. (Courtesy: Israel Government Press Office.)

human figures, all in stucco, as well as frescoes. Adjoining the palace was a large public mosque, mostly open to the sky, and an elaborate bath suite, including a bath hall, a large square basilica, with a raised pool (once filled by Walid with rosewater, musk and tumeric!) and a series of hot rooms, reception rooms, furnace rooms and latrine. An elaborate geometric mosaic in marbles covers the entire floor of the bath hall and an even more exquisite mosaic, imitating an oriental carpet, that of a small domed reception room. It depicts a tree of life with animals. The palace complex was enclosed within a large walled hunting park, and water for the baths was brought from a spring 2 mi. away by aqueducts running across bridges. Examples of the fine stucco work may be seen in the Rockefeller Museum in Jerusalem, which also displays some of the finds from Tell es-Sultan; others are in the Archaeological Museum, Amman, Jordan.

JERUSALEM

Capital of Israel, holy city of the Jews, Christians and Muslims, situated high in the Judean hills between Tel Aviv and the Dead Sea. Within the present metropolis is the so-called Old City whose magnificent walls, built by Sultan Suleiman the Magnificent in the 16th cent. roughly following the perimeters of the Roman city of Hadrian, are still so complete that it is possible to walk almost all the way around them on their tops. The Old City is still dominated on its east side by the massive platform, the Haram es-Sharif, built by Herod for his Temple, with the mosque of the Dome of the Rock rising above the site of the ancient Jewish temples. Within the city and in the surrounding hills are numerous Christian sites, some genuine, some legendary.

Jerusalem has been inhabited since prehistoric times and has been built on top of remnants from all periods of history. It is of course very much a living,

Jerusalem the Golden. The golden dome of the Umayyad mosque, Dome of the Rock, dominates the Temple Mount and city walls. The great platform on which the mosque rests was built by Herod the Great for his Temple, a successor to Solomon's Temple on the same site, then called Mount Moriah. It rose just north of the City of David. (Courtesy: Israel Government Tourist Office.)

growing city today; thus excavation is difficult. Nevertheless the Israelis, superb archaeologists, with extensive help from other nations have done a remarkable job since the creation of their state in revealing more and more of Jerusalem's rich buried history. Three major excavations and many minor ones have been concluded or are currently in progress, the more important ones being turned into attractive archaeological parks when completed. These are carefully signposted, with judicious restoration, so that the tourist is well served. Innumerable tours of the city's relics and museums are also available. The present chronological summary will therefore attempt to clarify the principal discoveries from the earliest period up through the Byzantine, leaving, for instance, the fine Mamluk remains (13th to 15th cents. AD) in the Muslim Quarter—not often visited—as well as most of the Christian sites around the hills to other, less archaelogical guides. (See, for instance, the excellent *The Holy Land*, by Jerome Murphy-O'Connor, Oxford University Press, 2nd ed. 1986, which devotes about one-third of the volume to Jerusalem alone.)

The original City of David lay on a long narrow ridge on the lower slopes of the Ophel hill, extending south from the Temple Mount and well outside the walls of the later Old City. It was flanked by two vallies, the Kidron and the Tyropeon, the latter now largely filled in. Settlers were attracted to the site as early as the Copper Age, perhaps about 3300 BC, by the copious flow of the Gihon spring at the foot of the eastern slope, still today an important source of water. The small but easily defended site became a town by about 3100 BC. The city of Urusalim, or Urusalima, is mentioned in the archives of Ebla in Syria (about 2400–2250 BC) and in the 19th cent. BC Egyptian Execration Texts and the *Amarna* letters of the 14th cent. (see EGYPT). The unimportant Canaanite city of Jebus, bypassed in the original Israelite conquest of Palestine, was seized from the Jebusites by David about 1000 BC as the site of his new civil and religious capital, conveniently located between the northern tribes of Israel and the southern in Judah. A threshing floor on Mt. Moriah to the north of the city, purchased by David as a High Place for his altar and shrine of the Ark of the Covenant, became the site of his son Solomon's temple and palace. The Temple, a rather small structure probably similar in plan to the earlier temples at *Hazor* and the later temple at *Arad*, was built and luxuriously furnished by Phoenician craftsmen (Kings, 6). Any remains of this temple are now lost beneath Herod's great platform.

When Israel, the Northern Kingdom, seceded from the monarchy after the death of Solomon, Jerusalem remained the capital of Judah. Later Israel succumbed to the Assyrians, and an expanded Jerusalem was refortified under Hezekiah and withstood an Assyrian siege in 701 BC. But in 586 it fell to Nebuchadnezzar of Babylon who savagely destroyed the city and the temple and marched most of the survivors into exile. Under the liberal Cyrus, founder of the Persian Empire, the exiles were allowed to return to the ruined city in 538 BC. A small group did return and gradually rebuilt the Temple, then in the 440s, under the single-minded Nehemiah, walled in a much smaller city. Falling under Seleucid (Macedonian) control after Alexander's conquests, a profanation of its temple by Antiochus IV in 168 BC led to a revolt of the Jews under the Maccabean family. For 100 years thereafter the Maccabeans, also called the Hasmonaeans, maintained a virtually independent rule, fortifying the city, which expanded greatly to the west and north, until it was taken by the Romans under Pompey in 63 BC. Eventually in 37 BC it came under Herod the Great, an Idumaean (Arab) client king of Rome, who practically rebuilt the city during his tumultuous reign of 33 years, including the magnificent Second Temple on its great platform.

Jesus spent the last days of his life and was crucified in Jerusalem during the disturbed times that led up to the bitter Jewish revolt against Rome. The revolt was put down by Vespasian and then his son Titus, who captured and ruthlessly destroyed the city and Temple in 70 AD. (The spoils from the Temple are depicted on the Arch of Titus in Rome). The city did not recover for some 60 years. After the second revolt under Bar Kochba (132–135 AD), Hadrian barred the Jews from Jerusalem and rebuilt it as a Roman city, Aelia Capitolina, with a temple of Jupiter on Herod's platform. The city, however, revived when the empire turned Christian under Constantine in 331 AD, and pilgrims flocked to the new churches and shrines. Captured by the Sassanian Persians in 614 AD, Jerusalem fell to Caliph Omar in 638 and thereafter was an Islamic city, except for the interlude of Crusader rule after 1099 AD.

There have been excavations in Jerusalem for well over 100 years, the first systematic campaign being carried out by Charles Warren, a British army engineer, between 1864 and 1867. Many other digs followed. Among the most important and conclusive discoveries were made by Kathleen Kenyon from 1961 to 1967, driving a wide trench from the summit of the City of David hill down to the Gihon spring at its foot. Since 1967 the three major Israeli excavations have been, first, a further investigation on a large scale of the City of David under Yigel Shiloh; next, the Ophel dig to the north by Benjamin Mazar just south of the Temple Mount, which in 20 years of excavation has turned up much interesting Herodian material (the Haram itself, in Muslim hands, cannot be touched); and finally the widespread excavations in the Jewish Quarter by Nahman Avigad, which have revealed among other finds the Byzantine *cardo* or main north-south street. The Ophel and City of David digs are forming one interconnected archaeological park; digging still continues (1988) in the Ophel sector.

Kenyon's excavation, carried well down the steep eastern slope, opened up a short stretch of the Middle Bronze Age Jebusite wall (of about 1800 BC) just where it turned up the hill, thus defining the northern limits of David's Jebusite city. It must have been smaller than thought, only about 15 acres in all. Just above the ancient wall, made of heavy boulders and in use well into the Israelite period, a parallel wall was found built by Hezekiah in the 8th cent. BC. Resting on this wall, a series of residential terraces rose to the summit, connected by stepped alleyways and with covered drainage channels. The terraces carried comfortable houses, mostly of Hezekiah's period and later, but all before the destruction of 586 BC. The later digs uncovered more houses on the top terrace, preserved in parts to their full height under a Hellenistic glacis, (including a four-room house with a toilet at the back), and a large public structure of Hezekiah's time, just outside the walls to the south. In all these digs sherds and other finds were turned up dating from the Copper Age, from all periods of the Bronze Age, and some from the city of David and Solomon, including cultic stands and fertility symbols (the goddess Astarte), attesting to the prevailing "idolatry" so often preached against in the Old Testament.

Altogether 25 layers of settlement were uncovered during the seven-year City of David dig, ranging from the Early Bronze Age into the Middle Ages. These included the discovery in 1984 of a large structure belonging to the period of David and Solomon, and remnants of the buried Canaanite citadel destroyed by David, as well as the early Israelite citadel. As a fitting climax to this major project, before the site began to be prepared as an archaeological park, the earliest houses of this very ancient city were discovered in 1985 underneath some Canaanite houses of the early 18th cent. BC (Middle Bronze Age II). Built directly on the bedrock, the three 5,000-year-old houses, narrow rectangular structures, each with a simple bench, were dated at about 3000 BC (Early Bronze Age I) in a little-known period when the cities of Palestine were just beginning to grow from villages into cities.

David occupied the Jebusite city but did little building. His son Solomon, however, seems to have extended the city north, building a platform on Mt. Moriah for his temple and palace. A section of a casemate wall, typical of Solomon's times, was found some time ago in the northern part of the City of David and may have been part of Solomon's extension of the city walls to connect with the Temple Mount. A broken proto-Aeolian capital was also found here that undoubtedly once adorned Solomon's palace. Then in 1980 Shiloh's large dig (30 staff and 250 international volunteers) began to uncover, between the remains of Canaanite and Israelite houses, a huge stepped-stone structure of rough ashlar masonry, as tall as a five-story house, and dating from Solomon's times. This astounding discovery is thought to be part of Solomon's underpinning for his acropolis, carrying his citadel. The structure is by far the most monumental so far found in Israel.

Israelite Jerusalem had three different water systems (access to water was crucial in any siege), all tunneled into the rock and emanating from the Gihon spring. These have been partly cleared and studied in detail by Shiloh's team. Possibly Solomonic is the rock-cut channel leading down the bottom of the east side of the hill, with openings for the release of water to irrigate the small fields in the Kidron valley. The famous tunnel of Hezekiah, which snakes through the rock of the hill to reach the Siloam pool on its opposite side, was dug when Jerusalem was threatened by the Assyrians in 701 BC, as attested by part of an inscription found deep inside it as well as by passages in the Bible ("Why should the kings of Assyria come and find much water?" said the king). This tremendous engineering feat, about 2,000 ft. long, can still be waded through (flash-

The City of David dig in 1983, looking northeast across the village of Silwan to the Mount of Olives. The small city of Urusalima, belonging to the Jebusites of Canaan, was located on a narrow ridge just south of the later Temple Mount. It was seized by David as his capital about 1000 BC. The important excavations by Kathleen Kenyon in the 1960s were followed by a massive 7-year project (shown here) which was climaxed in 1985 by the discovery of the earliest houses of the ancient city, dating back to about 3000 BC at the dawn of civilization in the Middle East. (Courtesy: Israel Government Press Office.)

lights and boots highly recommended!). The third and oldest system, called Warren's shaft for its discoverer, consists of a 110 ft. tunnel driven down through the rock beneath the ancient city and under its wall to a point where a vertical shaft drops straight down some 42 ft. more to a tunnel leading to the spring, which was outside the walls. Shiloh employed professional alpinists to climb up the shaft and study the tunnel. Warren's shaft, once thought to be the Jebusite "gutter" through which, according to the Bible, David's troops entered the city, has now been updated to David's City in the First Temple period. Now open to the public, it is well worth a visit.

Under pressure from the Assyrians Hezekiah not only rebuilt the walls of David's City and dug the water tunnel, but extended the massive city wall to enclose a new residential quarter that had been growing up on the western hill. Archaeology has shown that Jerusalem underwent a sudden and tremendous population explosion in his time and the next century, undoubtedly because of a flood of refugees from Israel, captured in 722 BC, and from elsewhere in Judah as Assyria encroached. This explains the new quarter as well as the difficult terracing on the eastern slope to extend the City of David as far as possible.

In 1970 Professor Avigad uncovered a curving stretch of Hezekiah's new western wall, the Broad Wall, in the Old City's Jewish Quarter that proved that the city had indeed expanded to the west far earlier than thought. In 1975 he found the foundations of a heavy tower of the same defenses, incorporated into a later wall. At its base were four Babylonian arrowheads in a layer of ashes, testimony to Nebuchadnezzar's fierce destruction of 586 BC.

Across the Kidron valley from the City of David, in the Arab village of Silwan, are a number of rock-cut tombs dating from this period. Notable are the "Tomb of Pharaoh's Daughter," a freestanding building cut out of the solid rock, of definitely Egyptian inspiration, and "The Tomb of the Royal Steward," which according to an inscription housed the bodies of a local magnate and his slave wife.

Well west of the old City of David, nine burial caves were discovered and excavated, beginning in 1979, on the slopes of the Hinnom valley ("Gehenna"). Mostly from the First Temple period, these caves helped to define the western extent of the city walls of the time—for burials were always placed just outside the walls. Although most of the burials belonged to the period before the destruction of Jerusalem in 586 BC, some were later, indicating, surprisingly, that wealthy Jewish families continued to occupy Jerusalem after the destruction. The location of the caves also suggested that the walls had enclosed a far larger city in the late First Temple period than had been previously recognized. Moreover, one rich burial deposit in particular, dating from the mid-7th cent. BC and luckily preserved intact for 2,600 years under a fallen roof, included many objects of gold and silver, pottery and glassware providing a precious glimpse into the life of a city far wealthier as well as larger than had been supposed. Among the objects two tiny silver scrolls of the mid-7th cent., unwrapped with great difficulty only in 1986, were found to be inscribed in ancient Hebrew with a familiar prayer from Numbers 6:24–26, "The Lord bless you and keep you . . ."—the oldest biblical verse ever found, 400 years older than the Dead Sea Scrolls (see Qumran). The verse also indicated that 2,600 years ago the Jews were indeed already familiar with the earlier parts of the Old Testament, long thought to have been compiled around this time.

The Babylonian exiles came back to repopulate a shrunken city. Little is left of this Persian period and the following Hellenistic and Hasmonaean periods, except some house foundations, numerous pottery vessels and inscribed jar handles, and several large rock-cut cisterns that can still be viewed. Nehemiah's walls, built in 52 days in 440 BC, were found to underlie the later Hasmonaean walls running along the top of the City of David ridge, with a heavy glacis below the walls—the old walls down the hill being abandoned. These walls enclosed what was now called the "Lower City" of David and the new "Upper City" to the west. As the city expanded during the 2nd and 1st cents. BC, the City of David became the "old city" of the time, and under Herod the Great (37–4 BC) the newer city grew rapidly both west and north beyond the Temple Mount. In Hadrian's time David's city was finally left beyond the walls altogether.

Herod, the great builder, turned Jerusalem into a magnificent capital city, with a huge palace and fortress, encircling walls, aqueducts, substantial houses and public buildings and his great new temple. A detailed model of Herodian Jerusalem may be seen at the Holyland Hotel today in the New City. To accommodate his much-enlarged temple Herod built the massive 36-acre platform that still dominates the Old City today. Covered porticos ran along all four sides. These have disappeared, but the lower courses of the heavy Herodian walls may still be seen, constructed without mortar of huge blocks weighing up to 400 tons, with beautifully finished double margins. Seven courses are visible at the famous Wailing Wall (now the Western Wall), and 19 more, resting on bedrock, have been opened up south of it in Dr. Mazar's excavations. In recent years the entire length of the Western Wall has been exposed and is open to the public.

The Antonia fortress and a huge reservoir adjoined the platform on the north (the courtyard of the Antonia, with Roman graffiti, can be seen in the crypt of a church off the Via Dolorosa). Monumental staircases approached the entrance-ramps on the north and south leading up into the interior courtyard of the temple platform. One of these broad staircases, on the south, with its plaza has been excavated and reconstructed by Dr. Mazar, whose dig has also elucidated the origin, long a puzzle, of "Robinson's arch," the stump of an arch high on the western wall of the platform. It was part of another monumental staircase that led down to the lower level, turning south on a pier over a broad street running along the western wall, with four little ancient "souvenir" shops under it facing the street. This main street of Herodian Jerusalem, paved with enormous slabs, has also been uncovered in part. "Wilson's arch" to the north is a relic of an exit leading from the temple over the street on arches to the western hill.

In rebuilding the walls Herod also paid much attention to the vulnerable pool area at the lower tip of the City of David hill (including the Siloam pool), fed from the Gihon spring. Here he erected a heavy wall, explored by Dr. Shiloh, which also served as a dam. All that remains of Herod's fortress-palace in the western quarter is the lower masonry of his Phasael tower (called "David's Tower"), one of three he built, and now in the Citadel near the Jaffa Gate. The Citadel, housing an interesting civic museum and a center for sound-and-light shows and other entertainments, dates from all periods up to the 16th cent., beginning with the Hasmonaean walls and towers, the foundations now visible in the courtyard. Herod's magnificent palace, judging from a few remains, extended south of the Citadel over most of the present Armenian Quarter. Here Pilate judged Jesus, Titus camped his troops on the ruins after 70 AD, and the Crusader kings of Jerusalem lived.

In the Jewish and Armenian quarters about 10 mosaic floors from luxurious houses of this period have been found, including several substantial houses destroyed in 70 AD, one with a ritual bath and footbath, another with frescoed walls and carved stucco ornamentation. Herod's family tomb, where members of his murdered family were buried (he himself was presumably buried in the *Herodian*) is just south of the King David hotel. Behind the entrance, closed by a great round stone, are four empty rock-cut chambers.

The savage Roman destruction of Jerusalem in 70 AD is well-documented throughout the city in smashed buildings, layers of ashes and debris. The "Burnt House" in the Jewish Quarter, now open to the public in a basement, was in the Upper City and belonged to a family of Temple priests. A number of rooms, a kitchen and a pool in its basement have been cleared, one area being left as it was found, broken pots, ashes, charred wood and the skeletal arm of a young woman amid tumbled stones from the upper stories. More recently three houses and an alley near the City of David and the Siloam pool were excavated. It was found that the whole area was littered with dismembered human bones. We know from Josephus that the rebels, defeated at the City of David, tried to flee, but weakened by famine were "all massacred and their bodies flung to dogs."

On the whole little is left of Roman Jerusalem, including Hadrian's Aelia Capitolina. Dr. Avigad has found a palatial mansion of the 1st cent. AD in the Jewish Quarter. It awaits restoration. Some of the forum wall south of the Church of the Holy Sepulcher survives, and the famous Ecco Homo arch over a part of the Via Dolorosa is now thought to be the remnants of a city gate built by Herod Agrippa I (37–44 AD) and the pavement around it part of a Herodian forum. The present walls of the Old City, however, do follow roughly the bounds of Aelia Capitolina, and its grid plan is suggested in the present street pattern of the Old City—especially the *cardo*, or main north-south street, which was 40 ft. wide and bordered by colonnades on either side. Visitors today can walk through a stretch of it. This ran south from the present Damascus Gate almost to the Church of the Holy Sepulchre. The Damascus Gate incorporates some of the masonry of the Roman gate under it.

This ancient gate has been excavated in an underground operation that also discovered a Roman guard tower still standing 36 ft. high and filled with rubble and concrete by the builders of the Damascus Gate, all of which had to be cleaned out. The famous 6th-cent. mosaic map of Jerusalem from Madaba in Jordan clearly shows the gate, the broad colonnaded *cardo* and just inside the gate a spacious plaza with a tall column (like that of Trajan in Rome) at its center, topped by a statue, presumably of Hadrian. The archaeologists, looking for the column, dug south of the gate and came across the paving of the plaza, then extending the underground dig, joined with that of the gate, making an entire underground museum. There was no trace of the column, though its emplacement was found, so a large hologram of a reconstruction of the column now centers the museum. It is just possible that a large round crushing stone, part of a later olive press found inside the guard tower, may be a section of the column. It's the right size and shape. Just outside the Damascus Gate and between it and Herod's Gate, a vast cavern—the so-called Solomon's quarries, a maze of galleries open to the public—runs over 700 ft. underground into the Old City. It may well have been the quarries for Solomon's temple, or perhaps that of Herod.

Numerous Hellenistic and Roman tombs survive or have been found on the outskirts of old Jerusalem. A fine example, north of the Damascus Gate, is the so-called "Tombs of the Kings," actually the tomb of Queen Helena of Adiabene (in northern Mesopotamia), a Jewish convert of the 1st cent. AD who moved to Jerusalem. It is noted for its fine Classical facade. A large forecourt, fully 100 ft. long, with steps, leads through a vestibule and entrance (closed by a rolling stone) into the antechamber, off which are a number of tomb chambers, two unfinished. The queen's sarcophagus was found hidden below the tomb floor.

Further north is the "Tomb of Simon the Just," identified by an inscription as that of Julia Sabine, a Roman matron. Considerably further out lies the "Sanhedrin Tombs," a rock-cut catacomb fronted by a richly-carved pediment (1st cent. AD) and spacious court. A number of tomb chambers containing shaft graves on different levels number 70 burials. In the New City, west of the Jaffa Gate, is the interesting Tomb of Jason, discovered in 1956, a wealthy supporter of the Hasmonaeans in the early 1st cent. BC, and several generations of his

family down to 31 BC, when the tomb was shattered by an earthquake. Three
courts precede a porch with a (reconstructed) pyramid over it. There were eight
shaft graves in the burial chamber. On the porch are unusual drawings of warships in charcoal and an inscription.

Among tombs in the Kidron valley is the striking "Tomb of Absolam," a freestanding Classical building of the 1st cent. AD cut in part out of solid rock. It is
surmounted by a tall conical spire, and a catacomb of eight chambers lies behind it. Very similar is the pyramid-topped "Tomb of Zechariah" nearby, possibly
dated to the 2nd cent. BC, as is the tomb of the priestly family of Beni Hezir,
with its Doric facade. The Mount of Olives rising above the Kidron valley was
for centuries a traditional burying ground for Jews, and numerous tombs, cemeteries and catacombs have been found in its southwest end, as well as Christian and Muslim cemeteries. Some can still be seen, others have been reburied.
A 1st cent. AD cemetery was found further east around the traditional tomb of
Lazarus in the village of Bethany, where a series of four churches with mosaics
(4th cent. AD on) was excavated 1949–53. Excavations closer to the Old City in
1954 uncovered an immense cemetery near the Dominus Flevit church, in use
from 100 BC to 135 AD and again from 200 to 400 AD. A few examples of the
tombs have been left on view.

Pilgrims flocked to a revived Jerusalem after the empire became Christian
and numerous churches and monasteries and many new public buildings and
houses appeared. In the 6th cent. AD there were 24 churches on the Mount of
Olives alone, most of them surrounded by monasteries. Today many of the surviving churches throughout the city have Byzantine foundations, and a splendid
Byzantine house with mosaic floors has been uncovered on the Ophel hill. Dr.
Mazar has also found other Byzantine buildings at the south end of the Temple

*The so-called Tomb of Absalom in
the Kidron valley southeast of the
great platform of Herod's Temple
Mount. The tomb actually dates from
the 1st century BC and its spire rises
over a burial catacomb with eight
chambers. The monument is partly
cut out of solid rock. (Courtesy: Israel
Ministry of Tourism.)*

The Byzantine extension of the Roman cardo or main street of Jerualem, excavated and restored, with some of the Byzantine and Crusader shops that lined it put back into use again. Such restorations are one of the most attractive results of the recent large-scale urban excavations in Jerualem. Other sites have been turned into outdoor archaeological parks. (Courtesy: Israel Government Press Office.)

Mount, some preserved to a height of three stories, and a Byzantine church foundation and that of another building have been uncovered at the Pool of Siloam.

However the most striking features of prosperous Byzantine Jerusalem have been uncovered by Dr. Avigad in his excavations in the Jewish Quarter. The southern half of the *cardo*—which proved to be Byzantine—has been excavated and cleared, some of its portico columns re-erected, and Byzantine and Crusader vaulted shops on either side cleaned out and some restored to their original purpose. Hezekiah's Broad Wall, the Israelite tower and Hasmonaean fortifications can now be seen in deep cuts off the *cardo*, itself well below the modern level of the Street of the Jews that parallels it.

The Byzantine southern extension of the *cardo* was apparently built, possibly by Justinian, as a processional way to link the Church of the Holy Sepulcher close to the bottom of the Roman *cardo* with Justinian's great New Church of the Holy Mother of God, called the Nea, further south up against the walls. The Nea was known from Procopius and is clearly shown on the Madaba mosaic map; but it was Dr. Avigad who found what was left of it in 1970—part of its southern wall and the foundations of the northern apse. More has since been located, and an inscription has definitely confirmed its building by Justinian in 543 AD. The church lies partly under the Ottoman walls and was immense. Each of its massive stones, Procopius wrote, were carted to the site by 40 oxen. It was destroyed by the Arabs after 638 AD.

The Church of the Holy Sepulcher as it now stands, small dark and crowded with the clerics and followers of competing Christian sects, is essentially a medieval building (12th-cent. Crusader) and thus outside the purview of this guide. Briefly, however, the traditional tomb of Jesus, now enclosed within it, was originally cut into the walls of a disused quarry of the early 1st cent. AD, then outside the city walls. The site was venerated from early times, attesting to its authenticity, but in 135 AD the emperor Hadrian, attempting to eradicate the

The Church of the Holy Sepulcher, essentially a medieval Crusader building, much rebuilt; it houses the Holy Sepulcher itself, traditionally the tomb of Christ, as well as a slender rock pillar, all that is left of Calvary, the rocky hill on which Jesus was traditionally held to be crucified. The site, originally a 1st century AD disused quarry, then outside the city walls, had long been venerated until Hadrian deliberately built a pagan temple over it in 135 AD. With the triumph of Christianity, Constantine the Great destroyed the temple and built a basilica, attached to a rotunda around the tomb whose shape still exists, though the basilica has gone. The far smaller Crusader church is now a dark jumble of elements contributed by all the Christian sects who worship there today. (Courtesy: Israel Ministry of Tourism.)

native culture, built a large pagan temple on the site, fronted by a forum. When the empire turned Christian under Constantine, the latter tore down the temple and cut away the cliff around the tomb to isolate it, leaving one slender rock pillar from the rocky hill of Calvary nearby, traditional site of the Crucifixion. Around the tomb he built a circular rotunda and a large basilica to the east, beyond an open courtyard in one corner of which stood the Calvary pillar. The shrine, dedicated in 335 AD, was all but wrecked by a Fatimid caliph in 1009.

The rotunda was restored in 1042 under the Byzantine emperor Constantine Monomachus, but the basilica and atrium in front of it were never rebuilt. In 1099 the Crusaders captured the city and thereafter built a Romanesque church joined to the rotunda, over the former open courtyard which included the Calvary pillar. This is roughly the complex existing today, all medieval except for the lower parts of the walls of the rotunda and other details dating from the 4th cent. AD. Since Constantine's shrine was far larger than the present church, some interesting remains from it may be seen in the nearby Russian mission and Ethiopian monastery. These include fragments of a triumphal arch and a bit of the pavement dating from Hadrian's temple on the site.

Of the early Islamic sites, a few must be mentioned. The exquisite octagonal Dome of the Rock on the Temple Mount, with its golden dome, a Umayyad mosque of 691 AD, is one of the earliest and most completely preserved of Islamic monuments. Naturally it is very Byzantine in conception, and the mosaics (those on the inside are the original ones) were done by Syrian Christian craftsmen. In its interior is an outcrop of bedrock from which, in Islamic tradition, Mohammed ascended into heaven. The rock probably underlay the central parts of Herod's and Solomon's temples. The El-Aksa mosque on the south side of the Mount, built 705–715, is of less interest because it has been almost entirely rebuilt. It was the residence of the Crusader king of Jerusalem, and then of the original Templars order. Below the south side of the Mount, and again in Dr. Mazar's dig, a large Umayyad palace and two hospices have been uncovered. The palace, filling the entire space between the Ottoman wall and the Temple Mount, was built partly of reused materials from Herod's Temple.

Jerusalem has a number of museums, the most important being the Israel Museum, largest in Israel, which also houses the Bronfman Biblical and Archaeological Museum and the modernistic Shrine of the Book, a dome-shaped structure in which is displayed the famous Dead Sea Scrolls (see *Qumran*) as well as scrolls and documents from other sites such as *Navel Hever* and *Masada*. The Rockefeller Museum (also known as the Palestine Archaeological Museum) displays a vast collection of Middle Eastern antiquities. Lesser museums include the Pontifical Biblical Institute, (visit by appointment), the Herbert Clark Collection of Middle East Antiquities, the Musée de l'Ecole Biblique et Archaéologique Française, and the Hebrew University's Museum of Prehistory.

Near Jerusalem is the Ein Yael project. Excavations on the site have revealed an Israelite farm and Roman villa and baths. The ultimate purpose is to create an open-air "living" museum of rural life with visitor involvement in carrying out ancient crafts. Nearby, at Er Ras (Manahat), is an excavation of a farm dating from the First Temple period. An appointment is necessary, from the Israel Department of Antiquities and Museums, to visit both sites. See *Ramat Rahel* for another site on the southern outskirts of the city.

JIB, EL-	See *Gibeon*.
JOTAPATA	See *Yodefat*.

KEBARA

Prehistoric cave site on the western slopes of Mt. *Carmel*, 1 mi. S. of Zikhron Ya'akov police station and about 2 mi. from the sea, excavated 1931, 1951–65 and 1987. The site gives its name to a late (Upper) Paleolithic stone industry, the Kebaran (about 20,000–16,000 BC) excavated here, characterized by composite microlith tools such as barbed spears and javelins, or reaping knives made with several little blades cemented in with resin or bitumen. There are also Mesolithic (Natufian) remains here such as fishhooks, harpoons and sickle hafts. Of the latter, four are decorated, one carved in the form of a gazelle. Altogether five levels were excavated in the cave, down to the Mousterian period.

In renewed excavations (1987) an important discovery was made of the partial skeleton burial of an undoubted Neanderthal man from about 60,000 years ago. The fact that *Homo sapiens* remains have been found both earlier and later than this burial indicated to the excavators that Neanderthals arrived in the Levant rather late on a temporary basis to escape the encroaching cold of the ice ages in western Europe. For instance, the recent discovery of fossils of early modern man in Qafzeh cave just north of Kebara, dated by thermoluminescence applied to burnt flint from their hearths, came to 92,000 years ago!

Also in recent years (1984–85) the burial of a Kebaran man was discovered and excavated just south of Haifa near the coast—only the second burial of the period to be discovered. He had been entombed deliberately under a stone amidst scattered tools and other evidence of a Kebaran settlement at the site.

Several large mortars used by these hunter-gatherers to grind wild wheat and barley were buried with the man—an early stage on the way to Neolithic farming. See also *Carmel, Mount* and *Nalal Oren* for more on the prehistoric caves.

KEFAR BARAM   See *Meiron*.

KELEIFAH, TELL El-   See *Ezion-Geber*.

KERAZEH   See *Capernaum*.

KFAR NAHUM   See *Capernaum*.

KHAN EL-AHMAR   Ruins of a Byzantine monastery in the Judean desert off the Jerusalem-Jericho road and just beyond Mishor Adummim, one of 130 monasteries that flourished in Byzantine times in the desert east of Jerusalem. In 428 AD St. Euthymius, an early leader of the monastic movement, founded a *laura* here, a group of cells centering on a church. After his death his cave became his tomb and that of his companions and a new church was built (478–82 AD) over the old one underneath it, which became a refectory. There was a strong tower for defense and other buildings, including a huge runoff underground cistern outside the walls. Although abandoned in the 12th century, much of this can still be seen at the site, including some of the mosaic floors of the later church. Excavations are currently (1988) taking place.

KHAREITUN, WADI   See *Wadi Khareitun*.

KHIAM, EL-, TERRACE   See *Wadi Khareitun*.

KHIRBET AL-MAFJAR   See *Jericho*.

KHIRBET ED-DEIR   Remote and lonely ruins of a monastery in the Judean desert, about 9 mi. straight E. of Hebron, one of the 130 monasteries that were once scattered through the desert between Jerusalem and the Dead Sea in the Byzantine period (4th to 6th cents. AD). In a lovely situation on the sides of a tributary running into the Nahal Arugot, off the road from Tuqa (Tekoa) to the Dead Sea, a visit involves a side road and a long hike up the wadi to the tributary on the left. Nothing is known about the monastery, whose remains are partly carved into the cliff and partly built against it. One of the largest caves served as the church. It is floored with mosaics in geometric and floral patterns, and a tower rising above it served as a refuge in case of attack. There are several other mosaic floors here, one with a Greek inscription, a row of five cells for the early monks built against the cliff, a central cistern fed by an aqueduct from above and gardens below watered by the overflow. The large kitchen building with oven once had the refectory over it, now disappeared. Crude steps beside a reservoir lead up to the top of the cliff where there are traces of more structures, one with a cistern.

KHIRBET EL-MINYA   Ruins of a Umayyad palace on the N. shore of the Sea of Galilee, 8½ mi. N. of *Tiberias*. The palace was almost square, with a round tower on each corner and half towers on three sides in between and a large domed gateway on the fourth (E.) side. Though not all excavated, digging in the interior (1932–39) did uncover a mosque, throne room, and five rooms paved with mosaics in geometric patterns. See also *Jericho* (Khirbet al-Mafjar).

KHIRBET ER-RABUD

The biblical Debir, a large and important city in the Judean hill country S. of Jerusalem, about 7½ mi. S. of Hebron. Sporadic occupation during the earlier millennia preceded the first walled city here in the Late Bronze Age (14th–13th cents. BC), covering about 15 acres. The excavators turned up four separate strata covering this period. Taken by the invading Israelites, Debir remained small until the 9th cent. when it gained a new wall enclosing about 12½ acres. Later an unwalled suburb grew up outside the city. This large city was destroyed, probably by Sennacherib in 701 BC, but was soon rebuilt with a city wall almost doubled in size—only to disappear from history when the Babylonians destroyed Judah in the 6th cent. BC

KHIRBET ES-SALAM

See *Gamla*.

KHIRBET KERAK

See *Beth Yerak*.

KHIRBET KERAZEH

See *Capernaum* (Chorazin).

KHIRBET RUHEIBEH

See *Rehovot*.

KHIRBET SHEMA

See *Meiron*.

KHIRBET SUSEYA

A hilltop in the Judean hills, about 9 mi. directly S. of Hebron and a few mi. S. of Yatta, reached by a rough road. Here stand the remains of an exceptionally well-preserved synagogue of great architectural merit adorned with much marble, excavated 1971–72. It was in use between the 5th and 9th cents. AD, and later a mosque was built over part of it. Its walls are still standing to a considerable height, and its mosaic floors—geometric, biblical scenes, a zodiac, Jewish religious symbols, with four inscriptions—are now protected by a roof. It stood between two hills covered with the remains of a Jewish settlement, probably 3rd to 4th cents. AD, which may have been Carmel. One house of the town was excavated in 1978, and the settlement as a whole more fully in 1984–85. A fortified town with a massive gate, its substantial buildings were constructed of ashlar masonry and arranged around courtyards, with large cisterns. Natural caves, somewhat rebuilt, were used in part for storage, and one large cave, over 60 ft. long, had been a wine cellar. Outside it was a large wine press. Olive presses were also uncovered, suggesting the town's twin economy.

A mile or two to the southwest another synagogue of the 4th or 5th cent. can be found in the village of Eshtemoa, a large Jewish village of the Roman-Byzantine periods. The synagogue, excavated 1935–36 and more fully in 1969–70, is again architecturally superior with mosaic floors and evidence of rich ornament on the exterior. The site has been identified with Es-Semu.

KISAN, TELL

Very large mound in the Plain of Akko (*Acre*) covering an ancient city, about 6 mi. inland from that port city. The latest excavation was by the Ecole Biblique (French) from 1971 to 1980. The city, in a richly fertile area and benefiting from trade between the inland and the coastal areas, enjoyed a most unusual several thousands of years of relative peace and prosperity with no check in habitation.

The earliest Early Bronze Age Canaanite town covered 25 acres and was walled in brick; the Middle Bronze Age town, though only 15 acres, was protected by Cyclopean walls and was equally prosperous and important. It came under Egyptian influence in the early Late Bronze Age, was peacefully infiltrated by Sea Peoples and fell under Phoenician influence from the coast. It was only destroyed, quite violently, about 1000 BC. Much later the town enjoyed a revival under Assyrian control after the fall of the northern Israelite kingdom in the 8th cent. BC, and its new prosperity was only lost when it was sacked in the second half of the 7th cent. Thereafter there was a Persian occupation and a new Hellenistic town on the site, which has left little trace, until the mound was abandoned in the 2nd cent. BC. A small Christian village and church on the mound in later centuries was wiped out by Saladin in 1191 AD.

KORAZIN

See *Capernaum* (Chorazin).

KUNTILLET AJRUD

An Israelite caravan station and cult center of about 800 BC, in the Sinai (see EGYPT).

KURNUB

See *Mamshit*.

KURSI

Or Gergesa, a Byzantine monastic center, the largest in Israel, on the eastern shore of the Sea of Galilee, a few mi. N. of *En Gev*, excavated 1970–72. A heavy rectangular plastered wall with a fortified gate facing the lake surrounds the whole. There are traces of paintings on the inside of the wall. The church (5th cent.), much restored, is approached by a basalt-paved road from the gate, and centers the compound with remnants of the monks' quarters to its north. Inside the church the floors of its sanctuary are laid in mosaics, mostly geometric but with animals and plants of the region depicted in the side aisles (the animals had been mostly destroyed by iconoclasts). A burial crypt and a cistern lie under the church. Traces of a Roman period village with breakwater and port can be discerned between the enclosure walls and the lake.

KYPROS

See *Jericho*.

LACHISH

One of the major fortified cities of both Canaan and Judah, guarding the approaches to the hill country from the south. The huge mound of Tell ed-Duweir in the Shepelah lies halfway between *Hebron* and *Ashkelon* and 25 mi. southwest of Jerusalem. An important excavation by the British in 1932 was terminated in 1938 when its leader, James L. Starkey, was brutally murdered by Arab brigands. After excavations by Yohanan Aharoni in 1967–68, intensive long-range excavations by the Israelis resumed in 1973 and restoration work is still going on (1989). The site was occupied from the Copper or Chalcolithic Age until about 150 BC. Upper Paleolithic flints, found on the plain below the mound, bring the record even further back. The Copper Age people (4th millennium BC) lived in caves, enlarged for use, in the rock of the original hill. In the next millennium, the Early Bronze Age, the first city grew up here, the earlier caves being used for burials. But late in the period (about 2400–2000 BC) urban life faltered, as it did elsewhere, and the only evidence from this seminomadic period was found in rock-cut tombs. Urban living was not resumed until the 18th century (late Middle Bronze Age) when, judging from the rich tomb contents, the city was again a prosperous one. A dagger found in one of the tombs was inscribed with four symbols thought to be, along with a sherd from *Gezer* and a plaque from Shechem (see *Nablus*), one of the earliest known attempts at alphabetic writing. About 1700 BC the city was heavily fortified with a mud brick city wall around the top of the mound, a vast sloping glacis of the Hyksos type on its sides, and a revetment wall and fosse or ditch at the bottom.

The Late Bronze Age was the peak of Lachish's prosperity as a Canaanite city. As a vassal of mighty Egypt, it was wealthy and secure. Letters from its kings are found in the 14th century tablets from *Amarna* in EGYPT, including one addressed to Pharaoh Akhenaten by its king, Shipti-baal. Traces of a palace were found, and its tombs yielded a rich assortment of grave goods, and even richer offerings were found in the "Fosse Temple" in the disused Middle Bronze Age ditch (the fortifications were destroyed, apparently by the Egyptians, about 1580 BC). This temple (15th–13th cents.) went through three main phases until its destruction, which sealed in a remarkable collection of ritual offering vessels, many imported from Cyprus and Mycenae, Egyptian glass and scarabs, ivory carvings, clay figurines, and jewelry. A bin beside the altar was filled with animal bones, almost all the right forelimbs of the sacrificed animals, the traditional priest's portion both in Canaan and Israel. Nothing is now to be seen of the temple.

About 1230–1220 BC the city and the temple were violently destroyed, perhaps by Joshua (who according to the Bible took Lachish) or more likely in an Egyptian punitive raid. The archaeological evidence indicates that the city was unfortified at the time. Lachish then lay crippled for over 200 years. Around about 1000 BC David or Solomon erected a large stone platform, 23 ft. high, on the top of the mound that served as the base of a citadel with a mud brick palace, now disappeared, and later as the principal citadel of the Israelite city and its governor's residence. Solomon's son Rehoboam refortified the city and it was further fortified under Asa, eventually becoming one of the strongest and largest cities of Judah. These defenses consisted of two massive walls with towers, one around the top, the other halfway down the slope of the mound, connected by a strong gate complex with three guard chambers on a side in the main gate.

These were the formidable defenses that faced Sennacherib of Assyria in 701 BC when he ravaged Judah and invested Jerusalem. Perhaps then, in preparation for his approach, the inhabitants, like those of Jerusalem under Hezekiah, started to dig a huge internal water shaft, 82 ft. wide and 62 deep. It was not yet finished when the attack came. For Sennacherib, according to his own inscription, took the city by assault "by means of well-stamped ramps, and battering rams brought near, attack by foot soldiers, mines, breeches as well as sapper work." All of this was pictured in graphic detail in a relief in his new palace at Nineveh (now in the British Museum), and the accuracy of his war artist has been recently amply confirmed, not only by biblical references, but also by the archaeological findings around the gate complex and sections of the walls. Evidences of a huge conflagration, countless slingshots and arrowheads were found in deep beds of ashes, and on the slopes pits filled with the remains of some 1500 humans, as well as animals, obviously from the clearance of the devastated city.

Over the next hundred years Lachish slowly recovered and the fortifications were restored and improved. Then came another epic siege during the campaigns of Nebuchadnezzar of Babylon in which he took Judah and destroyed

Jerusalem, marching the survivors off into exile. Lachish (in 588 BC) and nearby Azekah were the last cities taken before Jerusalem fell. To capture Lachish Nebuchadnezzar cut trees for miles around and built huge fires against the walls to weaken them—the abundant ashes have turned up in the excavations. A dramatic find in 1935 was 21 sherds, in a guardroom of the gate, inscribed in early Hebrew in black ink. They were messages to the commander of Lachish during the siege from an officer in an outpost between the city and Azekah. One was poignant: "And let my lord know that we are watching for the signal fires of Lachish, according to all the indications that my lord has given, for we no longer see the signals of Azekah."

Nebuchadnezzar put an end to Lachish's grandeur. For almost 300 years it lay almost deserted. Revived somewhat under the Persians, a mansion, of which only a few traces are left, was built on the old citadel platform, probably for the governor, and the remains of a temple have been found. In the Hellenistic period a small temple was built, possibly Jewish but more likely for a pagan solar cult. By about 150 BC the site was abandoned for good. Much of this can be seen on the site today, including the Assyrian siege ramp.

The finds from Lachish are divided between the Rockefeller Museum in Jerusalem and the British Museum in London, where the rich finds and records from the 1932–38 Starkey excavation have been acquired and put on display. The collection documents every aspect of the ancient city's history, and the pottery especially is abundant, technically superior and aesthetically pleasing, highlighted by the Late Bronze Age pottery from the Fosse Temple.

LAISH

See *Dan, Tell*.

MAMPSIS

See *Mamshit*.

MAMRE

See *Hebron*.

MAMSHIT

Mampsis in antiquity, and in Arabic, Kurnub, 26 mi. SE of *Beersheba*. Out of the half dozen Nabataean "ghost cities" identified in the Negev desert, Mamshit is one of the three that have been excavated, partially restored and carefully signposted for the extensive tourist trade (see also *Avdat, Shivta*). An attractive and well-preserved site, Mamshit was systematically excavated from 1965 to 1967 and again in 1971, and is notable for its buildings of beautifully dressed stone, so solidly built that many of them were in use for centuries. Mampsis was founded, perhaps as early as the 1st cent. BC, by the Nabataeans of Petra in Jordan. It was a caravan center channeling spices and exotic goods from further east and, unlike the other towns in the Negev, never had to resort to desert agriculture when the trade routes were displaced. Mamshit came under the Romans in 106 AD when a garrison was posted in the town, and later was a Byzantine center, but it never lost its Nabataean character. The end of the city seems to have come at the hands of desert marauders at the end of the 5th cent. AD.

Most of the remains on view date from the late Nabataean period (about 100–150 AD), though the walls, enclosing 10 acres with towers and two gates, were built by the Romans in the 4th cent. and strengthened by the Byzantines. The ruins of a large caravanserai outside the north gate may also belong to the Byzantine period. Blocks of spacious houses, centering on inner courtyards, line the streets. Most have stairways that led to upper stories and were roofed, in the scarcity of wood, with arches supporting stone slabs—the springs of the arches may still be seen. There were many cisterns filled with rainwater carefully channeled from the roofs and streets, and a large pool to feed the baths. Elaborate stables in two houses suggest that horse-breeding was important.

A large two-storied house in the western part of the town, with pillared courtyard, was probably the governor's mansion. A stairway and part of the upper story is preserved here. Next to it is a two-storied square tower still standing 17 ft. high, with a staircase. Around it are storerooms and a cistern. It may have served as an administrative center and observation post. The visitor may now view the ruins from its reconstructed upper part. South of it there was a large mansion, now partly covered by the Byzantine West Church, with stables and a large well-preserved cistern in its courtyard. More houses are on the east side, especially the Roman-period House of the Frescoes with Nabataean features and wall paintings of people and mythological characters. A hoard of 10,500 Roman silver coins in a bronze jar was found here. North of it is a large reservoir with a typical small Roman bathhouse next to it, added later.

Two Byzantine churches, both of the basilica type with atriums and fine mosaic floors, were built in the southeast and southwest parts of the town. Various subsidiary buildings surrounded both. The columns and eastern apse of the West Church are well preserved, and a Greek inscription in a mosaic shows it was built by St. Nilus of Sinai about 400 or 450 AD. The East Church may be considerably older. Cemeteries surround the town, Nabataean, Byzantine and a Roman military cemetery with Latin tombstones. And down below in the wadi reconstructed dams, protected by three watch towers, indicate how water from the brief rainy season was stored by the inhabitants. See also *Elusa, Nitzana, Rehovot.*

MARESHAH

The Arabic Tell Sandahanna, ancient town about 18 mi. E. of *Ashkelon*, close to *Lachish*. Excavations on the mound in 1898–1900 uncovered the Hellenistic-period town called Marissa. The dig has been covered up and nothing is now visible. In the area are ruins of three Crusader castles, the Crusader church of St. Anne, and some 3,000 bell-shaped caves that may be visited—actually chalk quarries worked during the Christian centuries and perhaps earlier, presumably to provide mortar and plaster for Ashkelon on the coast. One enters through a small hole cut into the hard surface crust to enter the caves. A mile north of Mareshah lies Beth Guvrin, once a village outside Marissa, then a thriving city taking the place of Marissa after it had been destroyed by the Parthians, in 40 BC.

Marissa had a long history, though there were few remains of its earlier periods. A town in ancient Judah, it was fortified by Rehoboam about 920 BC, destroyed by Sennacherib in 701 BC and by the Babylonians in 587. After the captivity it was resettled by Edomites and became part of Idumaea, and may have been the birthplace of Herod the Great. The Phoenicians established a colony here in the 4th cent. BC and in the 3rd the Ptolemies settled some Hellenized Sidonians in the city, which prospered on the slave trade with Egypt. It was forcibly Judaized by the Hasmonaeans about 115 BC. The city was laid out on a grid plan, with paved streets, blocks of houses, some arranged around a central court, a sewage system, and a town wall with towers. In this Hellenized city one large block of rooms around a spacious courtyard was apparently the government headquarters of the town, possibly with a temple. Another block shared a courtyard-market and a caravanserai. The finds, oddly enough, included six lead figures (used in witchcraft?) and 51 limestone plaques inscribed in Hebrew, Greek and some unknown script.

Two painted tombs have been discovered east of the town. A large tomb with urn recesses in three burial chambers was constructed for the head of the Sidonian colony (3rd and 2nd cent. BC) and was in use into the 1st cent. The paintings have faded away, but an intriguing Greek inscription was scrawled on its walls by two star-crossed lovers. The smaller Tomb of the Musicians on the southern side of a little valley, containing a painting of a flute-player and harpist, is also dated to the 2nd cent. Some 60 of the quarry caves are clustered around Mareshah. They have been used as houses, wine- or olive presses, or columbaria for the dead (or perhaps for the raising of domestic doves?). Nearby Beth Guvrin grew into a prosperous city honored by the emperor Septimius Severus in 200 AD with the name of Eleutheropolis. Mosaic floors from a Roman villa and a Byzantine chapel, uncovered here, are now in the Israel Museum, Jerusalem.

MARISSA

See *Maresha*.

MASADA

Spectacular Herodian fortress-palace on the top of a huge mesa that rises some 1,300 ft. in the gaunt, rocky Judean desert, 2 mi. W. of the Dead Sea. Masada was the scene of the last stand of the Zealot rebels in 73 AD, at the very end of the first Jewish revolt against Rome, three years after Jerusalem had fallen. Of the defenders—men, women and children—960 died, having killed each other after the Romans had breached their wall. Only two women, with five small children, hidden in a water pipe, survived to tell the story to the historian Josephus, whose graphic account of the siege and detailed description of the site was of enormous help to the excavators of Masada.

In an epic 11-month campaign in 1963–1965, with a force of 300, including volunteers from 28 countries, Yigael Yadin overwhelmingly confirmed Josephus' account in every detail, including the finding of about 28 bodies of the Zealots, most of them tossed into a cave, and a rich profusion of the remnants of their clothes, kitchen gear, weapons, jewelry, as well as unexpectedly elaborate architectural remains from Herod's time. Masada has now become not only an immensely popular tourist site but also a kind of national shrine of modern Israel, symbolizing the determination of the Jews to survive despite enormous odds. Young recruits of the armored units of the Israeli army are sworn in at Masada with the moving oath, "Masada shall not fall again."

Masada may be approached from the west on a new road from *Arad*, followed by a climb up the Roman siege ramp to the top, or from the more dramatic Dead Sea side. A cable car here takes one up to the east gate, or the hardier visitor may climb up the ancient Snake Path to the top. On the flat top, 2,000 by 1,000 ft. in area, about one-third of the excavated buildings have been reconstructed. Each one is well marked with explanatory signs and there are tourist facilities, including souvenir shops at the bottom and a youth hostel that also has an interesting museum of the finds. But the stark desert beauty of this great site, with its eerie silence, has not been spoiled.

A small fort was first built on Masada by Alexander Jannaeus the Hasmonaean (103–76 BC). It was to this fort that Herod first brought his family for safety when he fled from the Parthian invaders in 40 BC. Realizing its value as a refuge

The dramatic fortress-rock of Masada in the Judean desert west of the Dead Sea, now virtually a national shrine of modern Israel as well as a spectacular tourist site. It was at Masada that a band of Jewish rebel Zealots held out against the Romans in 73 AD until the end, when all committed suicide. The fortress, however, was the creation of Herod the Great, whose "hanging palace" on three levels can be seen on the left built over the chasm below. The mammoth excavation of the site in the 1960s left the Herodian remains for all to see as well as many pathetic relics of the Zealot occupation. In the dry desert below, the eight camps built by the Romans for the siege still stand out clearly. (Courtesy: Israel Ministry of Tourism.)

King Herod, fearing his own people—for he was a usurper—as well as Cleopatra's attempts to do away with him, turned it into the palace-stronghold we see today, between 39 and 31 BC. The top was enclosed within a double (casemate) wall with 38 towers, except at the north end where Herod daringly built his own private palace on three levels down the cliffside. There was also a larger, official palace near the West Gate, storehouses packed with food, weapons and other supplies, and other buildings, and a series of huge water reservoirs cut deep into the rock. After Herod's death the Romans occupied Masada, but at the beginning of the great revolt in 66 AD it was captured by the Zealots under Menachem. After his assassination, his nephew, Eleazar ben Ya'ir, took over the command.

Mopping up after the capture and destruction of Jerusalem in 70 AD, the Romans first took the forts of *Herodion* and Machaerus (north across the Dead Sea), then probably in 72 AD Flavius Silva, the procurator, under orders from Titus, marched on Masada with the 10th legion, its auxiliary troops and thousands of Jewish prisoners to do the menial work—perhaps upwards of 15,000 men. Determined to take the fortress by storm, he first built eight camps around the mesa, two large, the others smaller, whose remains are still quite visible today in the dry, unoccupied desert—though only one so far has been excavated. Next a stone wall, 6 ft. thick and reinforced by 12 towers in the eastern sector, was built entirely around the rock to keep the defenders from escaping, and finally a huge ramp of beaten earth and large stones was raised up the western side almost to the top, where a further platform of heavy stone, now entirely disappeared, was built. The ramp is still there, and a narrow path up it affords easy access to the ruins.

Somehow a huge tower, iron-plated against fire, with a heavy battering ram inside and catapults on the upper part, was dragged to the top and succeeded

Looking down over the second and third platforms of Herod's Hanging Palace to the desert far below. The second terrace contained an ornate round pavilion whose foundations can be seen, and several small rooms in back. The third terrace, with an elegant square pleasure house and small bath, was supported by tall retaining walls built up the cliffside below. (Courtesy: Israel Government Press Office.)

in breaching the wall near the Western Palace. The Zealots ingeniously plugged the hole with a structure of heavy beams and earth that would absorb the large artillery stones. Bringing torches, the Romans fired the beams, but the wind blew the fire back at the Romans, disastrously threatening all their work. Then the wind changed around, and both sides realized it was the end. When the Romans, retiring that night before the final assault, climbed onto the top next morning, they were met, according to Josephus, by "a terrible solitude on every side . . . and a perfect silence." The Zealots were all dead. After a rousing speech by Eleazar, 10 men were chosen by lot to kill all the others, then one by lot to kill the survivors. The last man fired the palace and drove a sword into himself. After the victory the Romans garrisoned Masada for at least 40 years, as the archaeological record shows. In the Byzantine period, when so many monks retreated to the Judean desert, a group settled on Masada.

The North Palace, Herod's own private retreat, was built on three terraces, one below the other, well-sheltered from Masada's fierce winds and sun. The upper terrace of this "hanging palace," shielded at the top from the other buildings by a high plastered wall, contained living quarters in a rectangular structure—four rooms and corridors, once lavishly decorated, and a small bathhouse. Simple geometric mosaic floors were preserved in some of the rooms. In front a semicircular terrace looked out over the spectacular view, probably bordered by columns (whose drums were found elsewhere). On the middle terrace, reached by a covered stairway, a round pavilion, its double circular walls once supporting columns, was backed by a series of rooms whose walls were once painted, though little remains. Evidently this and the lowest terrace were used for relaxation and pleasure only.

To build on the final narrow terrace, retaining walls up to 80 ft. high had to be built up the cliffside over the abyss (and excavation was equally difficult). Here was a square pleasure house with columns around a central courtyard. Wall paintings on the lower panels, imitating stone and marble, were well preserved under the fallen rubble and have since been laboriously restored. Above them rose fluted columns with gilded Corinthian capitals—the whole undoubtedly most sumptuous in effect. To one side was Herod's private bath suite in which was found the skeletons of a Zealot warrior, a young woman with nicely preserved plaited hair and elegant sandals, and a child—possibly the final warrior to die, with his family.

Below the North Palace a series of huge cisterns had been cut out of the cliff down the slope, ingeniously filled by aqueducts carrying water from two dams in two nearby wadis during the flash floods of winter. From here the water was carried up by hand to higher cisterns, including one for the palace. There was another huge rock-cut cistern at the southern end of the plateau.

On the flat top just south of the hanging palace was a complex of long narrow storehouses, a large communal bathhouse and a rectangular administrative building. The complex had only one entrance, on its western side, and at a strategic spot well inside this entrance 11 small sherds were found, each inscribed with a name, including that of "Ben Ya'ir," the commander himself. Undoubtedly these were the lots cast among the last survivors to determine who should kill the others.

The storehouses, with the help of a crane, were laboriously cleared, partly reconstructed, and then excavated. Needless to say thousands of small finds were uncovered here and elsewhere—jewelry, shekels (coins), lamps, vessels of stone, bronze and pottery, basketwork, bone and ivory utensils, dried food, stocks of tin and other metals. The excavated bathhouse proved to have the usual Roman steam room, with underfloor heating system and pipes in the walls, a cold room, tepid room, robing room and courtyard, the walls and roofs plastered and frescoed, and black-and-white mosaics on the floor.

South of this complex a square structure with rooms around a courtyard (in which was a later Byzantine addition) was excavated. It was obviously an "apartment house" for officials or garrison officers, with apartments consisting of a closed court and two small rooms each. Two hordes of rare silver shekels from the revolt period were also discovered here. More silver shekels were also found in one of the rooms in the casemate wall that was probably used as a dump by the Romans. The first scroll—a fragment of the Psalms—was found here. More scrolls turned up in other casemate rooms and in a wall tower, including a specialized scroll identical to one found among the Dead Sea Scrolls at Qumran and peculiar to the Essenes. This and other evidence indicated that at least a large number of the Essenes from Qumran had joined the rebellion and the rebels at Masada. Another rare scroll of Ecclesiasticus from the Apocrypha was found in another casemate room.

And more scrolls turned up in a rectangular structure projecting eastward from the wall on the west side. This proved to be a small synagogue, in its original Herodian plan the earliest found to date in Israel. There were six pillars in the interior. The Zealots built clay-plastered benches around most of the inside walls and a cell-like room on one side. The scrolls, parts of Ezekiel and Deuteronomy, were buried in Geniza-like pits below the floor. Altogether, parts of 14 scrolls were found at Masada. They are now housed in the Shrine of the Book in the Israel Museum, Jerusalem.

Obviously the defenders were devout Jews, as was shown by the discovery of a *mikveh* or ritual bath built into the southern wall, and later another in the administration building. Two top Hassidic rabbis, heavily clothed, climbed all the way up to Masada to measure the first *mikveh* and pronounce it kosher according to the age-old Talmudic laws. There were around 110 rooms in the casemate walls, as well as towers, and excavation and reconstruction of the entire wall—over 4,000 ft. long—was an arduous though rewarding task. For the Zealots used the rooms as dwellings, and also altered the existing buildings, erecting flimsy additions against them and the walls. The casemate rooms were found just as the Zealots had left them, after burning all their possessions and going off to die. Stoves and cooking pots were in place, and there were lamps, utensils, buckles and charred clothing, jewelry and cosmetics—and in the siege ramp area hundreds of stone missiles fired by the Romans, as well as huge stones prepared by the Zealots to roll down on the Romans but mostly never used.

Herod's Western Palace, some 36,000 sq. ft. and the largest building on Masada, was also used by the Zealots. This sumptuous, truly royal palace consisted of a living section with throne room and small bathhouse, a service wing, administrative building, and storerooms—in which remains of sophisticated palace wares were found. The whole had been set on fire by the last Zealot. The most remarkable find was part of an elaborate colored mosaic floor in the reception room in geometric patterns—and small colored mosaics in the bath suite. These were very similar to those found at Delos of the same period in Greece. Five smaller villas, some lavishly decorated, were located around the palace, obviously for the king's family members. Most were poorly preserved. Among them was a large swimming pool with steps at one end and niches for the bathers' clothes. To the south a round Herodian building with many niches inside in its walls was probably a columbarium for cremated bodies.

Between the apartment building and the Western Palace the ruins of a 5th cent. AD Byzantine chapel has long been a conspicuous landmark here. Its walls, curiously decorated with chips of sherds and stones in patterns, still stand high. There is a central hall with an apse at one end; the hall's mosaic floor has disappeared, but a fine mosaic, largely complete, was excavated in a side room, with medallions enclosing various fruits. A mosaic workshop was also found here.

MASOS, TELL A group of dispersed ruins around ancient wells and the wadi Beersheba in the Negev, representing widely separated eras, about 8 mi. E. of Tell *Beersheba*, excavated by a German-Israeli team from 1972 to 1975. The remains of an early Iron Age settlement at Khirbet el-Meshash north of the wadi are underlain by cave dwellings or subterranean houses of the late Copper Age, belonging to the Beersheba culture (3500–3200 BC). South of the wadi, two successive Bronze Age settlements of the 17th cent. BC near some wells were discovered by the codirector, Yohanan Aharoni. Both were fortified and neither lasted very long; little is left of either except parts of the protective embankment and house remains from the later one. The rest of this settlement had been destroyed by erosion.

More extensive and of greater interest is the early Iron Age settlement north of the wadi overlying the Copper Age huts. It lasted over 200 years (early 12th to mid-10th cent. BC), from the earliest peaceful settlement by the seminomadic southern Hebrew tribes, who began by living in tents, until the early years of the Israelite monarchy. This unfortified village, illustrating the crucial transition from seminomadic to sedentary existence, is the largest so far found in the Negev. It rapidly became a trading and metalworking center, especially in copper, and was in touch with Egypt and the Phoenicians, and as the finds indicate was directly influenced by Canaanite culture. Later it came under the control of the Philistines on the coast until the rise of David and the monarchy. Aside from three- and four-room houses, a house of Egyptian design also was found, and another of Canaanite type, apparently occupied by a Canaanite metalworker who left his anvil, stone tools and a collection of imported ceramics behind him. Many other such imported wares and objects of copper and bronze, as well as local unpainted wares—cooking pots, jars etc.—and a tiny lion head carved in ivory by some Phoenician and an Egyptian scarab of the period of Seti II (1204–1194 BC) were found.

The site lay deserted until the 7th cent. when under King Josiah a small fortress was erected south of the Iron Age settlement. It was destroyed by the Edomites in the 6th cent. BC; then much later a Nestorian monastery was established here, possibly after the Arab conquest of 638 AD, because the heretical Nestorians had been persecuted by the orthodox Byzantines before that date. A chapel, incorporated into the monastery, was carefully paved in limestone and may have been domed. Fragments of Syrian inscriptions were found here and seven graves in a crypt. The monastery was violently destroyed by bedouins in the 8th cent. AD.

MEGIDDO

Major fortified city of both Canaan and ancient Israel, the renowned Armageddon of the Bible, dominating the important Way of the Sea and the plain of Jezreel at a pass on its route from Egypt to Syria and beyond, about 20 mi. S. of Haifa. A natural battleground on the approaches to Galilee, the great warrior Tuthmosis III of Egypt smashed a coalition of Canaanite kings at Megiddo in 1468 BC. Here in 609 Pharaoh Necho killed King Josiah of Judah; here Napoleon in 1799 and Allenby in 1918 defeated the Turks, and Israel stopped the Arab drive on Haifa in 1948. No wonder St. John of Revelation placed the ultimate battle at Armageddon—Hebrew for the "hill of Megiddo." The 15-acre mound has been extensively excavated—in 1903–1905, then on a large scale by the Oriental Institute of Chicago in 1925–39, and by the Israelis since 1958 and 1960–70 by Yigael Yadin, including some restoration. The site is now a national park and the combined museum, snack bar and reception center outside the entrance ramp contains a useful model of the city in ancient times.

With 25 occupation levels (with subdivisions), the stratigraphy is complex. After a possible early Neolithic background, the settlements begin with the Early Bronze Age. From its later centuries the traces of a simple temple may still be seen. Still in the Early Bronze Age a mud brick wall was followed by a massive town wall of stone, 26 ft. thick in places. Possibly also from this period dates the often-photographed "High Place," a round stone altar base in the open, later (probably in the Middle Bronze Age) flanked by a Canaanite temple and then two more—a double temple, presumably for twin deities. The foundations may still be seen in a deep trench. In the Middle Bronze Age the town was enclosed by a rampart and glacis. Some houses were uncovered, and the earliest palace next to the north, or main, gate. Remains of a narrow Middle Bronze Age gate, the earliest, and a later chariot-width gate may be seen here. In the Late Bronze Age the city prospered. After Tuthmosis III captured it in 1468—his description of the battle, in which his booty included 924 enemy chariots, may be seen at Karnak (see *Thebes*) in EGYPT—Megiddo became an important Egyptian outpost for at least 100 years. Letter from its king, Biridiya, turned up in the 14th-cent. *Amarna* archives in EGYPT.

From the Late Bronze Age comes what may have been a fortress-temple. The

Megiddo, the famed Armageddon of the New Testament (Revelation) where the ultimate battle is to be fought, shown at the time of Ahab (9th cent. BC) in a model at the site. The great fortified city was indeed often a battleground. Excavated and reexcavated from 1903 to 1970, it revealed complex remains in 25 main strata ranging from the Early Bronze Age up to the 4th cent. BC when it was abandoned—though the decline began after the Assyrian attack of 732 BC. The long buildings called "Solomon's Stables," actually built under Ahab, were probably storehouses, or possibly stables. If stables, they could have housed 492 chariot horses. (Courtesy: Israel Government Press Office.)

palace was enlarged, and in one of its rooms a magnificent hoard of jewelry and ivories was found. These famous "Megiddo Ivories," mostly carved plaques of the 13th and 12th cents. BC, form the largest Canaanite collection ever found. Another interesting find from these levels, in 1955, was forty lines from the famous Gilgamesh epic of Sumeria, inscribed on a fragment of an Akkadian clay tablet. The city was destroyed at the end of the Late Bronze Age, perhaps around 1200 BC. The Philistines apparently occupied it for a time as they pushed inland. Joshua, according to the Bible, took Megiddo, but if he did he could not hold it.

Eventually it was occupied by the Israelites and under Solomon became a major administrative and military center. According to Kings, Solomon built the walls of Hazor, Gezer, and Megiddo. The typical casemate walls and Solomonic gate, with three guardhouses a side, were indeed found at Megiddo (one half of the gate is still to be seen); later at Hazor, Yigael Yadin found the same Solomonic complex, then predicted, on the basis of the Bible passage and an earlier archaeological report by Macalister, that it would also turn up at Gezer, when excavated. And it did. Solomon also built a northern palace, presumably for his governor, Baana ben Ahilud, and another in the south for himself, as well as other public buildings. All of this was destroyed in 924 BC by Pharaoh Shosheng of Egypt.

After a period of recovery the city was refortified, probably under Ahab of Israel, another great builder, in the 9th cent., and even more lavishly adorned. The gate was rebuilt with two guardrooms a side, a new solid zigzag wall erected around the city, and on the site of the north and south palaces of Solomon the famous "stables," still called "Solomon's Stables," though they are now definitely attributed to Ahab. These long narrow structures with two rows of supporting columns down the center, could have accommodated 492 horses, if they were stables. But judging from similar buildings elsewhere they could have been storehouses. Ahab also constructed a massive water system to replace a concealed water passage of Solomon's leading down the hill to a spring outside the walls. A vertical shaft 75 ft. deep was sunk into the hill to the water level, then an underground passage led 200 ft. further to the spring, which was blocked from the outside. Tourists can now traverse this mammoth project with the help of steps and lights. A governor's palace was also built (in which five proto-Aeolic column capitals were found, similar to those recovered in *Hazor*, *Jerusalem*, *Ramat Rahel*, and *Samaria*). The existing huge grain silo with steps circling down two sides was probably built in the 8th cent. BC.

In 732 the city fell to Tiglath-Pileser III of Assyria, who made it capital of the Assyrian province of Magiddu, giving it a new grid street plan and spacious houses. But it declined in the 7th cent., became a mere small fortress, and by the 4th cent. BC was abandoned.

MEIRON

Or Meron, ancient town just S. of the modern village of the same name (Meron) in the Upper Galilee, 6 mi. W. of Safed. It lies on the slopes of Mt. Meron, highest mountain in Israel. The Meiron project of the American Schools of Oriental Research, Philadelphia, has been investigating ancient village life and the synagogues of the Meiron area during the 2nd to 6th cents. AD for a number of years. When Jerusalem was closed to the Jews after the second revolt against Rome in 135 AD, the center of Jewish life moved north to this fertile area, which became famous for its export of fine olive oil. The local villages prospered and a number of fine synagogues were built, joining those of *Capernaum* and Chorazin to the southeast near the Sea of Galilee. The synagogue of Meiron itself is the largest in Galilee. One of the rebel leaders, Rabbi Simeon bar Yochai, lived in Meiron, and his supposed tomb there in later years became a point of annual pilgrimage, particularly after the Cabalists of Spain, mystics whose work, the *Zohar*, was based partly on his sayings, settled in nearby Safed in the 16th cent. AD. In Meiron, abandoned about 350 AD and revived in the 8th cent., the 3rd-cent. synagogue was excavated and partly restored in the 1970s; a 3rd- to 4th-cent. industrial complex and some wealthy houses were also excavated, and are on view.

Khirbet Shema, south across a wadi on a nearby hill, became an independent village when Meiron expanded. It has its own pilgrimage site, the monolithic tomb attributed to Shammai, a Jewish teacher of the time of Herod the Great. Here a 3rd-cent. AD synagogue has been carefully excavated and restored, a ritual bath or *mikveh* discovered, and a large winepress investigated. The synagogue, built about 284, was destroyed in an earthquake in 306 AD, rebuilt, then destroyed again and abandoned with the village in 419. It is the first discovered to have a basilica-like internal arrangement of columns. A large entrance stairway, a gallery, for women perhaps, and under the gallery a room frescoed in red and green, perhaps for storage of ritual objects, have been found, and an adjoining guesthouse. Another synagogue at Gush Halav, about 7 or 8 mi. north of Khirbet Shema—a village known for its native son John of Gischala, arch-foe of Josephus the historian—was excavated in 1978 and partly restored. This synagogue, constructed in the mid-3rd cent. AD, was in use for three centuries.

Finally, at Kefar Baram (or Biram), northwest of Gush Halav and 7 mi. northwest of Safed, another 3rd-cent. synagogue stands in the midst of a deserted Christian village. Its facade, partly restored, has three doorways, two windows above at each side and an arch over the central door, and is the best-preserved in Galilee. An unusual columned porch ran along the front of the facade, and the interior arrangement with rows of columns was similar to that of *Capernaum*. Traces of another synagogue nearby suggest a flourishing Jewish settlement here in the 3rd cent. AD.

MESAD TAMAR

Or Massad Tamar, the late Roman fort of Tamara in the Negev, lies in the Dead Sea area of Sodom, about 15 mi. S. of Arad. It was excavated and restored in 1973–75. The *castellum* was built in the mid-3rd cent. AD in an area once inhabited by Nabataeans; it was a unit in the frontier *limes* of Roman Palestine. It continued in use, with several rebuildings, until the 7th-cent. Arab conquest. The fort is square, about 120 ft. to a side, with projecting square towers at each corner and a single gateway. The interior structures, all built against the walls, surrounded a central court with cistern. These consisted of barracks, regimental shrine (*sacellum*), the headquarters buildings (*principia*), commander's quarters (*praetorium*), storerooms and a bakery. There are watchtowers on the surrounding hills.

MICHAL, TELL

See *Tel Aviv-Jaffa*.

MICHMORET

See *Tell el-Efshar*.

MIQNEH, TELL

The ancient city of Ekron, one of the five principal Philistine cities, about 10 mi. inland from the modern Mediterranean port of *Ashdod* (also once Philistine), near Kibbutz Revadim. Investigation of this inconspicuous low mound in a heavily farmed area—it proved to be merely the tip of a huge tell buried in the surrounding alluvial deposits—led to trial excavations in 1981, revealing 13 occupation levels, and finally a full-scale Israeli-American 10-year project which, with a staff of 75, carried out its first full season in 1984. Digging was still continuing in 1988. Early results show that Ekron was a Canaanite city with roots in the Copper Age. This city was destroyed by the Sea Peoples from the Aegean at the end of the 13th cent. BC, and was subsequently rebuilt and fortified by the Philistines, a branch of the Sea Peoples, as an outpost close to the Judean hills. Eventually it covered over 60 acres, the largest biblical site known in Israel. However it remained a small walled city of about 10 acres, overshadowed by the powerful Judean kingdom, until 701 BC when it was conquered by the Assyrians and became a vassal state. Under Assyrian protection it grew rapidly into a major city, funneling trade from inland to the coastal ports. It was finally and utterly destroyed by the Babylonians in 603 BC and was apparently abandoned.

The final city was divided into four areas—the fortifications, an industrial zone, the public buildings and a residential quarter. In the first few digging seasons a great many large olive oil-pressing installations have been identified—one in particular, the largest found in Israel, complete with presses, vats and stone weights. Fragments of 1,000 smashed oil jars have also turned up. The oil was pressed from olives obtained from Judah (no longer an enemy state) and was widely exported through the Philistine ports on the Mediterranean, amounting to one of the largest industrial operations in the Middle East of the 7th cent. BC. The oil installations may have been used for textile dyeing in the off season, since thousands of loom weights have been found in the rooms. The excavators also uncovered parts of what may have been an Aegean type of palace of the 11th cent. BC—several rooms, apparently cult shrines, and a court-yard. A massive mud brick wall, and a hoard of iron agricultural tools, intact pots and horned altar, sealed near the city gate in the final destruction, also turned up. An unsolved mystery is the presence in the oil installation rooms, of a dozen small four-horned altars of a type found nowhere else. See also *Ashkelon, Gaza.*

MITZPEH YIRON

Meaning "The Yiron Lookout," Acheulian (Paleolithic) site on the Yiron plateau above the Dishon River valley in Upper Galilee, the largest of eight sites discovered in 1979–80 on the plateau. Acheulian hunters roamed the plateau for tens of thousands of years after about 150,000 years ago, leaving behind them ample scatters of their flint hand axes. Though there are springs and rivers in the area, no traces of habitation sites were found. However, along the eastern edge of the depression in which the site lies, nine clusters of basalt stones were found, obviously gathered by human efforts. These earliest "constructions" were probably used by the small bands of 10 to 15 hunter-gatherers at different times to support shelters against the wind and the strong summer sun of Upper Galilee.

MIZPAH

See *Tell en-Nasbeh.*

MOR, TELL

See *Ashdod.*

MOUNT CARMEL

See *Carmel, Mount.*

MOUNT EBAL

See *Ebal, Mount.*

MUNHATA

Neolithic site on a terrace above the Jordan River, near Kibbutz Gesher, 9 mi. S. of the Sea of Galilee. Six strata were uncovered here in French excavations of 1962–63, the lower three dating from the Pre-Pottery Neolithic B, or PPNB (see *Jericho*) with a radiocarbon date of about 7200 BC. The last three were later pottery phases. The earliest PPNB domestic buildings were rectangular, later replaced by round structures. Finds of flint tools and implements and of limestone bowls, querns, sickle blades, grindstones and pestles suggest the harvesting of wild cereals along with hunting, though there is no evidence for actual cultivation of grain. The earliest pottery phase included an unusual circular structure, about 65 ft. in diameter—a central pebble-paved courtyard with rooms around it in which some fired pottery was found. The later ceramic phases yielded oval sunken huts (giving way later to rectangular houses), storage pits, burnished and painted pottery, and a series of figurines of the type found at *Sha'ar ha-Golan*, as well as pebbles roughly shaped in human form.

NABLUS

Modern city in an important E.-W. pass between Mts. Gerizim and E*bal*, 40 mi. N. of Jerusalem, one of the largest settlements today on the West Bank and militantly Arabic. It was founded in 72 AD as a military colony for Titus' veterans, called Flavia Neopolis (hence Nablus in Arabic). Nablus has a small (about 250) Samaritan colony, one of two remaining in Israel where there used to be many thousands. Mt. Gerizim is their sacred mountain, where the Passover pilgrimage takes place with the ritual slaughter of sheep according to the strict injunctions of the Torah, the only part of the Old Testament recognized by the Samaritans. They are descended from the Jews of Israel who escaped the Baby-

Ionian exile and mixed with colonists sent from the east by the Assyrians after the destruction of Israel in 721 BC. Abhorred by the Jews of Judah and Jerusalem as schismatics, they have also been persecuted by Greeks, Christians and Arabs alike.

In time Neopolis became a major city with a considerable Christian population as well as its Samaritan majority (who dominated and oppressed the Christian minority!). Justin Martyr, the early apologist, was born in Neopolis about 100 AD. The city was granted the high status of a Roman colony in 244 AD. No systematic excavation of the site has been undertaken; however in Nablus the remains of a hippodrome, an amphitheater and several large tombs have been found. On the eastern slopes of Mt. Gerizim the city's large theater (2nd to 6th cent. AD) was excavated in 1979. It was lavishly built of fine ashlar masonry with lower seats of the best white limestone, some inscribed in Greek with the names of the family owners, and an orchestra paved in colored marbles. The theater could hold 6,000–7,000 spectators. Sculptural fragments found in the ruins apparently came from a highly decorated stage building.

The Samaritan's temple lay on the northern peak of Mt. Gerizim above modern Nablus at Tell er-Ras. Built in the 5th or 4th cent. BC, it was destroyed by the Hasmonaean John Hyrcanus in 128 BC. In Hadrian's time a temple of Zeus was built here, presumably over the site. This temple, excavated in 1964 and 1966, was graphically illustrated on Roman coins of the period. It was found to be sited on a huge platform above 65 rock-cut steps leading up from the valley, just as shown on the coins. There were vaulted buildings or cisterns alongside the stairway and more buildings below it, also as depicted on the coins. Under the platform the scant remains of a Hellenistic building, probably the last Samaritan temple, were discovered. Some finds from the excavations are in the Rockefeller Museum, Jerusalem.

The predecessor of Neopolis (Nablus) was the famous biblical city of Shechem at the mouth of the pass, now Tell Balata, an eastern suburb of Nablus. It has been excavated by the Germans from 1913 to 1934, and by the Americans in 1956–66. Shechem was last occupied by the Samaritans in the 4th cent. BC and was razed to the ground by John Hyrcanus in 107 BC, to be replaced by Neopolis 35 years later. The visible remains are those of the important Canaanite and Israelite city, a cult center in both periods, which was finally destroyed by the Assyrian King Shalmaneser in 724 BC. The earliest city is mentioned in several Egyptian texts. The nomadic Abraham first reached Canaan at Shechem; his grandson Jacob purchased land there; Joshua called the tribes together to the city to make a covenant with God; and the city became the first capital of the rebellious northern state of Israel in the 10th cent. BC. See also *Samaria, Tirzah*.

Excavations have shown that Shechem was first settled in the Chalcolithic or Copper Age, and received a wall in the Middle Bronze Age (1750–1650 BC). In this period an acropolis area with four successive temples was enclosed within its own wall. Destroyed in 1650 BC, Shechem's most splendid period followed when it became a Hyksos fortress-city defended by a huge Cyclopean wall (built of boulders) surmounted by a sloping glacis and a wide casemate wall on top of that. Two strong gates, the eastern and northern, have been found, and in the acropolis area near the northern one a massive fortress-temple, or *migdal*, one of the largest found in Israel, was excavated. Its foundations are so heavy as to suggest thick walls and perhaps several stories. From this period, too, came an important stone plaque with one of the earliest alphabetic inscriptions known. The Hyksos city was violently destroyed by the avenging Egyptians in 1550 BC, after driving the Hyksos out of Egypt.

The fortress-temple went through four phases, having been rebuilt, with the city, in the Late Bronze Age. It had several sacred standing stones in its front courtyard, and in the final version a very large stone outside the temple, which has been re-erected by the excavators. From the Late Bronze Age a public square, paved with plastered cobblestones, was uncovered with a wide flagstone avenue leading to it. The city seems to have been taken over peacefully by the Israelites, and it may well have been the rebuilt gate and the fortress temple that figure in the biblical story of Abimelech, son of Gideon, and his capture of the city. House remains, silos, and a large public granary built later over the fortress-temple date from the Israelite period. The site was virtually abandoned after the Assyrian conquest of 724, until the Samaritans settled there.

NAHAL HEMER

Truly astonishing discovery of a cache of well-preserved 9000-year-old Neolithic materials in a small dark cave in the southern Judean desert near the lower Dead Sea, 30 mi. S. of Jerusalem. The cave entrance was rifled by bedouin in the frantic search for more Dead Sea Scrolls (see Qumran) after the initial discovery in 1947, but they neglected the interior, which was dark and dry, and here the new discovery was made and excavated in 1983 by Israeli archaeologists. They uncovered a cache of partly ceremonial objects remarkably well preserved in the cave's conditions, including organic materials such as textiles, probably the earliest known, objects of wood, bone and leather, and basketry of various kinds, providing a rare insight into the lives and rituals of a group of pastoral goat herders who apparently used the cave for thousands of years. Extensive radiocarbon tests of the organic materials in 1984 confirmed dates from 9,100 to 8,300 years ago in the very early Pre-Pottery Neolithic B period. See also Atlit-Yam, Jericho, Munhata.

Among the ritual materials were three stone masks, one decorated with red and green stripes, three adult skulls, one with a criss-cross pattern of leather straps cemented with bitumen, and three tiny figurines of bone with features painted in red and green. Materials of daily life included small sections of fabric, woven, twined and knotted in 11 different intricate designs, wickerwork baskets coated in bitumen, net baskets and mats, a wood and flint sickle, flint knives, arrowheads of flint and wood and wooden digging sticks, ornaments and jewelry, including beads of stone, clay and wood, the latter painted in red and green, animal bones and a collection of sea shells that must have come from the Red Sea or Mediterranean. The study of this unprecedented collection is throwing new light on early weaving and religious rituals.

NAHAL HEVER

One of the deepest canyons in the Judean desert, running W. off the Dead Sea about 3 mi. SW of En Gedi. The discovery of the Dead Sea Scrolls near Qumran in 1947 sparked an intensive search of the Dead Sea region for more scrolls. The deep caves in the side of the canyon were explored in 1953 by Y. Aharoni. Excavations followed in 1960–61 in a number of the caves, under Yigael Yadin and Aharoni, after the dramatic discovery of two of the caves once used by rebels of the second, Bar Kochba revolt against Rome in 132–35 AD— and earlier in the Chalcolithic period. The remains of two Roman camps were also found directly above the caves, used by the implacable besiegers of the rebels below. The larger camp, above the famous Cave of the Letters, was walled on three sides, with an entrance on the north. Outside it the footings of tents were found, and within the camp the foundations of other buildings.

The Cave of the Letters lay some 335 ft. below the Roman camp and about 650 ft. above the canyon bottom. Its three large halls contained a variety of finds hidden beneath stones and in niches and crevices, as well as the skeletons of 17 of the rebels who had died there. The most important find was a bundle of 15 dispatches to the rebel leaders in the En-Gedi region, signed by Bar Kochba himself and written in Hebrew, Aramaic and Greek. There were also fragments of biblical scrolls (Psalms and Numbers), a leather purse belonging to a woman called Babata containing 35 documents (dated 93 to 132 AD) concerning her property and legal affairs, written in Nabataean, Greek and Aramaic, and another bundle of six documents in Hebrew and Aramaic dealing with the administrative affairs of the Bar Kochba government. A basket contained 19 bronze vessels and utensils; and everywhere were other baskets, utensils, objects of wood and leather, fragments of clothing, keys and glass plates. The Bar Kochba letters were found inside a waterskin that also contained the jewelry, purses, mirror and balls of wool belonging to some unfortunate woman.

More domestic possessions were found in the so-called Cave of Horror, 265 ft. below the cliff top, where some 40 skeletons of the refugees were discovered—men, women and children—as well as some fragments of parchment and papyri. The finds from both caves are in the Shrine of the Book in the Israel Museum, Jerusalem.

NAHAL MISHMAR

More Dead Sea caves were investigated in 1960–62 in this canyon about 6 mi. S. of En-Gedi, which had also been used (see *Nahal Hever*) by the rebels of the Bar Kochba revolt who left behind them many evidences of their presence. But the importance of the caves lay elsewhere. Of the five investigated, four yielded rich finds of Copper Age (or Chalcolithic) materials—fireplaces, pottery, utensils, a variety of ornaments, leather articles (a coat, sandals), wooden objects, a straw sieve, remains of cloth, a loom, and food (grain, lentils, onions, olives, garlic and dates), all remarkably preserved in the dry climate. The most astonishing

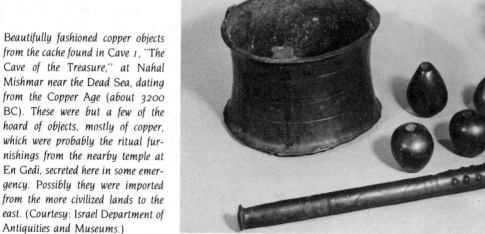

Beautifully fashioned copper objects from the cache found in Cave 1, "The Cave of the Treasure," at Nahal Mishmar near the Dead Sea, dating from the Copper Age (about 3200 BC). These were but a few of the hoard of objects, mostly of copper, which were probably the ritual furnishings from the nearby temple at En Gedi, secreted here in some emergency. Possibly they were imported from the more civilized lands to the east. (Courtesy: Israel Department of Antiquities and Museums.)

find, however, was a secondary deposit in cave 1, concealed under a stone and quite unrelated to the living materials around it.

Cave 1 is 165 ft. below the top of a towering cliff almost 1,000 ft. high, and is accessible only by rope from the top. Here were 429 objects, mostly of copper and carefully wrapped in a straw mat before being hidden. The arsenic used in the copper to improve its quality and hardness must have been imported. The workmanship, artistic quality and casting of these objects is superb. There were 240 "mace heads," 20 chisels, 80 scepters or standards (some topped by well-fashioned human faces or ibex figures), 10 "crowns," most of them profusely ornamented with faces, birds and other motifs; vessels, hammers and implements. The cache also included six ivory objects (hippopotamus and elephant ivory), and maces of haematite and limestone.

It is thought that the cache from this Cave of the Treasure had been the ritual furnishings of a temple, most probably from the Copper Age temple discovered at En-Gedi nearby (though other open-air oval "temples" or cult places of the period were found on the plateau above the cave). The dates are right (3500–2800 BC); the temple at En-Gedi was deliberately abandoned about 3200 BC, probably after an enemy raid, when the cache could have been concealed here. The objects themselves are now in the Israel Museum, Jerusalem. They may have been, it is fair to say, imported from Mesopotamia or even Iran.

NAHAL OREN

Prehistoric cave and settlement on the western slope of Mt. *Carmel*, on the north side of the Oren valley on a few mi. N. of the Valley of the Caves, and not far from *Haifa*. Like other caves on Mt. Carmel, extensive early occupation here in the cave and on its slopes dates from the Upper Paleolithic (Kebaran) to the Pre-Pottery Neolithic B period (PPNB), a range from about 18,000 to 7000 BC. The site was excavated in 1942, 1954–60 and by the British from 1969 to 1971. In the Natufian period and extending into the PPNB the presence of many gazelle bones seems to indicate possible herding of the animal, or at least selective hunting. Crops were not grown—the land is hardly arable—but the gathering and processing of wild plants grew in importance. The earliest occupation was in the cave; in the Natufian period an artificial terrace was constructed outside the cave to hold a group of oval huts. An early Natufian cemetery of some 50 burials around a hearth was also excavated. It contained a few grave goods—carved stone and bone objects, notably a gazelle head. The round houses of rough stone with a central hearth and floors of beaten earth, built on the Natufian terraces, continued into the PPNA period—these changed in the PPNB period into rectangular houses of limestone, or semicircular ones, still built on the same terraces. See also *Jericho, Kebara*.

NAHARIYA

Delightful seaside resort, founded by German Jews in 1934, about 15 mi. NE of *Haifa* and about 3 mi. S. of *Achzib*. The area, as numerous finds in the vicinity attest, was settled from Middle Bronze Age times to the Byzantine, and the local mound, now covered by the town, has revealed some evidence from the Middle Bronze, Iron Age and Persian periods. But the most important find was in a small mound behind the beach, which proved to be a well-preserved Canaanite temple from the Middle Bronze Age (18th–17th cents. BC), its walls after excavation still standing in places almost 4 ft. high. A rectangular hall, flanked by smaller rooms, with others in the northeast, revealed sacred standing stones (*mazzevot*) and an altar, and in a dump outside the temple ritual objects and

Stone mold and bronze statuette of a goddess cast from it, found in the Bronze Age temple (18th–17th cent. BC) at Nahariya, a coastal town northeast of Haifa. The goddess was probably Astarte, goddess of the sea, also worshipped by the later seafaring Phoenicians. (Courtesy: Israel Department of Antiquities and Museums.)

statuettes. Near the temple a *bamah*, an outside "High Place," was uncovered. It had been erected over an earlier temple with its own *bamah*. From excavations here in 1947 and 1954–56 numerous offerings to Asherah or Astarte, goddess of the sea, were retrieved, including a large collection of figurines, animal and female—both schematic silver plaques and molded and cast figurines of silver and bronze—as well as miniature vessels, beads, and jewelry of gold, bronze and silver. The local museum is in the town hall.

NASBEH, TELL EN-

Ancient city on a mound, 7½ mi. NW of Jerusalem, generally identified as the small, heavily fortified city of Mizpeh, in which the survivors from Jerusalem, including Nehemiah, took refuge after its destruction by Nebuchadnezzar in 586 BC. Mizpeh had apparently opened its gates to the enemy and was not destroyed. The mound was excavated in five campaigns between 1926 and 1935. The site had been briefly occupied in the Early Bronze Age but then lay deserted until settled by the Israelites about 1000 BC and occupied until the 4th cent.

King Asa of Judah heavily fortified the town in the early 9th cent. with an offset-inset wall of roughly shaped stones, plastered, and almost 45 ft. high. Below this was a sloping stone glacis ending in a dry moat, 7 ft. deep by 16 ft. wide, the only such construction found in Israel. The wall was strengthened with 10 towers and a gate of a new pattern, set into an overlap in the wall and flanked by two towers, the outer one massive. Parts of the wall and the gate in particular have been remarkably well preserved. The remains of numerous houses, mostly small and poorly built, with a few more substantial ones, have also been excavated, as well as 53 small cisterns. The site also yielded an important sequence of Israelite pottery and many cult objects.

NAZARETH

In Lower Galilee, boyhood home of Jesus and a Christian holy city. Nazareth is now a largely Christian community with a plethora of churches of all denominations, and is largely given over to the care and feeding of pilgrims and tourists. Occasional archaeological soundings have indicated that a village of great antiquity existed on the hill on which the Basilica of the Annunciation and Church of St. Joseph now stand, and on its western slopes graves of the Roman-Byzantine period have been uncovered. The Basilica of the Annunciation, dedicated in 1969, is the largest and most splendid church in Israel. It is the fifth on the site, all built over the Grotto of the Annunciation, traditional site of the visit of the angel to Mary.

A church built by the Franciscans in 1730 was pulled down in 1955 to construct the present one, which displays through an octagonal opening in the floor of the upper church the extensive remains of the older churches excavated below the lower church, as well as the Grotto itself. The first church was apparently a simple synagogue type of the 3rd cent. AD (see *Meiron*), and the pillars now standing in front of the Grotto may have come from it. The second was a Byzantine church of the 5th cent. with a small monastery adjoining it. Its apse may still be seen, and the mosaic floor outside the Grotto comes from the same period. In the 12th cent. the Crusader Tancred, Prince of Galilee, built a far larger basilica whose triple apse and some walls are still extant. Notable are the carved column capitals on display, sculpted for the church in northern France but never used after Saladin drove out the Crusaders.

NESSANA

See *Nitzana*.

NICOPOLIS

See *Imwas*.

NITZANA

Or Nizzana; Arabic: Auja el-Khafir. The ancient Nessana was a Nabataean-Byzantine town in the Negev (like *Avdat*, *Elusa*, *Mamshit*, *Rehovot* and *Shivta*) located close to the Egyptian border 32 mi. SW of *Beersheba*. Of the two parts of the site, connected by a flight of steps, the lower Byzantine town along a wadi has not been excavated; the upper citadel was excavated in 1935–37. Little is left of the city's founding as a Nabataean outpost in the 3rd cent. BC, except the remains of a Hellenistic period fort with round towers at the corners, and a retaining wall in the south. Nessana languished during the Roman period but, like the other Negev towns, flourished again in the Byzantine period after the 4th cent. AD. Early in the 5th cent. (or late 4th) a large fort (about 115 by 285 ft.) was constructed on the acropolis. A casemate wall with towers at the corners and on each side enclosed a large rectangular courtyard with rooms on two sides.

Remains of earlier churches displayed beneath the modern Basilica of the Annunciation in Nazareth, boyhood home of Jesus. The basilica is the fifth church on the site and the largest in Israel today. The columns shown probably belonged to the first, 3rd cent. AD church, the mosaic floor to a later 5th-cent. Byzantine church. In the background is the Grotto of the Annunciation, traditional site of the angel's visit to Mary. (Courtesy: Israel Ministry of Tourism.)

Around 600 AD the fort became part of a monastery. To the north and south of it were two churches; SS Sergius and Bacchus to the north (5th cent.) was built over the Hellenic fort and was later enlarged with rooms and courtyards. The southern church (early 7th cent. AD) was dedicated to the Virgin Mary. Among the finds were numerous Byzantine inscriptions, mostly in Greek; in rooms near the churches a cache of 6th–7th-cent. papyri (the "Nitzana Papyri") was found— some literary, most legal and business records—in Greek but some in Arabic.

OBODA	See *Avdat.*
PHILOTERIA	See *Beth Yerah.*
QAFZEH CAVE	See *Kebara.*
QASILE, TELL	See *Tel Aviv-Jaffa.*

QUMRAN

Religious community buildings in the desert, close to the NW end of the Dead Sea, about 12 mi. S. of Jericho. Its identification and excavation was sparked off by the discovery of the first of the Dead Sea Scrolls in 1947 by a shepherd boy in a cave less than a mile from the site. Eight clay jars in the cave contained bundles of parchment scrolls that proved to be among the earliest Hebrew copies of the Old Testament ever found (1st cent. BC-1st cent. AD) and other manuscripts copied by or concerned with the Essenes, one of the three major sects of Judaism at the time, though little known compared to the Pharisees and Sadducees. The Essenes were an otherwordly, messianic group devoted to religious purity in reaction to the established Judaism of the Temple in Jerusalem in Herod's time. These first scrolls found their way to Jerusalem and to the United States for sale. There they were purchased for Israel in a surprise move by Eliezer Sukenik—the father of the famous archaeologist Yigael Yadin. An intensive search of the Qumran area thereafter turned up many more scrolls in 10 other caves; the ruins of the Essene community center (previously thought to be the remains of a Roman fort) were excavated by Father Roland de Vaux and G. Lankester Harding from 1951 to 1956.

The complex site as now revealed gives a clear picture of the life of this high-minded desert community. Around 150 BC a group of Essenes took over an abandoned 8th-cent. fort and cistern here, and enlarged it as their community grew to a maximum of about 200 members (out of the 4,000 or so Essenes scattered around the country). The buildings were tumbled in an earthquake in 31 BC, but some 30 years later the Essenes returned, rebuilt them, and lived there until, during the first revolt in 68 AD, the Romans destroyed the community. The Essenes' library and archives were presumably secreted in the caves as the Romans approached. During the second revolt in 132–135 AD the buildings were briefly occupied again by the rebels.

Central to the ruins is a tower for defense and the long refectory where the white robed members gathered for communal meals, breaking bread and offering wine in a ritual reminiscent of early Christianity. Next to the refectory was a kitchen-pantry in which ovens and hundreds of stacked pottery bowls, plates and beakers were found. Plentiful water was supplied by an elaborate system consisting of a dam in a wadi and a tunnel and aqueduct, leading water by gravity into a series of large cisterns inside the enclosure. These fed two baths in constant use for the ritual baths taken before every meal by these purity-minded people. A complete pottery workshop with two kilns supplied the kitchen ware and the large storage jars, over 1,000 of which were found in a storeroom. Some of them, with lids, exactly matched the jars in which the scrolls were found in the caves. There was a council room, and on the upper story the long scriptorium where the scrolls had been copied. The excavators found its long writing table and inkwells spilled into the room below when the floor had collapsed. Other facilities included storerooms, workshops, a mill and cattle pen, but no bedrooms because the members lived in caves, tents, or huts dug into the marl all around. A cemetery nearby contained 1,100 graves, all of youngish men except for seven women and two children. A contemporary structure, a large building with courtyard and rooms, was excavated in 1958 at Ein Feshka springs, now a nature reserve on the Dead Sea less than 2 mi. south of Qumran. It may have housed another religious community.

The Qumran caves have now yielded over 500 manuscripts in Hebrew, Aramaic and some in Greek, as well as private documents; the best are displayed in the modernistic Shrine of the Book, part of the Israel Museum in Jerusalem. All the books of the Old Testament except one, some of the Apocrypha and other books, and a 7-ft. roll describing the maxims and messianic theology of the Essenes are represented. Pride of all the scrolls is an almost complete copy of the Book of Isaiah (about 100 BC), over 10 ft. long. Cave 4, close to the community center, yielded fragments of hundreds of separate manuscripts, which are still being assembled and studied. From Cave 3 came copper scrolls of the 1st cent. AD. The Old Testament scrolls proved to be remarkably close to the previously known versions from hundreds of years later, and the overall study of the scrolls has provided immensely important information for Old Testament studies and on the origins of Christianity.

RABUD   See *Khirbet er-Rabud*.

RAMAT EL-KHALIL   See *Hebron*.

RAMAT RAHEL   Or the Hill of Rachel, a prominent hill (2,685 ft.) in the southern outskirts of Jerusalem from which fine views of Bethlehem and Jerusalem may be seen. The kibbutz here of the same name was the scene of fierce fighting in the recent War of Independence and the Six-Day War. Excavations from 1954 to 1962 by Yohanan Aharoni have uncovered a most interesting palace-fortress of the period of Judah. The first settlement here, of which little remains, was a royal stronghold built in the 8th cent. BC, surrounded by gardens and farmhouses. The most interesting find was a collection of about 150 royal seal impressions. At the end of the 7th cent. the entire top of the hill was turned into an impressive royal citadel and palace, probably built by King Jehoakim of Judah (609–598), son of Josiah, who was placed in power by Nebuchadnezzar of Babylon and then revolted against him. It was probably to the king and his palace that Nehemiah referred when he wrote: "Woe to him who builds his house by un-

One of six proto-Aeolic capitals excavated from the ruins of a sumptuous palace of a king of Judah at Ramat Rahel, just south of Jerusalem, dated at the end of the 7th cent. BC. The palace was burned, probably by Nebuchadnezzar of Babylon when he destroyed Jerusalem in 586 BC. The capitals probably adorned columns at the gates of the palace's citadel. (Courtesy: Israel Department of Antiquities and Museums.)

righteousness, and his upper rooms by injustice . . . , who says 'I will build myself a great house with spacious upper rooms,' and cuts out windows for it, panelling it with cedar, and painting it with vermilion." (22:13–14).

The outer citadel, covering above 4 to 5 acres and little excavated, was enclosed by a solid inset-offset wall and was apparently devoted to the army and its chariots. The upper citadel, within a rectangular casemate wall of ashlar masonry with a fine gate to the east, consisted of a paved courtyard, a palace, sleeping quarters and storerooms. The whole had been burned in a fierce fire, probably set by Nebuchadnezzar when he destroyed Jerusalem in 586 BC. The remains of six proto-Aeolic capitals of the late type (found also at *Hazor, Jerusalem, Megiddo* and *Samaria*) probably decorated the citadel gates. Interesting fragments of a small columned balustrade similar to the many ivories of the "Woman at the Window" found in Assyria and elsewhere had apparently fallen from an upper window. Traces of red paint showed that the balustrade had been "vermilion" in color! Another rare find was a sherd painted with an elegant depiction of a seated king.

Scant remains from the Persian-Hellenistic period, mostly seal impressions, indicate that the site had become a Persian administrative center, and in Herodian times a mere settlement, destroyed by the Romans in 70 AD along with Jerusalem. In the later Roman period the 10th legion was stationed here, and a villa and bathhouse were built on the hill. A 5th-cent. church and monastery and finally some occupation in Arab times ended the story of Ramat Rahel. There is a small museum at the site.

RAS, TELL ER-	See *Nablus*.
REHOVOT	Or Ruheibeh, site of ruins of a Nabataean-Byzantine town amidst sandy hills in the Negev, about 20 mi. (35 km.) SW of *Beersheba*. Many scholars identify the site with Rehovot (the biblical Rehoboth) because of the similarity of its Arabic name, Khirbet Ruheibeh, but the identification has never been proved. The site was excavated by Hebrew University from 1975 to 1979; excavations then resumed in 1986 with an American partner. The town was apparently founded in the 1st cent. BC by the Nabataeans as a caravan way station, but attained its maximum size in the 4th to 7th cents. AD when it covered 22 acres and was one of the largest towns in the Negev. After the Arab conquest it was abandoned to squatters.

From its more prosperous period a large building, 90 ft. square, has recently been excavated. Possibly a caravanserai, it was built around a central court with a cistern and contained a stable like those at Mampsis (*Mamshit*). Exploration of the residential area showed that the houses were substantially built of stone, close together, in effect creating a wall around the town. Four churches have been found. The Central Church, dated by a Greek inscription to the mid-6th cent. AD, was built over an earlier, smaller church, and building blocks below that may have been from a Nabataean temple. It was a single-apsed basilica, paved with marble slabs. The North Church, with three apses, was even larger and more ornate. It was entered through a spacious atrium and under it was a small crypt, built of ashlars faced with marble, possibly once containing the relics of a saint. Around it were chapels and the rooms of a monastery. Excavation of some 30 graves in the Christian cemetery, some of them marked by carved gravestones, yielded intact skeletons, well preserved in the dry desert conditions—even to the remains of a full beard! These are being studied by a physical anthropologist. The finds included many remnants of columns, building stones and architectural elements attesting to the wealth of the town, as well pottery, coins, bits of metal and decorated glass objects, and Greek inscriptions from the 5th and 6th cents. AD. See also *Avdat, Elusa, Nitzana, Shivta*.

RUHEIBEH

See *Rehovot* (above).

RUJM EL-HIRI

Also known as Gilgal Rephaim. Probably the most enigmatic site in Israel, in the Golan Heights E. of the northern end of the Sea of Galilee and about 3 mi. E. of *Gamla*. After initial surveys in 1968 the site is only now beginning to be investigated in earnest. Here is a strange circle of three massive concentric stone walls, the outer circuit wall over 500 ft. in diameter, and at the center a huge pile of stones rising to over 16 ft. with a perimeter at the base of over 65 ft. This tumulus is enclosed within still another, though slighter, arc-shaped wall. The three main circuits of walls still stand over 9 ft. in places and include huge megaliths up to 6 ft. long in their masonry—especially on the east side.

Moreover, radial walls run out from the center of the site, four of them bordering what looks like entrance passages on the northeast and southeast from the outside of the monument to the center. Each passage also has another, though smaller, pile of stones within it. In the summer of 1988 an Israeli-American team began preliminary excavations at the northeast entrance, soon unearthing the remains of a 13-ft.-wide paved gate. And the pile of stones in this entrance passage proved to be the tumbled remains of a large structure, possibly with two stories.

Many guesses have been hazarded as to the purpose of this extraordinary site—a ceremonial center, a defensive enclosure, an astronomical observatory. As for its age, a handful of sherds discovered in the excavations belonged to the 3rd millennium BC, which seems to indicate a possible date for the whole site. The next season is to tackle the huge pile of stones at the center.

SABA, TELL ES-

See *Beersheba*.

SAFADI

See *Beersheba*.

SAINT GEORGE OF KOZIBA

See *Jericho*.

SAMARIA

Ancient capital of the Kingdom of Israel in the 9th and 8th cents. BC, a magnificent site high on a hill commanding views in all directions, about 6 to 10 mi. NW of *Nablus* and Shechem. It was excavated principally in 1931–35. Omri, the sixth king, chose the strategic hill for his capital in 876 BC, moving from *Tirzah*, the previous capital. He purchased the hill for "two talents of silver" and named it after its owner. Eventually the entire region became known as Samaria. Omri fortified the hill and built a palace before he died, which was enlarged by his son Ahab in luxurious fashion. The palace complex, called "the house of ivory" in the Bible, had walls and furniture decorated with exquisite plaques of ivory in many different designs of Phoenician type. Ahab's elegant and sophisticated queen, the much-maligned Jezebel, was the daughter of the Phoenician king of Sidon. Since Jezebel imported the worship of Baal and Astarte into Israel, she and Ahab were hated and reviled by the shrill prophets of the Bible, Elijah in particular. In the century after Ahab's death Samaria reached the peak of its prosperity under Jeroboam II (787–747 BC), developing a powerful and luxury-loving aristocracy whose wealth and ways further angered the fundamentalist Hebrews. Constantly menaced by the growing power of Assyria, the city was finally destroyed by Sargon II in 721 BC and the inhabitants of the city and kingdom, some 30,000 of them—the "lost tribes of Israel"—were marched off into Assyria. They were replaced by foreigners from Mesopotamia, and the mix of these with local people produced the Samaritans.

Samaria was rebuilt as the administrative capital of the region under the Assyrians, and later the Babylonians and Persians, and fell to Alexander the Great in 331 BC as he marched east from Egypt. He removed the Samaritans to Shechem, where some still live (see *Nablus*), and colonized Samaria with his Macedonian veterans. Now a Hellenistic city, it was razed by the Jewish Hasmonaean king John Hyrcanus in 108 BC, but its Hellenism was renewed by Herod the Great, to whom it was given by Augustus. That cruel man and great builder renamed it Sebaste (Greek for Augustus) and built there a huge temple to the emperor, repeopling the city with foreign mercenaries. Sebaste suffered in the Jewish revolt and its citadel was razed by Vespasian in 68 AD. Septimius Severus, trying to revive the city, made it a colony in 200 AD and rebuilt the Herodian monuments; nevertheless, decline set in. Byzantines and Crusaders were attracted to the site by a cult of John the Baptist. Surviving from this period is a small Byzantine church below the acropolis, well preserved though much rebuilt, and the 19th-cent. mosque in the village of Sebastiye (note the Herodian name), built over a 5th-cent. Byzantine church and a 12th-cent. cathedral. The "tomb of John the Baptist" beneath it is actually a late Roman tomb. Another of the same period is exposed in a deep trench nearby.

The acropolis is dominated by a handsome flight of steps built under Septimius Severus that led up to Herod's (rebuilt) Temple of Augustus, of which little is left except a retaining wall. The temple was built over the palace area of Israelite Samaria, where excavations have brought to light the remains of the palaces of Omri and Ahab and other buildings, as well as a tower and pool. The masonry is of exceptionally high quality. The main palace consisted of a central courtyard surrounded by rooms. East of it was Ahab's "house of ivory," easily identified by a concentration of the innumerable fragments of carved ivory that litter the whole area. These famous Samaria ivories, in sophisticated designs of palms, flowers, sphinxes, Egyptian gods and human figures, had ornamented the walls, the entrances, the drinking couches and other furniture within these luxurious palaces. Three proto-Aeolic columns, probably from the enclosure gates, were also found (see *Ramat Rahel*), and to the west a storage house in which 63 Hebrew ostraca in clay jars, dating from the time of Jeroboan II, were found. These listed shipments of oil and wine to the palace.

The acropolis with its palaces was originally protected by a solid rectangular defensive wall, strengthened by Ahab and supplemented by a casemate wall. Outside this the lower city, little excavated, spilled down the slopes. Stretches of the Israelite wall around the city have been exposed, on the acropolis and lower down towards the village, as well as traces of a massive eastern gate. Close to the Israelite wall here is a Hellenistic reinforcing wall connected with a massive Hellenistic round tower, one of three found, which still stands 28 ft. high and is probably the most impressive monument of the period in Israel.

Samaria was at its most prosperous in Roman times. A great open area above the village marks the Roman forum with seven of its 24 columns still standing from the colonnade that bordered it. The Severan basilica at its upper side is indicated by two more rows of columns. A rectangular stadium, probably Herodian, is now marked by a hollow north of the forum. To the west of the forum a Roman theater is cut into the northern slope of the acropolis just below the Hellenistic tower. Further north of the acropolis the remains of a Hellenistic temple of Kore were discovered. The whole area, about 170 acres, was encircled by a new, larger wall in the Roman period, and the Hellenistic western gate was rebuilt by Septimius Severus. It is well preserved, with three towers, one built on a Hellenistic base, and there are also traces of the Hellenistic wall here. The remains of a residential section have been uncovered on the western slopes of the acropolis inside the wall, while a long colonnaded street ran from the western gate along the base of the acropolis through the business district in the direction of the present village; 600 of its columns have been excavated, and a stretch of it, with small Roman shops on each side and (originally) a covered sidewalk, has been preserved.

SAMRAT, TELL ES-

See *Jericho*.

SCYTHOPOLIS

See *Beth-Shan*.

SEPPHORIS

See *Zippori*.

SHA'AR HA-GOLAN

Neolithic site about 8 mi. SE of *Tiberias*, just S. of the Sea of Galilee and near the Jordan border, close to the kibbutz of the same name. It is located on an ancient river terrace of the Yarmuk River, which runs to the S. of it. Discovered in 1943, it was excavated until 1959. The seven strata of the site proved to be contemporary with the Pre-Pottery Neolithic A at *Jericho* (after about 8500 BC) and the Early Neolithic at *Byblos* in Lebanon, called here after the river the Yarmukian culture, along with a few remains from the Middle Bronze Age I. The site was abandoned at the end of this Neolithic period, possibly owing to river flooding. Its economy was based on agriculture with some fishing and hunting, and its early "art" has been judged outstanding. For instance, of two half-buried huts uncovered, one had been turned into a burial with a cairn over it, but the other proved to be a workshop, unique in the Near East, for the production of flint implements but also of a remarkable series of human fertility figurines, mostly fashioned from pebbles and representing females and sexual organs. There was also a group of grotesque figurines made of clay mixed with grit or chaff, similar to those found at *Munhata*, not far south on the Jordan's banks. Finds from the site are exhibited in a local museum.

SHAMIR

An area around Kibbitz Shamir in the valley of the Jordan N. of the Sea of Galilee, 16 mi. NE of Safed, where one of the largest concentration of megalithic monuments in ancient Palestine can be found. There are other large concentrations in the Golan region just to the east and in the Bashan region of Jordan, as well as in the lower Jordan River valley around the Dead Sea, and in the Negev. Since most have been disturbed or reused in later times, precise dating is impossible. At Shamir these probably Neolithic stone monuments, over 100 of them, fall into two types: short gallery graves and simple dolmens or chamber tombs. The roof slabs on the latter are often marked by clusters of small cup marks.

SHARI'A, TELL EL-

Or Tell Sera, a horse-shaped mound, possibly the biblical Ziklag, in the NW Negev, 12½ mi. NW of *Beersheba*, overlooking the N. bank of the wadi (or Nahal) Gerar. Excavations from 1972 to 1976 revealed a long history of occupation here, from at least the Middle Bronze Age to early Islamic times. It seems to have first emerged as a Canaanite city in the 17th cent. BC, but the earliest architectural remains date from the 13th–12th cents. BC (Late Bronze Age) when the city was probably under Egyptian control. A massive structure over 80 ft. long, its walls still standing in places 7 ft. high, may have been the Egyptian governor's residence. Its many small rooms and corridors, some paved in mud brick, yielded Egyptian imports such as alabaster vases, scarabs, bronze and ivory objects, and a rare find of ostraca (sherds) in New Kingdom hieratic script listing taxes paid by the Canaanite citizens to some local temple or fortress— possibly a sanctuary within the building. Other finds of this period included imported Cypriot and Mycenaean vases. The city was destroyed in the 12th cent. BC.

It rose again in the 11th cent. as a Philistine settlement characterized by four-room houses of a common type that persisted through the next occupation, which was Israelite. Various buildings, public and private, were unearthed from the early Israelite period (10th–9th cent. BC), including a typical well preserved four-room house with a row of pillars dividing the central courtyard. In the later period (7th–6th cent.) two citadels were built on the mound, north and south. This fortified city was destroyed by fire in the late 7th or early 6th cent., possibly by Egypt or more likely by the Babylonians when they conquered Judah.

Many grain storage pits survived from the period of Persian dominance, including a well-preserved brick-lined silo about 16 ft. in diameter. In the Roman period a villa (1st cent. AD), with frescoed walls, was built on the mound and a large tower in its northeast part, and the mosaic floor of a Byzantine church or monastery (5th–6th cent.) was uncovered. Across the Nahal Gerar many scattered remains from the Roman and Byzantine periods indicate heavy settlement in the area at the time. These included plastered cisterns and a bathhouse that was in use right up to the 5th or 6th cent. AD.

SHARUHEN, TELL

See *Tell el-Farah South*.

SHECHEM

See *Nablus*.

SHIKMONA, TELL

See *Haifa*.

SHILOH

Small mound of about 12 acres, in Arabic Khirbet Seilun, covering the ancient cultic center of the early Israelites in the days of the conquest of Canaan; briefly excavated by the Danes from 1926 to 1929. It lies about 18 mi. N. of Jerusalem. Excavation of the mound was resumed in the 1980s by an Israeli team. A Canaanite town occupied the site from the Middle Bronze Age through the Late Bronze Age. It may have been deserted when the invading tribes of Israel chose it for the resting place of the Ark of the Covenant, the sacred religious symbol of all the tribes, where it remained for about 100 years and was the center of an annual pilgrimage. It was here that Samuel was called to the Judgeship, and in a battle with the Philistines, then at the height of their power, in the 11th cent. BC near Eben-ezer (see *Izbet Sartah*), the Israelites brought the Ark of the Covenant from Shiloh to encourage them, only to have it captured by the enemy in the ensuing rout. Shortly thereafter, about 1050 BC, the triumphant Philistines from *Tell Aphek* apparently destroyed Shiloh itself. When the Ark of the Covenant was eventually recovered, David took it to his new capital of *Jerusalem* and Shiloh lost its importance.

There is little to see in the excavations, but the findings do suggest the persistence of a religious tradition at Shiloh over a very long time. Intensively occupied in the Roman and Byzantine periods, a section of a town wall and Roman graves have been uncovered, and the remains of two Byzantine churches (5th–6th cents.) near the mound—the Basilica and the Pilgrim's Church—are now crudely restored in concrete to protect their mosaic floors. Moreover there are two open-air *weli*, Muslim sacred areas near the mound, and excavation of one of these, Jama Settin (Mosque of the Sixty), suggests that before the Arab conquest it may have been a synagogue. Only a few house remains from the Canaanite and Israelite periods have so far been found, and a Middle Bronze Age defensive wall. If there was a temple here to house the Ark of the Covenant, no trace of it has yet turned up.

SHIQMIN

See *Beersheba*.

SHIVTA

Or Subeita in Arabic, site of impressive ruins of one of the three Nabataean-Byzantine towns in the Negev out of a half dozen or so that have been extensively restored in recent years and are now on the tourist routes (see also *Avdat* and *Mamshit*). It lies about 25 mi. SW of *Beersheba*, between Avdat and *Nitzana*, another Nabataean-Byzantine town. Although founded by the Nabataeans in the late 1st cent. BC, Shivta's existing ruins are almost entirely that of the Byzantine town and are the best preserved of all the Negev towns. Excavated originally by a joint Anglo-American team, 1934–38, the restored ruins now form a national park.

Today Shivta is like a miniature Pompeii with its streets of stone-built houses, its three churches—and a mosque, since the town was peaceably occupied by the Arabs during the early years after the conquest. The town, once an unfortified agricultural settlement, centers around a large double reservoir; the preoccupation with water in this desert land is evident everywhere. Water was channeled from the public squares, down the streets and off the flat roofs into the town cisterns, and the houses, with scarcely any outside windows, were built around inner courtyards, again each with its cistern. More water was channeled in from the surrounding areas of terraced fields, which were also so ingeniously irrigated that in Byzantine times vines could be grown, and a number of large winepresses survive inside and outside the town. In this treeless land the upper stories of the houses, some still extant, were made of stone slabs supported on stone arches. One such house still has its stone table and chairs in one corner.

From the Nabataean town, which occupied the southern third of the Byzantine town, little survives except a reservoir, a tower with staircase, and a house with stables similar to that at Mamshit. Of the three churches, all with nave and side aisles, the South Church (the earliest, 4th–6th cent. AD) had an interesting cruciform font cut from a single stone. The small mosque, with its *mihrab*, was built right on to this church. The Central Church, north of a town hall, is the

Wine-settling tanks used in conjunction with large Byzantine wine-presses, on the citadel of Shivta, southwest of Beersheba, best preserved and extensively restored of the Nabataean-Byzantine towns in the Negev. The ruins now form a national park. The Byzantines, and the Nabataeans before them, employed many ingenious devices to conserve and use water in this desert land and to promote agriculture, including viniculture. Modern Israelis have learned much from the ancient methods used here. (Courtesy: Israel Government Press Office.)

latest and has three apses. The North Church, the largest and most elaborate, was squeezed in at the outer edge of the town. It has a large entrance atrium, a monastery alongside it, a chapel with a lovely mosaic floor, and a baptistery containing 7th-cent. graves of the clergy. Less than a mile from the parking lot a Byzantine farm has been reconstructed with its complex water system, and Israeli scientists, constructively learning from the past, now grow varied crops here, using the old methods. See also *Elusa, Rehovot.*

SKHUL ES- (Cave)   See *Carmel, Mount.*

SUBEITA   See *Shivta.*

SULTAN TELL ES-   See *Jericho.*

SUSITA   Much overgrown ruins of a once flourishing Greco-Roman-Byzantine town, situated on a rocky promontory jutting out from the Golan Heights, over 1,000 ft. above Kibbutz En Gev below it on the eastern shore of the Sea of Galilee. From the heights one may still see the Roman road ascending a wadi on its way to Damascus. Susita grew prosperous as a staging point on this road. The town, excavated from 1951 to 1955, was founded by the Seleucids in the Hellenistic period. Little remains from that time, since in 63 BC the conquering Roman general Pompey took it over and rebuilt it on a grid plan of streets, a plan that persisted until Susita was abandoned at the Arab conquest. It was known to the Greeks as Hippos, and later as Susita in Aramaic, both meaning horse—nobody knows why. It was made part of Pompey's Decapolis, the 10 Greco-Roman cities he organized in the area. Briefly held by Herod the Great in his lifetime, it was then returned to the province of Syria, and in Byzantine times became the seat of a bishop.

The ancient walls of the town are best preserved on the southern side, along with the main East Gate. Stretches of the basalt paving of the east-west Roman main street, are visible here and there, and along it were four Byzantine churches, three on the north side and the larger cathedral to the south (excavated), with mosaic floor and an unusual baptistery with three apses. Remains of an aqueduct leading from a spring 2 mi. away to the East Gate and thence under the main street to a Roman nymphaeum, as well as Byzantine houses, bathhouse and an underground cistern, were also excavated.

TAANACH

Or Tell Ta'annek, ancient Canaanite and Israelite city overlooking the N. end of the plain of Jezreel, 5 mi. SE of *Megiddo*, best known for the biblical account of the battle in which Deborah and Barak challenged Sisera and the Canaanites. The Israelites ". . . then fought the kings of Canaan in Taanach by the waters of Megiddo . . . They fought from heaven; the stars in their courses fought against Sisera." (Judges, 5:19–20). Excavations at the 16-acre mound in 1901–1902 by the Austrians and again by Americans in the 1960s showed that Taanach had long been a Canaanite city, dating from about 2700 BC. In this Early Bronze Age period it was defended by walls and a huge glacis. Abandoned about 2400 BC, it was reoccupied about 1700, at first as a campsite, which later became a substantial settlement. Finds from the Late Bronze Age included remains of a palace and other buildings, a number of Akkadian cuneiform tablets, and Mycenaean pottery. This city was destroyed by Tuthmosis III of Egypt in 1468 BC and not reoccupied until the late 13th cent. BC. It was again destroyed about 1125 (by the Israelite tribes?). By the 10th cent. Taanach had become an Israelite religious and administrative center, and from this period date some defenses, the ruins of royal stables, and a cultic temple with a number of sacred standing stones. In 924 Shoseng of Egypt destroyed this city along with Megiddo. Apparently it was never reoccupied.

TABGHA

See *Heptapegon*.

TABUN, ET-

See *Carmel, Mount*.

TAMAR

Or Tamra. See *Mesad Tamar*.

TEL AVIV-JAFFA
(Yafo in Hebrew)

Largest city in Israel and its commercial and industrial center, on the Mediterranean coast 35 mi. NW of Jerusalem. Tel Aviv, built on the barren sand dunes S. of the Yarkon River, has grown in much less than a century from nothing to a bulging metropolis of well over 1,200,000 people, engulfing in its expansion the old Arab city of Jaffa to its S., one of the most ancient ports on the coast; and the city is now creeping beyond the river to the north. The area of Tel Aviv has been inhabited since the 5th millennium BC, as chance finds of graves, houses and walls here and there indicate. Represented are Neolithic Yarmukians (see *Sha'ar ha-Golan*), the Copper or Chalcolithic Age, all periods of the Bronze Age, walls from the Persian period, Hasmonaean fortifications near the Hilton Hotel and much more. In its spread Tel Aviv has overrun a number of ancient sites, of which Jaffa, the ancient Joppa, takes pride of place.

Joppa was an important Canaanite port until it was taken by the warrior pharaoh Tuthmosis III in 1468 and became an Egyptian stronghold. When Egypt weakened it fell into the hands of the Philistines around 1200 BC, then under David and Solomon became a port of entry for Jerusalem. Presumably the cedar

Jaffa (Yafo), the ancient Canaanite-Israelite port of Joppa, now engulfed by the huge modern metropolis of Tel-Aviv-Jaffa. In the open spaces in front of St. Peter's monastery on the former citadel, built over a Crusader castle, one can discern the excavations that uncovered bits and pieces of the Canaanite and later towns on the site. (Courtesy: Israel Ministry of Tourism.)

of Lebanon for Solomon's temple was imported through here (though some favor Tell Qasile to the north—see ahead). Under the Persians it was controlled by the Phoenicians of Sidon; it became autonomous under the Ptolemies and was captured by the Hasmonaeans. Jonah, embarking at Jaffa, encountered his whale at sea and St. Peter visited the city. Finally it became a key port for the Crusaders, and was destroyed by Napoleon in 1799.

On the old citadel today stands St. Peter's monastery on top of the substantial foundations of a Crusader castle. In the square in front of the church, overlooking the old harbor, limited excavations since 1950 have uncovered bits of the Canaanite town dating from the Middle Bronze Age on: sections of walls, a heavy glacis of the Hyksos period (18th cent. BC), an imposing citadel gate set in a wall, its door jambs inscribed with the name of Ramesses II, a pre-Philistine temple, and mere traces of the Philistine and Israelite settlements. A large building, probably a temple and ironworks, dates from the Persian period, and from the Hasmonaean, remains of a wall and square fortress. Very little is left from Roman times. The dig is well signposted, and the rich finds from the excavations and from the area are in the Museum of Antiquities just behind the excavated site.

Another early settlement engulfed by Tel Aviv is the Philistine town at Tell Qasile, just north of the Yarkon River and a mile or so inland. The 4-acre mound now lies in the extensive grounds of the Israeli National Museum, or Ha'aretz Museum, a complex of nine separate museums. Excavated by Benjamin Mazar from 1949 to 1951 and 1959, and by his nephew from 1971 to date, 12 levels have been uncovered, starting with a Philistine settlement on virgin land of the 12th cent. BC that was destroyed, probably by the Israelites under David, in the 10th cent. It had parallel streets and blocks of four-room houses with courtyards, traditional to the region (one has been reconstructed), a public building containing a large hall with benches in Aegean style, and was fortified.

But the most interesting find, in 1971, was the only Philistine temple to be discovered up to 1974, with a small open-air shrine beside it. It lay in a large sacred precinct including two courtyards and an outdoor altar. There were actually three superimposed temples on the site, the latest built with heavy mud brick walls on stone foundations, an antechamber and main chamber, the latter with a raised altar platform (*bamah*), and behind it a small storage chamber that was found filled with pottery cultic vessels. The temple was quite small, its roof upheld by two cedar pillars on stone bases. Were these the type of pillars Samson pulled down in Gaza? The settlement was rebuilt by the Israelites, again with four-room houses (a public building was also identified), but was destroyed by Egyptians, or by the Assyrian Tiglath-Pileser III in 732 BC. It was little occupied until Persian times, and there are other traces of occupation up to at least Byzantine times. The finds are in the nearby museums.

Still another site overrun by Tel Aviv is Tell Gerisa (or Jarisha) on the southern bank of the Yarkon River in the hilly suburb of Ramat Gan, about 2 mi. inland from Tel Aviv proper. Extensive excavations in 1927 and 1950, 1976 and since 1982 on a mound that once held a camp of Napoleon's in 1799 uncovered the remains of a major Canaanite river port dating back to the Early Bronze Age. Buildings from the Middle Bronze Age (Hyksos period) with an unusually well-preserved glacis from the fortifications on the slopes of the mound (18th–17th cents. BC) were revealed. The settlement was destroyed in the 17th cent. BC, rebuilt, then razed again, like Jaffa, about 1200 BC by the Israelites or the Philistines. The latter established a town here, a rival to Tell Qasile (above), later taken by the Israelites, probably under David, and later destroyed at the end of the 10th cent. BC by the Egyptians, when the site was abandoned.

About 6 mi. north of Tel Aviv, in the seaside resort of Herzliya, more recent excavations at Tell Michal have uncovered the largest Persian-period site on the coast, a major wine production center near a small anchorage. The site was occupied from the late Middle Bronze Age up to the Arab conquest. Among finds here were an Israelite cult center (9th–8th cent.) and eight winepresses, four from the Israelite period, four from the Persian-Hellenistic period (4th to 2nd cent. BC), including the largest Hellenistic winepress so far discovered in Israel. A Roman fortress from the 1st cent. AD, square with rooms around a courtyard and an unusually early central tower, was excavated in 1978–80 and has been partially reconstructed.

TELL EL-FARAH NORTH   See *Tirzah*.

TELL EL-FARAH SOUTH   In the Negev, an ancient border city 15 mi. S. of and inland from Gaza and about 16 mi. W. of *Beersheba*, usually identified with Tell Sharuhen, excavated by Sir Flinders Petrie in 1928–29. Often mentioned in early Egyptian sources, the site was almost continuously occupied from the Middle Bronze Age into the Roman period (1st cent. AD). The earliest settlement was established by the Hyksos (about 1750–1650 BC) and was characteristically defended by a wall, glacis, and a ditch on its western side. A well-preserved gate of mud brick, flanked by two towers, was uncovered at the southern end of the mound. This was in use into the Late Bronze Age. The city was often under Egyptian control, and the most striking find from the Late Bronze Age was a massive residence from the late 13th cent. BC, presumably the governor's, about 66 by 75 ft. with rooms around a central courtyard, and very similar to the building uncovered at nearby *Tell el-Shari'a*. The city was taken over by the Philistines, probably in the 12th or 11th cent. BC, and then by the Israelites, and in the Iron Age levels a massive mud brick wall was excavated, as well as a house and other remains. A fortified structure from the Hellenistic-Roman period with rooms around three sides of its courtyard was unearthed, as well as houses, a large hall, and two parallel walls, perhaps the remains of a gate.

About 350 tombs were excavated north, south and west of the mound, one site containing graves from the 13th to 12th cents. BC. But the most interesting was a Philistine cemetery, and here five graves were particularly rich in grave goods—fine Philistine pottery, bronze bowls, daggers and spears—and some weapons and jewelry of iron, among the earliest objects of this metal to be found in Palestine (see also *Tell Jemmeh*). Two "Philistine" anthropoid coffins were also discovered, similar to those found at *Beth-Shan* and *Deir el-Balah*.

TELL ER-RAS	See *Nablus*.

TIBERIAS

Modern capital of the Galilee, a flourishing resort on the western shore of the Sea of Galilee, and one of the four holy cities of the Jews (including *Jerusalem*, *Hebron* and Safed). Founded by Herod Antipas, son of Herod the Great in about 20 AD, it was named after his patron, the emperor Tiberias. Some overgrown ruins from the Roman city survive, but Tiberias is better known as a famous seat of rabbinical learning and of the Sanhedrin when the center of Judaism moved north after the failure of the Bar Kochba revolt in the 2nd cent. AD. The actual rabbinical school here was founded around 220 AD by Rabbi Jochanan ben Nappaha, a disciple of Rabbi Judah ha-Nasi (see *Beth Shearim*), and here the Palestinian Talmud, comprising the Mishnah of Rabbi Judah with the Gemara, was completed, and a number of Jewish sages were entombed—among them the great Maimonides and Rabbi Akiva, tortured and executed by the Romans after the second revolt.

The Roman city extended south of the present city to the hot springs of Hammat Tiberias. The most recent excavations were carried out in 1973 to 1976. Most notable is a Roman gate dating from the time of Herod Antipas. On its southern side two round towers of basalt masonry project from it, and on the north the road to Tiberias, paved with basalt blocks, can be discerned leading out of it. The walls near it were built later. Remains of a colonnaded street and, closer to Tiberias, the overgrown ruins of a late Roman basilica and a huge Byzantine bath are visible, the latter with mosaics. South of the gate a group of substantial houses of the Arab period (8th to 11th cent. AD) have been excavated, and some shops closer to the gate.

Hammat Tiberias, south of the gate, with its hot springs, is still a medicinal spa. With Tiberias it had its share of rabbinical scholars, and the tomb of an earlier sage, Rabbi Meir, is here. Most noteworthy is a 4th cent. AD synagogue, excavated 1961–63. It was often rebuilt, with extensive mosaics from its founding in nave and aisle, beautifully restored and very Classical in style and subject, and far more realistic than those of *Beth Alpha*. Again there is a depiction of the Ark of the Law, and an elaborate zodiac surrounding the Greek sun god Helios, and inscriptions in Greek and Aramaic. The synagogue is well signposted for the tourist. Other mosaics from it and finds from Tiberias can be found in the Municipal Museum of Antiquities.

The waterfront of modern Tiberias, a resort on the western shore of the Sea of Galilee. Founded about 20 BC by Herod Antipas, son of Herod the Great, it was named for his patron, the emperor Tiberias. After the 2nd century AD Tiberias became a center of Jewish rabbinical studies. The mosaic floor of a 4th century AD synagogue (below) at Hammat Tiberias south of the city is one of the finest and earliest examples of the craft, purely Classical in conception. A roundel with signs of the Zodiac (with the four seasons at the corners) surrounds the sun god Helios. At the top is the Ark of the Law and other symbols of the long-lost Temple at Jerusalem. The inscriptions, Aramaic and Greek, give the names of the donors. (Courtesy: Israel Government Press Office; Israel Ministry of Tourism.)

TIMNA

Desolate valley in the wadi Arabah region, about 18 mi. N. of Eilat on the Gulf of Aqaba, and close to the Jordanian border. Here a huge rocky formation of Nubian sandstone, all reds and purples, has been the site of intermittent copper mining for some 6,000 years, including recent sporadic mining by the Israelis. The formation is fronted by tall weathered columns called "Solomon's Pillars," rising from the desert. The ancient mining operation here is the largest so far discovered. The cliffs are seamed with thousands of shafts and tunnels, and the remains of many ancient mining camps are scattered over a wide area. Long thought to have been the site of "King Solomon's Mines," popularized in the novel by Rider Haggard, excavations by Dr. Beno Rothenberg from 1959 to 1961 and since 1964 have found no evidence whatsoever for any mining in Solomon's time. Instead, the most systematic enterprise was that of the pharaohs of Egypt's New Kingdom from about 1300 to 1150 BC—long before Solomon.

Thousands of years before that the Chalcolithic or Copper Age people here (around 4000 BC) established a copper-smelting operation on the top of a hill. About 2 mi. north of Timna itself an Early Bronze Age settlement and smelting establishment has been excavated. Much later came the Egyptians, who left numerous shafts, galleries, workshops and large camps, some walled, and a rock-cut frieze. Finally the Romans came, and at Beer Ora, about 5 mi. south of Timna, the archaeologists found a 2nd cent. AD copper-smelting plant, including remains of furnaces, workshops and the largest slag heaps in the whole mining area.

Conclusive for the dating of the extensive Egyptian workings was the discovery in 1969 of a small, crude shrine to the Egyptian goddess Hathor, often rebuilt, directly under one of Solomon's Pillars (its remains may now be seen behind a fence). It has a small cella and open court and was dated from the many cartouches and inscriptions found there from Seti I to Ramesses V. Built in the 14th cent. BC, it was abandoned in the 12th and was taken over as their sanctuary by the Midianites from northwest Arabia who had been employed in the mines. They threw some 11,000 votive objects into a corner where Dr. Rothenberg found them, and erected five of their own standing stones, or *massebahs*. In the cella was found a beautifully worked Midianite copper serpent with a gilded head, a common fertility symbol. The standing stone and the serpent suggest an interesting connection with early Hebrew cultic practices as alluded to in the Old Testament. After all, Moses married the daughter of a Midianite priest. Another small Midianite shrine can also be visited.

TIMNAH

The mound of Tell Batash, identified as the biblical city of Timnah in excavations by American-Israeli teams from 1977 to 1979 and since 1981. The city, about 27 mi. directly W. of Jerusalem in the Sorek valley, just W. of *Beth Shemesh*, lay on the border between Philistia and Judah, and after a Canaanite period there was a lengthy occupation by the Philistines (it figures in the biblical Samson stories), then by the Israelites. Excavations on the mound, 10 acres overall, indicated that the first, Middle Bronze age city had been defended by a massive rampart of earth and pebbles topped by a mud brick wall, the rampart so large that the mound still has a concave appearance. Apparently a wide moat was dug outside the ramparts. Five Late Bronze Age strata (1550–1200 BC) were also identified, each city burnt in turn. An impressive house, possibly the governor's, had also been burnt, possibly around 1200 BC. It had a large two-row pillared hall and a second story, and in its ruins were found storage jars filled with carbonized grain, olives and almonds, as well as a collection of bronze weapons and tools, household vessels, and scarabs and cylinder seals of the 14th cent. The Philistines then moved in, reusing many of the Canaanite houses. Parts of a heavy wall, a tower and the massive remains of what may have been a fort indicated that the city had been heavily defended.

A new Israelite town was built on the site in the 10th cent., leaving two square towers in the gate area and characteristic pottery. Destroyed by Pharaoh Shosheng of Egypt in 924 BC, the city seems to have lain derelict in the 9th cent., though possibly reoccupied by the Philistines, until it was again seized by the Israelites, probably under Uzziah, in the early 8th cent. Massive new fortifications could not hold out against Sennacherib the Assyrian in 701 BC–at the time when Jerusalem under King Hezekiah was invested (but held out). However, the city was soon rebuilt and flourished until its final destruction in the early 6th cent. BC in one of the Babylonian forays.

The most visible remains today date from the Israelite occupations. A series of gates were built on the massive Philistine "fort," the earliest gate set into a new city wall. With an outer gate on the slope and an inner gate on the crest of the mound, with four guard chambers, these fortifications were comparable in complexity to those of *Lachish*. After 701 BC the gate complex was rebuilt in a simpler, shortened version, with only two guard chambers in the main gate, and the wall system was altered. From the earlier period too came a series of storerooms of a type known elsewhere in Judah in this period. After 701 they were replaced by a large public building. Several houses on a wide street along the northern wall yielded a collection of over 30 complete Judean vessels and a large oil press installation with weights and vats. The pottery, reflecting a frontier city, also included Philistine and Phoenician types. The final occupation was that of a meager small settlement during the Persian period.

TIRZAH

Or Tell el-Farah North, Canaanite and Israelite town that was the capital of the northern kingdom of Israel during its first half-century, until Omri moved the capital to *Samaria* (about 10 mi. W.) in 876 BC. The mound lies abut 7 mi. NE of Shechem (see *Nablus*). Excavations by the French under Roland de Vaux from 1946 to 1960 showed scanty occupations by Neolithic and Copper Age people (one pit hut discovered), but about 3100 BC a new people moved in and built a substantial fortified town. From this Early Bronze Age period well-built houses, a temple, two potters' workshops and streets with drains were excavated, as well as stretches of a stone-built wall with a glacis, and two square hollow towers guarding the gate. Abandoned about 2500 BC, the town was deserted for nearly 600 years until in the Middle Bronze Age it was partly reoccupied, and about 1700 a new, shorter wall was built, eventually given a glacis below it. The southwest quarter of this town was well preserved, yielding the remains of workrooms, storerooms, and an interesting subterranean sanctuary in which for centuries (1750–1550) young pigs were sacrificed to the gods of the underworld. The gate complex, many times rebuilt, and the defensive wall served the city right up to the end in the late Israelite period—about 1,100 years!

According to the Bible, Tirzah was taken by Joshua, but the earliest Israelite remains—the usual four-room courtyard houses—date from the time of David and Solomon (10th–9th cent. BC). A fierce assault on the town in the 9th cent. accords perfectly with the biblical account of Omri's capture of Tirzah from the Usurper Zimri in 882 BC, after which Omri was proclaimed king of Israel. He ruled here six years, and again the biblical account is confirmed by the discovery of a large building, probably his palace, of which only the foundations were laid, with a cut stone found ready to be positioned. The palace was never completed, for in 876 Omri moved to Samaria, taking the court and most of the inhabitants with him, where he built another palace. By the 8th cent. Tirzah had been intensively reoccupied, and as at Samaria the visitor may still see the ruins of opulent houses from the time of Jeroboam II (784–748) next to the hovels of the poor. Destroyed, along with the Northern Kingdom, by the Assyrians in 723 BC, Tirzah declined and by 600 BC was abandoned. Much of this can still be seen on the mound.

TULUL ABU EL-'ALAIQ   See *Jericho*.

UBEIDIYA   Very early Paleolithic site near Kibbutz Afiqim in the Jordan valley, about 2 mi. S. of the Sea of Galilee. Here in 1960–74 was excavated one of the earliest human sites known outside Africa, dating from as early as 1.2 million years ago. An immense quantity of stone tools ranged from primitive pebble-choppers resembling those from the Olduvai Gorge in Africa (Olduwan) to the earliest primitive hand axes, similar to the Abbevillian in the pre-Acheulian period (Lower Acheulian). Human teeth and (literally) fragments of a human skull were found, but not enough to identify the physical type.

UMM NAQUIS CAVE   See *Wadi Khareitun*.

UMM QATAFA CAVE   See *Wadi Khareitun*.

WAD, EL   See *Carmel, Mount*.

WADI AMUD   See *Amud Caves*.

WADI KHAREITUN   This deep wadi, about 1 mi. SE of the *Herodion*, crosses the road from Bethlehem to the Dead Sea. On its sides are a number of caves occupied by prehistoric people typical of others found in the Judean desert. Most of them were excavated by R. Neuville in the 1930s, with occasional later excavations. In the Wadi Khareitun the most important cave is the large Umm Qatafa, first occupied in the Lower Paleolithic period (500,000–120,000 BC) at the time of the ice ages in Europe, though the climate here was temperate. A circle of stones around a hearth provides the earliest evidence for the use of fire in Palestine. A series of rock-cut basins was found below the cave.

Irq el-Ahmar cave was occupied in the Upper Paleolithic (from about 80,000 BC), while the upper layer showed Natufian remains, including the burial of an adult and the finding of three skulls. The Umm Naquis cave, with four levels, was prehistoric only in the lower two—Mousterian of the Middle Paleolithic and a small layer from the Upper Paleolithic. Finally, lower down the wadi a terrace was excavated (el-Khiam) yielding remains from the Lower Aurignacian in the Upper Paleolithic age, and near the surface Natufian deposits.

YARMUTH, TELL   Important site, identified with the biblical city of Yarmuth, in the Shepelah about 19 mi. SW of Jerusalem and a few mi. S. of *Beth Shemesh*. Under excavation since 1980 and currently, by Pierre de Miroschedji on behalf of the French Research

Center in Jerusalem and the Institute of Archaeology of the Hebrew University of Jerusalem, the mound covers one of the largest Early Bronze Age cities in Israel, an outstanding example of early urbanization in the Middle East. The mound covers about 40 acres, with a small acropolis and a large lower city. While the acropolis was occupied into the Byzantine period, after probable reoccupation in the Late Bronze Age, the city as a whole was first settled at the end of the 4th millennium BC and was continuously occupied only until the end of the Early Bronze Age, about 2300 BC, when it was abandoned, as were many cities of the time (see for example *Arad*).

At its height the city was defended by the largest and most complex fortifications of the Early Bronze Age known to date in Israel. The fortifications consisted of a huge stone rampart reinforced by glacis-like stone buttresses, monumental stone platforms, and an outer wall made of cyclopean masonry, still standing some 21 ft. high at the city gate. The gate has an indirect approach up a long plastered ramp. Inside the city the excavators have uncovered both living quarters and an area of public buildings, including a probable sanctuary consisting of a large columned hall, a courtyard with rooms opening off it, as well as an "industrial" area. Notable also is the impressive Early Bronze Age system of terraces covering the whole lower city, with retaining walls up to 15 ft. high. Prominent among the finds were several human figurines and a number of large vessels, especially red-burnished platters of unusual size. The most recent excavations on the acropolis have revealed an Iron Age I destruction level—from about the 11th cent. BC.

YIN'AM, TELL

Ancient site consisting of a small mound and a large terrace settlement, 5 mi. W. of Kinneret at the southern tip of the Sea of Galilee, between Kinneret and Kfar Tabor. Excavated since 1976 and into the 1980s by the University of Texas, the site was occupied from the Late Bronze Age into the Early Iron Age (until about 1000 BC). The most interesting discovery here was a possible iron smelter of the 13th cent. BC in a large building, probably belonging to the local ruler. If it is an iron smelter—and some scholars doubt it because of the absence of sufficient slag and iron ore around it—it is most unusually early; for the introduction of iron-working into Palestine is usually credited to the Philistines a century later. Two Mycenaean vessels from the same period as the smelter were also found, as well as rare imported items from Egypt and Assyria.

YODEFAT

Modern village close to the scanty ruins of the ancient fortified town of Jotapata, 12 mi. SE of *Acre* at the northern foot of Mt. Azmon. Jotapata, situated on a high ridge with a cliff and deep gorge on its southern side, is interesting for its associations. It was a rebel stronghold near the beginning of the Jewish revolt of the 1st cent. AD against Rome. Its commander, Joseph ben Matthias, a young priest from Jerusalem, later became the famous historian of the Jewish war, Flavius Josephus, who has given us a detailed account of his defense of Jotapata against the troops of Vespasian himself. In 67 AD, during a 47-day siege, the Romans, as at *Masada*, built a ramp on the north side of the fortress-town in order to breach the walls with a battering ram. Taking the town, they "knew neither mercy nor compassion," killing many of the rebels and taking 1,200 prisoners. Josephus, in hiding, finally gave himself up and joined the Romans, eventually writing his histories in Rome. See also *Gamla*.

ZIPPORI   Jewish name of the important ancient city of Sepphoris in the Galilee, traditional home of Mary, mother of Jesus, 4 mi. NW of *Nazareth*. It was excavated in 1931, and then in major excavations from 1985 to date by two separate teams, American and Israeli-American. The site is ½ mi. N. of the present village of Zippori, and is marked by an 18th-cent. Turkish fort and ruins of a Crusader castle on a hill, both built of reused Roman materials. The city's roots go back to the Israelite monarchies, but the town became important in the Hasmonaean period and during the Herodian dynasty. Under Herod Antipas it was briefly capital of Galilee before *Tiberias*, and during the Roman period it became an important market town and administrative center where Jews, Christians and pagans all lived in harmony, as attested by the numerous inscriptions found in Greek, Hebrew, Syriac and Latin scripts. After the destruction of the Second Temple in Jerusalem the city became the seat of the Sanhedrin and its leader, Judah ha-Nasi (Judah the Prince), compiler of the Mishnah, who lived and taught here for 17 years (see nearby *Beth Shearim* for more on him). Sepphoris, renamed Diocaesarea by Hadrian, who gave it its autonomy, lasted as a prosperous city into the Byzantine period. It appears to have been destroyed by an earthquake in 363 AD.

A large public building of the Roman period has been excavated on the city's eastern acropolis, most likely a large villa or palace with plastered walls, some still adorned with frescoes, standing in places 6 ft. high. Among the building's mosaics is the recent discovery of a particularly fine and large mosaic depicting episodes in the life of Dionysos, the scenes labeled in Greek. The floor, dated to the late 3rd or early 4th cent. AD, was probably that of a triclinium or dining room. Nearby an elaborate Roman villa has been excavated. It was in use, with alterations, for over 500 years, and underneath it and an adjoining building was an enormous complex of underground cisterns and storage caves. A 4,000 seat theater, partly excavated in 1931, is still being uncovered and restored, while an aqueduct and large reservoir of the same period has been discovered. The Jewish presence is indicated by a large number of ritual baths. Plans call for the possible opening of the site in future years as a national park.

EGYPT

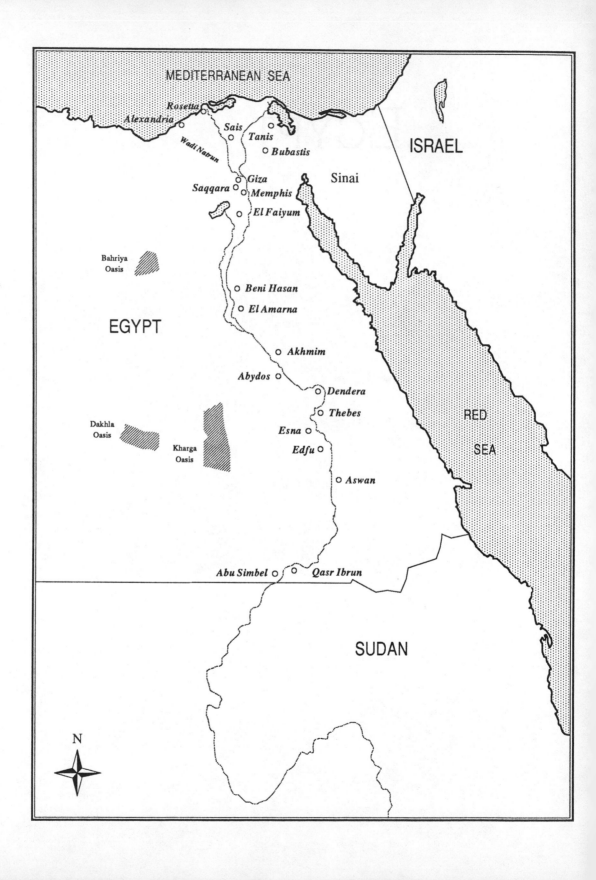

The Archaeology of Egypt

There could not be a greater contrast in every way between the archaeological histories of Israel and Egypt. From earliest times Israel, sandwiched between the two great power centers of Egypt and Mesopotamia, became a crossroads of influences and incursions. In contrast, Egypt, largely in isolation from other nations, developed a distinctive culture and held to it for over 2,000 years. Typical of Israel are the many mounds or tells covering the remains of the towns and city-states, which, in shifting alliances, were the power centers of that ancient land. In Egypt few towns were built or have survived; instead, the archaeological landscape consists largely of temples, pyramids, tombs and statues—all focused in one way or another on the central power of the divine pharaoh. In Israel the lives of the people from high to low are equally laid bare in excavating the remains of the squabbling city-states, whereas in Egypt it is hard to find much evidence at all of the lives of the common people—except in the workmens' villages attached to the construction sites of pyramids or tombs (see *Tell el-Amarna, El Lahun* or *Der el-Medineh* under *Thebes*) or in the wall paintings in the tombs of commoners or the little wooden models of daily life popular especially in the Middle Kingdom (see *Beni Hasan*).

Even the history of archaeology in the two countries is in sharp contrast. In Israel most of the digging, with increasingly sophisticated methods, has taken place during the last century—and the greater part of it since the creation of the modern state of Israel in 1948. Egypt on the other hand has been looted of its treasures for millennia past. The Romans were not backward in removing many Egyptian treasures to Rome. Then in the 16th and 17th cents. more and more travelers began to visit Egypt, recording its monuments and adding many ancient objects to their own collections of antiquities. In the 19th cent., interest in ancient Egypt and its antiquities was spurred on by the work of the team of draftsmen and experts Napoleon took along with him on his expedition to Egypt in 1798—the soldiers called them "the donkeys." The Rosetta Stone, a trilingual inscription of Ptolemaic times found during the expedition, gave Jean François Champollion the key to his final decipherment of the ancient hieroglyphic writing in 1822–24—which really began the discipline of Egyptology. However it was not until the second half of the 19th cent. that digging for objects began to be replaced by digging primarily for archaeological knowledge. In the earlier part of the century, archaeological looting had gone on apace, some practitioners not disdaining to use gunpowder to further their labors!

The application of scientific methods to Egyptian archaeology really began with pioneers like Auguste Mariette (1821—81), who under the ruling khedive excavated many sites and founded the important Egyptian Museum as well as the Antiquities Service. Above all, the greatest pioneer was the indefatigible W. M. F. Petrie (1853-1942), who after 1880 excavated innumerable sites and contributed greatly to the organization of knowledge about the sequence of events and periods in early Egyptian history. Since Petrie's time there has been a great deal of new digging, mostly, until recently, by foreign teams from many countries. Many of the previously excavated sites have been meticulously revisited to elucidate new problems. Indeed archaeological investigation in the 20th cent. has been characterized by much quiet but valuable work, little publicized, in the study of standing monuments and the recording of decorated tomb interiors, punctuated by a few sensational finds like Howard Carter's opening of King Tutankhamun's tomb in the Valley of the Kings in 1922 (see *Thebes*).

The building of the first dam at A*swan* in 1902, its heightening in 1907, and particularly the building of the great High Dam (1960–69) occasioned extensive excavation, removals and surveys of threatened sites in the area of the dams in Egypt and nearby Nubia. The removals were funded by UNESCO. The High Dam has eliminated the age-old annual inundation of the Nile, leading to some unexpectedly dire results for the survival of the standing monuments. For such reasons, and under the continuous onslaught of innumerable tourists, as well as the encroachments of settlements on valuable sites, such as that of *Memphis*, the already fragile ancient monuments and tombs are in constant danger of irreversible deterioration. And the menace of looting continues.

The history of Egypt from the beginning has been determined in a most decided manner by the country's peculiar geography. Everything has always depended on the Nile, which cuts its way through the desert northward on its way to the Mediterranean Sea, the river edged all along its course by a narrow strip of fertile land. This strip the ancient Egyptians called the Black Land, and the desert uplands on either side the Red Land. Until the building of the Aswan High Dam the Black Land was fertilized each year by the floods originating way south in Africa, which deposited a new layer of rich silt. Since rainfall in Egypt is minimal, a season or two of low floods could spell famine and disaster. As it neared the sea, the Nile divided into a number of branches, forming the triangular delta, again rich in deposited silt. A difficult, marshy area, the delta also to a large extent protected the heart of Egypt from invaders from abroad, while in the far south the first of six cataracts, at A*swan*, usually marked the limits of civilized Egypt. However there were numerous forays into, and periods of domination, of Nubia, south of the first cataract.

Egypt was a self-contained narrow land, over 700 mi. long, well-protected on all sides and with the Nile forming the only artery of communication from one end to the other. The Red Land, the desert, had its uses as well as the Black Land in building Egypt's unique civilization. The eastern desert was rich in natural resources and was mined for copper, turquoise and various minerals, for gold and for the marble and other stones quarried for use in building the great monuments. Cemeteries were usually sited in the desert, just outside the settled area, and trade routes ran across it, notably Wadi Hammamat in the east, leading to the Red Sea. On the west other routes ran through the desert to Libya, and here there were four principal oases, usually outlying pockets of Egyptian civilization. The western desert, as well as the delta, were great hunting grounds in antiquity.

The peculiar oasis-depression called the Faiyum, west of the Nile and south of Cairo, was in antiquity almost covered by Lake Moeris, which has since dwindled to the far smaller Lake Garun. The Faiyum was extensively settled in ancient times and its fertility increased by engineering works, especially during the Middle Kingdom and in Ptolemaic times.

Though Egyptian civilization flourished for thousands of years within these natural borders, there was a tendency to disunity even within this narrow land, especially the ancient division between Upper Egypt to the south and Lower Egypt, including the delta—the ancient "Two Lands". The dividing line was somewhere in the neighborhood of ancient Memphis, just south of Cairo. The two lands tended to break apart in periods of weakness or anarchy, whereas in stronger periods Egypt was always unified under a single central administration, whether north or south, and power then flowed outward into conquests abroad, for instance the New Kingdom empire in Syria and Palestine. The two most notable periods, the Old Kingdom and the New, were centered respectively in Memphis and at Thebes in Upper Egypt.

Following periods of weakness and disunity, the tough and resilient civilization of ancient Egypt always seemed to recover until, slowly and gradually, it was overwhelmed by invaders from the outside—the great empires of Assyria, Persia, Greece, Rome and finally the Arabs. Yet even as a province in the Roman Empire, and later under Byzantium, Egypt still managed to retain much of its characteristic art, architecture and religion. In fact the continuity of Egyptian culture over some 2,000 years, from the Old Kingdom to Cleopatra and beyond, seems remarkable when compared to other countries. Viewed as a whole one seems to find roughly the same formalized architecture and art forms, the same centralized administration and complex religion over the entire history of Egypt.

Yet looked at more closely there were actually greater differences from period to period than one would realize. The pyramid age was succeeded by that of rock-cut tombs, architectural forms developed and changed, sculpture and art varied in content, quality and style—notably of course during the brief "revolution" of the heretic king Akhenaten—and in religion the complicated pantheon of gods and their worship shifted about like a kaleidoscope from age to age. Even the all-embracing concept of the divine pharaoh, sole mediator between the gods and the people, went through many transformations, though officially maintained right up through the Macedonian period when the rulers, even though Greek, formally took on the traditional role of pharaoh.

Ancient Egyptian history has traditionally been divided into three main periods, the "Kingdoms," separated by a number of eras of disunity called Intermediate Periods. Within these periods the sequence of 31 dynasties is based on a list compiled by the priest-historian Manetho, who lived under the early Ptolemies. Preceding the list is the Predynastic Period, followed by the Early Dynastic, or Archaic, just before the Old Kingdom. All present authorities roughly follow this scheme, but with wide differences in dates and even in the placing of the dynasties within the periods. For instance, does the Third Dynasty belong in the Early Dynastic Period, or is it the First Dynasty of the Old Kingdom? Or do the Thirteenth and Fourteenth dynasties belong at the end of the Middle Kingdom, or in the following Second Intermediate Period? There is no agreement. I have therefore tried to construct below a simplified scheme for ancient Egyptian history that represents a reasonable consensus of the schemes in a number of reputable sources. This will help the reader to place the monuments described in the following alphabetical entries in an approximate chronological framework.

Periods	Approximate Dates	Dynasties
Prehistoric	up to about 5500 BC	
Predynastic	5500 to 3100 BC	
Early Dynastic	3100 to 2700 BC	First and Second
Old Kingdom	2700 to 2180 BC	Third to Sixth
First Intermediate	2180 to 2040 BC	Seventh to Tenth
Middle Kingdom	2040 to 1780 BC	Eleventh and Twelfth
Second Intermediate	1780 to 1570 BC	Thirteenth to Seventeenth
New Kingdom	1570 to 1080 BC	Eighteenth to Twentieth
Late Dynastic	1080 to 332 BC	Twenty-first to Thirty-first

A confused final period ending with the Macedonian ascendancy. Some experts place a Third Intermediate Period after the New Kingdom (1080 to about 700 BC), including the twenty-first to twenty-fourth dynasties.

Ptolemaic	332 to 30 BC
Roman	30 BC to 395 AD
Byzantine	395 to 641 AD
Early Islamic	641 AD into the 14th cent.

Prehistoric and Predynastic Egypt

During much of the Paleolithic era, all of North Africa, including what was to become Egypt, enjoyed the same uniform, mild climate and bands of Stone Age hunters roamed impartially over the whole area. Then from perhaps 15,000 to 10,000 BC the climate changed. While the Sahara gradually dried up, the Nile cut its long valley south to north through the increasingly arid land, and Egypt was created, roughly as we know it today. The hunters moved away from the desert into and near the valley, leaving a number of their transient camps for the archaeologists to discover. One of the most intriguing aspects of the period is some highly controversial evidence for the seasonal planting and harvesting of crops by these still nomadic people, from about 18,000 to 12,000 years ago—far earlier than anywhere else in the Middle East (see Wadi Kubbaniya). Typical of the Paleolithic seasonal camps are those found along the Nile at Nekheb (see El Kab) dating from the late Paleolithic (6400 to 5980 BC).

Much more is known, chiefly from the cemeteries, about the Predynastic or Archaic Period, which equates roughly with the Neolithic (the first farmers) and what we would call elsewhere the Copper Age, or Chalcolithic. The earliest sites of these first farmers and herders, found in Middle Egypt and the *Faiyum*, are designated the Badarian after *Badari* (about 5500–4000 BC). These people already made crude objects of copper as well as fine pottery and simple human figures out of terracotta. The Tasian (from *Deir Tasa*) seems to have been merely a phase of the Badarian. For other Neolithic sites see *Helwan* and *Hemanieh*. One of the most interesting of these villages is the large farming settlement of *Merimde* in the delta, settled about 4880 BC, with its round wickerwork houses and reed fences.

The principal cultures of the period, however, are known as Naqada I and II, first discovered at *Naqada* in the late 19th cent. Naqada I (also known as Amratian from *El Amra*) was a more advanced village culture (about 3800–3500 BC) characterized by polished pottery sometimes showing simple incised scenes of hunting and the like. It was relatively widespread, but nothing like Naqada II (3500–3100 BC; also known as the Gerzean from *Girza*) which appears to have spread over the entire country in its later phases. Naqada II, judged from its rich grave goods, represented an astonishing leap forward in every way, probably under strong influences from Asia through trade and other contacts, for which there is much evidence. Even an invasion from the east is not ruled out. The early capital cities of Naqada II were *Hierakonpolis*, Coptos (see *Qift*) and *Abydos* as well as Naqada. In late Naqada II, two confederations, north and south, may have developed—at least according to tradition—with the king of Upper Egypt wearing the white crown and the king of Lower Egypt wearing the red crown. On the famous slate palette of King Narmer (now in Cairo) the two crowns are combined, heralding the unity of the entire country and the beginning of the dynastic periods.

The Early Dynastic Period

Traditionally the two kingdoms were first joined together under Menes of the First Dynasty, a Greek name which does not occur in contemporary inscriptions but is equated either with Narmer or with King Aha (a tomb from Aha's reign is the earliest found at Saqqara in *Memphis*). However there is much disagreement among scholars over this misty period, for the written and material remains are decidedly scanty. It is possible, for instance, that there were earlier periods of unity under Naqada II, after the two confederations of Upper and Lower Egypt had appeared, and that unity was actually a gradual, on-and-off process. However the history of Egypt does begin with the First Dynasty, signaled by the strengthening of the central administration and the founding of the capital city of *Memphis*, of "the white walls," deliberately located at the boundary between Upper and Lower Egypt—marked, too, by the spread of the art of writing, perhaps originally stimulated by contacts with Mesopotamia in the late Naqada period.

Certainly the early civilization of Egypt grew rapidly in this period, as indicated by superbly crafted objects of copper and stone found in the cemeteries of *Abydos* and Saqqara (*Memphis*), the first the royal cemetery, the second that of royal officials. It is now agreed that the royal tombs were moved to Saqqara in the Second Dynasty. The role of the pharaoh was by now well established, hieroglyphic writing had become a flexible narrative instrument, and the peculiar conventions of Egyptian art had already evolved. Trade with Africa and Asia grew apace, and there are hints of military expeditions into Sinai and Nubia. The long-lived civilization of Egypt was rapidly taking on its characteristic shape.

The Old Kingdom

Egyptian civilization reached its first full flowering during the Old Kingdom, and one of its first and finest monuments is the famous Step Pyramid of King Djoser of the Third Dynasty at Saqqara in the necropolis of *Memphis*. It was the first pyramid, and with its complex of ritual buildings around it the first royal tomb to be built entirely in stone. Its architect was Imhotep, the brilliant prime minister who was so revered in his own time and later that in the Greco-Roman period he was worshiped as a god. Later Egyptians indeed looked on the period of Djoser and Imhotep as a golden age, and the Step Pyramid complex still radiates, as it did to them, an aura of newly found power, and technical skill of a high order—a far cry from the squat mud brick mastabas in which kings and officials had hitherto been buried.

The Step Pyramid, however, with all its grandeur, was but a prelude to the famous pyramids of the Fourth Dynasty at Giza, also in the necropolis of *Memphis*. The Step Pyramid was actually a tentative structure—it was begun, it seems, as a mastaba and was then elaborated. The final achievement of the true pyramid, exemplified by the Great Pyramid of Khufu (Cheops) at Giza, still the largest stone structure in the world, was not easy. Earlier faulty attempts at the true pyramid by Snofru, father of Khufu, can be seen at Dahshur (*Memphis*) the "Bent Pyramid" where the angle of construction had to be lowered in midstream, and the North Pyramid, unacceptable squat in proportions—and at *Medium*, where parts of the structure actually collapsed. There are many other royal pyramids, 15 at Saqqara alone, but by the Fifth and Sixth dynasties and into the Middle Kingdom the pyramids grew smaller and flimsier in construction, and finally pyramid building was abandoned, largely because they were too easily robbed. In the Fifth Dynasty sun worship by the pharaohs—the god Re with open-air temples (see Abu Gurab under *Memphis*)—became briefly popular.

During the Old Kingdom trading or punitive military expeditions, often combined, were increasingly mounted into Nubia, Libya, the Sinai and Asia, and even to Punt way down the coast of East Africa. In the arts the Old Kingdom produced remarkably competent and realistic sculpture, especially during the Fourth Dynasty, some in wood, as well as fine painting and painted reliefs in the tombs. In tomb furniture a high level of craftsmanship was employed. As the central power weakened, especially during the 94-year reign of Pepy II at the end of the Sixth Dynasty, decentralization grew apace. The tombs of the nobles, for example, once clustered humbly around the great pyramids, moved away, became more ostentatious, and some are found in the provinces (nomes), indicating a falling apart of the country into regional powers, a prelude to the first major period of political anarchy.

The First Intermediate Period

Little is known about this chaotic period of about 130 years in which provincial leaders (nomarchs) fought with one another for power and territory. There was poverty and famine, perhaps brought on by a series of low inundations of

the Nile. Out of the welter two lines of kings appeared, one based at Heracleo-
polis in northern Egypt (the Ninth and Tenth dynasties), of which virtually nothing survives today, the other in southern Egypt (Eleventh Dynasty) at Thebes,
later to become the capital of the New Kingdom. Inevitably the two clashed,
and eventually Thebes won out, unifying the country again under Nebhepetre
Mentuhotpe II (remnants of whose mortuary temple are at Deir el-Bahri; see
Thebes: the Necropolis).

The Middle Kingdom

Under the long reign of Mentuhotpe II the unity and strength of the country
were revived and continued to gain strength under the succeeding Twelfth Dynasty. The Libyans and bedouins were chastised, Lower Nubia up to the second
cataract was annexed and a series of strong forts built to hold down the restless
natives. A well-organized standing army even made expeditions into Palestine.
Trade was renewed, expeditions again being sent through *Wadi Hammamat* to
the Red Sea and down again to Punt. A strong central government with an
efficient bureaucracy managed to curb the power of the once-strong provincial
governors, or nomarchs. Deserting Thebes, the Twelfth Dynasty moved to a new
capital at It-towe near *Memphis*—of which nothing survives except some temples
and pyramids in its neighborhood.

Despite all this activity the remains of the Middle Kingdom are scanty, because the temples and other buildings were mercilessly robbed for their stones
by New Kingdom and later pharaohs (see, for instance, *Memphis* and *Tanis*). Only
two temples of the Middle Kingdom survive, at *Medinet Madi* and *El Tod*. Moreover the pyramids, in order to save labor and expense, were built either mostly
of mud brick or with stone or brick-filled compartments and consequently are
now usually shapeless mounds. *El-Lisht* was the main necropolis of the Twelfth
Dynasty, and Middle Kingdom pyramids are also found at *El-Lahun* near the
Faiyum and at Dahshur (see *Memphis*). At both these sites buried caches of exceptionally fine jewelry were found, of gold and precious stones, beautifully
crafted. The Middle Kingdom artists and craftsmen had revived the high standards of the Old Kingdom. Mentuhotpe's mortuary temple at Deir el-Bahri, for
instance, was decorated with fine colored reliefs (now in many museums), and
the elegant reliefs on a little chapel of Senwosret I, its disassembled stones
excavated at Karnak (*Thebes*) and now reconstructed, became models for New
Kingdom artists. Royal sculptures reached a new high of realism, and the little
wooden models of daily life, found for instance at *Beni Hasan*, have delighted
countless modern museum-goers.

The Second Intermediate Period

This long interregnum of some 260 years was characterized at first by little
of the debasing of artistic standards and loss of political control of the First
Intermediate Period. Instead the royal authority of the Thirteenth Dynasty kings
only very gradually weakened as one insignificant pharaoh after another came
and went; the bureaucracy became top-heavy, and only a line of strong viziers
kept things afloat. But the gradual weakening of central control led eventually

to the loss of Lower Nubia, while in the delta, settled earlier by masses of Asiatics, a new group of these arose and, possibly with outside help, seized power. The Asiatic Hyksos (Fifteenth and Sixteenth dynasties) in the end controlled much of Lower Egypt from their delta capital of Avaris (see *Qantir*), but their influence extended over most of the country. Like the later Greek Ptolemies they ruled as Egyptian pharaohs but seem to have introduced technical innovations like the potter's wheel, a method of making bronze, and in warfare the light chariot and horse and the composite bow.

Later in this period several independent dynasties arose, chiefly again that of the native Theban princes (Seventeenth Dynasty) who finally dominated much of Upper Egypt. Inevitably they clashed with the Hyksos in the north, since the Thebans claimed the throne of all Egypt. The struggle was protracted and reached a climax under Kamose, who regained Lower Nubia and fought the Hyksos all the way to their capital at Avaris. But the final expulsion of the Hyksos came much later, under Kamose's successor Ahmose, first king of the great Eighteenth Dynasty.

The New Kingdom

Ahmose not only captured Avaris, driving the Hyksos from Egypt, but chased them all the way into Palestine. At his death he left behind him a united country with a strengthened economy, a revived Egypt so exuberant in its newly restored confidence that under Ahmose's successors of the Eighteenth Dynasty it became the greatest power in the Near East. The great warrior king Tuthmosis I, with a strong standing army, brought the new empire to its fullest extent, reaching beyond the fourth cataract in Nubia, which thereafter became an Egyptian colony, and in Asia reaching the Euphrates in his campaigns against the Mitanni. Tuthmosis I was the first king to be buried in the Valley of the Kings at *Thebes*, which thereafter became the royal burial ground for the New Kingdom. In Palestine the rulers of the petty states became client kings under Egyptian supervision, and the Libyans to the west were beaten back. Trade was energetically pursued, and, with Nubian gold, accounted for the wealth of the country. Substantial sums, for example, went into renewed building of temples, especially at Karnak (*Thebes*), and this in turn stimulated a revival of the arts and a notable increase in the power of the priesthood of Amun.

Tuthmosis III ascended the throne as a youngster with his aunt, Hatshepsut as regent. In time, as co-regent, she declared herself pharaoh and ruled the land for about 20 years; only at her death did Tuthmosis III take full control. It was not until late in his reign that he turned vindictively against the memory of his aunt and ordered her name, images and statues to be obliterated. Hatshepsut's beautiful mortuary temple at Deir el-Bahri (*Thebes*), one of the handsomest creations of Egyptian architecture, was apparently the work of her brilliant and powerful steward, Senenmut. As full pharaoh, Tuthmosis III also became a lavish builder and campaigned vigorously in Nubia and in Syria against the Mitanni, extending his conquests far across the Euphrates and north to the Hittite border.

In succeeding years, especially under Amenhotep III, the high point of the early empire was marked by relative peace, with only a few military excursions to "show the flag." Peace with the Mitanni was sealed by the importation of a number of Mitannian princesses as minor wives of the pharaoh. Egyptian contacts now extended over the entire Near East, as shown by the remarkable find at *Tell el-Amarna* of a cache of diplomatic correspondence from the reigns of Amenhotep III and his son. Amenhotep III took to building on a scale only exceeded by the later Ramesses II, and to the fostering of the arts, especially sculpture, most of which was of high quality. Among other monuments he was responsible for the great palace and artificial harbor at Malkata (of which little remains), the lovely temple at Luxor, and the Colossi of Memnon, which fronted his mortuary temple, now disappeared (all under *Thebes*).

Under Amenhotep III the worship of the sun god Re had been growing, reminiscent of the Middle Kingdom sun worship (see Abu Gurab under *Memphis*). His son, Amenhotep IV, who became the famous "heretic king," was a strangely shaped, brilliant but wayward religious fanatic. With his beautiful wife, Nefertiti, he devoted his life to the cult of the sun disk Aten of the god Re, changing his name to Akhenaten and building an entirely new capital for himself and his god at *Tell el-Amarna*, which he named Akhetaten. He also forbade the worship of the state god Amun of Karnak and Luxor. How much this had to do with the growing wealth and power of the priests of Amun, which were increasingly impinging on the prerogatives and power of the pharaoh is an open question. Akhenaten also furthered a revolution in the arts resulting in the charming "Amarna" style. But his revolution was short-lived and was never popular. After his death the religious capital was returned to *Thebes* under the "boy king" Tutankhamun and the priesthood of Amun again flourished. *Memphis* once more became the administrative capital.

Eventually the power behind the throne, Tutankhamun's general Horemheb, became pharaoh (he was buried at Thebes, but his magnificent tomb, prepared for him at *Memphis* before he became king, has recently been discovered). His reign, as a commoner, marked the transition between the Eighteenth Dynasty and the Nineteenth, which began with Ramesses I. This period was devoted to the restoration of the Asiatic empire, increasingly threatened by the rising power of the Hittites and which had fallen apart under Akhenaten's neglect. The temples were refurbished and there was much new building, notably the splendid Osiris temple at *Abydos*, built by Ramesses' son, Seti I. And so we come to the great Ramesses II, Seti's son.

Ramesses II was an able but egotistic self-aggrandizer whose long reign of 67 years was marked by more building than that of any other pharaoh of Egypt, much of the later work bombastic and crude (see for instance *Abu Simbel*). The Ozymandias of Shelley, Ramesses also erected innumerable statues of himself all over the land, some colossal. Early in his reign he confronted the Hittites in a battle at Qadesh in Syria that seems to have been a draw but which he celebrated as a great victory, depicting it in a number of large temple reliefs (for instance in the Temple of Osiris at *Abydos* and the Ramesseum, his mortuary temple in the necropolis of *Thebes*). A later treaty with the Hittites left the Asiatic empire in peace for many years. He also moved his capital to Pi-Ramesse in the delta (see *Qantir, Tanis*).

After a period of dissension and confusion, Ramesses III of the Twentieth Dynasty, the last strong pharaoh of the New Kingdom, reestablished order and in the course of his reign beat off attacks by the Libyans and the Sea Peoples, the latter sea-rovers from the Aegean and Asia Minor, both of whom had been attacking Egypt with mounting ferocity for many years. One of the great sea battles off the delta was memorialized in a relief in Ramesses III's great mortuary temple at Medinet Habu (see *Thebes*). Ramesses III was succeeded by eight kings named Ramesses, a period which saw the loss of Nubia and the Asiatic empire and the ominously growing power of the priests of Amun at Karnak. Egypt was no longer the greatest power in the Near East and its history, except for a few periods of resurgence, was all down hill from then on.

The Late Dynastic Period

The long, troubled period down to the Macedonian ascendancy, beginning in 332 BC, is one of confusion as Egypt struggled to maintain its independence against invasions by the great powers from the outside and constant disruption from within. Along with several periods of renewed unity there were, more often, several different dynasties ruling separate areas at the same time. Even at the end of the Twentieth Dynasty, Egypt was already effectively divided between the virtual rule of the High Priest of Amun in Upper Egypt at *Thebes* and the ruler of Lower Egypt based at *Tanis* in the delta.

The first period of disunity from the Twenty-first to the Twenty-fourth dynasties is sometimes called the Third Intermediate Period. Shoshenq (Shishak), one of the stronger kings of the Twenty-second Dynasty in this period, carried out an extensive campaign in Palestine (see ISRAEL), and in 1939 a sensational discovery was made of the untouched royal tombs, lavishly furnished, of the Twenty-first and Twenty-second dynasties at *Tanis*. Centuries of divided rule and even civil war followed until the country was again brought into a shaky unity for half a century under the Nubian kings of the Twenty-fifth Dynasty, when there was a considerable artistic revival, especially under Taharqa. But the Nubians were soon hard-pressed by the rising power of the Assyrians, who in three campaigns overran the country between 671 and about 660 BC.

For many years there had been rivalry between the Nubians and the kings of *Sais* in the delta in Lower Egypt. After Nubian rule of Egypt had disintegrated into the usual welter of local rulers, one of the princes of Sais, Psammeticus, again united the country in 656 BC with the help of Greek mercenaries. He inaugurated the Twenty-sixth Dynasty, or Saite period, under which the artistic and cultural revival of the Nubian kings was brought to new heights and the economy improved—one of the last efflorescences of traditional Egyptian culture. There were now many Greeks in Egypt and a later king, Amasis, favoring them, granted them *Naukratis* as a trading town.

But Egypt was by now fatally open to aggression by the great empires of the Middle East. The latest menace was the Persian empire. In 525 BC Cambyses mounted a massive assault and conquered the country. Persian rule thereafter, for about 121 years under the familiar Darius, Xerxes and their successors, is counted as the Twenty-seventh Dynasty. There were abortive revolts against the Persians in the delta, and finally they were driven out and in 404 BC the country became briefly independent again under the Twenty-eighth to Thirtieth dynasties. The Persians returned in 343 and ruled Egypt as the Thirty-first (and last) Dynasty until their empire collapsed at the hands of Alexander the Great of

Macedon. In 332 BC Alexander took over Egypt peacefully, as a liberator from
the hated Persians.

The Greco-Roman Period

After the death of Alexander in 323 BC one of his generals, Ptolemy Lagus,
became satrap of Egypt. By 304 he had made himself king of an independent
Egypt, the first of a line of some 16 Ptolemaic pharaohs who ruled the country
until 30 BC when the last "pharaoh," the notorious Cleopatra VII, lost her life
and her country to Rome. As absolute monarchs, the Ptolemies ruled Egypt in
their own interests, favoring the Macedonian elite and the Greek settlers while
the native Egyptians were subordinated and oppressed—though their traditional culture was allowed to survive. In the minor arts Egyptian styles were
curiously combined with Greek forms. State monopolies were set up, the army
modernized, and agriculture and commerce encouraged, the latter flowing through
the great port city of *Alexandria* out to all the Mediterranean lands. Alexandria
founded by Alexander, was actually a Hellenistic city imposed on Egyptian soil
and became one of the greatest metropolises of the Greek world. With its great
library and museum, it was famed as a seminal seat of learning; unfortunately,
little is left of all Alexandria's splendor, lost under the modern city.

To provide continuity the Ptolemies adopted all the trappings of the traditional pharaohs, commissioning numerous reliefs and statues of themselves
sculpted in the traditional Egyptian manner. It was their policy to support the
temples and priesthoods and their pantheon of ancient gods, rebuilding and
redecorating the older buildings and erecting substantial new temples, again
strictly in the traditional style—a practice continued by their Roman successors.
The most famous of these are the beautifully preserved temples along the Nile,
now ironically viewed as *echt* Egyptian by countless tourists (see *Dendera*, *Edfu*,
Esna, *Kom Ombo* and *Philae*). Egyptian gods, notably Isis, became popular all
through the Mediterranean world, and one new composite Greco-Egyptian god,
Serapis, "invented" by the Ptolemies, was worshipped chiefly at Alexandria in
the great Serapeum. Animal worship reached its height in the Ptolemaic period,
the mummified birds and animals buried in huge catacombs—baboons and
ibises at *Hermopolis*, a pilgrimage center for both Greeks and Egyptians, the sacred Apis bulls and other creatures at *Memphis*.

If the Ptolemies ruled Egypt for their own benefit, Rome, with a mere prefect
in charge, exploited its wealth for the sake of Rome. As time went on, heavy
taxation and official coercion of both Greeks and Egyptians caused increasing
poverty and distress. But the persistent traditional culture of Egypt kept some
semblance of itself all through the Roman period. Aside from the occasional
temples and fragmentary remains of the period, a remarkable insight into daily
life in Egypt, mostly in the Roman period, was provided by the discovery of
masses of papyrus writings at *Oxhrhynchus*, formerly a Greco-Roman town.

The coming of Christianity in the 4th century AD dealt a severe blow to the
traditional culture and its monuments, including deliberate mutilation of some
of the temples. Alexandria, especially in Byzantine times, became one of the
seminal centers of early Christianity. In 383 Emperor Theodosius closed all the
pagan temples in the Roman Empire—though the worship of Isis at *Philae* man-

aged to survive somehow into the 6th cent.! Few early Christian remains are to be found in Egypt: two 5th-cent. basilicas are known, one at *Hermopolis* and another at *Deir Abu Menas* in the western desert. An unexpected glimpse into the writings and beliefs of the early Gnostic heretical Christians in Egypt was provided by the discovery of the papyrus books at *Nag Hammadi*.

Byzantines and Arabs

The official date for the beginning of the Byzantine empire is 395 AD, when the eastern and western parts of the Roman Empire separated. Egypt of course fell under Constantinople and the long-lasting eastern empire. In Egypt the remains of the Byzantine period consist mostly of monasteries; in *Cairo*, however, there are interesting survivals of a number of early Coptic (Egyptian Christian) churches, some founded in the 7th cent. Towers and a gate of the old Roman-Byzantine fortress of Babylon, ancestor of modern Cairo, also survive in the city. Monasticism actually began in Egypt when St. Anthony and other early hermits fled to the western desert, their cells eventually becoming monasteries. A large number of monasteries once existed in the western desert, up to 50 alone in the area of *Wadi Natrun*, a few dating back to the 4th cent. AD. Only four inhabited monasteries now remain in Wadi Natrun. The remains of another Christian town and monastery complex may be seen at *Deir Abu Menas*, also in the western desert. At *Aswan* is the large and well-preserved 6th-cent. monastery of St. Simeon, while the famous monastery of St. Catherine's, deep in the wild mountains of the Sinai, was built for the monks by the great Byzantine emperor Justinian in the 6th cent.

In many ways the Byzantine period in Egypt was an extension of the old classical Greco-Roman civilization—though by this time the old Egyptian religion had died and its monuments lay derelict. The real turning point, as almost everywhere in the Near East and North Africa was the Arab invasion, bringing a new religion and a new culture to the entire area. In Cairo the old fortress of Babylon was stormed by the fanatical armies of Islam in 641 AD and the last Byzantine governor managed to escape through the fortress' water gate on the Nile—which still survives and is shown to tourists today.

Egypt was now a province of the far-flung Arab empire, and except for the Coptic Christians, who still exist today, has been an Islamic country ever since. Almost all the monuments of early Islam in Egypt, however, are to be found in *Cairo*, which boasts some of the finest early mosques in any Arab country. The ruins of one of the earliest is to be found in the old area of Fustat, founded by the conquering Arabs in 641, one of a number of small towns that later made up Cairo. The jewel of Cairo, however, is the 9th-century mosque of Ibn Tulun, lovingly restored, built by the leader who achieved the independence of Egypt in 868 from the Abbasids, the last united empire of the Arabs. The original *Cairo* was founded by the Fatimids, who captured the site in 969 and built their capital city there. Walls, gates and mosques still survive from the Fatimid period, especially the much rebuilt Al-Azhar, still center today of the greatest Islamic university in the Arab world.

Saladin, the principal opponent of the Crusaders, captured Cairo for his capital in 1171, founding the Ayyubid dynasty. He melded all the smaller towns into a larger Cairo and built the original citadel. The Ayyubids were succeeded by the "slave" sultans, the Mamluks, in 1250 AD, who ruled Egypt for centuries thereafter. Most of the Islamic buildings and mosques in Cairo date from the Mamluk period. Among the many mosques from Mamluk times, the massive Sultan Hasan should be singled out. And with the Mamluks we leave Egypt, for the writ of this guide extends no further.

ABGIG

See *Faiyum*.

ABU GURAB

See *Memphis*.

ABU MENA Monastery

See *Deir Abu Menas*.

ABU ROASH

See *Memphis*.

ABU SIMBEL

Famous Nineteenth Dynasty rock-cut temples, on the left bank of man-made Lake Nasser, in Nubia about 170 mi. S. of Aswan. In a widely-publicized international rescue operation sponsored by UNESCO, begun in 1964 and costing $40 million, the temples were sawn into pieces and reassembled inside concrete domes about 200 ft. up the cliff of Abu Simbel to save them from the rising waters of Lake Nasser, created by the construction of the High Dam at *Aswan*. This was part of a larger operation that rescued 14 other Nubian temples for posterity. The work, posing immense technological problems, was carried out behind a coffer dam and was successfully completed by 1968. Now tourists may once again admire the rather heavy work of the mighty warrior-king Ramesses II, the Great (about 1300–1233 BC), who reigned 67 years, sired over 100 children, and whose monuments and statues exceeded those of any other pharaoh in quantity, size and pomposity. Be it noted, however, that the monumentality of Abu Simbel was clearly designed to overawe the restless Nubians. Visitors today are also shown inside the concrete domes behind the temples to see the details of the engineering feat that made it all possible.

The temples, among the largest rock-cut buildings in the world, have been famous ever since they were first described by Johann Burckhardt, discoverer of Petra in Jordan, in 1813. They may be visited now most easily by airplane from Aswan. The Great Temple of Ramesses II and his gods Re-Harakhte, Amun, and Ptah, is flanked by a smaller one dedicated to the goddess Hathor and Ramesses' queen, Nofretari. Four huge, 67-ft.-high statues of Ramesses enthroned, flanking the doorway of the Great Temple (one somewhat damaged) suggest a three-dimensional version of the usual temple facade, or pylon, as the rock-cut interior is a simplified version of the usual temple plan. Nestled close to the feet of the four statues are tiny ones of the royal family, and above the doorway is an inset statue of Re-Harakhte, the sun god. A row of 20 adoring baboons tops the facade. Eight heavy pillars line the great hall just inside the cliff, faced with statues of the king as Osiris. Its walls are decorated with scenes of war, including one of the indecisive battle of Qadesh in Syria, which Ramesses celebrated as a victory. On either side are rock-cut storerooms. Beyond it is a second pillared hall with religious reliefs leading into the antechamber and finally the sanctuary at the very back, a niche with four small enthroned statues

The colossal statues of Ramesses II and his queen at Abu Simbel, known worldwide for their sheer size and virtuosity. Flanking the main temple (above) is another with statues of the queen and royal children, as well as the pharaoh. The statues are carved out of solid rock and behind each group is a rock-cut temple deep in the hill, the statues acting as a facade or pylon to the temple proper. The whole immense assemblage was moved to a new site betwen 1964 and 1968 to escape the rising waters of the Aswan High Dam. (Courtesy: Lehnert & Landrock, Cairo; Rhett Austell.)

of Ramesses and his gods. The whole temple is so oriented (and still is, despite its removal) that at the semi-annual equinoxes the rising sun penetrates all the way into the sanctuary to illuminate the statues. The smaller temple is fronted by six niches containing more colossal statues—four of the king, two of the queen, with smaller princes and princesses. Inside it a hall with Hathor pillars leads through three doorways into an antechamber with side rooms, and to the sanctuary.

ABUSIR

See *Memphis.*

ABUSIR

See *Taposiris Magna*.

ABYDOS

Greek name for the ancient Ebodu (or Abedju), an important town and religious center throughout the history of ancient Egypt, 7 mi. W. of the Nile and 90 mi. N. of Luxor. It was established in Predynastic times (3200–3100 BC) as a royal burial ground and religious center for the earliest kings of Egypt. By the Middle Kingdom it had become a national shrine for the popular cult of Osiris, whose death and resurrection were celebrated in elaborate open-air rituals, attracting pilgrims from all over Egypt. Worshippers, and later kings too, began to erect small brick cenotaphs as well as stelae at the site. Growing more elaborate, these cenotaphs culminated in the great mortuary temples of Seti I and his son Ramesses the Great of the New Kingdom, the principal monuments at the site. There are also Middle and New Kingdom necropolises at Abydos, as well as burial grounds of sacred animals from the Late Dynastic and Greco-Roman periods, when the animal cults became popular.

Little is left of the earliest part of Abydos, Kom el-Sultan, where the original walled town of Thinis clustered around the famous Temple of Osiris. Although the temple, frequently rebuilt, was in use through the whole of Egyptian history, starting probably with the First Dynasty, it was built of brick and has long ago disappeared. The remains were excavated by W. M. F. Petrie. To the South, at Umm el-Gaab, lies the cemetery of the First and Second dynasties, the Thinite kings, with tombs or cenotaphs of all the former and two of the latter. Their real tombs (or again, cenotaphs) may be at Saqqara (see *Memphis*). Only the underground, brick-lined chambers are left, fronted by finely carved stelae bearing the king's name. Finds in the pits included fragments of objects and furniture of precious materials, beautifully worked. Near the temple are also mysterious large rectangular structures with towered gateways and traces of buildings within, which have been called funerary castles because, like the tombs, they were surrounded by subsidiary burials. They may have been early funerary enclosures like the later enclosure around the Step Pyramid at Saqqara.

Among the monuments at Abydos, the Temple of Seti I of the Nineteenth Dynasty is outstanding. Unusually L-shaped, it is entered through two pylons and two courts, the first, built by Ramesses II (his son) now lost. Beyond are two hypostyle (columned) halls, and at the back of the second one seven chapels, side by side, dedicated to the king, to Osiris, and to five other gods. Beyond these are secret rooms connected with the Osiris cult, while the L-shaped wing contains other cult chapels and storerooms. The painted reliefs, detailing the entire priestly Osiris cult carried out within the temple by the king, are not only one of the finest examples of the genre in Egyptian art but give a rare insight into Egyptian ritual. In the temple, too, is an important king list, which helped in a reconstruction of Egyptian chronology. Nestling against the L-wing was a brick-built palace and long storerooms, and behind the temple is the Osireion, the cenotaph proper of Seti I, an enigmatic tomb-like structure, once underground though now uncovered, approached by a sloping corridor and partly filled with water. One hall imitates the primeval island of the creation story, another a sarcophagus. The smaller temple of Ramesses II, southwest of the Temple of Seti I, was built on much the same plan, though only the lower walls survive. its fine painted reliefs are well preserved, and on the outer walls are carved another account of Ramesses' Battle of Qadesh in Syria, the famous "Poem of Pentaur."

AKHETATEN

See *Amarna, Tell el-*

AKHMIM

On the E. bank of the Nile across from Sohag, 55 mi. SE of Asyut, the ancient Ipu, or Khant-min, also called Panopolis. Once an important provincial town and cult center of the god Min, it was long ago destroyed, with its temples. To the northeast, however, at el-Salamuni, there is a rock-cut temple of Min, dating probably from the reign of the Eighteenth Dynasty Tuthmosis III, with reliefs, 1,000 years apart, dating from the Eighteenth Dynasty and from the reign of Ptolemy Philadelphus. Akhmim was later an important Coptic Christian town and its extensive necropolis, little investigated, extends for some 2 mi. along a hill over the Nile. Some excavations here have uncovered fine examples of Coptic textiles of wool, linen and silk, which, reconstructed, are to be found in the museums of Berlin, London, Brussels, Trier and Mainz. An important monastery, founded by the early Christian St. Pachomius (d. 346 AD), once stood at Akhmim.

ALEXANDRIA

Chief port of modern Egypt and its second largest city, at the western end of the Nile delta, 110 mi. NW of Cairo. Alexandria was also the greatest city of the Hellenistic world, and after 30 BC a wealthy port of Roman Egypt—and always a major cultural center. It was the first megalopolis, with a population of some half a million, a cosmopolitan city of Greeks, Jews, Egyptians and others. Facing Egypt across Lake Mareotis and with two fine harbors on the Mediterranean, it tapped the wealth of Egypt as well as much of the maritime trade of the Mediterranean.

The city was founded as a colony by Alexander the Great in about 332 BC on the site of a fishing village. After his death it became the new capital of Egypt under the Macedonian Ptolemies, and was honored under Ptolemy the founder, one of Alexander's generals, with the embalmed body of Alexander in a glass coffin. He had hijacked the body from Babylon, where the conqueror died. No trace of Alexander's tomb survives. Under the autocratic rule of the Ptolemies, Alexandria quickly became the commercial and cultural capital of later years. Its great library contained some 700,000 volumes, and with the museum adjoining it attracted the leading scholars, scientists and men of letters of the day, who were handsomely supported by the government. Outstanding thinkers such as Eratosthenes, Euclid, Hero and Apollonius Rhodius brought letters and scholarship, and especially mathematics, astronomy, geography and medicine, to a level only exceeded in modern times. Though Alexandria managed to survive up to the Arab conquest, despite sieges and massacres and uprisings of the volatile population and other disasters, its greatest period was its earlier years as a Hellenistic city—although it was also a seminal center of early Christianity during the Byzantine period.

Built in effect on a peninsula between lake Mareotis (now Mariut) and the Mediterranean, the ancient city was centered on a handsome, exceptionally broad avenue. A long mole, the Heptastadion, linked it to the island of Pharos on which a suburb developed and on whose eastern end stood the famous lighthouse, 220 ft. high, one of the Seven Wonders of the World, built in 279 BC. The site is now occupied by a 15th-cent. mosque and a fort. The mole divided the harbor of Eunostos on the west and the Great Harbor on the east, along whose shore lay the principal buildings of the city—the Caesareum, theater, Emporium and palaces of the Ptolemies, and probably the library and museum.

Of the meager remains of the ancient city buried under the modern metropolis, most lie in the suburbs and include a number of necropolises. The most interesting area is around the so-called "Pompey's Pillar" in the southwest district, a granite column 99 ft. high, actually erected around 300 AD in the time of Diocletian. It seems to have been part of the complex of the ancient Ptolemaic-Roman Serapeum, dedicated to a Greek-Egyptian god, Serapis, invented by the Ptolemies. Parts of the Serapeum, including underground chambers, have been excavated west of the Pillar and a number of statues are on view, and in the same area a large tract is also being excavated, which, among other finds, revealed the remains of a Roman amphitheater in 1963. Nearby are the famous catacombs of Kom es-Shugafa, a necropolis of the 2nd cent. AD cut three levels deep, the largest such Roman complex in Egypt. Consisting of chambers with sarcophagi, urns in niches, and chapels, remarkably preserved, much of it is decorated with a curious blend of Greek, Roman and Egyptian designs and motifs.

Excavations near the center of the ancient city in the 1960s, at Kom el-Dik, turned up the well-preserved remains of a marble-seated Roman theater or odeon that could hold 700 to 800 spectators, as well as the foundations of 3rd cent. AD Roman baths (rebuilt in the 6th cent.), now being restored, and some townhouses. Out near the western end of the Pharos island, near the Ras el-Tin palace, is the rock-cut Anfushy necropolis of the 3rd and 2nd cents. BC (i.e., Ptolemaic), its tombs, each with antechamber and mortuary chapel, opening onto a common atrium. The decoration is in the local Ptolemaic Greco-Egyptian style: Classical art forms used to illustrate Egyptian funeral practices. Two more Ptolemaic necropolises were found near the shores beyond the eastern harbor (near the Chatby baths and at Mustafa Pasha), and still more in what was the eastern extension of the ancient city. Near these, in the present-day New Latin Cemetery, lies the richest Hellenistic tomb yet discovered, restored in 1936—a series of chambers built of huge blocks of alabaster. There have been recent Polish excavations in the area of the ancient ports.

These meager remains sum up all that has been found of the ancient city, once so glorious. Moreover hardly a trace of the many early churches and early Islamic monuments known to have existed have survived. A better idea of the riches of ancient Alexandria can be obtained by a visit to the Greco-Roman Museum.

AMADA

A small temple in good condition, built by Tuthmosis III and Amenhotep II of the Eighteenth Dynasty, with later additions. It stood originally on the Nile's W. bank over 100 mi. S. of Aswan, and opposite it on the E. bank at El-Deir was another temple, rock-cut, dedicated to Re-Harakhte by Ramesses II. With the construction of the High Dam at Aswan both temples were removed to higher ground about 1½ mi. away from the original site of Amada. The Amada temple was dedicated to Amun-Re and Re-Harakhte and consists of a portico of fluted columns, a vestibule and three sanctuaries. The decoration is outstanding and the painted portions well preserved, and there are two important historical inscriptions describing campaigns of Amenhotep II and Merneptah. The rock-cut el-Derr temple resembles Ramesses II's Great Temple at *Abu Simbel* in plan, though without the colossal statues. The color on its restored reliefs is unusually bright. The enthroned statues in the sanctuary were of Ramesses II, Re-Harakhte, Amun-Re and Ptah.

AMARNA, TELL EL-

Most commonly used modern name for ancient Akhetaten, the short-lived capital of Akhenaten (Amenhotep IV), the famous "heretic king" of the Eighteenth Dynasty, laid out along the E. bank of the Nile about 186 mi. N. of *Thebes*, the traditional capital of the New Kingdom, and 58 mi. N. of Asyut. Akhenaten was an aesthete and visionary, impelled by a religious fervor for his one god, the Aten, the sun's disk, in whose honor he changed his name. In founding Akhetaten early in his reign, he was also determined to challenge the growing power of the priesthood and bureaucracy of Amun-Re, entrenched at Thebes and posing a mounting threat to the supremacy of the pharaoh. He would have his own capital, his own god, the Aten—a new version of the Old Kingdom sun god (see Abu Gurab under *Memphis*)—and he himself would be the Aten's priest. In the event, his revolution also included a remarkable loosening up and humanizing of the age-old traditional art forms of Egypt. The result was the entrancing "Amarna art." Akhetaten itself only lasted about ten years, until Akhenaten's death, when his revolution, already faltering, collapsed and the capital, under the famous "boy king" Tutankhamun, was returned to Thebes. The triumphant priesthood of Amun-Re eventually supplied a line of pharaohs themselves. Akhetaten was deserted, and later deliberately destroyed, its stones being used for nearby monuments (a boon to the archaeologists, who have identified many of them). However, excavations of part of the site, beginning under Petrie in the 1890's, have enabled scholars to reconstruct one of the few known cities of ancient Egypt, never built over, and all conveniently on one habitation level.

Representing one of the high points of Egyptian civilization, Akhetaten was a notably civilized city, spacious, orderly and elegant, a city of temples, luxurious palaces and low-lying comfortable houses with open courts and columned porticos. Gardens were everywhere, with palms, willows and sycamore trees, lotus ponds and colorful flower beds. The upper-class inhabitants, so well portrayed in Amarna art, wore flowing robes of pleated linen and elaborate wigs. And over all presided the king, a strangely misshapen figure, and his beautiful and powerful queen, Nefertiti. The city, long and narrow, almost 10 mi. long, lay on both sides of the royal road flanking the Nile, and was situated on a flat plain bordered inland by cliffs, into which the tombs were cut. It had no walls, but the sacred area of the city was marked out by 14 stelae, some on the west bank. The city itself consisted of a central area containing the palaces, temples, government offices and magazines; a South City, the residential quarter; and a northern suburb and business area. In the central city the columned coronation hall and harem of the royal palace lay on the Nile side, with terraced gardens leading down to the Nile landing stage. It was connected with the king's private palace on the other side of the royal road by an arched bridge. Outlying palaces included the enchanting pleasure palace of Maruaten, south of the city, and a North Palace. South of the king's palace in the central city was the royal temple, and north of it the huge great Temple of Aten (both quite unlike the traditional temple), consisting of a large precinct open to the sun, with a series of open courts dotted with hundreds of offering tables leading to the high altar in the sanctuary.

The site of Akhetaten first came to light in 1888 when a peasant found an invaluable hoard of clay tablets, the famous Amarna letters, in the remains of the Record Hall behind the king's palace. Written in cuneiform in the Akkadian language (the lingua franca of the day), they were copies of correspondence of the Egyptian court with outlying cities of Egypt-dominated Syria and Palestine, as well as cities in Mesopotamia and Asia Minor. Excavation followed, though the site has never been fully explored. Work on it has now resumed. For the tourist, visiting on foot or by tractor or donkey, it is disappointing, for little above 3 ft. high survives and that is often buried in sand. However, much detail has been recovered. The private houses in the South City were generously designed with porch, vestibule, central hall, living room and family apartments with bathrooms and privies, and occasionally second stories and loggias. In the house of the royal sculptor Tuthmosis, many of his pieces were found, including the famous and elegant bust of Nefertiti, now in West Berlin, and practice busts of plaster. Another house belonged to the vizier Nakht. Southeast of the city, up against the cliffs, a neat walled rectangular workmen's village of five streets and simple houses was found, and in the cliffs themselves the 25 rock-cut tombs of the priests and nobility, in two groups, north and south, and the tomb of Akhenaten himself (now empty) in between. They consist of an open court and several chambers. The decoration of these tombs in the free-wheeling style, with interesting views of the city and its life, is worth a visit, though only a few can be seen. See also *Deir el-Ballas*.

AMRA, EL-

A small predynastic site about 6 mi. E. of *Abydos*, on the W. bank of the Nile, which gave its name to the early Amratian culture (about 4000–3500 BC). The culture however is now better known and in a larger context as Naqada I, from the larger site of *Naqada*. The Amratians seem to have been early agriculturalists and animal herders who used copper to make pins, harpoons and beads, and gold for ornaments. Their culture is characterized by sophisticated polished red ware incised in white, red burnished pottery with blackened tops, cosmetic palettes and the earliest stone vases.

ANTINOOPOLIS, or Antinoë

See *El-Sheikh Ibada*.

ARMANT

Ancient Iuny, Greek Hermonthis, a major center of the cult of the war god Montu, 8 mi. S. of Luxor on the W. bank of the Nile. From at least the Eleventh Dynasty there was an important temple here, often rebuilt with additions. It was destroyed in the Late Dynastic Period and all that remains is a pylon of Tuthmosis III. A second temple, begun under the Thirtieth Dynasty (4th cent. BC) and continued under the Ptolemies included a lake and birth house only recently destroyed. Two gates of Roman times have been found. Armant is surrounded by cemeteries, including the burial galleries of the Buchis bulls (the Bucheum) and cows sacred to Montu, in use from the 4th cent. BC until the reign of Diocletian.

ARSINOE

See *Faiyum*.

ASASIF

See *Thebes*.

ASHMUNEIN

See *Hermopolis*.

ASWAN

Attractive southern frontier city on the boundaries of Nubia, just N. of the Nile's first cataract and the Aswan High Dam. The modern town lies on the E. bank opposite Elephantine island, which was the site of the ancient town and temple area from the beginning of the Early Dynastic Period. Although in a barren area, ancient Aswan flourished from earliest times as a garrison town and center for the trade in ivory and other products from lower Africa, and was the home of the ram god Khnum. Situated at the southern end of the island, the town is now undergoing a new and extensive program of excavation. Remains of temples from nearly every period have been found here, including the unusual shrine of a deified local governor of the island (Sixth Dynasty), one Heqaib, whose worship continued into the Middle Kingdom, a newly reconstructed Temple of Satet, built by Queen Hatshepsut of the Eighteenth Dynasty, and Greco-Roman–Period burials of the sacred ram of Khnum. There is evidence, too, for the existence of a large Jewish community of the 7th to 5th centuries BC on the island, with its own temple dedicated to Yahweh (Jehovah). Across the Nile from the northern end of the island, at Qubbet el-Hawa, are the rock-cut tombs of the notables of Aswan ("Tombs of the Nobles") dating from the Old to the New Kingdom. They are reached by ancient stairways cut into the cliff. The decoration is interesting but somewhat provincial in style. There are groups of family tombs, notably that of a father, Harkhuf, and his son, from the Sixth Dynasty, and the tomb of the deified Heqaib. At the SE end of the island is the famous Roman Nilometer, a stone shaft for measuring the height of the Nile floods, and well-preserved Roman quays of the Temple of Khnum, while in modern Aswan, opposite, are the remains of a Roman aqueduct ("Cleopatra's Bath"). There is little else to see in modern Aswan except a small Ptolemaic temple to Isis; however, there is an interesting small museum on the island.

The famous quarries of red granite lie south and east of Aswan, with a huge unfinished obelisk (about 130 ft. long) still in its bed, and a half-buried colossal statue, as well as interesting ancient graffiti. About 7 mi. southwest of Aswan, near the airport and overlooking the High Dam, is the very large Temple of Kalabsha (the "Temple of Mandulis"), from the Roman period though built out of a New Kingdom temple, and dedicated to a local god. It was moved here from the west bank over 30 mi. south of Aswan by a German team in 1962–63, after the building of the High Dam, and beside it are two other small "rescued" temples. Its decoration is interesting in content if not in style. About ½ mi. southwest of the Tombs of the Nobles is the famous monastery of St. Simeon, founded in the 6th cent. AD, one of the largest and best preserved of Coptic buildings. Within its 20-ft.-high walls are a three-aisled church, cells for the monks, and storerooms. Some frescoes still survive. See also *Philae*.

ASYUT

The major modern city of Upper Egypt, 235 mi. S. of Cairo, on the Nile's W. bank. As ancient Lycoplis, or Zawty, Asyut was the center of the cult of the jackal god Upwaut. Plotinus, famous Neo-Platonic philosopher of the 3rd cent. AD, was a native. Nothing survives from the ancient city except its necropolis, to the west of modern Asyut, with rock-cut tombs dating from the Middle Kingdom, and some from the New—now in a military zone. The best of these is the unfinished Twelfth Dynasty (Middle Kingdom) tomb of Hapi-djefa, with open court, three large chambers and underground burial chamber. In Asyut the American College has a small museum devoted to Pharaonic and Coptic antiquities. Another small museum has material from the tombs of Asyut and Meir.

AVARIS

See *Qantir*.

BADARI	Prehistoric cemetery on the E. bank of the Nile in Upper Egypt, close to that of *Deir Tasa*, 20 mi. SE of *Asyut*. Both sites gave their names to the Badarian and Tasian cultures (about 5000–4000 BC)—now thought to be all one culture—the first farming and herding people of Upper Egypt. The Badarian is characterized by well-made brown or red pottery with black tops, and by delicate hollow-based arrowheads, beads of shell and stone, ivory spoons, human figures of baked clay, animal amulets and carved throwing sticks. Some 300 graves were excavated at Badari in 1922–25, many long ago robbed. Some contained objects of copper, and there were small luxury objects—malachite for eye paint, and shells—-imported from the Sinai, Nubia, the Red Sea. See also *Merimde*.
BAGAWAT, EL-	See *Kharga Oasis*.
BAHNASA, EL-	See *Oxyrhynchus*.
BAHRLYA OASIS	The Northern Oasis of antiquity, 70 mi. W. of the Nile and some 186 mi. SW of Cairo, exhibiting a miscellaneous set of ruins, mostly around el-Qasr, the capital. Close to it is a temple of the Twenty-sixth Dynasty with a well-preserved chapel of King Apries; also the ruins of a Roman triumphal arch, destroyed only in the 19th cent. A mile or two south is the oldest site, a decorated tomb of a governor of the oasis in the late Eighteenth or early Nineteenth Dynasty. At El-Bawiti, still further south, is a necropolis of tombs belonging mostly to the Twenty-sixth Dynasty, many painted, and an Ibis catacomb. Still farther south is an impressive Temple of Alexander the Great with outlying buildings within a temenos (sacred precinct) wall. Finally some 30 mi. further on one finds a late Roman (5th–6th cents. AD) settlement with a military camp, a church and houses decorated with Christian motifs. See also the oases of *El-Dakhla*, *Kharga* and *Siwa*.
BALAT	See *Dakhla, El-*
BAWITI, EL-	See *Bahriya Oasis*.
BEHBEIT EL-HAGAR	In the central delta, 6 mi. W. of El-Mansura, chaotic ruins of one of the most important temples of Isis in Egypt, begun by the rulers of the Thirtieth Dynasty (380–343 BC), whose town of origin lay nearby, and finished in Ptolemaic times. It is the only surviving example of a Late Dynastic Period monument built entirely in hard granite with paving of basalt. Either an earthquake, or perhaps determined stone robbing, have so tumbled the blocks that the plan can scarcely be discerned; the advantage however is that the exquisite relief carving on the blocks and some fine Hathoric column-capitals can be seen close up and in good light, which is usually not possible in other temples.
BENI HASAN	Important Middle Kingdom rock-cut cemetery on the E. bank of the Nile, 14 mi. S. of El-Minya. Here on the side of a cliff are 39 rock-cut tombs, mostly of the nomarchs, or local princes, of the Eleventh and Twelfth Dynasties. Most consist of a spacious chapel with pillars and a statue niche at the back. A few have an outer court and portico. The burial chamber was at the bottom of a shaft sunk vertically outside the chapel. The tombs were painted throughout with highly informative scenes of daily life, of hunting and fishing, and especially of warfare

and sieges—typical of the disturbed times. The objects found in the tombs included many of the engaging and equally informative little wooden models—ranks of soldiers marching, or servants at work in a kitchen—now found in many museums in the world. Only four tombs are now worth visiting (by donkey), including the tombs of Khnumhotpe, an important noble of the Twelfth Dynasty, and of Amenemhet, both with open courts in front. In the former is the well-known scene of Semitic nomads arriving from the east, often used to illustrate the biblical Exodus story—though actually far too early. South of the tombs is a rock-cut temple at Istabl 'Antar, called in Greek times Speos Artemidos, dedicated to the goddess Pakhet by Queen Hatshepsut of the Eighteenth Dynasty and finished by Seti I of the Nineteenth. In it is the queen's curious inscription describing her loathing of the Hyksos.

BIYAHMU

See *Faiyum*.

BUBASTIS

Classical form of the ancient Bast (now Tell Basta), once an important city in the eastern delta, about 1 mi. SE of Zaqaziq. Bubastis was not only the chief city of Lower Egypt's 18th nome (province) but was also the cult center of the cat-goddess Bastet ("she of the city of Bast"). The city and shrine reached their height under the Twenty-second Dynasty (about 940–720 BC), whose rulers belonged to a "Libyan" family of Bubastis. Herodotus in the 5th cent. BC describes the waterborne pilgrimages to the sanctuary of Bastet accompanied by the music of flutes and castanets. The sanctuary itself was excavated by E. Naville in 1887–89 and the remains are still impressive. The court and monumental entrance gateway of Osorkon II (Twenty-second Dynasty) led into a hypostyle hall, its columns topped by capitals of palms and Hathor heads. Beyond was the inner shrine and chapels, elegantly decorated under the Thirtieth Dynasty. Many of the reliefs are still in situ; others are scattered among the museums of Cairo, London, Berlin, Paris and Boston. In 1906 a rich treasure of ritual objects of gold and silver used in the temple was found at Bubastis. Remains of about seven small temples from different periods, including the Roman, have been excavated on the site; also an Old Kingdom (Sixth Dynasty) chapel and other evidences of Old Kingdom structures, as well as the tombs of important officials of the Nineteenth, Twentieth and Twenty-second dynasties. In the outskirts of Zaqaziq was an extensive animal cemetery, chiefly of the sacred cats of Bastet.

CAIRO

The capital of modern Egypt and an enormous metropolis, the largest city in Africa, situated on the E. bank of the Nile at the southernmost point of the triangular delta. The remains of ancient On, once one of the most important religious centers of ancient Egypt, lie under its northern suburb of *Heliopolis*. On was destroyed in the 6th cent. BC by the Persians, who had built a fort to its south. This strong point, called Babylon and rebuilt and fortified by the Romans and Byzantines, now lies at the center of Old Cairo. In 641 AD it was captured by the Arabs, whose encampment to the north of the fort gave rise to a new Islamic town, Fustat, the actual ancestor of modern Cairo. As capital of Arab Egypt, Fustat was taken by the Fatimids in 969 AD who built still another city, el-Kahira (Cairo: "The Victorious One") as their capital. Expanding north, Cairo fell to the Ayyubids (1171–1250), and under the famous Saladin all the separate settlements were united in one. After 1250 the city flourished even more grandly under the Mamluks, who ruled Egypt into the 16th cent, and then under nominal Turkish rule until 1798. Thereafter Cairo declined until its modern renaissance, chiefly after World War II.

Excavations of the remains of Fustat in Old Cairo have revealed a tight network of buildings on narrow streets, with many cisterns and oil presses. The remains of the old Roman fort of Babylon lie within the compound of the Coptic Museum nearby, both recently restored and refurbished. Built under Augustus in 30 BC and rebuilt under Trajan, it was remodeled again in 395 AD under Arcadius. Two of its towers mark the entrance to the Coptic Museum, and the fort's southwest gate, flanked by two massive bastions, can be reached by stairs leading down below the old Coptic church of El-Muallaqa, the "hanging church," which is built over ("hangs over") the passage into the fortress, its two ends resting on the bastions of the gate, which originally gave on to the Nile. El-Muallaqa, dating from the 7th cent. AD (though the present fabric is only from the 9th) and reached by a high flight of steps, is the largest and finest of seven old Coptic (early Christian) churches within the museum compound that may be seen. The Abu Serga church next to the museum, dedicated to two Roman martyrs, is built over a subterranean crypt where the Holy Family is supposed to have stayed during the flight into Egypt. It dates from a rebuilding in the 11th cent. A gate in its garden leads to the 12th-cent. Jewish Ibn Ezra Synagogue built over a Coptic church of the 7th cent. St. Barbara also dates from the 7th cent., although rebuilt in the 10th.

The numerous Islamic monuments of Cairo—there are over 500 mosques alone—are among the finest in the world. The most venerable of the mosques is that of 'Amr ibn el-As at the site of Fustat, the first holy mosque of Islamic Egyptians, its foundations dating back to the 7th cent. though it has frequently been rebuilt. The next oldest and largest of Cairo's mosques is the Ibn Tulun, built by Ibn Tulun, who achieved Egyptian independence from the Abbasids in 868 AD. The original fabric of brick, dating from 879 AD, is well preserved and skillfully restored. With its clean lines, early pointed arches, bold kufic inscrip-

The Ibn Tulun mosque in Cairo dating from 879 AD, one of the earliest of Cairo's many splendid Islamic mosques. The clean lines and austere beauty of the mosque have been skillfully preserved in a restoration. Its minaret was probably inspired by a famous early example in Samarra, Iraq, itself reminiscent of the Sumerian ziggurats of Mesopotamia. (Courtesy: Lehnert & Landrock, Cairo.)

The huge and ornate 14th-cent. mosque of Sultan Hasan in Cairo (left in upper photograph), and a closer view (below) of its principal minaret. The mosque to the right is modern. Built by the Mamluk Sultan Hasan, the mosque was never finished; for he was assassinated, like so many of the bloodthirsty Mamluk rulers, before he could be buried in his domed mausoleum at the rear. (Courtesy: Lehnert & Landrock, Cairo; Rhett Austell.)

tions along the walls and intricate stucco carving, it is one of the most admirable examples of early Islamic architecture. Its minaret was probably copied from the ziggurat-like example in Samarra, Iraq.

The Fatimids have left sections of the city walls with high curtain walls and square towers and gates, of which three are still standing—Bab el-Futuh, Bab en-Nasr and Bab Zuwaila. The Fatimid mosques included El-Akmar, built in 1125, El-Hakim near the old walls, begun in 990 and modeled on Ibn Tulun (now mostly in ruins though being restored) and above all Al-Azhar, first built in 970–71 but often rebuilt and enlarged, the center of the largest and most prestigious Islamic university in the world. Established in 988, the university today still teaches many thousands of Muslim students from many different Islamic countries. It is often called the oldest university in the world. From the Ayyubid period little remains except parts of the walls, the Citadel, begun under Saladin but chiefly a Mamluk structure, and two madrasahs (schools).

The largest number of Islamic monuments in Cairo were built under the Mamluks, "slave sultans" who dominated Egypt until the end of the 18th cent. Among the earliest were the mosques of the great warrior Baybars in El-Zaher square and the Qala'un complex of mosque, madrasah, hospital and mausoleum, both begun in 1269. The latter is in ruins, except for the mausoleum of Sultan Nasir, Qala'un's son. From the 14th cent. come the mosque of Nasir on the Citadel, and especially the huge and imposing mosque of Sultan Hasan, his son, at the foot of the Citadel, begun in 1356 and never fully completed.

Built in a cruciform plan to accommodate the four Muslim schools of law grouped around a spacious courtyard with fountain, the mosque is distinguished by its huge entrance porch, 85 ft. high, its intricate decoration and magnificent fittings, and its large domed mausoleum, never used by Sultan Hasan, who like so many of the fractious Mamluks, was assassinated. Also from the 14th cent. are the mosque of El-Barquq near the Qala'un, and the mosque of El-Aqsunqur, known as the Blue Mosque for its Persian tiles. The mosque of El-Muayyad was finished in 1420 and extensively restored in the 19th cent. Its immense bronze gates were taken from the Sultan Hasan, and its minarets rise curiously from the two bastions of the earlier Zuwaila gate in the southern walls. Finally we might mention the madrasah and mausoleum of El-Ghuri, completed in 1503, and in the extensive Muslim cemeteries called the City of the Dead (with numerous mosques, decorated tombs and mausoleums) the mausoleums of Barquq, and especially the opulent domed mausoleum of Sultan Qait Bey with its minarets, built in 1474. The last great Islamic shrine, the "Alabaster Mosque" of the 1830s, stands inside the Citadel.

Among Cairo's many museums, two are preeminent: the crowded Egyptian National Museum, containing the world's greatest collection of ancient Egyptian antiquities, including the finds from the tomb of Tutankhamun, and the Museum of Islamic Art, arguably the richest and most comprehensive collection of Islamic art in the world. The Coptic Museum, refurbished, is attractive. Most unusual of the museums is the Papyrus Institute, housed partly in houseboats on the Nile and devoted to the recent rediscovery and research into papyrus making. There is a small museum attached.

COLOSSI OF MEMNON   See *Thebes*.

COPTOS   See *Qift*.

CROCODOPOLIS	See *Faiyum*.
EL-DABA, TELL	See *Qantir*.
DAHSHUR	See *Memphis*.

DAKHLA, EL-

One of the four larger oases far in the western (Libyan) desert, inhabited from Paleolithic times into the Roman period and usually under Egyptian control when the central government was strong. The oases also acted as havens for refugees and a "Siberia" for political prisoners. At Dakhla, 120 mi. northwest of Kharga oasis, many Old Kingdom settlements and cemeteries have been found, especially at Balat, and cemeteries and temple remains from later Pharaonic and the Roman periods at other sites. At Deir el-Hagar is a ruined Roman temple of the 1st cent. AD and at El-Smant El-Kharab a small Roman temple and settlement. See also *Bahriya Oasis, Kharga Oasis, Siwa Oasis.*

DEIR ABU MENAS

Or the Abu Mena monastery, in the western desert, about 50 mi. W. of Alexandria and about 8½ mi. S. of the town of Bahig, the ruins of a once flourishing Christian town and monastery of the Byzantine period, at a time when the desert was a refuge for thousands of monks (see also *Wadi Natrun*). The town and monastery, a center of pilgrimage until the 8th cent., was named for St. Mena, a Christian soldier of the 3rd cent. AD, and was well known for its curative waters. The site, rediscovered in the 19th cent., includes the ruins of several churches, baths for the pilgrims, monks' cells, catacombs and remains of the town itself. The outstanding monument is the Basilica of Arcadius, reputedly the oldest extant Christian building in Egypt, said to have been built in the early 5th cent. AD by the emperor Arcadius in thanksgiving for the cure of his son in the waters of Abu Menas.

DEIR ABU MAKAR	See *Wadi Natrun*.
DEIR AMBA BISHOI	See *Wadi Natrun*.
DEIR EL-BAHRI	See *Thebes*.

DEIR EL-BALLAS

Village about 20 mi. N. of Luxor and Thebes, on the western bank of the Nile, embraced within the river's great bend. A royal palace and settlement here—very much like that of Akhetaten at *Tell el-Amarna* though about 300 years earlier—was partially excavated by George Reisner in 1900. A new survey of the site since 1980, with limited excavation, has led to the current seasons of full-scale excavations. The survey established the plan of the settlement, one of those rare examples of urban planning excavated in Egypt to date such as Malkata (see *Thebes*) and Pi-Ramesses (see *Qantir*). In the middle of the settlement rose the huge North Palace, built out of extra-large mud bricks. It had an unusual two-storied central block surrounded on the ground level by columned courts and halls decorated with paintings and faience tiles. The whole lay within a vast enclosure wall. Groups of houses, most very different than those of Akhetaten, were detected to the north, west and south of the palace. These ranged from small two-room houses to large villas with courtyards and outbuildings.

Also south of the palace was what appeared to be a workmens' village, with small houses similar to those of Deir el-Medineh (see *Thebes*) and Akhetaten, with buildings on the hillside that appeared again to be like the chapels of Akhetaten. Also on the south was a group of tightly grouped large structures resembling the administrative center at Akhetaten. Finally, a large structure with broad steps leading up to an elevated platform at the southernmost end of the city may have served as a military observation post during the wars with the Hyksos. For Deir el-Ballas, as inscriptions reveal, was briefly occupied at the end of the Second Intermediate Period by the Theban princes, who were squeezed between the Nubians to the south and the Hyksos to the north who controlled northern Egypt. When the Hyksos were driven out by Ahmose of Thebes (1570–1546 BC), the founder of the powerful Eighteenth Dynasty, the temporary palace and militarized settlement at Deir el-Ballas was abandoned as no longer necessary.

DEIR EL-BARAMUS   See *Wadi Natrun*.

DEIR EL-HAGAR   See *Dakhla, El-*

DEIR EL-MEDINEH   See *Thebes*.

DEIR EL-SURYANI   See *Wadi Natrun*.

DEIR TASA   Neolithic site on the plain E. of the Nile opposite Abutig, about 20 mi. SE of Asyut in Upper Egypt. It gives its name to the Tasian culture of about 5000 BC, now considered a local variant of the Badarian culture, named for nearby *Badari*. These primitive farming people buried their dead in shallow pits in a protracted position, covered over with skins, matting or cloth. With the corpse were buried offerings of food and drink in pots, palettes of stone or alabaster for the grinding and mixing of eye paint, stone implements, and ornaments of ivory and shell from the Red Sea such as beads and bangles.

DENDERA   The ancient Tantere, Greek Tentyris. Here on the W. bank of the Nile, about 40 mi. N. of Luxor, stood a city that was once the provincial capital of the 6th nome (province) and an ancient religious center dedicated to Hathor. The town has disappeared, with Qena on the E. bank taking its place. Now there is only the famous temple of Hathor here, all alone on the edge of the desert. One of the best preserved temples in Egypt, it is unusually late, having been begun under the Ptolemies about 125 BC and continued, though never entirely finished, under the Romans until about 60 AD. Its decoration, including reliefs of the notorious Cleopatra on the back wall, is lavish but, like its traditional architecture, frozen in time, stiff, lifeless. Nevertheless it is possible to see here—along with the equally well preserved Ptolemaic temple at *Edfu* further south—a perfect and classic example of the Egyptian temple plan, and without the alterations and accretions of the ages. Dendera, however, has no pylon. The temple lies within an enclosure of mud brick, almost square, with a monumental Roman gate (of Domitian and Trajan) leading into it. The east gate is also Roman. The massive temple, with its Hathor-headed porch, lies behind a large court. Two (late) hypostyle halls, again with Hathor-headed columns—the first decorated with offering scenes on the walls and astronomical reliefs on the ceiling, the second much smaller—lead through two vestibules to the sanctuary

A relief of the king making offerings to Hathor in the birth house at Dendera, one of the auxiliary buildings surrounding the main cult temple of Hathor. The birth house dates from the reign of the Roman emperor Trajan and the temple itself, one of the best preserved and decorated in Egypt, was begun under the Ptolemies and not finished until about 60 AD. Here is the traditional art and architecture of Egypt, lifeless, unchanged as late as the Roman period, frozen in time. (Courtesy: Lehnert & Landrock, Cairo.)

at the end, surrounded by chapels. Scenes of the Hathor ceremonies decorate the sanctuary walls.

The temple's thick side walls contain within them curious crypts on three levels, used for storage and priestly gear, 12 on each side, with access from the temple interior only through concealed holes. The walls also conceal processional stairways on each side leading to the roof, where in a small kiosk the ritual of the goddess' union with the sun disk was performed. Also on the roof are two shrines of Osiris with reliefs throwing much light on the Osiris ritual. Within the precinct two birth houses used for the Hathor ritual, the larger one Roman, the other Thirtieth Dynasty and Ptolemaic, stand close to the temple with a Coptic church between them. To one side was a mud brick sanatorium with baths and cells for the pilgrims. Immediately south of the temple are the ruins of a small Roman temple of Isis, and to the southwest was the sacred lake, now dry. The antiquity of Dendera as a religious center is attested by the remnants of a number of earlier temples found on the site, and the necropolis investigated by Petrie, which contained mastaba tombs from the Old and Middle Kingdoms. A small Eleventh Dynasty chapel, now reconstructed in the Cairo Museum, was also found on the site.

DENDUR

Small temple, reassembled inside the Metropolitan Museum of Art in New York City as a gift from the Egyptian government. It was dismantled in 1963 to save it from the rising waters of Lake Nasser in its original location about 50 mi. south of Aswan. Built by Augustus (23–10 BC) to honor two local princes, who had perhaps drowned in the Nile, it may have been a thank-offering for the loyalty of their father to Augustus a few years earlier. A separate pylon stands in front of the main building with its columned porch, vestibule and sanctuary. The reliefs show Augustus in the guise of a pharaoh.

EL DERR

See *Amada*.

DIR (DRA) ABU EL-NAGA

See *Thebes*.

EDFU

The Greek Apollinopolis, imposing temple of the falcon-headed Horus, almost entirely preserved after 2,000 years. It lies on the W. bank of the Nile, 70 mi. S. of Luxor and almost the same distance N. of Aswan. Like *Dendera* a very late

Entrance to the hypostyle hall of the temple of Horus at Edfu, its columns topped by plant forms. The powerful statue of the hawk-headed Horus is one of three here, carved from gray granite. Like Dendera, Edfu is late Ptolemaic in date, begun in 237 BC and finished in 67 BC. It is the best-preserved temple in Egypt and masterfully exhibits the traditional plan of an Egyptian temple, progressing from the light-filled outer court to the dim mysterious light of the sanctuary deep inside the building. (Courtesy: Lehnert & Landrock, Cairo.)

Ptolemaic structure, it was built in stages between 237 and 57 BC on the site of a smaller temple of Ramesses III. Though the abundant reliefs are rather lifeless, the building as a whole presents a perfect example of the age-old plan of the Egyptian temple, particularly the artful deliberate progression from the full light of the open courtyard through the dim columned halls into the semi-darkness and seclusion of the god's sanctuary within. Passing through the massive pylon, the entrance flanked by a magnificent pair of falcons in gray granite, the visitor enters the outer court—the only large one preserved—with its surrounding columns topped by elaborate and varied floral capitals. Beyond rise the columns of the great hypostyle hall, with another colossal falcon statue at the entrance. The hall is followed by a smaller one with 12 columns, two vestibules, and finally the darkened sanctuary enclosed within a monolithic naos (shrine) of polished granite, with chapels grouped around it. As at Dendera there are stairways leading to the roof for sun rituals, and a ruined birth house across the forecourt from the pylon. The reliefs include details of the temple's construction and rituals, including a depiction of the ritual drama of Horus' slaying of the evil god Seth, which must have been enacted on a platform in front of the temple, much like a medieval mystery play performed in front of a cathedral. The ancient town was formerly the capital of the 2nd nome (province) of Upper Egypt. Much of it lies under the modern town, but parts have been excavated to the west, revealing Greco-Roman remains as well as Old Kingdom mastaba tombs and other remnants.

ELEPHANTINE

See *Aswan*.

EL-LAHUN

See *Lahun, El-*.

ESNA

The ancient Iunyt, Greek Latopolis, a Greco-Roman temple, 36 mi. S. of Luxor on the W. bank of the Nile, dedicated to Khnum, the potter god who fashioned mankind on his wheel. Only the hypostyle hall, built under Claudius, survives and now rests some 30 ft. below the street level of the modern town. Its back wall is Ptolemaic. The hypostyle hall, almost perfectly preserved, contains 24 columns over 43 ft. high with a variety of different capitals, and valuable inscriptions giving two hymns to Khnum and describing the cycle of festivals carried out annually at the temple. The decoration on the walls dates from the 1st to 3rd centuries AD, for Esna is the latest major temple to have survived in Egypt. See also *Wadi Kubbaniya*.

THE FAIYUM

Largest of the western oases, 75 mi. SW of Cairo, with salty Lake Qarun (Lake Moeris in antiquity) in its NW corner. A large and extremely fertile region, the Faiyum is connected with the Nile by a westward branch of that river. Originally the lake filled almost the entire area, and even through Ptolemaic times it was still quite large. Today, lying well below sea level, it is much shrunken and reduced. Paleolithic finds have been located in the Faiyum, and hunting and gathering people lived there in the Neolithic period, about the same time (around 4500 BC) as the Badarian and Tasian people on the Nile (see *Badari, Deir Tasa, Merimde*). The Faiyum first came into prominence when the Twelfth Dynasty pharaohs of the Middle Kingdom pursued extensive building, irrigation and dam works there, reclaiming much rich land from the lake. Later the New Kingdom Eighteenth Dynasty pharaoh Amenhotep II reclaimed more land by building a dam about 10 mi. long. Under the Macedonian Ptolemies the Faiyum was even more intensively cultivated, becoming one of the richest and most heavily populated regions of Egypt.

The chief town and capital of the Faiyum is Medinet el-Faiyum, called Crocodilopolis in ancient times since it was the center of the cult of the crocodile god Sobek; crocodiles abounded in the marshy region. Under the Ptolemies the town was known as Arsinoë. The ruins of the ancient settlement, now reduced to rubble after centuries of stone-robbing, lie to the northwest of the modern city, where fragments of a pharaonic temple and a Greco-Roman shrine, both dedicated to Sobek, have been unearthed, and Hellenistic and Coptic buildings. An obelisk of Senwosret I of the Middle Kingdom, which once lay broken at Abgig, now stands outside Medinet el-Faiyum, and at Byamu, about 4 mi. north the huge bases alone survive from two colossal statues of Amenemhet III of the Middle Kingdom (1842–1797 BC). See also the Faiyum localities of *Hawara, Kom Aushim, El-Lahun, Medinet-Madi, Qasr Qarun* and *Umm el-Breigat.*

GEBEL DUKHAN

Just inland from the Red Sea, about 30 mi. southwest of the scuba diving capital of Hurghada. Here was the source of the famous red porphyry used to decorate innumerable Roman baths, temples, basilicas and villas. Called Mons Hadrianus by the Romans, there were some 15 quarries here and a busy small town with a fort, camps, stables, a well and cistern, and a temple built of granite with Ionic columns. The equally prized white granite came from Mons Claudianus, now Gebel Farita, about 30 mi. to the south. Here, too, was a town, walled, with a temple and the remains of heated baths, and an aqueduct near its entrance gate.

GEBEL FARITA

See *Gebel Dukhan.*

GEBEL SILSILA

Sandstone quarries on the Nile, about 40 mi. N. of A*swan*, which supplied stone for the great New Kingdom monuments of Middle and Upper Egypt, from the Eighteenth Dynasty into the Roman Period. Here the sandstone comes down in cliffs on both sides of the Nile, replacing the limestone to the north of Silsila that was more popular with the Old Kingdom builders. Most of the quarries are on the east bank. On the west bank are also inscriptions, stelae, graffiti and some 30 rock-cut commemorative chapels of the kings and nobles of the New Kingdom. The largest is that of Horemheb, Tutankhamun's general and himself later pharaoh, called the "Great Speos." Behind an entrance with four pillars lies a vestibule and a sanctuary in which seven deities were honored, among them Horemheb. The decoration, in particular the scene of the triumph of Horemheb, is notable.

GIRZA

Large Predynastic cemetery on the Nile E. of the Faiyum. Its name was given to the Gerzean culture, now generally identified with Naqada II (about 3500–3100 BC), which developed out of the Amratian (Naqada I) (see El *Amra, Naqada*). This was the crucial period of cultural flowering that gave rise to the distinctive civilization of Egypt, beginning in the Predynastic period. A strong Asiatic, even Mesopotamian, influence became increasingly evident, either through quickening trade, conquest, or both, with cylindrical seals, use of mud brick, and the relatively sudden appearance of writing. The Gerzeans made beautifully fashioned flint implements, and beads of copper and gold. They ground superb stone vessels and palettes, manufactured faience for the first time, and produced pottery decorated with red line drawings from nature, especially of boats. The dead were buried in oval or rectangular graves. See also *Hemamieh*.

HAWARA

At the eastern entrance to the *Faiyum*. Near it, about 6 mi. SE of Medinet el-Faiyum, are the remains of a brick pyramid of Amenemhet III (1842–1797 BC) of the Middle Kingdom's Twelfth Dynasty, who also built a larger pyramid at Dahshur (see *Memphis*). To defeat grave robbers, the passage into the interior of the pyramid was a complex series of dead-ends, sliding trap doors, and chambers filled with stone. It led to the burial chamber hollowed out of a single huge block of quartzite. But to no avail; the tomb was robbed anyway. South of it was the mortuary temple, excavated by Petrie, called the Labyrinth by the Greeks for its complex of many rooms, and mentioned both by Herodotus and Strabo. A fine statue of Amenemhet III in the Cairo Museum came from the site, of which little is left today. In 1956 the tomb of Amenemhet's daughter, Neferu-ptah, was found about one mile south of the pyramid. Along the road nearby pit graves contained mummies of the Roman Period from which the famous "Faiyum" painted portraits came, rare and lovely examples of the classic realistic portrait painting of the period.

HELIOPOLIS

"City of the sun" in Greek, the renowned and ancient city of On, center of the cult of the sun god Re or Ra, which became one of the "state religions" of Egypt. The site of On, marked by an obelisk of Senwosret I of the Twelfth Dynasty, lies now in the spacious modern suburb of *Cairo*, also called Heliopolis, where underground water and modern building have hampered excavation. Two other obelisks from On, the New Kingdom "Cleopatra's Needles," ended up in London and New York, via Alexandria. Two more are in Rome. On and the cult of Re go back at least to the Fifth Dynasty of the Old Kingdom, when On became one of the most important religious centers in the country. Though in the New Kingdom the city itself lost preeminence to *Thebes*, its cult and creation myth gradually absorbed those of *Memphis* and *Hermopolis* to become a royal state religion.

HELWAN

About 15 mi. S. of Cairo, on the E. bank of the Nile across from Memphis, a spa town with an interesting wax museum depicting the highlights of Egyptian history. It is also near several interesting archaeological sites. About 1 mi. to the north is the Neolithic site of el-Omari, actually a complex of three sites and two cemeteries discovered in 1924. The site of Omari A proved to be a Neolithic village of about 4000 BC consisting of some 100 circular or oval huts with floors below the ground, each in a yard with reed fences, much as at the Neolithic site of *Merimde*. Burials within the settlement had few grave goods. Very different was the somewhat later Neolithic farming village at Maadi, about 6 mi. north of Omari in a residential suburb of Cairo. Excavated 1930–35, it was dated about 3600–3000 BC, just on the edge of the Early Dynastic Period. Here there was evidence for metallurgy and extensive trade, including foreign contacts. Pottery from southern Palestine was found here and the unusual underground house type had apparently been imported from the same area (see *Beersheba*, ISRAEL). Specialized storage areas were found at the opposite ends of the site: underground cellars with the remains of grain, carnelian beads and well-made stone vessels, and the other area with large storage jars (pithoi) that once contained foodstuffs and other items. At Maadi also some of the earliest remains of the domesticated donkey were found.

Southeast of Maadi a Predynastic cemetery of 468 burials was found. Another rich cemetery dating to the Archaic or Early Dynastic Period (about 3100–2700 BC) was excavated from 1942 to 1954 about 2 mi. west of Helwan. Some 10,000 tombs, probably belonging to the lesser nobility of the early *Memphis* court, some of them resembling the Archaic tombs of Saqqara on the other side of the Nile beyond Memphis, were investigated here. The remains of an Old Kingdom dam were excavated about 6 mi. south of Helwan at Wadi Gerrawi, stretching for 79 yds. It was originally enormously thick and some 10 yds. high. Finally, at Tura, below Maadi and about 8 mi. south of Cairo, were the famous quarries that provided the fine white limestone used for the outer casing of the pyramids.

HEMAMIEH

Predynastic site about 10 mi. SE of *Badari* on the E. bank of the Nile, excavated in the 1920s and important because it is one of the few well stratified Predynastic sites so far studied. The sequence begins at the lowest and earliest levels with the Badarian (thermoluminescent dates: 5580 ± 420 to 4360 ± 355 BC), moves on through the Amratian, with small circular houses (about 4000–3500 BC) to the Gerzean (up to 3100 BC). See also *Amra, El, Girza, Hierakonpolis, Merimde, Naqada*.

HERMOPOLIS

In Arabic El-Ashmunein, site of the ancient Khmunu, called Hermopolis by the Greeks, on the W. bank of the Nile 22 mi. S. of Minya. Hermopolis, chief city of the 15th nome (province) of Upper Egypt, was the cult center of the Ibis-headed god Toth, god of healing and writing, and from most ancient times had been one of Egypt's premier religious centers, often called the "City of Eight" because in its creation myth Toth had engendered four couples (eight gods) before the creation of the world. In the Ptolemaic period the Greeks worshiped Toth as Hermes, hence Hermopolis became a pilgrimage center for Greeks and Egyptians alike. Glimpses of the heavy mud brick walls and broken bits of temples standing up above mounds of rubble in a palm grove now mark the site of Khmunu's sacred area, and the fact that excavations have revealed nothing very ancient in this ancient site is merely an accident of survival. In fact the most prominent remains here are the granite columns of a late Roman (5th cent. AD) basilica—one of the few large buildings of the type to have survived in the country. For the rest, parts of the monumental gates of various temples have been identified, including one of Amenemhet II of the Twelfth Dynasty and others from the New Kingdom and Ptolemaic periods. The foundations of a pylon of a temple of Rameses II yielded over 1,500 blocks plundered from the temples of Akhnaten's city (Akhetaten) at *Tell el-Amarna* nearby, which helped in the investigation of that site. Two colossal statues of baboons, an animal sacred to Toth, now stand in front of the old excavation building. There is a good museum of finds from Middle Egypt in the nearby district capital of Mellawi.

The extensive late necropolis of ancient Hermopolis lies several miles to the west in the desert at Tuna el-Gebel. Just north of it the northernmost boundary stela of Akhenaten's city at Tell el-Amarna, along with a rock-cut shrine, may be seen. South of it are the miles of underground burial catacombs of the baboons and ibises sacred to Toth, dating mostly from the Greco-Roman period. Animal mummies and other finds may be seen in a small museum in the nearby town of Mellawi. The well-preserved Ptolemaic tomb of Petosiris, of about 300 BC, a priest of Toth, is unique in that it resembles a small Egyptian temple with a columned entrance, cult sanctuary and underground burial chambers. It is decorated with reliefs, in content Egyptian but in style heavily influenced by the Greek. South of it lies the Greek "City of the Dead," streets of tombs and chapels in the form of houses, again Greco-Egyptian in style, dating from the 3rd cent. BC to the 2nd cent. AD and decorated with colored funerary scenes.

HIERAKONPOLIS

Modern Kom el-Ahmar, the ancient Nekhen. The site, with little now to see, lies on the W. bank of the Nile about 11 mi. N. of Edfu in Upper Egypt. With its twin city of Nekheb (see Kab, El-) across the Nile, it was one of the oldest cities in Egypt, a center of the ancient cult of the falcon-headed Horus and probably the chief city of the White Kingdom of Predynastic times. From here its leaders may have conquered the Red Kingdom of the South to unite Egypt under the First Dynasty about 3100 BC. One result of the unification was probably the founding of the new capital, Memphis, strategically placed on the borders of both kingdoms.

Extensive and important Predynastic (or late Gerzean) settlements and cemeteries lie along the edge of the desert to the west of the site for a mile or so. Some 200 tombs were excavated here, yielding typical Gerzean painted pottery (see Girza), superbly worked flint knives and animal-shaped palettes, buried with contracted skeletons. Among a group of five larger tombs found in the 1890s was the famous brick "Tomb 100" (now disappeared), its west wall decorated with the earliest tomb painting known in Egypt, depicting boats, warriors and animals. The tomb was probably that of a local Predynastic king. At the start of the First Dynasty a new town enclosure, its mud brick walls now shapeless heaps, was built further towards the Nile, with a temple complex in one corner. At the site, now known as Kim el-Ahmar, a notable cache of older votive objects was discovered in the remains of the earliest brick temple. The finds included palettes, stone vessels, mace heads and other objects, many of them referring to and dating from the period of the unification of Egypt. These included the macehead of the Scorpion King (now in Oxford) wearing the crown of the White Kingdom, and the famous palette of King Narmer of about 3100 BC, of dark green slate. It is now in the Cairo Museum. It depicts the king on one side wearing the crown of Upper Egypt while ritually bashing in the head of an enemy, and on the other, wearing the crown of Lower Egypt, passively viewing his beheaded opponents. Also in the cache was a fine sculpture of King Kha'sekhem of the Second Dynasty (about 2670 BC) and from the Sixth Dynasty two unique large copper statues of King Pepy I and his son Merenre, as well as a fine falcon head of hammered sheet gold with inlaid eyes (Egyptian Museum, Cairo). Many other decorated rock-cut tombs dating from the Sixth to Eighteenth dynasties have also been found here along the edge of the desert. The complex stratigraphy of the site was greatly elucidated by the American Museum of Natural History expedition, starting in 1969. New excavations in the Predynastic cemeteries continue (1988).

KAB, EL-

The ancient Nekheb, on the E. bank of the Nile about 12 mi. N. of Edfu, known to the Greeks as Eileithyaspolis, twin city with Hierakonpolis, or Nekhen, on the W. bank. Both cities were very ancient. The history of Nekheb, center of the cult of the vulture-headed goddess Nekhbet and at one time chief town of the 3rd nome (province) of Upper Egypt, runs from about 6000 BC to the Roman Period. Excavations here in 1967–68 have uncovered a sequence of three late Paleolithic seasonal riverside camps, dated from 6400 BC to 5980 BC. The main archaeological sites center on the town itself on the banks of the Nile, enclosed within massive mud brick walls (10th cent. BC?) within which the ruinous temple complex dedicated to Nekhbet included the main temple, subsidiary buildings, smaller temples, birth house and sacred lake. There is evidence of Early Dynastic building here, but the principal structures included works from the Eighteenth Dynasty on up through the Twenty-ninth and Thirtieth (the most abundant) and even a Roman temple.

Outside the walls were two chapels from the Eighteenth and Thirtieth dynasties, now gone, and about 10 rock-cut tombs, mainly of the Eighteenth Dynasty. Two of these in particular, numbers 2 and 5, are well known for their historical inscriptions describing the expulsion of the Hyksos and other campaigns, while another, the tomb of a mayor of Nekheb, has fine reliefs. Closer to the river is a decorated Ptolemaic tomb. Further into the rocky desert are the "desert temples," partly rock-cut: the Ptolemaic sanctuary of the goddess Shesmetet, a chapel called "el-Hammam," built originally under Rameses II, and finally the small Eighteenth Dynasty temple of Hathor and Nekhbet. Near the latter is the "Vulture Rock" covered with Old Kingdom and earlier inscriptions.

KALABSHA   See *Aswan.*

KARNAK   See *Thebes.*

KHATANA, EL-   See *Qantir.*

KHARGA OASIS   Southernmost of the four larger oases in the western desert that were generally under the control of the government of ancient Egypt, 80 mi. W. of the Nile and *Thebes,* and about 40 mi. E. of the smaller oasis of El-Dakhla. There are nearly 100 archaeological sites in Kharga, of which the best known is the Temple of Hibis, a few miles north of Kharga town, built in the Egyptian manner and dedicated to Amun by the Persian king Darius I (521–486 BC). Restored in 1908, it is well preserved and is the only example from the period. The usual monumental gateway fronts a colonnaded court and three hypostyle halls, the last surrounded by chapels. On one of the entrances is a 69-line inscription in Greek dating from the reign of Galba (69 AD). At el-Bagawat, two to three miles north of the temple are the remains of a Roman town and a Christian cemetery of some 200 domed tombs of mud brick, aligned along a street. Wall paintings on a few depict Old and New Testament scenes, allegorical figures and floral motifs. At Nadura, a mile or two south of the temple are two Roman temples (2nd cent. AD) with interesting column capitals. South of Kharga town are more temples: a Ptolemaic temple of Amun at Qasr el-Gheuida, a Ptolemaic-Roman temple at Qasr Zaiyan, and a Roman temple of Serapis and Isis at Qasr Dush. See also *Bahriya Oasis, Dakhla, El-, Siwa Oasis.*

KHOKA   See *Thebes.*

KOM EL-AHMAR   See *Hierakonopolis.*

KOM AUSHIM

In the *Faiyum*, about 15 mi. N. of Medinet el-Faiyum, the large excavated site of a Ptolemaic town, the ancient Karanis, with agora and house remains clustered on a hill. The site lies behind a small museum holding antiquities from the area. There are also two limestone temples here, the southern one, from Ptolemaic and Roman times, dedicated to a local crocodile god, the date of the other uncertain.

KOM OMBO

One of the great Ptolemaic temple-sanctuaries, occupying a commanding height overlooking a wide bend in the Nile just S. of Kom Ombo, 30 mi. N. of *Aswan*. It was dedicated to two principal deities, the crocodile god Sobek and the falcon-headed Haroeris (the elder Horus) and their attendant gods; this is reflected in the unusual dual plan: two gateways, aisles and sanctuaries at the back. There is evidence for an earlier Eighteenth Dynasty temple on the site, and later decorations and additions to the Ptolemaic temple were made in Roman times. Though much ruined, some of the walls, richly decorated with interesting scenes, stand to a considerable height and a number of columns have been reerected, so that the whole is impressive in its proportions and grandeur. The temple is tightly enclosed within double walls with corridors between (the duality again), the outer wall, added in Roman times, embracing a colonnaded courtyard in front. Beyond this are the first and second hypostyle halls, three vestibules and the two sanctuaries, side by side, each approached by an aisle. Numerous small rooms along the back of the inner wall and in the temple itself complicate the plan. A ruined birth house stands near the Nile, and on the south side of the temple a tiny Roman shrine of Hathor—now housing crocodile mummies and sarcophagi found in a nearby necropolis. There is a substantial Ptolemaic well and two more of the Roman Period, and there was a monumental Ptolemaic gateway on the Nile. One column of a Coptic church still stands on the site. See also *Wadi Kubbaniya*.

KOPTOS

See *qift*.

KUNTILLET AJRUD

Interesting if enigmatic Judean site in the extreme eastern Sinai, about 25 mi. E. of El-Kuntilla. Dating to about 850 BC, it was excavated by the Israelis in 1975–76 during the Israeli occupation of Sinai. A rectangular structure on an isolated hill, enclosing a courtyard and storerooms, it was first thought to be a Judean fortress built to protect the rich trade routes to the port of *Ezion-Geber* (now Eilat) and biblical Ophir beyond, but it is now considered a caravan station and cult center. For the finds included a large number of votive inscriptions in both Hebrew and Phoenician scripts on pottery, stone vessels and on some of the inner plastered walls invoking the blessings of several gods. One refers to the Israelite god Yahweh and his "Asherah," possibly referring to an Israelite goddess, a divine-consort not included in later biblical tradition.

LAHUN, EL-

Brick pyramid of Senwosret II of the Twelfth Dynasty (1897–1878 BC), 11 mi. SE of Medinet el-Faiyum at the eastern end of the entrance to the *Faiyum*. Sited on a rocky knoll, the pyramid was built in the Middle Kingdom core or compartment method of construction to save expense and labor—stone retaining walls radiating from the center, the intervals in between filled with mud brick. The pyramid originally had an outer casing of Tura limestone, now gone; consequently it is now an almost shapeless mass of mud brick. When new, it measured 350 ft. on a side at its base. Unlike other pyramids, the entrance, leading into a complex of shafts and corridors, was on the south side. The funeral chamber, built of granite slabs and not centered, still contains a fine sarcophagus of pink granite and an alabaster offering table. Around the pyramid are graves and mastabas of almost all periods, and the small queen's pyramid. Three other shafts on the south side of the main pyramid lead down to the tombs of princesses; and in one, that of princess Sat-Hathor-Yunet, the king's daughter, was found a splendid treasure of jewels consisting of diadems, necklaces, pectorals and bracelets, now in the Egyptian Museum (Cairo) and the New York Metropolitan Museum of Art.

At less than a mile east of the pyramid are the remains of the valley temple and close to it a remarkable town (sometimes called Kahun), excavated by Petrie. Here lived the priests, officials and workers connected with the pyramid. Laid out in a neat checkerboard of streets and houses, the town had several quarters separated by walls: a luxurious quarter of large houses of up to 80 rooms for the dignitaries, a workers' quarter of uniform small houses, and an "acropolis" area, perhaps for the king himself while the pyramid was building. A set of papyrus archives, found in a small temple here and remarkably preserved, have yielded invaluable details on many aspects of Middle Kingdom life.

LISHT, EL-

The principal necropolis of the Twelfth Dynasty kings of the Middle Kingdom, at the edge of the desert to the W. of the Nile, about 19 mi. S. of *Memphis*. It was close to the royal capital of It-towe, which probably lay to the east, though no trace of it has been found. The principal monuments, surrounded by smaller pyramids of the royal family, mastabas and cemeteries, are two now shapeless pyramids. That of Amenemhet I, founder of the dynasty. is a mere mound, hardly worth a visit, though excavations have determined that many decorated stones, robbed from Old Kingdom temples at Memphis, were used in its construction. The pyramid of his successor, Senwosret I (1971–1926 BC), originally 200 ft. high and 350 ft. on a side, is now a sand-covered mound 80 ft. high. Constructed like that of Senwosret II at *El-Lahun*, its 16 compartments between heavy stone retaining walls were filled with rough limestone blocks. It, too, had a casing of white Tura limestone, and the entrance to the burial chamber (now flooded with water) was on the north. A surrounding wall of Tura limestone encloses a small subsidiary pyramid and the mortuary temple, with its sanctuary up against the pyramid. The causeway from the valley led to a pillared court in front of the temple with 10 statues of the king (found in a cache and now in Cairo), the whole temple complex being copied from that of Pepy II at Saqqara. Within a larger enclosure were nine smaller pyramids of the royal family, each with its own temple. The interesting mastaba tombs belonged to various court viziers, stewards, a Mistress of the House, Senebitsy, and two high priests (that of High Priest Senwosret-ankh of Memphis, contains a version of the Pyramid Texts). The finds are in the Egyptian Museum (Cairo) and the Metropolitan in New York.

LUXOR

See *Thebes*.

LYCOPOLIS

See *Asyut*.

MAADI

See *Helwan*.

MALKATA	See *Thebes*.

MEDAMUD

Site of ancient Madit, or Madu, a cult shrine of Montu the war god, on the E. bank of the Nile, 5 mi. N. of Karnak. In the Old Kingdom there was a sacred grove here, walled, with two tumuli inside it. The first temple, now destroyed, was built during the Middle Kingdom, probably by Senwosret III of the Twelfth Dynasty. Much building and rebuilding followed up through the Late Dynastic Period, and there are indications that an early Ptolemaic temple stood in a corner of the enclosure. The present ruins date from the Greco-Roman Period. Tiberius built a brick enclosure wall, which was approached by an avenue of sphinxes. The facade and first hypostyle hall are late Ptolemaic, the court in between by Antoninus Pius, who rebuilt the temple. Its exterior walls were decorated under Domitian and Trajan. Somewhere within the temple were rooms for the sacred bull of Montu, and to its south a sacred lake.

MEDINET EL-FAIYUM	See *Faiyum*.
MEDINET HABU	See *Thebes*.

MEDINET MADI

Once a flourishing Greco-Roman town in the *Faiyum*, about 15 mi. SW of Medinet el-Faiyum. The chief interest here however is a small Twelfth Dynasty temple, built by Amenemhet III and IV (about 1840–1790 BC), its nucleus well preserved despite Ptolemaic and Roman additions. Excavated by an Italian team from Milan, it was dedicated to the serpent goddess Renenutet and to Sobek. It is one of the two non-funerary Middle Kingdom temples known (see also *El-Tod*), since the avid New Kingdom builders destroyed most of them for the stone. A sacred way lined with sphinxes and lions leads to a kiosk in front of the temple, which is rectangular in plan with a porch of two papyrus columns, a vestibule, and a sanctuary with three chapels. See also *Umm el-Breigat*.

MEIDUM

Or Maidum, Old Kingdom pyramid, the first attempt at a true pyramid, which collapsed because of faulty construction. Situated on the Nile's west bank below *Memphis* and opposite the northern Faiyum, it now towers above a huge mound of rubble like an immense fortress. Perhaps begun by the last pharaoh of the Third Dynasty, Huni, it was finished by and is usually attributed to Snofru (Sneferu), founder of the Fourth Dynasty (2575–2551) who built two other pyramids at Dahshur (see *Memphis*). The pyramid was begun as a step pyramid like that at Saqqara, then the usual type, with seven steps, later eight. Then the builders decided to add a smooth casing of limestone, turning it into a true pyramid 250 ft. high. Unfortunately the bonding and/or the foundations of this casing were faulty and at some unspecified time the casing collapsed down the sides, leaving the central core one now sees with 250,000 tons of fallen limestone heaped around the base. At Dahshur, Snofru's architects continued to experiment with the true pyramid, with odd results in the "Bent" and "Red" pyramids.

The Meidum pyramid can be entered through a sloping shaft into the north face, which leads down to several chambers then up again to the ground-level burial chamber inside the pyramid. In 1891 a well-preserved small mortuary temple was found on the pyramid's east side. To the north and east lie a number of large, early Fourth Dynasty mastaba tombs, including those of Nefermaat and his wife, Itet, and of Prince Rehotpe and his wife Nofret. From the latter came the astonishingly realistic seated limestone statues of the pair, now in the Egyptian Museum (Cairo), with the painted details still fresh. Both tombs were the first to be decorated with scenes from daily life.

MEMNON, COLOSSI OF   See *Thebes*.

MEMPHIS   The famous city, heartland, royal residence and religious center of the Early Dynastic and Old Kingdom Period, with its enormous necropolis stretching for nearly 20 mi. N. and S. along the edge of the western desert. Memphis, on the west bank of the Nile, remained an important metropolis throughout Egyptian history. Founded about 3000 BC, it became the Old Kingdom capital called "White Walls," the residence of the kings and center of the worship of the god Ptah. Although during the New Kingdom *Thebes* became the capital, Memphis continued to be an important administrative and religious center, in particular rebuilt and adorned by the great Ramesses II, who built a new and splendid temple of Ptah. Memphis continued to flourish thereafter as one of the greatest and most cosmopolitan cities of the ancient world and only began a slow decline about 1000 BC. With the founding of Ptolemaic *Alexandria* in the 4th cent. BC it began to lose its population, and in the later Roman Period it was devastated by the burning of many of its stones for lime, while its importance as a religious center suffered with the coming of Christianity. After the Arab conquest many more of its stones were hauled off to help build the new city of *Cairo*. Thereafter its tumbled remains slowly disappeared under the alluvial soil brought down by the annual Nile flood.

Of the once-great city, whose center must have shifted around from period to period, very little is still visible, and only a tiny part of its vast area has been excavated. However there have been many accidental discoveries in recent times and spot excavations here and there. In the 1980s large-scale surveys and excavations were begun by various institutions in the face of serious encroachments by the land-hungry villages on or near the site—for the rich alluvial soil is much coveted by local farmers. Participating are the Egyptian Antiquities Organization, the University of Pennsylvania and other American teams, and above all the vast survey of the whole site inaugurated by the British-based Egypt Exploration Society in 1982 and still continuing. One of its principal aims is to record the numerous inscriptions, but it is also taking a multidisciplinary approach to the problems of Memphis.

The great temple enclosure of Ptah with the temple of Ramesses II, only partially excavated, is once again being surveyed by the Egypt Exploration Society teams, starting in 1987. This huge temple enclosure was perhaps as large as Karnak (see *Thebes*) and to date has yielded blocks and remnants from the Middle Kingdom and New Kingdom temples on the site, the most numerous being those of Ramesses II, who built the west pylon, hypostyle hall and north and south gates—typically placing colossal statues of himself outside them. One is now housed in a small building on the site, where there is also an alabaster sphinx of the New Kingdom, and another stands in front of the Cairo railway station. An embalming house for Apis bulls (see Saqqara below) inside the enclosure, a temple of Hathor, a chapel of Seti I, a palace of Merneptah, have been identified and excavated, as well as a few tombs.

The former magnificence of Memphis is suggested rather by the sheer immensity of its necropolis along the desert to the west, which includes over 20 known pyramids, including those of Giza and Saqqara. The principal areas of the necropolis, named for nearby local villages, will be discussed here in alphabetical order. All but the first site—an interesting temple in the midst of the area—belong to the necropolis proper:

Abu Gurab   About 1 mi. N. of the Fifth Dynasty pyramids of A*busir* was the Sun Temple of Abu Gurab, built by King Neuserre of the same dynasty; for these kings favored the sun god of *Heliopolis* to the north. Like a pyramid complex, a covered causeway led up from the valley temple to the entrance of the shrine, a large court on a raised platform, open to the air like the later sun temples of Akhenaten (see *Amarna, Tell el-*). In the middle of the court a large alabaster altar faced the symbol of the sun at its back, a stubby masonry obelisk originally 114 ft. high, raised on a truncated pyramidal base. Around the sides of the court were magazines and slaughterhouses for sacrifices, with large stone basins to catch the blood. A corridor around the temple and a small chapel tucked under one side of the obelisk were decorated with ritual scenes, and in a "Room of the Seasons" were beautifully executed reliefs of the countryside and of animals during the seasons of the year. A brick imitation of the sun god's boat was found south of the platform. The temple was excavated at the turn of the century and the reliefs dispersed abroad long ago. Another sun temple, the earliest known, simpler in design and with no reliefs, was built by Userkaf, founder of the Fifth Dynasty. Lying between Abu Gurab and Abusir, it was investigated by the Swiss.

Abu Roash   A plateau about 4 mi. N. of Giza. On it are the isolated remains of the northernmost pyramid of the Memphis necropolis, and indications that it had also been a necropolis for some lost center of the early kings of the First Dynasty, Aha and Den. King Radjedef of the Fourth Dynasty, successor to Khufu (Cheops), began a large pyramid here which was unfinished since he only reigned eight years. Excavations of the pyramid and its mortuary temple, however, yielded parts of about 20 statues of high quality, carved from hard red granite. No other pharaoh built here.

Abusir   About 1½ mi. N. of Saqqara there are three delapidated pyramids of the Fifth Dynasty and the beginnings of a fourth, with mortuary and valley temples connected by causeways. The best preserved (though it has lost its Tura limestone casing), still 143 ft. high (originally 250 ft.), is that of Neferirkare. Its inner step-pyramid construction has been exposed. Next to it the pyramid of Neuserre is badly ruined, while that of Sahure, because of slipshod inner construction and the loss of its casing, is a heap of rubble only 50 ft. high. Though the pyramids were poorly built in comparison to those of the Fourth Dynasty, the Fifth Dynasty mortuary complexes were sumptuous creations, built of local and Tura limestone with columns of red granite and black basalt pavements. The best preserved and most thoroughly investigated (at the turn of the century) is the mortuary complex of Sahure. Judging from surviving fragments, the decoration, in low relief and once painted, was outstanding in quality and in originality of subject matter, showing activities of the king's reign, including the earliest known depiction of Egyptian seagoing vessels, returning from Asia. The unfinished pyramid probably belonged to Raneferef, who only reigned a few years. Recently Czech archaeologists have excavated one of the accompanying mastaba tombs, largest of the Old Kingdom, that of Ptahshepses, vizier and son-in-law of Neuserre.

Dahshur   Pyramid field, southernmost of the Memphis necropolis, about 6 mi. S. of Saqqara, now in a military zone and thus inaccessible. There are two Fourth Dynasty pyramids here and three smaller Middle Kingdom pyramids, randomly placed. The field is dominated by the two huge pyramids of Snofru, founder of the Fourth Dynasty and father of Khufu (Cheops) of the Great Pyramid at Giza. They are of particular interest because they illustrate, along with the pyramid at *Meidum*, stages in the bold transition from step pyramid to true pyramid (the Great Pyramid) accomplished at this time. Why Snofru appears to have built three pyramids, including that at Medium, is not known. The earliest at Dahshur, planned as a true pyramid, is the "Bent Pyramid," the "bend" caused by a sharp reduction of the angle of the slopes when less than half built—perhaps because of miscalculations or the discovery of faults, either here or at the Meidum pyramid contemporary with it. The North or "Red" pyramid at Dahshur (its stones are reddish in color), the first completed true pyramid, was built cautiously at the low angle of the upper part of the earlier Bent Pyramid, giving it an unpleasant squat appearance. Nevertheless its base dimensions (715 and 725 ft.) are only exceeded by those of the Great Pyramid (755 ft. on a side). The Bent Pyramid is unique in having two separate entrances and burial chambers, on its north and west faces, and much of its outer Tura limestone casing is still in place. Its valley temple, and a small mortuary temple, have been excavated, yielding remarkable reliefs, and statues of the king. A small subsidiary pyramid stands beside it.

The smaller Middle Kingdom pyramids include those of Senwosret III and of Amenemhet III (who also had a smaller pyramid at *Hawara*), both of mud brick, and in between the much ruined stone pyramid of Amenemhet II—all kings of the Twelfth Dynasty. The pyramid of Amenemhet III still stands about 100 ft. high, and that of Senwosret III about 90 ft. high. The tomb chamber of the latter was protected by a maze of underground passages. Near both, and within a vast enclosure wall, are the usual tombs of notables and of princesses, interconnected. And in the latter was found a treasure-cache of exquisite jewelry of gold and precious stones, comparable to those found at El-*Lahun*. The jewelry is now in the Egyptian Museum (Cairo). The stone pyramid of Amenemhet II was built in the compartment method, as at El-Lahun and El-*Lisht*, and hence is now a heap of rubble. Outside the enclosure wall a rare cache of six wooden boats was found, now in the Cairo museum.

Giza   The three Great Pyramids and the Great Sphinx, of the Fourth Dynasty, at the edge of the desert 9 mi. W. of Cairo. Though a modern four-lane highway now speeds the tour buses out through the Cairo suburbs to the hill on which the Great Pyramids stand, these huge structures still exercise their fascination as they have since the earliest years of human civilization when they were built. Dating from the years around 2600 BC, they culminated a generation of bold experimentation with pyramid building (see Dahshur [above], *Meidum*, Saqqara [below]), and are remarkable for the skill and accuracy of their planning and construction. The pyramids, moreover, are memorials as much as tombs, embodying the order, the stability, the magnificence of the Old Kingdom of Egypt.

The noble silhouettes of the three great pyramids of Giza, near Cairo. Their size and perfect form has intrigued and fascinated untold generations for over 4,500 years. Much has been made of the "mystery" of these pyramids. There is no mystery, for they were clearly tombs as well as temples, expressing the divinity of the pharaoh and the stable grandeur of the Old Kingdom of Egypt. (Courtesy: Lehnert & Landrock, Cairo.)

With its fall the glory departed, but over 1,000 years later, under the New Kingdom, the site once more became a place of pilgrimage. And under the last dynasties of independent Egypt over 2,000 years later there is evidence for a renewed veneration of the already ancient site. In the 5th cent. BC Herodotus, the early Greek historian, gave us a vivid glimpse of the pyramids. Then again the glory departed, but the pyramids remained, though largely despoiled of their shining limestone casings. About 150 years ago serious study and excavation of the site began and now, amidst swarms of tourists, still continues on these great structures already some 4,500 years old.

The Great Pyramid of Khufu or Cheops, is still the largest and most impressive stone structure in the world. Covering 13 acres, it is 450 ft. high (originally 480 ft), measures 755 ft. on a side, and contains about 2½ million tons of stone, all quarried, transported, shaped and positioned by fairly small but skilled gangs of peasants during Khufu's long reign of 23 years. It has three burial chambers, indicating changes of plan, the first below ground level, the second (the so-called "Queen's Chamber") inside the pyramid, and the final one ("King's Chamber") higher up inside it, reached by an impressive ascending corbelled passage, the Great Gallery. The burial chamber has two air shafts, and above it was a series of five weight-relieving chambers. Only the massive granite sarcophagus was found in the chamber, rifled centuries earlier.

Of Khufu's pyramid complex, the valley temple is lost beneath the nearby village, the causeway has disappeared, and only a basalt pavement close to the pyramid marks the site of the mortuary temple. For Khufu's queens there were three small pyramids on the east side, and beyond them and also to the west of the pyramid regular rows of many large mastaba tombs for the dignitaries of his court. Close to the queens' pyramids a sealed vertical shaft found in 1925 contained the burial goods of Queen Hetepheres, wife of Snofru and mother of Khufu, with an empty sarcophagus—probably buried here after the pillaging of the original tomb, presumably at Dahshur. The jewelry and exquisite furniture

A close view of the base of the Great Pyramid of Khufu (Cheops) at Giza (above). This impressive monument is the largest stone structure in the world. It is 450 feet high, and an estimated 2½ million tons of stone went into building it. In the main burial chamber inside it the king's huge granite sarcophagus was found, but his mummy had long ago disappeared. The famous Sphinx (below), close to the pyramid of Khephren, Khufu's son, was probably fashioned in that king's likeness. A large Fourth Dynasty temple has been excavated at its base. (Courtesy: Rhett Austell; Lehnert & Landrock, Cairo.)

(now reconstructed and in Cairo) represents the only major find of such articles from the Old Kingdom.

Another major discovery was made close to the south side of the pyramid in 1954—a perfectly preserved boat, probably used to carry Khufu on his last journey, dismantled into 1,224 pieces and sealed in a pit under 41 huge stones. After years of patient reassembly, the boat, 142 ft. long, now rests in its own special museum on the pit site—closed to all but specialists. Another boat pit lies near it. In 1987 it was examined by remote means and found to be rather decayed; hence it was left alone, unexcavated.

The Pyramid of Khephren or Khafre, Khufu's son, is about as tall as the Great Pyramid, but measures only under 700 ft. on a side. At its cap much of the Tura limestone facing is preserved, and two entrances pierce the north face. Its mortuary temple under the pyramid is reasonably well preserved, and the 500-ft.-long causeway leads down to the impressive valley temple—square, with two entrances and a pillared hall, largely unadorned but with door frames and columns of polished granite. Both temples held many fine statues of the king, the best of them now in Cairo. His face may also adorn the Great Sphinx near his valley temple. In front of this famous but enigmatic monument, 240 ft. long, the remains of a Fourth Dynasty temple with a vast pillared courtyard has been excavated. Another temple was erected nearby when the site became a place of worship in the New Kingdom. Among the stelae here is one of Tuthmosis III between the Great Sphinx's paws, commemorating an early clearance of the sand around the monument—the first of many.

The third pyramid, that of Menkaure, or Mycerinus, son of Khephren, is far smaller (originally 218 ft. high) and had two interior corridors and burial chambers, and three small pyramids on its eastern side. The basalt sarcophagus found in the lower chamber was lost at sea while on its way to England. Evidence shows that the pyramid was refurbished, probably in the Late Dynastic Period when the cult of the Giza kings was revived. Menkaure's two temples were made of mud brick, but the remains did yield a remarkably fine collection of royal sculpture, now in Cairo. Southeast of the pyramids, in the former quarries, are many rock-cut tombs, the earliest in Egypt, now mostly closed to the public. The Great Pyramids not only have a sound-and-light show (reported to be excellent) but also a museum at the foot of the Great Pyramid. South of Giza, at Zawyet el-Aryan, are the scanty remains of two uncompleted pyramids of the Third and Fourth dynasties.

Saqqara   The large central area of the Memphis necropolis, 17 mi. S. of Cairo, extending over 4 mi. N. and S. opposite Memphis itself. The site is dominated by the great Step Pyramid of King Djoser, probably the second king of the Third Dynasty. This admirable and revolutionary structure, rising in six steps within its vast enclosure, dates from after 2630 BC, and is the earliest major stone monument in the world and the first of Egypt's pyramids. According to Manetho, the 3rd cent. BC historian of Egypt, it had been built some 2,400 years earlier for his king by Djoser's prime minister, Imhotep, a genius so renowned that in later centuries he was worshiped as a god. During the 1920s excavations Imhotep's name was in fact found in the Step Pyramid enclosure, thus confirming Manetho. It was Imhotep then who was largely responsible for the coming of age of Egyptian civilization as celebrated in this monument, which set a style for the future. But it also looked to the past, for its severe and elegant architecture, lovingly restored today by the French archaeologist Jean-Philippe Lauer, reproduces in stone the mud brick recessed walls, the reed columns, the wooden roof beams and door frames of earlier structures. Investigations have shown, moreover, that the pyramid was begun as a traditional mastaba tomb, then went through six building stages, the daring last two turning it into the first step pyramid, of four then of six steps, like a series of mastaba tombs piled on top of each other. Thus most later true pyramids contain a step pyramid as the inner core. The Step Pyramid was originally about 200 ft. high and was finished in Tura limestone.

The Step Pyramid of King Djoser of the Third Dynasty at Saqqara, Egypt's earliest pyramid and still an impressive tribute to its builder, Imhotep, the brilliant prime minister. It started as a low mastaba, then went through six building stages to emerge as the first step pyramid. Surrounded by a huge enclosure of ritual buildings, the pyramid complex was the first to be built entirely in stone, and reflects the newfound glory of Egypt's first coming of age. (Courtesy: Lehnert & Landrock, Cairo.)

The walls of the huge enclosure, over 1,640 ft. long, are still 15 ft. high in places, imitating in Tura limestone the recessed mud-brick walls of towns and palaces, with over 200 bastions and 14 imitation doors. The actual covered entrance on the southeast leads through interesting colonnades into the Great South Court facing the pyramid on the north. The buildings within, devoted to the well-being of the king in the hereafter and to his cult, include another court with empty mock-ups of the special buildings used for the *sed* festival, the periodic rejuvenation of the king through a curious ritual foot-race (two blocks in the Great Court probably mark the course of his sprint); also his mortuary temple north of the pyramid; and a full-scale tomb complex at the bottom of a 90-ft. shaft next to the southern enclosure wall. Here were found a maze of chambers with delicate reliefs, including one of Djoser running the *sed* race. Under the pyramid itself was a similar tomb complex, again with a deep shaft and corridors and chambers, long ago robbed, in which were found many precious alabaster vases, but no bones or grave goods. It cannot now be entered. The reason for having two tombs is not known. Queens and princes were also buried under the pyramid. Next to the mortuary temple an Archaic statue of the king, earliest of a long line of royal statues, was found in his *serdab*, or private statue room. It is now in Cairo, though a copy now stands in its place. So venerated was this earliest pyramid complex that 14 centuries later Egyptians of the Nineteenth Dynasty scratched their admiration for it on its walls, and the Twenty-sixth Dynasty pharaohs tried to restore it, sinking a new shaft into the pyramid.

Altogether, 15 royal pyramids are known in the Saqqara necropolis, around and south of the Step Pyramid, as well as hundreds of mastabas, other tombs, temples and other structures. Only a fraction of the site has been scientifically excavated, although much earlier digging and looting took place. There are monuments and tombs here from every period of Egyptian history, though most date from the Old Kingdom. As late as 1950 the remains of another unfinished step pyramid inside a huge enclosure were found under the sands southwest of the first step pyramid. It belonged to Djoser's successor, Sekhemhet, and in the usual maze of corridors beneath the pyramid foundations more stone vessels were found and an empty alabaster sarcophagus in the burial chamber. West of this, aerial photographs have disclosed another, even larger, enclosure, so far unexcavated, and possibly still another one nearby. They probably belonged to the Third Dynasty.

Of the other pyramids here, little is left of that of Userkaf, first king of the Fifth Dynasty (about 2460 BC), just northeast of the Step Pyramid enclosure. The pyramid of Wenis, or Unas, last king of the dynasty, is more interesting. Just southwest of the enclosure, it contains within it the first example of the magical Pyramid Texts designed to further the ruler's immortality, and along the walls of its causeway leading from the much-ruined mortuary temple to the valley temple a few interesting reliefs survive showing boats transporting architectural blocks from *Aswan* to the pyramid. The pyramid of Teti, founder of the Sixth Dynasty (about 2320 BC) well to the northeast is poorly preserved, but around it—as with all the pyramids—are many mastabas of the nobles of his court; and these are the largest in the necropolis. Notable is that of the vizier Mereruka, with 30 rooms decorated with interesting reliefs of daily life. More reliefs are found in the mastaba of Kagemni. Just east of Teti's pyramid, an unexcavated pyramid probably belongs to Merykare of the Ninth-Tenth (Herakleopolitan) dynasties.

The numerous private tombs at Saqqara represent at least all the first ten dynasties of Egyptian history. The earliest are the large mud brick mastabas of the First Dynasty, perhaps the earliest monumental buildings in the world, heavy structures with the burial chamber and subsidiary rooms sunk into the ground, with a brick superstructure with many storerooms above it. Much of interest has been found in these storerooms—copper objects and a great many assorted stone vessels. In the last years of the dynasty they were given staircases and a rudimentary small mortuary temple—the prototype of the later pyramid complex. They lie along the eastern edge of the Saqqara plateau. Much damaged, they were excavated by W. B. Emery from 1936 to 1956. Some may have been royal tombs or royal cenotaphs (see *Abydos*), the earliest dated to the time of King Aha, but they were more likely the tombs of Memphis notables. Behind them to the west are tombs of the Second and Third dynasties, and rock-cut gallery tombs of the Second Dynasty have been found under and near the pyramid of Wenis. These may well have been royal tombs.

A necropolis of the Third to Fifth dynasties, excavated long ago and the tombs now sanded up, lies to the north of the Step Pyramid. To the west of this is the notable Fifth Dynasty mastaba of Ti (or Ty) containing exceptional painted reliefs and a cast of the owner's statue as found in his serdab. Considerably to the south is another important Fifth Dynasty mastaba, that of Akhtihotpe and Ptahhotpe. Some 250 more Old Kingdom tombs, both rock-cut and mastabas, lie along the causeway of the pyramid of Wenis. Among them are the mastaba of Nebet, a queen of Wenis, and the Sixth Dynasty mastabas of Idut, a royal princess, and of the vizier Mehu. Others nearby contain lively paintings, including the "tomb of the birds," the rock-cut "butcher's tomb" and the tombs of the chiefs of the court singers and chiefs of the court manicurists. From the Old Kingdom mastabas have come famous statues—the *Sheik el- Beled*, (Egyptian

There are many private tombs at Saqqara, mostly large squat mastabas, some dating from the earliest dynasties of Egypt. Saqqara is only one part of the vast necropolis of Memphis. The pleasing relief shown here, of herded steers and a gaggle of very typical geese in a rural setting, comes from the notable Fifth Dynasty mastaba tomb of Ptahhotpe and Akhtihotpe. Delicately carved panels like this were fashioned to accompany Ptahhotpe, a necropolis official, to remind him after his death of the peaceful rural scenes he cherished in life. (Courtesy: Lehnert & Landrock, Cairo.)

Museum, Cairo) and other wooden statues, the Fifth-Dynasty Seated Scribe (Louvre, Paris), the statue of Ranofre (Cairo) and others.

Memphis was again the administrative capital of Egypt in the late Eighteenth and early Nineteenth dynasties (with Thebes as religious center), consequently the almost total lack of New Kingdom standing monuments at Saqqara is puzzling. Presumably the tombs of the Memphis officials and priests, many of them rock-cut, have been destroyed or now lie beneath the sands. A joint British-Dutch expedition began the search in 1975 and immediately discovered, south of the Wenis causeway, the magnificent tomb of Horemheb, the great army commander, the power behind the throne during the brief reign of young Tutankhamun, and himself pharaoh from 1335 to about 1308 BC. His royal tomb is at *Thebes*; this tomb was prepared for him before he became king. Samples of its fine reliefs, found earlier, were known in various museums. The tomb, of plastered mud brick and limestone slabs in the interior, consisted of a series of open and colonnaded courts, a statue room, others for offerings, a three-chapel sanctuary and the burial chambers below. The magnificent painted reliefs, in the free realistic style inherited from the recent *Amarna* period—depicting, most unusually, actual campaigns and incidents in the commander's life—form a high point in Egyptian art. Other New Kingdom tombs are now beginning to come to light.

At the western edge of the plateau is the curious Serapeum, underground burial galleries for the sacred Apis bulls from the Temple of Ptah at *Memphis*, excavated by Auguste Mariette in the 1850s. From the time of Amenhotep III (1391–1353 BC) the Apis bulls—one about every 14 years—were buried at Saqqara. About 100 years later Ramesses II began the first gallery (the "Lesser Vaults"). Another gallery at right angles was added much later under Psammetichus I of the Twenty-Sixth Dynasty (the "Greater Vaults"). These still contain 24 massive bull sarcophagi of polished granite, but no carcass remains. The galleries were used into the Ptolemaic period. Above ground little remains of the various temples and an avenue of sphinxes (Thirtieth Dynasty) leading to Memphis, with Ptolemaic temples at the end and a small temple of Nectanebo II along the route. At its west end, near the Rest House, is a curious semicircle of statues of Greek philosophers, erected by Ptolemy I. Here, too, were burial grounds of sacred cows, falcons, baboons and ibises, as well as jackals and cats from the late Dynastic Period, excavated since 1964. Late Period and Greco-Roman tombs, some rock-cut, have been found near the Step Pyramid enclosure, along the avenue of sphinxes and elsewhere. An intrusive ruin at Saqqara is that of the 5th cent. AD Monastery of St. Jeremiah, east of the Tomb of Horemheb. It was destroyed by the Arabs in the 10th cent. AD.

Eight pyramids are known in the southern part of the Saqqara necropolis, the largest number dating from the Sixth Dynasty. The most unusual, far to the south, is that of Shepseskaf, last king of the Fourth Dynasty (about 2460 BC), a highly unusual mastaba-like structure built of huge blocks in the shape of an enormous sarcophagus. Its mortuary temple is much ruined. The pyramid of Djedkare Izezi of the Fifth Dynasty still stands some 80 ft. high. Latest of the Old Kingdom funerary complexes is that of Pepy II, last important king of the Sixth Dynasty, who ruled some 94 years. There is a pyramid, mortuary and valley temples connected by a causeway, a satellite pyramid, and three small pyramids for his queens. Little is left of the other Sixth Dynasty pyramids of Pepy I and Merenre, or of the little-known Ibi of the Eighth Dynasty. The two southernmost pyramids, of mud brick, belonged to Khendjer (or Usarkare) of the Thirteenth Dynasty, and an unknown king of the same dynasty.

MENDES

Greek name for two large tells, or mounds, a few mi. apart in the central Nile delta, around 13 mi. SE of Mansura. They were in succession the capital of the 16th nome (province) of Lower Egypt. The northern one, Tell el-Rub'a, was ancient Mendes proper, center of a ram god cult. Sarcophagi of the sacred rams have been found here. The earliest remains of ancient Mendes are those of late Old Kingdom mastaba tombs. There are indications of Ramessid monuments, though none has been found. The high point of Mendes was in the Late Dynastic Period, however, and the site is dominated by a huge naos (a shrine for divine statues) of red granite built by Amasis of the Late Period Twenty-sixth Dynasty (6th cent. BC), and some walls of his temple survive. Later, Mendes may have been the capital of the twenty-ninth dynasty (4th cent. BC), whose rulers probably came from there.

The southern mound, Tell el-Timai, the ancient Thmuis, succeeded Mendes in the Greco-Roman Period. Fragmentary brick remains of the Hellenistic-Roman city, including houses, shops, public buildings and industrial areas have been found. Both tells were excavated in the 1960s and 1970s by the Institute of Fine Arts of New York University.

MERIMDE

Large Neolithic site in the western delta, 37 mi. NW of Cairo. Covering 44 acres, it was excavated by the Vienna Academy of Sciences from 1928 to 1938. Some confusion in their reading of the stratigraphy has reduced the value of the findings. Merimde seems, however, to be the earliest large farming village in Lower Egypt, settled first about 4880 BC and occupied in three phases for some 650 years. A median date might be 4180 BC. The rounded houses, more substantial in later phases, were built of mud, posts and wickerwork with reed fences, like those of Omari A (see *Helwan*). Leg bones of hippopotamuses were used as doorsteps. The dead were buried under the houses, with few grave goods. The people ate emmer wheat, vetch, pigs, cattle, sheep and fish, and hearths, grinding stones, baskets for storing grain, and sunken water jars have been found. The tools and implements were of stone, bone, ivory and horn, and huge quantities of plain handmade pottery, mostly straw-tempered, were excavated. See also *Badari*, *Deir Tasa*, *Faiyum*, *Helwan*, *Hemamieh*.

MIT RAHINA

See *Memphis*.

MONS CLAUDIANUS, MONS HADRIANUS

See *Gebel Dukhan*.

NADURA

See *Kharga Oasis*.

NAG EL-MADAMUD

See *Medamud*.

NAG HAMMADI

Town in Upper Egypt, about 20 mi. W. of Qena on the Nile at the western base of its great bend. It lies close to the Jebel el-Tarif, a mountain pierced by over 150 caves. Some of the caves were shaped and painted to serve as tombs during the very early Sixth Dynasty. Here, in December 1945, a peasant made by chance one of the most unusual and important discoveries in the history of Egyptian archaeology, the Nag Hammadi papyri. He and his brother were digging in the mountainside for the rich soil they used to fertilize their crops when one of them unearthed an earthenware jar, which they smashed, hoping it might contain gold. Instead it spilled out 13 papyrus books bound in leather, apparently hidden, as the scholars later presumed, by some monk in the 4th cent. AD at a time when the "true church" was intent upon destroying all heretical Christian books. He may have come from the nearby monastery of St. Pachomius. For almost all the texts, written in Coptic, the language of the Christian Egyptians, were concerned with Gnosticism, a widespread "heretical" sect of early Christianity. Gnosticism eventually lost out to the "orthodox" form of Christianity, which formulated the canon of the present New Testament.

When the peasants brought the books home their mother burned some of the loose papyri to fuel her oven, but the remaining books contained an astonishing 53 texts from the earliest years of Christianity, including the Gnostic Gospel of Thomas, other secret gospels, cosmologies, myths, poems and magic. The

Gnostic writings embodied an "inward-looking" mystical early type of Christianity (possibly with some Buddhist influence, for Buddhists were proselytizing in Alexandria at the time) certainly very different from the Christianity that finally prevailed and which we know today.

The rest of the story has to do with black market machinations and academic jealousies so that, unlike the Dead Sea Scrolls (see *Qumran* in ISRAEL), the translated texts of the papyri were not available to all until the 1970s. Since then there have been well over 4,000 publications concerned with these books, for they have literally created a revolution in our conception of early Christianity. Once the primitive church was conceived as a simple, pure form of the faith, but it is now seen as a period of extremely diverse teachings, much like the Protestant sects after the Reformation, all of them considered legitimate in their time—at least in their own eyes. The Coptic papyri were of course written in the 4th cent. AD, but a study of these Gnostic texts indicated that they were translations of earlier Greek texts, compiled in the 2nd cent. AD but probably containing "lost" Christian traditions possibly *older* even than the accepted date of the composition of the four canonical gospels of the New Testament (about 60 to 110 AD). The discovery of these remarkable writings by ignorant peasants in 1945 might be said to surpass, in scholarly importance at least, the famous opening of King Tutankhamun's tomb with all its treasures by Howard Carter in 1922.

NAQADA

Extensive Predynastic cemetery on the W. bank of the Nile, about halfway between *Dendera* to the N. and *Thebes* to the S., excavated by Petrie in 1895. The name of the village, about 5 mi. to the S., has been used to identify the two latest Predynastic cultures of Egypt: Naqada I (4000–3500 BC), a simple village culture also called the Amratian (see *Amra, el-*) and Naqada II (about 3500–3100 BC) also called Gerzean (see *Girza*). The two cultures are now seen as a continuous development, though in Naqada II there was a pronounced quickening of pace, probably owing to increased influences from Asia through trade and cultural interaction across the *Wadi Hammamat* route east of the Nile to the Red Sea. This may have contributed to the political unification of Egypt in the late Naqada II/Early Dynastic Period at the beginning of "history," about 3100 BC.

Petrie uncovered 2,149 graves here in a 17-acre area, the burials in rectangular pits once covered by a roof of branches and a mound of earth. The grave goods, even in the first period, were extensive, including beautifully worked flints, the increasing use of copper and some gold and silver, green slate grinding palettes with pigment stones, ornaments of imported shell and stone, finely crafted stone vessels, carved ivory plaques, clay figurines (with the first use of faience), and a variety of well-fashioned handmade polished red ware with animal and plant designs in white, and later a buff or gray with elaborate designs in red, including ships and hunting scenes. In the area Early Dynastic artifacts have also been found, and De Morgan in 1897 excavated a large Early Dynastic mastaba tomb, built in the times of King Aha, with an elaborate "palace" facade and many rooms inside. See also *Helwan; Hierakonpolis.*

NAUKRATIS

Greek trading town on Egyptian soil, in the delta on the W. (Canopus) branch of the Nile, about 50 mi. SE of Alexandria and 50 mi. from the sea. Founded in the late 7th cent. BC, Naukratis was largely populated by Greeks from Asia Minor and the eastern Aegean islands of Chios, Teos, Rhodes, Samos and Lesbos, as well as Aegina, the island off Attica. Much Athenian, Corinthian and Spartan pottery has been found here too, perhaps indicating a trading interest. The Greeks traded olive oil, wine and silver for Egyptian products, principally grain (in short supply in Greece). Under King Amasis of Egypt in the 6th cent. BC the town was given a monopoly of trade with Egypt. Naukratis was thus not a colony but a mercantile outpost of the Greek world in an ancient land, traditionally suspicious of foreigners, and as such it interested Greek poets, statesmen and historians such as Herodotus, who visited and wrote about it. The arts and ideas of ancient Egypt also penetrated the Greek world through Naukratis. A typical merchant who traded through Naukratis was a wine dealer from Samos, brother of the famous poetess Sappho. The town was somewhat eclipsed after the founding of Alexandria in the 4th cent., but did survive through the Ptolemaic and into the Roman Period.

An overgrown mound called Kom Qi'eif a few mi. from el-Niqrash now covers the site, and there is little to see. Naukratis was excavated by Petrie (1884–85), Gardner and Hogarth (1899 and 1903), revealing the foundations of Greek temples of Aphrodite, Hera, Apollo and the Dioscuri, a possible warehouse, a small faience scarab factory ("good luck" charms sold in Egypt and Greece), and the large Hellenion, mentioned by Herodotus, a sanctuary and administrative headquarters shared by the principal founding Greek states. There was also an Egyptian temple, probably of Amun and Thoth. American teams from the universities of Minnesota and Missouri began renewed excavations in the 1980s, investigating the Hellenistic and Roman periods at Naukratis.

NEKHEB   See *Kab, El-*

NEKHEN   See *Hierakonpolis.*

OMARI, EL-   See *Helwan.*

OXYRHYNCHUS   Once a flourishing Greek town in the Roman and Byzantine periods and a Coptic center, now the town of El-Bahnasa, about 125 mi. S. of Cairo on the W. bank of the Nile. It was the site of an early and major find of papyri in 1895—incredible quantities of papyrus rolls and fragments preserved in the dry air of Egypt—by two young Oxford dons. The finds dated from about 250 BC to 700 AD, though most were from the Roman Period. They consisted of discarded documents of all kinds, including literature, letters, accounts, contracts, tax receipts, census records and religious and magical texts, throwing a flood of light on every detail of daily existence, law, government, the economy, society and beliefs of people in all walks of life. They were written in Latin, Greek, Egyptian, Coptic, Hebrew and Syriac and included the earliest copy of the New Testament Gospels (about 100 AD), many works of Classical writers presumed lost (Pindar, Menander, Callimachus), as well as parts of ancient histories, and many papyri of Homer. Their continuing publication by expert papyrologists, with those of other, more recent papyrus finds, have vastly enriched our knowledge of the ancient world. See also *Nag Hammadi.*

PHILAE   Romantic island sanctuary of Isis and other gods at the first cataract of the Nile, between the old Aswan dam to the N. and the High Dam, about 5 mi. S. of *Aswan.* Philae was a favorite tourist attraction during the 19th cent. until the

The kiosk of Trajan on the romantic island of Philae in the Nile, near Aswan, with its lovely floral capitals. It served as an ornate river gateway to the Temple of Isis, goal of the yearly festival of Isis, which continued, unbelievably, into the 6th century AD. The small temple was approached by the pilgrims from the end of the island along a series of colonnades. The buildings on the island, mostly Ptolemaic and Roman, like the temples of Dendera and Edfu, were removed stone by stone between 1972 and 1980 to a nearby island to escape the rising waters of the Aswan High Dam. (Courtesy: Lehnert & Landrock, Cairo.)

building of the earlier dam at the turn of the century inundated it for most of the year. After the building of the High Dam the island was surrounded by a coffer dam in 1972 and the ancient buildings removed block by block to a nearby, higher island shaped to resemble the original long narrow island. The job was completed in 1980. The earliest standing work here is by Nectanebo I of the Thirtieth Dynasty (4th cent. BC) but most structures date from Ptolemaic and Roman times (though built in the Egyptian manner) when pilgrims flocked to Philae for the festival of Isis. Surprisingly, the Isis cult was celebrated at Philae right up into the 6th cent. AD, although there were two Christian churches of the 4th cent. AD on the north of the island. Apparently Christian and pagan coexisted happily together here for centuries.

Pilgrims landed at the southern end of the island, near the small columned hall of Nectanebo, proceeded north between two late colonnades, the western with 31 columns, the eastern one shorter—it was never completed—then up to the massive first pylon (60 ft. high). In front of it a gate of Ptolemy Philadelphus led east to the elegant small kiosk of Trajan, with its lovely floral capitals. Moving north again through the first pylon one entered a court, flanked by an oddly placed birth house on the left and a colonnade and rooms on the right, to face the second pylon. Placed on a different axis to conform to the shape of the island, this led into the temple of Isis proper, rather small. In the hypostle hall the paint on the capitals of the ten columns may still be seen. There are several Osiris shrines on the roof. A landing stage west and below the temple led up to the monumental Hadrian's Gate. Far to the northeast lay the Gate of Domitian, beyond the two churches and near a temple of Augustus. There is a small temple of Hathor, known for its reliefs of musicians, just east of the temple, a ruined temple of Horus west of it, and three small temples lay along the eastern entrance colonnade, two dedicated to Nubian gods and a third to Imhotep, deified vizier of the Fourth Dynasty thousands of years earlier (see *Memphis*: Saqqara). Needless to say all the temples are covered with the usual reliefs. An obelisk, now in England, once stood before the first pylon. It played an important part in the eventual decipherment of Egyptian hieroglyphics (see *Rosetta*).

PI-RAMESSE

See *Qantir, Tanis*.

EL-QALA

See *Qift*.

QANTIR

A village in the NE delta which, with El-Khatana and the tell or mound of El-Daba (all a few mi. N. of Faqus), lies in an area rich with puzzling remains. The largest site of the region is *Tanis* (San el-Hagar) about 11 mi. to the north. In most cases the ruins include stone elements robbed from other, earlier sites making identification difficult, for stone was a scarce item in the delta. Somewhere in the region were the Hyksos capital of Avaris, and the Nineteenth Dynasty Ramessid capital of Pi-Ramesse (Per-Ramses, or "House of Ramses"), a royal capital and residence often identified with the "place of afflictions" suffered by the Children of Israel in the biblical Exodus story. Modern opinion places Avaris at Tell el-Daba, and Pi-Ramesse near Qantir. At Tell el-Daba, for instance, there was evidence of occupation by Asiatics (i.e., Hyksos) during the Second Intermediate Period, as well as material from the twelfth and thirteenth dynasties of an earlier period and the remains of a large Ramessid temple from the succeeding period. Near Qantir the remains of a palace of the Nineteenth and Twentieth dynasties, of houses, stelae and other finds were uncovered, which were probably from Pi-Ramesse. In the palace foundations quantities of faience tiles in blue and polychrome, with designs from nature, were found as well as the faience factory where they were produced. And some of these tiles bore the names of Seti I and his son Ramesses II, while on some ostraca from the site the name "Per-Ramses Meriamum" was inscribed in hieratic. Incidentally, Pi-Ramesse was described by a contemporary poet as "beauteous with balconies and dazzling halls of lapis lazuli and turquoise . . .".

QASR, EL-

See *Bahriya Oasis*.

QASR IBRIM

A fortress and important civil and religious center of Lower Nubia from New Kingdom times into the 19th cent. AD. Once a walled citadel and town on a high bluff, it is now an offshore island across from *Abu Simbel* in the new manmade Lake Nasser, the only Nubian site still open for investigation after the flooding of the area by the Aswan High Dam. Excavations began in 1963 and still continue. The site is largely covered by the ruined houses of a Turkish (Bosnian) garrison, which occupied it from 1517 to 1812, leaving, it is said, blue eyes and blondish hair among the local inhabitants. Dominating it is the shell of a fine cathedral, originally built about 700 AD, later enlarged, then converted to a mosque in the 12th cent. AD. The remains of Bishop Timothy, consecrated in Cairo in 1371, were uncovered in its crypt in 1964. Approached by monumental steps, the cathedral had two aisles, granite columns and a semicircular apse.

Another church here was originally a temple, apparently built by Taharqa of the Twenty-fifth Dynasty (7th cent. BC) from which four columns and a damaged wall painting survive. In its earlier period Qasr Ibrim was mostly occupied by the Meroitic kingdom (about 300 BC to 320 AD), from which a massive structure, apparently a tavern, survives as well as a small temple, now inundated. The tavern lasted well into the succeeding so-called X-group period (350–500 AD) when the town prospered. Thereafter Nubia, and Qasr Ibrim, became Christian after 641 AD and remained so for some 700 years, despite the Arabic occupation of Egypt.

Remarkable finds of papyrus documents, preserved in the dry air, have been made at Qasr Ibrim, including a magnificent large Arabic scroll of the 8th cent. AD discussing the treaty between Muslim Egypt and Christian Nubia signed 100 years earlier. There were also Coptic letters addressed to a governor of Nubia and above all a copy of elegiac couplets by Cornelius Gallus, a soldier, famous poet and friend of Virgil and governor of Egypt under Augustus. Previously only one line of his verse was known. Gallus was born in Fréjus in southern France and as a soldier in Augustus' occupation of Egypt captured the notorious Cleopatra after the Battle of Actium. He was responsible for setting up an obelisk in Alexandria, now in St. Peter's Square in Rome. As governor, while Augustus was ruthlessly establishing the Roman Empire, he fell into disgrace and committed suicide in 26 BC. The papyrus was part of a book that may have come to Qasr Ibrim with the Roman soldiers who briefly occupied the fortress.

QASR QARUN

Near the western end of Lake Qarun in the *Faiyum*, a late Ptolemaic temple and town and a late Roman fortress. The well-preserved temple, once on the lake shore, was dedicated to Sobek, the crocodile god. It is a simple rectangular structure of two stories enclosing a sanctuary, with underground crypts. A sacred way, partly lined with the remains of townhouses, leads some 330 yds. to a kiosk. Near the latter is a small Roman mausoleum. A Roman fortress, built under Diocletian (4th cent. AD) stands northwest of the temple. Rectangular, built of brick, it has large towers at each corner and smaller ones in between. Inside it one can discern the outlines of the *principia* building and traces of other structures.

QIFT

A very ancient city, called Gibtu in Egyptian and Koptos in Greek, on the E. bank of the Nile, 13 mi. S. of Qena, with remains dating from all periods of ancient Egyptian history. Its situation at the western end of the caravan route and mining areas of *Wadi Hammamat* leading to the Red Sea made it one of the important early centers of Upper Egypt in the Predynastic (see *Naqada*) and Dynastic periods. It became the chief town of the 5th nome (province) of Upper Egypt and a cult center of the god Min, who was later joined by Isis and Osiris. The standing ruins, however, date only from the Late Dynastic and Greco-Roman periods. Excavated by Petrie (1893–94) and Weill and Reinach (1910 and 1911), materials from the Early Dynastic Period were turned up, but chiefly an enclosure area with three main temple groups, including a temple of Min and Isis, built in Ptolemaic times with Roman additions (by Caligula and Nero). It stood on the site of earlier temples of the Middle Kingdom and particularly of Tuthmosis III of the New Kingdom. Another Ptolemaic-Roman temple also had remnants of buildings of the Middle and New Kingdoms and the Twenty-second Dynasty, as well as a set of stelae with temple inscriptions from the Sixth and

Seventh Dynasties of the Old Kingdom. The relics of the third temple complex included a chapel of Cleopatra VII and gates from the Thirtieth Dynasty and the reigns of Claudius and Caligula. A small temple of Min, Isis and Horus northeast of the site, at El-Qala, also dates from the reign of Claudius.

QURNEH	See *Thebes*.
QUSTU	A Nubian site now under Lake Nasser. It was on the E. bank of the Nile below *Abu Simbel*, about 150 mi. S. of Aswan near the present Sudan border. Excavated in a rescue operation in the 1960s, it yielded a number of cemeteries of the New Kingdom and A-group period of Nubian archaeology as well as A-group tombs of Nubian kings of the 4th to 6th cents. AD. But the most important find was an early Predynastic royal cemetery, dating from about 3300 BC, of the kingdom of Ta-Seti ("Land of the Bow"), which revealed artifacts of Pharaonic-level civilization in the area some 200 years before the unification of Egypt under the First Dynasty. Although long ago plundered, 33 large tombs here still yielded around 1,000 painted vases, or fragments thereof, with geometric or linear patterns or stamped and incised decoration, over 100 stone vessels, palettes, ornaments and, of particular importance, incense burners of stone or a clay mixture, some incised with the *serekh*, a paneled palace facade, later a symbol of Egyptian royalty. One burner showed a royal sacrificial procession of three ships moving towards a *serekh*.
RAMESSEUM	See *Thebes*.
ROSETTA	Or Rashid in Arabic, town on the Rosetta branch of the Nile in the delta. Near here, in 1799, the famous Rosetta Stone, key to the decipherment of hieroglyphics, was unearthed while one of Napoleon's engineers was working on an extension to Fort St.-Julien. A bilingual inscription on black basalt, it recorded a public decree of 190 BC by Ptolemy V Epiphanes, inscribed in Egyptian hieroglyphics, in late Egyptian demotic (a cursive script), and in Greek. When Napoleon was driven from Egypt the stone fell to the British victors, who shipped it home in 1802. It is now in the British Museum. Working with a cast from the stone a Frenchman, Jean-François Champollion, succeeded in deciphering the hieroglyphics in 1822–24. His had been a lifetime passion. He knew many languages and learned Coptic (in which some of the ancient Egyptian words are still to be found) for the purpose. His achievement effectively opened up the field of Egyptology and added thousands of years to known history. A cast of the stone is in the Greco-Roman Museum in Alexandria.
RUB'A, TELL EL-	See *Mendes*.
SA EL-HAGAR	See *Sais*.
SAINT CATHERINE'S MONASTERY	Famous monastery in the wilderness, high up in the jagged red mountains of the desolate southern Sinai, built on the traditional site of Moses' burning bush. In the 3rd cent. AD the area became a refuge for persecuted Christians and hermits. By the 6th cent. when some 300 hermits, constantly menaced by the local tribesmen, were living on the mountain, the emperor Justinian built them the present monastery, tightly enclosed within massive walls, and sent a group

of his Slav Wallachian subjects to protect them. Today the local Jebaliya bedouin who, according to local tradition, are descended from the Wallachians, are still friendly with the monks.

A maze of narrow alleys lined with houses and chapels fills the interior of the monastery, whose chief feature is the ancient basilica, begun in 542 AD, with ancient doors of Lebanese cedar and an interior decorated with marble and porphyry, mother of pearl and gilding, icons, hanging lamps, and murals and mosaics. In the apse is a rare 6th-cent. mosaic of the Transfiguration (now difficult to see) that escaped, together with many early icons in the library, the destructive iconoclastic movement of succeeding centuries. Behind it is the Chapel of the Burning Bush and some relics of Saint Catherine, a 4th-cent. martyr. The basilica's recent bell tower (1871) overtops the minaret of a small mosque, now little used, built, it is said, in the 11th cent. to placate hostile Arabs. It has a minbar dating from 1106. Other points of interest are the old refectory, the charnel house with bones and skulls of former monks, and the library and icon gallery containing a priceless collection, one of the richest in the world, of books, illuminated manuscripts and icons well preserved in the dry air.

A few of the 5,000 items in the library are on display and 150 of the icons. Here in 1844 was found the famous Codex Sinaiticus, one of the earliest Greek manuscripts of the Bible (4th cent. AD), now in the British Museum, London. Mt. Sinai (Gebel Musa), where according to tradition Moses received the 10 Commandments, looms behind the monastery. It may be ascended by 3,750 huge steps, painfully hewn into the mountainside centuries ago by early monks. A visit to the monastery must be arranged in advance.

SAINT MACARIUS	See *Wadi Natrun*.
SAINT MENAS	See *Deir abu Menas*.
SAINT SIMEON	See *Aswan*.
SAIS	Capital of Egypt during the Twenty-sixth (Saite) Dynasty (7th–6th cents. BC), capital of the 5th nome (province) of Lower Egypt and cult center of the goddess Neith. Remarkably, nothing is left of the palaces, temples and tombs of the famous city in the western delta. Its site is on the east bank of the Nile's Rosetta branch, near the village of Sa el-Hagar. Although many objects from Sais are known from museums—almost all of them from the Twenty-sixth Dynasty—the site itself has not been systematically explored.
SAQQARA	See *Memphis*.
SERABIT EL-KHADIM	Principal site of Egyptian turquoise mining in the Sinai, with the remains of a temple of Hathor, on a desolate high plateau difficult of access. Mining here is attested from the Twelfth Dynasty through the New Kingdom, but no later. The earliest mining site in the Sinai is at Wadi Maghara, where rock inscriptions and reliefs from the Third Dynasty kings Zanakht, Djoser and Sekhemkhet have been found, as well as others from the Fifth Dynasty and a few from the New Kingdom. Recently a third center of turquoise mining has been located at Wadi Kharit with an inscription by Sahure of the Fifth Dynasty and a stela of Senwosret I of the Twelfth Dynasty. At Serabit el-Khadim the oldest part of the temple

of Hathor is a rock-cut cave entered through a court and portico, dating from the Twelfth Dynasty. In the New Kingdom the temple was enlarged with a pylon and 12 rooms, and a shrine of the god Sopd was built to the south. Along an avenue approaching the temple and in the temple itself are many commemorative stelae dating from the Twelfth through Twentieth dynasties.

SHEIKH'ABD EL-QURNEH   See *Thebes*.

SHEIKH 'IBADA, EL-   The Hellenized city of Antinoopolis, or Antinoë, founded by Hadrian in 130 AD in memory of his young male favorite, Antinous, who drowned himself in the Nile here. It lies on the east bank, about 5 mi. NE of *Hermopolis* across on the western side of the Nile. As late as the 19th cent. many temples, a theater, an arch, two streets, and an ampitheater and hippodrome were still discernible, but the site was recently despoiled to build new sugar factories and now little remains above ground. Excavations in the necropolis yielded many fine colored Coptic textiles, now in various museums. Remains from the earlier Egyptian settlement of Besa here include the remnants of a large temple of Amun, built by Ramesses II.

SILSILA   See *Gebel Silsila*.

SIWA OASIS   Westernmost of the oases in the Libyan desert, only 15 mi. from the present Libyan border. An enigmatic and picturesque area of eroded bluffs, springs and ponds, groves of date palms and olive trees, it is difficult of access; the 480-mi. trip from Alexandria must be made in convoy. Indeed in 525 BC the Persian conqueror of Egypt, Cambyses, led a disastrous expedition to Siwa, losing his army in the hostile desert (its armor and physical remains have been the object of continuing search). Siwa was incorporated into Egypt only in the Late Dynastic Period, and here in 331 BC Alexander the Great, who delivered Egypt from the Persians, visited the oracle of Zeus-Amun at Siwa and was told he was the "son of Amun," and thus a god. The remains of what was probably the oracle and temple, founded under the Twenty-Sixth Dynasty, are on the hill of Aghurmi to the east of Siwa town—merely an Egyptian-style facade with Ptolemaic Doric half-columns, two doorways and the sanctuary. Nearby at Umm el-Ebeida are the fragmentary ruins of a temple of Amun by Nectanebo II (360–343 BC), the last native king of Egypt. See also *Bahriya Oasis, Dakhla, El-, Kharga Oasis*.

SOHAG   Modern town about 60 mi. S. of Asyut on the Nile's W. bank. Near it on the edge of the desert are two Coptic monasteries of the 5th cent. AD, the "White" and the "Red." Deir el-Abiad, built of white limestone, a few mi. W. of Sohag, has a ruined church with lovely frescoes painted by an Armenian monk in 1137 AD. Deir el-Ahmar, built of red brick, lies 3 mi. further north.

SPEOS ARTEMIDOS   See *Beni Hasan*.

TANIS   A large site, the most important in the delta, a huge 32-acre tell 17 mi. N. of Faqus in the northeastern delta, the tell of San el-Hagar excavated by Mariette (1860–80), Petrie in the 1880s, and Pierre Montet from 1929 to 1951. Tanis was founded in 1085 BC by Smendes, first king of the Twenty-first Dynasty during the Third Intermediate Period and was his capital, while the high priests of

Amun ruled at *Thebes*. It was later capital of the Twenty-second and probably the Twenty-third dynasties as well. The chief feature of the site is the huge enclosure of the Temple of Amun, its walls exceedingly thick, with another enclosure inside that. The ground here is littered with loose blocks, statues, obelisks, columns and other debris dating from the Old, Middle and New Kingdoms. But most are dated to the reign of Ramesses II, which led Montet to identify the site with Pi-Ramesse, the Ramessid capital of the biblical Exodus. But later evidence indicates that Pi-Ramesse was more likely near *Qantir* to the south, and the many Ramessid remains here, as well as the earlier ones, were moved to the site by later dynasties to be reused, the usual custom in the stoneless delta. Excavations have shown no construction under the ground here earlier than the Twenty-first Dynasty.

A monumental gateway to the enclosure by Shoshenq III of the Twenty-second Dynasty, for instance, was partly built out of reused materials, and the East Temple inside the enclosure by Osorkon III of the same dynasty used column capitals from the Old Kingdom, which had been used again by Ramesses II and finally incorporated here. Within the enclosure these were at least three smaller temples and a sacred lake, the work dating from the Twenty-first Dynasty into the Ptolemaic Period, and another precinct, of 'Anta (Mut), and a chapel of Ptolemy Philadelphus outside the enclosure.

The most important discovery, by Montet in 1939, were six royal tombs of the Twenty-first and Twenty-second dynasties (around 1000 BC) within the enclosure, the only such tombs besides that of King Tutankhamun to be found relatively undisturbed. These were underground tombs below a shaft, some of the rooms decorated with painted reliefs and inscriptions, and in some cases containing more than one royal sarcophagus. The most spectacular finds were the coffins of pink and black granite and one of solid silver, and the magnificent gold funerary mask of Psusennes I, as well as a rich collection of jewelry, now in the Egyptian Museum (Cairo). Other finds from Tanis are in the British Museum, London.

TAPOSIRIS MAGNA

Remnants of a Ptolemaic town at modern Abusir (no connection with Abusir at Memphis), about 30 mi. along the coast W. of Alexandria. Standing out here are the ruins of an unfinished Ptolemaic temple in the Egyptian style, probably dedicated to Osiris, within a limestone enclosure with an entrance gate in the form of a pylon. A large animal necropolis lay nearby. The confusing remains of the town, which was most important in Ptolemaic times, include houses, baths, a stadium and a cemetery of 40 rock-cut tombs. On the coast a restored Roman lighthouse, said to be a miniature copy of the famed Pharos at *Alexandria*, was probably one of a chain along the western coast as far as Cyrene, in Libya.

TARIF, EL-

See *Thebes* (Qurneh).

TASA

See *Deir Tasa*.

TELL EL-AMARNA

See *Amarna, Tell el-*.

THEBES

Greek name for the ancient city of Waset or Weset, in southern Egypt 450 mi. S. of *Cairo*. Thebes was the resplendent royal capital of the New Kingdom, center of the national cult of Amun, and one of the greatest cities of the civilized

Middle East in ancient times. It first came to prominence at the end of the First Intermediate Period when its princes reunited the country under the Eleventh Dynasty (about 2133–1991 BC). Later princes of Thebes drove the Asiatic Hyksos out of Egypt (about 1560 BC) to create the New Kingdom under the Eighteenth Dynasty, when Egypt became an imperial power, extending its borders west into Libya, south into Nubia and Ethiopia, and into Asian Syria east to the Euphrates. The wealth of conquest flowed into Thebes and into the coffers of its pharaohs and the priests of Amun, whose vast temples became the national shrines of all Egypt. The city itself must have extended many miles along the east side of the Nile and on the west side too, where it abutted on the great Theban necropolis, with its royal mortuary temples and Valley of the Kings and Queens. The city's palaces, mansions, residential and artisan quarters, being built of perishable materials, have disappeared. The small but growing modern city of Luxor certainly lies on the southern part of the site, which must have extended north up to and beyond Karnak.

All that are left now are the tombs and the temples, notably of course the twin shrines of Amun, the lovely temple at Luxor and the monstrous temple complex, largest in the world, of Karnak about 2 mi. to the north. Though not always the capital, Thebes remained an important city until the 12th cent. BC when decline set in with plundering of the royal tombs, famine, corruption and disunity. But the power of the priests of Amun grew and in the Third Intermediate Period (from the 11th cent. on) they actually set up a southern theocratic state in the name of their god, counterbalancing the northern state based in the delta. By the Late Dynastic Period, Theban influence was no more. The city was sacked by the Assyrians in the 7th cent. BC, suffered earthquakes and, by the time of Strabo (63 BC-21 AD), had become a mere collection of villages.

The two temples of Amun, in different godly manifestations, at Luxor and Karnak were closely united, especially by the great annual festival procession of Opet during the Nile's inundation season, when Amun traveled from Karnak to Luxor by boat to visit his other temple. The sacred bark carrying his image was accompanied by the barks of Mut and Khons, while a companion procession, with the chanting of priests, the wailing of priestesses, drums and rattles marched along the shore. In lesser processions Amun often crossed the Nile to visit the temples on the west bank.

Of the two temples, Luxor is smaller but more appealing and most unusual in its long narrow shape, fully 850 ft. long. The temple proper was basically the work of Amenhotep III of the Eighteenth Dynasty, father of Akhenaten, and the heavier, later pylon and forecourt that of Ramesses II of the Nineteenth Dynasty. The shrine was connected with Karnak by an avenue of sphinxes, added in the Late Dynastic Period, which is gradually being excavated. The large pylon, by Ramesses, its reliefs and inscriptions telling the story of the Battle of Qadesh against the Hittites, was fronted by the usual colossal statues of Ramesses, originally six of them, and two tall obelisks. One obelisk is still in place; the other is in the Place de la Concorde in Paris. Ramesses' court behind the pylon, bordered by a double rank of pillars (74) and more royal statues at the southern end, encloses an earlier small shrine of the Theban triad of Amun, Mut and Khons. A 13th-cent. mosque (Abu el-Haggag) was built onto the east side at a much higher level—for before excavation the temple was buried deep in rubble.

Moving south into the temple we come to its most impressive and earlier part, the magnificent processional colonnade of Amenhotep III, two rows of huge

Luxor, sister temple of Amun (right) at Thebes a few miles south of Karnak. The great processional colonnade of Amenhotep III, with seven huge columns on a side, centers the long narrow temple. He was the father of Akhenaten, the heretic king. Behind the colonnade is a glimpse of the massive pylon of Ramesses II, main entrance to the temple. The minaret belongs to a mosque built later into a corner of the temple. Below (right) is a closer view of the colonnade, and on its left a relief, typical of many at Luxor. Note the Asiatic captives along the bottom of the relief, fruit of the imperial conquests of the time. (Courtesy: Lehnert & Landrock, Cairo; Lehnert & Landrock, Cairo; Rhett Austell.)

columns, seven on a side, leading into his great court, bordered again by tall double ranks of smaller columns. Reliefs by Horemheb and Tutankhamun showing the Opet procession decorate the side walls of the colonnade, and there are more statues. The forecourt merges into the hypostyle hall with 32 columns, then four antechambers and other rooms, with the sanctuary of Amenhotep III at the far end of the temple. In one antechamber, the birth room, reliefs explain how the pharaoh was actually fathered by Amun—for his royal parentage was dubious, his mother, for instance, being a Mitanni princess from Asia! Another antechamber, once the legionary sanctuary of a Roman fort built into the temple, was decorated with fine paintings of 300 AD—now faded. And Alexander the Great built a bark shrine before the sanctuary.

The main temple of Amun at Karnak is very different. The site today is a bewildering array of ruined temples, chapels, obelisks and statues covering some 250 acres, built and rebuilt over 2,000 years of Egyptian history but mostly dating from the New Kingdom. Often called "a great historical monument in stone," it has been excavated, reerected and restored by a succession of French archaeologists. Karnak is a temple city, dedicated chiefly to the Theban triad but playing host to many other gods, a national shrine equivalent to a Vatican and St. Peter's rolled into one. Though sometimes exquisite in detail, the architecture and decoration as a whole is too often grandiose and tasteless. Rather than of anything spiritual, it speaks of sheer power, the wealth and power of imperial Egypt. Nevertheless Karnak, the largest temple in the world, is impressive because of its sheer size. Within the precinct of the Temple of Amun alone there are 10 pylons and about 20 temples, shrines and halls—the main temple being on an east-west axis with a subsidiary section running at right angles to it. Outside the main enclosure are two more smaller ones, that of Montu the war god to the north (closed to the public) and of Mut, Amun's consort, to the south. The latter is connected with the main enclosure by an avenue of ram-headed sphinxes.

The main temple, once approached by a landing stage on a canal to the Nile and another avenue of sphinxes, is fronted by the huge first pylon, 370 ft. wide and the largest in Egypt, probably built in the 4th cent. BC under the Thirtieth Dynasty. Beyond it is the immense forecourt containing a single column in its center from a kiosk built by Taharqa (7th cent. BC), and again a small shrine of the Theban triad on the left, by Seti I of the Nineteenth Dynasty. Facing into the court on the S. is a complete temple of Ramesses III, dwarfed by its surroundings but actually of a good size. The second pylon, by Horemheb, leads into the colossal and famous hypostyle hall, a monument to imperial power, its 134 huge bulbous columns once supporting a roofed area almost as great as that of Notre Dame in Paris. The central aisle of 12 taller columns towers almost 70 ft. high, carrying stone architraves weighing 60 to 70 tons each. The imperial message is repeated in the decoration of the outside walls by Seti I and his son, Ramesses II, telling the story in text and reliefs of their campaigns in Palestine and Syria, and in particular again the Battle of Qadesh with the Hittites, celebrated here again in the pompous Poem of Pentaur (see also *Abydos*).

The third, fourth, fifth and sixth pylons, progressively smaller, stood closer together. They are now poorly preserved. In excavating the third pylon of Amenhotep III many blocks from earlier structures were discovered, enabling two of them to be reassembled in an open-air museum north of the hypostyle hall—a *sed* festival (ritual of royal regeneration) kiosk of Senwosret I of the Middle Kingdom (the White Chapel) and a chapel of Amenhotep I of the early New Kingdom. Behind the sixth pylon the remains of the earliest structures at Karnak, again by Senwosret I, were discovered. Between pylons four and five are the earliest standing parts of the temple, dating to Tuthmosis I of the early New Kingdom. Four obelisks of Tuthmosis I and III, marking the original entrance to the temple, stood behind the third pylon (only one still stands), and two more by Queen Hatshepsut behind the fourth pylon; the one remaining, of pink Aswan granite, towers nearly 100 ft. tall. Much of the rest of the temple was built by Tuthmosis III, including his columned festival hall behind the sanctuary. A bark shrine in the sanctuary was built under Philip Arrhidaeus, Alexander the Great's half-wit half-brother and successor.

At right angles to the main temple, stretching south from the third and fourth pylons, are four more open courts and four pylons. In the first "cachette" court a cache of thousands of statues from the temple, buried probably by the Ptolemies, was found in 1903. The first two pylons here were built by Tuthmosis III, the last two by Horemheb, who reused stones from a huge temple of Akhenaten whose outlines have now been traced by an American team east of the enclo-

Adding to the magnificence of the great temple-complex at Karnak is this avenue of ram-headed sphinxes that led from a landing quay on a canal up to the massive first pylon, the largest in Egypt. Each sphinx enfolds between its paws a miniature statue of the king. The pylon, main entrance to the temple, was never finished and its date of building is uncertain. (Courtesy: Frances Tilt.)

sure. A *sed* festival temple of Amenhotep II stood to one side of the last court. Elsewhere within the main enclosure were many small chapels and temples, including those of Ptah, Osiris-Hekadjet, and Opet. Close to the latter and a splendid Ptolemaic gate (Bab el-Amara) in the south side of the enclosure is the Temple of Khons, son of Amun, a typical temple with all its parts well preserved. The Great Sacred Lake, south of the main temple, has been restored and is a principal locus of an interesting sound-and-light show.

There are little but foundations in the small precinct of Montu north of the main enclosure. The Temple of Montu proper, originally by Amenhotep III but much rebuilt, was preceded by an earlier one (outside the precinct) by Tuthmosis I, discovered only in 1970. The later temple was approached from the north by an avenue of human-headed sphinxes. Several other small temples were in the precinct. In the far larger (20-acre) precinct of Mut to the south, little was visible, and there had been scant work on the site until 1976, when an American team began to excavate and elucidate the complex, a project which continues in the 1980s. At least six temples stood on the site, the largest the Temple of Mut, embraced by a crescent-shaped sacred lake on the south. The earliest work here seems to have been of the Eighteenth Dynasty, and there is a temple of Ramesses III of the Twentieth, but almost everything seems to have been heavily rebuilt in the Twenty-fifth Dynasty, when Mut became popular again, and there are still later additions. A new museum at Luxor was opened between Karnak and Luxor in 1975. It displays objects from the Predynastic to the Mamuk periods of Egyptian art, all attractively presented.

THEBES: THE NECROPOLIS

On the W. bank of the Nile, across from Luxor and Karnak, lies the immense necropolis of ancient Thebes, one of the most memorable archaeological sites in Egypt and in the world, containing over 450 painted tombs. From the Middle Kingdom on, but chiefly during the New Kingdom, the dead were ferried across the river to be buried in deep tombs cut in the arid rocky hills that rise beyond the area of cultivation, the royal families in their own valleys, the nobility and other important people throughout the area. At the edge of the hills were the mortuary temples of the pharaohs, facing Thebes. These were devoted to carrying out the cult of the dead. There were also a number of temples here dedicated to the gods. By this time the pyramid tomb, typical of the great earlier metropolis of *Memphis*, had been abandoned as too conspicuous, and now the rock-cut tombs of the pharaohs, unlike the earlier practice, were far removed in the hills from their temples. To keep the pharaohs company, numerous private tombs of nobles, officials and other dignitaries were also cut into the hills, most of New Kingdom date, though others range from the Middle Kingdom to the Late Dynastic Period.

These private tombs usually consisted of a forecourt, a transverse chamber and a long corridor leading into a chapel containing the statues of the deceased and his family—basically a small mortuary temple for the dead. The actual tomb chamber lay below a shaft under the floor. The walls of the tombs, unlike those of the pharaohs in which religious scenes predominate, were exuberantly painted with scenes that vividly bring to life the daily activities of that ancient time— the lord and his lady inspecting their estate, counting their cattle, hunting in the marshes, receiving bountiful offerings of food and drink, feasting and drinking. There are seductive scenes of near-naked Nubian dancing girls gyrating to the skirling and drumming of the music, or of artisans of every kind at work—

for to the Egyptians their tombs were considered "houses of eternity" in which every painted activity served to prolong the life hereafter. It was life and its continuance that they celebrated, not death.

The major sites of the Theban necropolis will be described here in alphabetical order:

Asasif   Some of the latest and largest private tombs in the necropolis, originally with elaborate chapels above them, are to be found on this plain southwest of Deir el-Bahri. That of Pabasa of the Twenty-sixth Dynasty is a large underground tomb decorated with scenes inspired by Old Kingdom prototypes. The tomb of Mentuemhat and of Pedamenope; both priestly officials of the Twenty-fifth and Twenty-sixth dynasties, are again decorated with Old Kingdom type reliefs, and texts from the sacred books (formerly reserved for royalty). The former is a huge labyrinthine tomb, usually closed to visitors; the latter, the largest in the necropolis, has a series of rooms and passages on three levels (a guide is necessary). From the New Kingdom comes the tomb of Kheruef, a steward of the Eighteenth Dynasty Queen Tiy, one of the finest of all with splendid reliefs (permission necessary to enter it).

Colossi of Memnon   Famous pair of colossal seated statues, standing all alone by the road to the Nile, well out into the cultivated area. Once guarding the entrance to the mortuary temple of Amenhotep III (1417–1379 BC), long disappeared, they depict the pharaoh but in Classical times were thought to honor Memnon, a legendary Greek hero. Tiny figures of the King's mother and wife flank the statues. Originally 75 ft. high, they have been a tourist attraction since Classical times and are covered with inscriptions from antiquity to the present, especially the northern one, which is reported to have emitted a singing sound at sunrise. An unusual sphinx with crocodile body has been unearthed nearby.

Deir el-Bahri   Here in an impressive natural amphitheater in the mountains, backed by tall cliffs, stands the mortuary temple of Queen Hatshepsut of the Eighteenth Dynasty, surely one of the most beautiful architectural creations of the ancient Egyptians. Built on three terraces, each faced with handsome colonnades, it is a building without parallel—except for the simpler temple on two terraces lying next to it, built 550 years earlier by Mentuhotpe of the Middle Kingdom. The earlier temple obviously inspired the queen's architect, her steward and favorite, Senenmut. Nowhere else does a building fit so naturally into its environment, the long low lines of the terraces echoing the long line of the cliff tops, the vertical columns of the colonnades matching the bold rising lines of the cliffs themselves.

Not much is left of the temple of Nebhepetre Mentuhotpe, who reunited Egypt under the Middle Kingdom. His causeway leading from a lost valley temple rises into a large walled forecourt, underneath which is a ceremonial tomb or cenotaph below a shaft, and a colonnade at the end. A ramp climbs up to a terrace on which was a now-ruined mastaba-shaped structure, probably a sun temple or a model of a tomb, all enclosed within an arcade. At the end of the forecourt and on the terrace were varied high-colored reliefs; only fragments remain, mostly in museums. Behind the terrace the king's shrine, rock-cut in the cliff, consisted of colonnaded vestibule and hypostyle halls on both sides of an entrance to an underground shaft leading to the tomb chamber, in which little was found. However the tomb of Meketre near the temple, a royal chancellor, yielded 24 lively wooden models of daily life—ships, houses and workshops, complete with many small figures, now in the Metropolitan Museum, New York.

The larger temple of Hatshepsut also has a causeway, once sphinx-lined, and her valley temple has also disappeared. There is again a forecourt, and two large ramps lead to two other courts on different levels, faced by three colonnades—a most harmonious design which must have been even more attractive when adorned with groves of trees, flower beds, fountains and statues. Under the colonnades are the well-known painted reliefs depicting the famous expedition to the exotic land of Punt (Somalia), the transportation of huge obelisks on barges along the Nile from Aswan to Karnak, and the divine birth of the queen. With the columns of the upper colonnade were colossal statues of Hatshepsut, and shrines to Anubis and Hathor flanked the second court. More shrines, of Hatshepsut, Tuthmosis I, Amun and Re-Harakhte are on the upper colonnaded

The mortuary temple of the famous female pharaoh, Hatshepsut of the Eighteenth Dynasty at Deir el-Bahri in the Theban necropolis. The harmonious plan of three ascending terraces and colonnades echoes the horizontal and vertical lines of the huge cliff above. This superb temple was designed by Hatshepsut's steward and favorite, Senenmut, who based it on an earlier and simpler temple of a similar design built by Nebhepetre Mentuhotpe, first king of the Middle Kingdom. Its remains may be seen to the left of Hatshepsut's temple. Although a woman, Hatshepsut adopted all the trappings of the traditional pharaoh during her long reign. (Courtesy: Lehnert & Landrock, Cairo.)

court, and at its end one entered the rock-cut sanctuary itself. Tuthmosis III, Hatshepsut's vengeful nephew, who mutilated many of her statues, reliefs and cartouches here, built another causeway, a kiosk, and at the end of a temple of Amun and a small chapel of Hathor. All these were sandwiched in between the two earlier temples and long ago destroyed in a rock slide.

Near the temple complex the underground tomb of Senenmut, its architect, has been found. Its reliefs are outstanding. And it was south of Deir el-Bahri in 1881 that an extraordinary cache of royal mummies from the Valley of the Kings (see below) was found in an old unused tomb at the bottom of a deep shaft, secreted there by priests in the Twenty-first Dynasty to protect them from the voracious grave robbers. Among them were the mummies of the greatest monarchs of the Seventeenth to Twentieth dynasties: Seti I, Ramesses II and III, Tuthmosis III and many others, including that of Seqenenre of the Seventeenth Dynasty who began the Theban struggle against the Hyksos that led to their expulsion. Obviously he died in battle, for his body was twisted and distorted with wounds on his neck and skull. The mummies are in the Egyptian Museum, Cairo.

Deir El-Medineh   A planned village for the workmen and officials who labored on the building and decorating of the noble and royal tombs of the Theban necropolis, conveniently situated between the Valley of the Kings and the Valley of the Queens. Deir el-Medineh has been meticulously excavated by a number of hands, most lately by the French, who completed their work in 1951. The village is of particular interest because its remains have richly documented our scant knowledge of the lives, habits and beliefs of the ordinary Egyptian. Founded during the reigns of Amenhotep I or Tuthmosis I, it was occupied for some 500 years, and although enlarged during this period it maintained its rectangular layout, with 70 houses at its most extensive tightly squeezed into a narrow area along a main street inside mud brick walls, with one entrance gate. Some 50 more houses were sited more freely outside the walls. The houses were one-storied, with four rooms, stone foundations, mud brick walls and wooden roofs; a few, perhaps for priests, were more substantial. There were also police posts and a water tank by the gate.

A sifting of the village's rubbish heaps has yielded many ostraca, papyri and other remains providing a wealth of information on life in the village. The workmen included painters, sculptors, builders, scribes and others. They lived in the village but, divided into gangs, camped and worked at the tombs for 10-day stretches. They received payment in kind, and occasionally mounted demonstrations when the rations were delayed, and even went on strike in the reign of Ramesses III, the first recorded incident of the kind. The ostraca and papyri included many letters, records of wages etc., and even sketches and amusing caricatures by the artists, freely and vividly drawn. The village tombs, underground chambers with a chapel and a hollow brick pyramid on top, lay outside the village. Some were elaborately and brightly painted, such as that of Sennedjem, or of Ipuy, a sculptor, both of the Nineteenth Dynasty. The latter includes in its paintings a scene of laundrymen plying their trade on a riverbank. At Qurnet Mura'i nearby are some more tombs, badly damaged, including that of Huy, a viceroy of Nubia under Akhenaten and Tutankhamun, which includes a painting of a procession of Nubian tribute-bearers. At Deir el-Medineh there is also a small Ptolemaic temple (about 210 BC) dedicated to Hathor and Maat, and traces of a number of earlier temples.

Dir (Dra) Abu el-Naga   The oldest part of the Theban necropolis, W. of Qurneh. There were burials here of the Eleventh Dynasty, and the Theban rulers of the Seventeenth Dynasty lay here in modest tombs. Altogether, there are some 60 tombs of the New Kingdom, probably including that of Amenhotep I, one of the earliest kings of the Eighteenth Dynasty, though his tomb has not been found. His successor, Tuthmosis I, was the first to be buried in the Valley of the Kings. Among private tombs are those of the priest Khaemuast of the Eighteenth Dynasty with scenes of a grape harvest and winepress, of the priest Amenmose of the Nineteenth with religious and funerary scenes, and of Pane-kesi with religious and agricultural scenes, again of the Nineteenth Dynasty.

Khoka   Another cemetery close to that of Dir Abu el-Naga holding tombs of many periods, but especially about 40 private tombs of the New Kingdom. The best known is the tomb of two royal sculptors (late Eighteenth Dynasty), Ne-bamon and Ipuky. Its walls show scenes of funeral processions and of carpenters, metalworkers and stoneworkers plying their trades.

Malkata   A new quarter of Thebes was developed here by Amenhotep III of the Eighteenth Dynasty, who was a prolific builder during one of the most prosperous periods of Egyptian history. A huge T-shaped artificial lake or harbor, Birket Habu, now traceable only by a line of mounds, was created here, possibly for mercantile as well as ceremonial purposes. On its banks, south of the king's mortuary temple (see *Colossi of Memnon*), Amenhotep III built an enormous palace enclosure, containing within it four separate palaces as well as parade grounds, villas for government officials, chapels, workrooms and workers' quarters. Here his son, later Akhenaten, must have grown up. Little of all this magnificence is left except foundations.

Medinet Habu   Huge mortuary temple of Ramesses III (1194–1163 BC) of the Twentieth Dynasty, the last great pharaoh of the New Kingdom. Enclosed within a vast enclosure, it included not only the squat, walled mortuary temple itself, modeled frankly on the earlier Ramesseum (see ahead), though smaller (about 500 ft. long), but also a brick-built palace to one side, as well as storerooms, houses and offices. Situated opposite modern Luxor, the complex was for several hundred years the administrative and economic center of Thebes, and in later troubled times, and even into the 9th cent. AD, was crammed with houses built within the strong defensive walls. The site of Medinet Habu was from early times associated with Amun, and in the Eighteenth Dynasty Hatshepsut and Tuthmosis III built a temple here to the god, much altered in later centuries, which Ramesses III included inside his enclosure between the east gate and the mortuary temple. What one sees today on the site as a whole are the well-preserved long inner walls of the mortuary temple itself, fronted by a massive broad pylon. Inside are the usual courts, second pylon, two hypostyle halls and the sanctuary behind. A canal from the Nile for the sacred barges once led to a quay just outside the east gate. The palace adjoining the temple, now merely excavated foundations, was connected with it by a large window of appearances in the temple wall, and was decorated with lovely faience tiles (see *Qantir*). Inside were a throne room, audience hall, bathroom and private apartments for the royal family when in residence.

Ramesses III came to the throne after a period of near anarchy and in his early years beat off three great attacks on land and by sea by the Libyans and elements of the Sea Peoples, piratical sea-rovers from the Aegean area after the siege of Troy and the breakdown of civilization there. He also made the usual forays against rebels in Palestine. The rest of his reign, the final years of the Egyptian empire, were peaceful and prosperous, though after his death Egypt began its long slow decline. Of particular interest at Medinet Habu were the reliefs, depicting his campaigns against the Libyans and Sea Peoples (among whom were the biblical Philistines), on the pylons and the north wall of the temple, especially the famous relief on the wall of the great sea battle off the delta. Inside the temple, however, the reliefs convey the usual religious themes. The reliefs in the upper rooms of the massive east gate, known as the "Pavilion," however, are of a different kind (the west gate is destroyed). They show the king dallying with the girls of his harem. The outside of the battlemented gate, modeled on a Syrian *migdol* or fortress (no doubt familiar to Ramesses), shows more reliefs on martial themes. Just inside the gate and the enclosure are the mortuary chapels of the Divine Adorers (Theban priestesses of Amun) of the Twenty-fifth and Twenty-sixth dynasties, as well as the remains of the Eighteenth Dynasty temple of Amun.

Qurneh   Here at the northeastern end of the Theban necropolis, south of the village of el-Tarif, lie the truncated remains of the mortuary temple of Seti I of the Nineteenth Dynasty, the so-called "Qurneh Temple," dedicated to him and to his short-lived father, Ramesses I, and completed by his son, Ramses II. The temple's two pylons and courts are gone; only a colonnade of papyrus columns is left, leading into a complex tripartite sanctuary. This consists of a central hypostyle hall with three shrines around it and a fourth dedicated to the sacred bark of Amun. The temple's reliefs are notable for their finely detailed execution.

Ramesseum   Mortuary temple of Ramesses II the Great of *Abu Simbel* and Karnak fame, the inner temple even larger than that of Ramesses III at Medinet Habu, which was modeled on it. The Ramesseum is in a far more ruined state, however, but enough can be discerned to indicate that here again sheer size and power rather than beauty is the architect's aim. For example, the prime tourist attraction here is the tumbled broken colossus of the king that stood at the back of the first court. It was about 58 ft. high, and was carved out of a single block of Aswan granite weighing over a thousand tons. Diodorus Siculus referred to it in antiquity as Ozymandias, thus giving Shelley a convenient name for his famous sonnet. Two smaller colossi stood at the back of the second court; the head of one is now in the British Museum, London, the other is still in situ.

The temple again lies within a vast enclosure, once filled with long brick vaulted workshops and offices as well as the palace (foundations only) to the south, with houses for the visiting court officials behind it. The palace was connected with the temple by a passage. The front courts were later used as quarries and only half of the first pylon and part of the second survive. Of the great

The much-ruined Ramesseum, mortuary temple of Ramesses II in the Theban necropolis (Ramesses was buried in the Valley of the Kings), a massive construction, impressive, like the statues of the king at Abu Simbel, because of its sheer size. In fact the upper part of another colossal statue, about 58 ft. high, still lies here within the temple. The torso inspired Shelley's famous poem, "Ozymandias." Within its heavy walls the Ramesseum contained a complete temple with two courts, hypostyle hall and sanctuary as well as rows of mud brick storehouses, a palace and other buildings. A similar but much better preserved temple, copied from the Ramesseum, is that of Ramesses III at Medinet Habu nearby. (Courtesy: Lehnert & Landrock, Cairo.)

hypostyle hall's columns, only 29 remain out of 48. Behind it are three smaller columned halls or antechambers, with interesting astronomical symbols on the ceiling of the first one. Of the inner sanctuary of the temple nothing is left. Alongside the great hypostyle hall to the north stood a smaller and earlier temple to Ramesses' mother, Tuya; its orientation forced the plan of the whole enclosure out of the true rectangular. Among the reliefs on the mortuary temple are two interesting ones, on the pylons, of Ramesses' Battle of Qadesh against the Hittites, and others of the festival of Min.

The foundations of other mortuary temples have been traced to the north and south of the Ramesseum—those of Tuthmosis III, Tuthmosis IV and of Amenhotep II of the Eighteenth Dynasty, and of Merneptah of the Nineteenth, Ramesses II's son and successor. In the court of the latter was found the famous Stela of Israel, the earliest reference to Israel in an Egyptian text: "Canaan is laid waste, Askalon despoiled . . . Israel is desolate and its people is destroyed. . . ."

Sheikh Abd el-Qurneh   An area in the hills of the W. bank between Deir el-Medineh and the *Ramesseum* especially rich in the private rock-cut tombs of the nobles and more important dignitaries of the Eighteenth and Nineteenth dynasties. These tombs provide such a wealth of enchanting painted scenes of daily life (and a few reliefs) that no tourist (with guides) can see more than a few examples. Most see little of them at all. The tombs lie in three groups. In what is called the Lesser Precinct in a hollow near Khoka the most noteworthy are those of Wah (a royal majordomo of the early Eighteenth Dynasty) with fine banquet scenes; of Djeserkaraseneb, an Eighteenth Dynasty scribe, again with banqueting scenes and especially graceful female figures; and in particular the famous, often-illustrated tomb of Nakht, an Eighteenth Dynasty scribe of the granaries. Its brilliant paintings depict scenes of plowing and harvesting, hunting and fishing, and of scarcely clothed dancing girls and the well-known blind harpist.

On the hill of Sheikh Abd el-Qurneh itself, the so-called Main Precinct, one finds the tomb of Menna, a royal land steward of the Eighteenth Dynasty, with farming, hunting and fishing scenes of unusual naturalism. Military life is depicted in the tomb of Thanuny, troop commander and scribe under Tuthmosis IV, and a famous scene of wild dancing in the tomb of Horemheb, a royal scribe of the Eighteenth Dynasty. The tombs of Nebamun and of Menkheperraseneb, a chief priest of Amun (both Eighteenth Dynasty) contained detailed scenes of foreign tribute-bearers (Cretans, Syrians, Hittites) carrying characteristic products of their lands. The tomb of Amenemhat, scribe and steward, offers paintings of outstanding quality in the severe style of the early Eighteenth Dynasty. One of the most attractive is the tomb of Sennefer, mayor of Thebes and overseer of the fields, cattle and gardens of Amun under Amenhotep II of the Eighteenth Dynasty. On its ceiling are clusters of purple grapes for the deceased to walk under as he had in life. Of more exalted rank was Rekhmire, governor of Thebes and vizier in the same period, whose famous tomb, one of the largest and finest, boasting a wide transverse hall with 32 columns, offers a variety of painted activities: his own investiture as vizier, more foreign tribute-bearers, craftsmen at work, hunting, funerary and banqueting scenes. The Main Precinct also holds a Middle Kingdom tomb, that of Antefoker, a vizier in the reign of Senwosret I, its wall paintings in the rather rigid style of the Middle Kingdom.

In the plain towards the Ramesseum, in the village of Old Qurneh itself, the best-known tomb is that of Ramose, governor of Thebes and vizier in the early years of the reign of Amenhotep IV (Akhenaten). Delicate reliefs, as well as paintings in the free *Amarna* art style grace the tomb, especially the lovely, often-illustrated painting of women mourners. Two Userhats are also buried here, one of the Nineteenth Dynasty, the other an Eighteenth Dynasty scribe, both tombs with fine paintings. Another tomb of a royal scribe of the Eighteenth Dynasty, Khaemhat (or Mahu), is decorated with elegant reliefs. The tomb of Sennutem near Deir el-Medineh, though not often visited, is worth a mention. He was a minister under Tutankhamun. His tomb is small but the profuse paintings, covering all the walls, are among the brightest and best-preserved in the necropolis.

Valley of the Kings   In Arabic Biban el-Muluk, desolate valley in the hills behind Deir el-Bahri where the pharaohs of the Eighteenth to Twentieth dynasties were laid to rest for over 400 years, from Tuthmosis I to Ramesses XI, in deep rock-cut tombs. Of the 62 tombs known here, not all royal, most lie in the East Valley, while those of Amenhotep III and Aya are in the West Valley or branch. All the tombs, except for that of the boy-king Tutankhamun—No. 62 and the last to be found—were robbed in antiquity, many not long after they had been closed. Graffiti in the most prominent tombs show that they had been visited by awe-struck tourists as early as Ptolemaic and Roman times, as they are today, by the busload (with an occasional maverick on a donkey or bicycle). In general, these tombs consist of a long (often over 300 ft.) rock-cut sloping corridor descending through one or more halls, occasionally with pillars, to the burial chamber and storerooms around it. In the earlier tombs the corridor was often bent at right angles and the decoration, exclusively religious, was painted.

Entrance to a typical rock-cut tomb of the New Kingdom in the desolate uplands of the vast Theban necropolis. The principal tombs here are the largely royal tombs in the Valley of the Kings and Valley of the Queens, although there were many others. Behind the tomb's entrance a long sloping passage led down through several halls to the burial chamber surrounded by rooms for the storage of the magnificent burial goods, such as those found in the only unrifled tomb, that of Tutankhamun. The easily robbed pyramids of the Old and Middle Kingdoms gave way to the rock-cut tombs of the New Kingdom, such as that above—but alas these were all entered and rifled long ago, all but that of Tutankhamun. (Courtesy: Rhett Austell.)

After the Eighteenth Dynasty the corridor became straight and the decoration was generally in relief. Aside from religious scenes, much play was made in the tombs with the texts from various sacred books, with accompanying illustrations, to aid the deceased on his journey through the underworld. The result is a certain repetitious, static quality of decoration compared with the lively, vivid scenes of daily life in the private tombs.

The most accessible of the tombs (those that can be visited) are usually equipped with electric lights, and are also generally the most interesting. Among these the largest and most elaborate is that of Seti I of the 19th Dynasty (see also *Abydos*), 328 ft. long, with 13 chambers, a concealed tomb chamber (which did not foil the robbers) and sumptuous paintings and reliefs. An interesting painted zodiac adorns the ceiling of an inner chamber. The king's mummy survives in Cairo and his lovely alabaster sarcophagus is in the Soane Museum, London. The most popular tomb among tourists is that of Tutankhamun of the Eighteenth Dynasty, far smaller but famous for its rich tomb furnishings, found almost intact by Howard Carter in 1922. A selection of the furnishings, now in the Egyptian Museum, has been seen by hundreds of thousands during traveling exhibitions. Their splendor merely hints at the inconceivable magnificence once enclosed in the larger tombs of the more important pharaohs. In the tomb itself the gilt-encased mummy still lies in the tomb chamber in the second of the three magnificent coffins found there. The wall painting, in the tomb chamber only, though not the best is fresh and bright. The tomb of Horemheb, army commander and power-behind-the-throne under Tutankhamun, later the last pharaoh of the Eighteenth Dynasty, is unfinished but worth visiting for its excellent decorations, some of which still show the stages, from rough sketch on the walls to finished relief, used by the artists. The sarcophagus is still in situ. An earlier, private tomb was prepared for Horemheb and has been found at Saqqara.

The tomb of Amenhotep II of the Eighteenth Dynasty, discovered in 1898, was robbed like the others, but it was the only one, aside from Tutankhamun's, in which the mummy was found inside its sarcophagus (Tutankhamun's is still in the tomb). A garland of flowers had been placed around the king's neck and his great bow lay at his side. Moreover, in side chambers of the tomb nine other royal mummies were found, placed there later by priests for safekeeping, including those of Tuthmosis IV, Amenhotep III, Merneptah, successor to Ramesses II, and three later Ramesses (IV, V, VI) of the Twentieth Dynasty. These complemented the larger cache of royal mummies found at Deir el-Bahri. All as usual had been slit open by robbers for their jewels, then rewrapped by the priests, some more than once. Difficult to reach but interesting for its complex plan is the tomb of the great warrior king of the Eighteenth Dynasty, Tuthmosis III, the earliest tomb here among those visitable. Finally, the later tomb of Ramesses VI, whose imposing large entrance effectively concealed with its debris the smaller entrance to that of Tutankhamun just below it, is worth a visit.

Valley of the Queens   In Arabic Biban el-Harim, behind Medinet Habu at the southern end of the Theban necropolis. Here were buried most of the queens and royal offspring of the Nineteenth and Twentieth dynasties, with a few burials from the Eighteenth Dynasty, some 70 tombs all told, many badly damaged, others quite small and simple. And all of course had been robbed. Only three can be visited. Unfortunately the finest, that of Queen Nefartari, chief wife of Ramesses II, is considered unsafe and temporarily closed. It is a complex of eight chambers with lovely painted reliefs, among the best in Egypt. The tomb of Prince Amun-Her-Khopeshef, one of the many sons of Ramesses III, has some fine paintings in unusual pastel colors. The tomb of Queen Titi, or Thyti, of the Twentieth Dynasty, wife of one of the later Ramesses, is worth a visit.

THMUIS	See *Mendes*.
EL-TIMNAI, TELL	See *Mendes*.
TOD, EL-	The ancient Tuphium of the Greco-Roman Period, about 13 mi. S. of Luxor on the E. bank of the Nile, a cult center of the hawk-headed war god Montu whose shrines were also to be found at Karnak (*Thebes*) and *Medamud*. Building effectively began here in the Middle Kingdom period when Senwosret I of the Twelfth Dynasty erected a shrine to Montu, whose remains have been found. It is one of the two known Middle Kingdom temples, the other being at *Medinet Madi*. The

New Kingdom pharaohs, starting with Tuthmosis III, built and embellished a shrine to Montu here, still partly preserved. Ptolemy VIII erected another temple and made a sacred lake, to which the Romans under Antoninus Pius (138–161 AD) added a court, small central hall and chapel dedicated to the goddess Tenenet. An important cache of the Middle Kingdom Amenenes II of the Twelfth Dynasty was discovered at El-Tod, which included cylinder seals and cuneiform inscriptions indicating important relations with Asia during the period. These are now in Cairo.

TUNA EL-GEBEL	See *Hermopolis*.
TURA	See *Helwan*.
TUSHKA	See *Wadi Kubbaniya*.

UMM EL-BREIGAT, TELL   At the extreme southern end of the *Faiyum*, about 13 mi. S. of Medinet el-Faiyum, a Ptolemaic temple and town on the Bahr el-Gharak canal, the ancient Tebtunis. Italian excavations here have uncovered the remains of a temple similar to the one at *Medinet Madi*, about 9 mi. to the northwest, but with an opposite orientation. There was a kiosk at the north end of a processional way, lined with stone lions and sphinxes, that led to the temple at the south end, of which almost nothing is left. However the mud-brick enclosure wall still stands sometimes 15 ft. high on three sides. Interesting papyri in demotic Egyptian and Greek were recovered here, as well as the remains of four Roman buildings of brick with many rooms and large halls, perhaps the priests' quarters. A cemetery with crocodile burials was discovered here in the 19th century.

VALLEY OF THE KINGS	See *Thebes*.
VALLEY OF THE QUEENS	See *Thebes*.

WADI HAMMAMAT   Important caravan route through the eastern desert to the Red Sea, leaving the Nile at *Qift* (ancient Coptos) or nearby Qus, about 20 mi. N. of *Thebes*. In early times it was one of the main routes bringing Asiatic cultural influences into Egypt through trade, or possibly conquest. In Dynastic times its quarries, about 60 mi. east along the route, provided the prized *bekhen* stone, a sandstone much used for statuary, and it was the route for expeditions down the Red Sea to Punt. The main quarry is marked today by large banks of waste along the wadi as well as unfinished columns and sarcophagi left in situ higher up. There are also a large number of inscriptions here, in hieroglyphic, hieratic and demotic Egyptian and in Greek and Latin, carved by travelers and quarry workers, many of which give details of various expeditions to collect the stone. One mentions a quarrying expedition of 17,000 men. The ruins of workers' houses, mainly Roman period, are also visible in the vicinity, and a badly ruined temple.

WADI KHARIT   See *Serabit el-Khadim*.

WADI KUBBANIYA   Six late Paleolithic sites in the area of this wadi where it abuts on the Nile, a short distance above Aswan in southern Egypt, excavated by an international team in the 1980s, yielded highly controversial evidence, in the form of charred grains of barley and einkorn wheat, of extremely early cultivation of these grains some 18,000 years ago—thus possibly upsetting the common assumption that food raising began in the wetter uplands of the Middle East 10,000 to 9,000 years ago. The grains used here were not native to the region. Apparently they were deliberately imported and planted on the moist slopes of dunes and in the floodplain itself, though the area was then as arid as it is today. It was the annual inundation of the Nile that made it possible. Presumably the inhabitants returned once or twice a year to tend and harvest it, then prepared it on grindstones, numerous examples of these having been found at the sites. The rest of the time they ate birds and large mammals and fish trapped in pools by the receding floods. Also contrary to Middle Eastern experience, the population here, despite this probable added food supplement, did not markedly increase for over 6,000 years.

Nearby sites at *Kom Ombo* to the north and numerous large sites at *Esna* even further north, dating from 13,000 and 12,000 years ago (all by radiocarbon dating), yielded similar evidence for intensive use of cereals as food. Finally, excavations in the 1960s at Tushka (now under water), on the former west bank of the Nile just below *Abu Simbel*, uncovered the remains of about 100 hearths, dated to 14,500 years ago, strewn with microliths, grinding stones and stone sickle blades, along with pollen from wheat-like grasses. A late Paleolithic cemetery with 21 burials was also found here.

WADI MAGHARA

See *Serabit el-Khadim*.

WADI NATRUN

An isolated oasis-valley in the western desert, close to the delta, 63 mi. SW of Alexandria. Natron (salts of sodium), used for cleaning, in the mummification process and for the manufacture of faience and glass, have been extracted from the salt lakes here from earliest times. In the late Roman Empire the area became a refuge for early Christian hermits, including St. Anthony, the chief founder of western monasticism, and there once may have been as many as 50 Coptic monasteries in the area. These in turn were only a few of the many monasteries that flourished in the western desert and along the Nile in the Byzantine period. In Wadi Natrun today only four monasteries are still inhabited, and permission from the Patriarchate in Cairo is necessary to visit them. Some date back to the 4th cent. AD. Destroyed in the Arab invasions, they were then rebuilt and fortified in the 9th cent.

The most interesting is Deir el-Suryni (not open to women). Of two churches within its walls, El-Adra displays notable carved stucco decoration of the 10th cent. AD, close to the early Islamic models. The British Museum in London has about 1,000 Coptic manuscripts purchased here in 1842. The monastery of St. Macarius (Deir Abu Makar) at the southern end of the Wadi Natrun, founded in the 4th cent. AD, resembles a stone fortress, with a fortified keep and three churches within its walls. A crypt, opened during renovations, contained what are believed to be the remains of St. John the Baptist. Until the controversy is settled the monastery is closed to visitors. Of the two other monasteries, Deir el-Baramus and Deir Amba Bishoi, the latter, lying just east of Deir el-Suryani, also has an interesting church inside it, a well-preserved keep and monks' cells of different periods, including the present. See also *Deir Abu Menas*.

ZAWIYET EL-ARYAN

See *Memphis* (Giza).

NORTH AFRICA

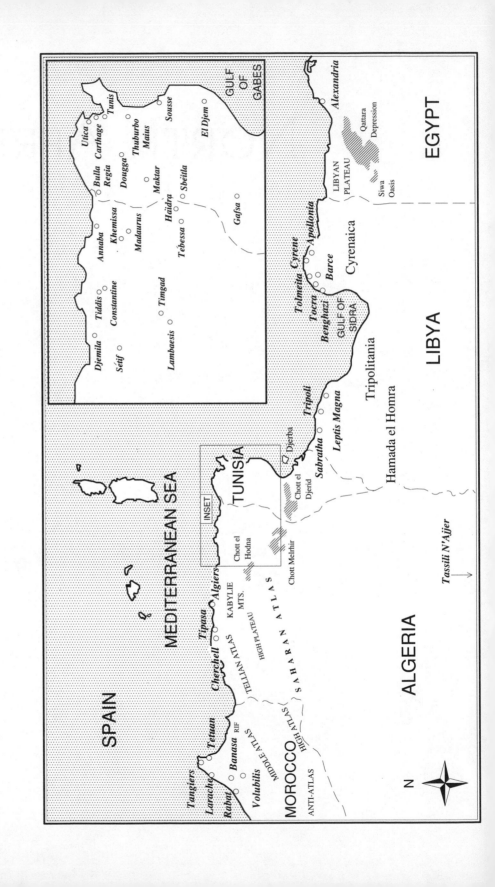

The
Archaeology of
North Africa

The long and varied history of North Africa up into the early Islamic period, here comprising Libya, Tunisia, Algeria and Morocco, presents an extreme contrast to that of Israel or Egypt, but in many ways it is just as interesting. In one respect there is a parallel with Egypt, for North Africa also had its "Red and Black Lands," its arable and its desert, the one a strip of arable land of varying width along the length of the Mediterranean coast, gradually merging (unlike Egypt) into desert towards the south as it approached the shifting sands of the Sahara.

This was not always so. Some 12,000 years ago, at the end of the Ice Ages, North Africa, including the Sahara, enjoyed a moist tropical climate, with big beasts—hippos, elephants, giraffes, giant buffalo—roaming the land. It was an environment that soon nurtured a succession of peoples who produced North Africa's first distinctive and original art, the abundant rock engravings and paintings of the Sahara that have been compared to the superb earlier cave paintings of France and Spain (though there seems to have been no connection between the two). This rock art first appeared with big-game hunters, then continued through various styles and phases for some 4,000 to 5,000 years, changing its content as the Sahara gradually dried up into the desert we know today.

But the Sahara with its incomparable art lies far to the south in wild and desolate lands reached today only by the hardiest tourists and most adventurous of tour operators. The more recent history of North Africa has left its mark chiefly along the Mediterranean coasts from Libya to Morocco. And here, archaeologically speaking, the landscape is dominated by the incredibly abundant and well-preserved ruins dating from North Africa's golden age during the high point of the Roman Empire in the 2nd and 3rd cents. AD. The ruins are not only abundant but are evocative of a past so civilized and luxurious that it is hard to believe. Even the smallest of these Romanized cities and towns enjoyed many of the Roman amenities—good roads, forums, temples, markets, innumerable bath establishments and aqueducts to feed them, amphitheaters, circuses for horse racing, elegant theaters and many-roomed, comfortable houses and villas adorned with fine mosaics and wall frescoes, marbles, precious stones, fountains and statuary, and even air-conditioning of a sort (see *Bulla Regia* in Tunisia). Other provinces in the empire enjoyed the same amenities—Gaul and Syria for instance—but almost nowhere else are the ruins so abundant, varied and complete. Viewing them, one can almost feel oneself back in those rare times of peace and plenty.

Emphatically we do not have here the jealous city-states typical of Israel, constantly at war or threatened from the outside, girdled by massive defenses. These cities of North Africa were all part of the same polity, both Romans and natives enriched by the shipping of grain, olive oil and other goods for the voracious appetites of the Romans across the Mediterranean. The prosperity of this wealthy North Africa was not entirely due to chance. Whatever one may think of the Roman Empire, the Romans were canny empire administrators, employing a set of shrewd if self-serving policies for the provinces, particularly well represented in North Africa with its Greek and Punic heritage and its often reasonably civilized native peoples. Once under Roman control, the natives were offered all the amenities of Roman life, and thus were usually Romanized in short order—and eventually offered citizenship and local or even imperial office.

Romanization went hand in hand with urbanization, for the Roman system centered on cities. New cities were built, peopled by veterans, and old ones adorned with the public buildings, baths and houses typical of any Roman city, while the land around the cities was intensively cultivated with olives and grain, the staples of the Roman diet. A measure of urbanization was even extended well south into what is now often arid desert, with elaborate irrigation projects to bring the land to life.

But the nomads of the interior were not always friendly, and there were from time to time revolts, particularly by those who resisted being settled down. Against these the usual Roman frontier defenses in depth, or *limes*, were gradually built up, eventually protecting most of the back country from Morocco to Libya—a flexible system of ditches, walls and forts linked together and with the coastal strip by a network of military roads. The roads of course also facilitated settlement. So successful in its time was this system that, unlike Israel, some of the Romanized cities were unwalled until late in the period. Behind these defenses peace and prosperity reigned, so that for much of the period only one legion, the Third Augustan, supplemented by auxiliary troops, sufficed to police the whole area.

These Romanized cities extended from Morocco in the west (see *Volubilis*) well into Tripolitania in Libya to the east, where stand the magnificent ruins of *Leptis Magna*, birthplace of the emperor Septimius Severus, a native. Further east, in Cyrenaica, there was a rather different region of once-Greek towns centering around wealthy *Cyrene*—still lovely in its ruins—a Greek colony dating all the way back to 632 BC and grown rich on the export of silphium, a much-prized medicinal herb (now extinct). Around 440 BC the historian Herodotus visited and reported on wealthy Cyrene. Here the underlying theme was Greek civilization and the Greek influence, not only from Greece itself but from the Macedonian Ptolemies of Egypt, who ruled Cyrene from 322 to 96 BC when it was willed to Rome. Greek ways and language in Cyrene lasted well into the Roman period.

In the same manner the underlying theme in the west—in what is now western Libya, Tunisia, Algeria and on into Morocco—was the earlier Punic civilization centered on Carthage, a great city founded, like Cyrene, in the colonization period in the 8th cent. BC or earlier by Phoenician seafarers from Lebanon. As early as the 6th cent. *Carthage* was a powerful city-state of some 300,000 or more with its own colonies, dominating an empire stretching from Libya to the Atlantic and on into Spain. Its great navigator, Hanno, explored well down around the great bulge of West Africa, if the narratives can be believed. In its time Carthage was by all odds the most powerful maritime empire in the Mediterranean. But the gradual eclipse of this great power, first at the hands of the Sicilian Greeks who inflicted a naval defeat in 480 and an abortive invasion in 310, and then of nascent Rome is well known. Before Rome finally destroyed Carthage after 100 years of bitter warfare (264 to 146 BC), the great Punic general Hannibal had brought Rome to its knees after his famous invasion over the Alps. It was a near-run thing. How different history might have been if the Semitic Carthaginians had humbled Rome in its early years!

Though Scipio leveled Carthage and sowed its site with salt in 146 BC, Punic civilization did not die but was merged into that of Rome, a vigorous mixture. Punic was still spoken in St. Augustine's Hippo Regius in the 5th cent. AD and the old Punic gods lived on, disguised under Roman names, like Saturn. Hundreds of stelae of the Saturn cult have been found in the Punic-Roman cities, and the many rich Romanized dignitaries, sometimes even wearing togas, who donated the splendid markets, theaters, temples, fountains in these attractive towns betrayed their origins by their native names on inscriptions.

An undercurrent in this fruitful mixture was made up of the real natives—called Libyans in the east, Berbers further west—who had long ago been overrun by Greeks, Phoenicians and Romans and had been absorbed—but never entirely so. Distinctive Berber royal mausoleums are found in Algeria and elsewhere (see *Dougga* in Tunisia; *El-Khroub*, *Medracen*, *Tiaret* and *Tipasa* in Algeria; and *El-Gour* in Morocco) some as late as the Vandal and Byzantine periods. The able Numidian king Masinissa (203–148 BC) played a central role on Rome's side in the third and final Punic War, and the Jugurthine War, later in the 2nd cent. BC, was provoked by another Numidian king, Jugurtha, who lost his life by defying Rome. Another native Numidian prince, Juba II (25 BC–23 AD), was installed as the puppet king of Mauritania by Augustus. He was Greek-educated, Roman in upbringing and Punic in culture, and married Cleopatra's daughter by Mark Antony. Finally, one of the more serious revolts (17–24 AD) by Tacfarinas, a native trained in the Roman army, upset the country for a time. Romanized after the 2nd cent. AD, these underlying strains of native Libyan, Berber, Numidian or what have you never ceased to enrich the vigorous culture of North Africa well into the early Islamic period.

The Vandals, a wandering Germanic tribe already Arian Christians, overran North Africa under their able leader Gaiseric and dominated it from 429 to 533–34 AD. Overall they seem to have had little effect on the tenacious Romanized civilization of North Africa—though they were a bit hard on the Catholic Christians. Sufetula (*Sbeïtla*) for instance, in Tunisia, seems to have lived through the period quite unscathed. The Vandals were easily expelled by the resurgent Byzantines under the eunuch general Solomon, in 533–34. Classical civilization in North Africa, now thoroughly Christianized, was again reinforced under the great emperor Justinian and for another century thereafter, and there was much new building. But as a sign of the times a great number of massive new forts were built, and some cities walled, for the times were insecure. Indeed the end of the empire was not far off. In the 7th cent. the Arabs swept westward, eventually subduing all North Africa to Islam; and it has remained Islamic to this day.

Though Roman Carthage, once again a large and important city, did not fall until 698, the Arabs had already built their splendid mosque at *Kairouan* in Tunisia in 670 AD, with its forest of reused Roman columns.

The tumultuous history of early Muslim North Africa will be described in some detail ahead. The various sects and dynasties, Berber and non-Berber, that moved across the map of North Africa in this initial Islamic period, ceaselessly contending with each other for power and territory, nevertheless left behind some notable buildings and interesting sites, many excavated and others restored to their original condition and thus worthy of inclusion in this survey of the archaeology of North Africa.

North Africa in Prehistoric Times

Scattered discoveries have revealed the presence of ancient man in North Africa from earliest times. Pebble tools like those found by Leakey in Olduvai Gorge in Tanzania, the earliest human tools known, have been excavated at Aïn *Hanech* in Algeria. They have been dated to 1 to 1.5 million years ago. Moving up the ladder of time and evolution we find *Homo erectus*, that precursor of modern man, represented by fragmentary skeletal remains at *Ternifine*, also in Algeria, where the bones of sabre-toothed tigers and giant apes were also found. The human bones have been dated at about 400–300,000 BC. More remains of *Homo erectus* have turned up in the regions of *Casablanca* and *Rabat* in Morocco—naturally dubbed Casablanca Man and Rabat Man. Tunisia's most ancient site is a former waterhole at *Sidi-Zin*. But probably the most important prehistoric site in North Africa is the great cave of *Haua Fteah* in Cyrenaica in Libya. Its 42 ft. of deposits have so far yielded artifact sequences from about 80,000 BC up to historic times, the earliest being those of big-game hunters. Later, about 40,000 BC, Neanderthal hunters left their tools and slaughtered game in abundance at a brief stopover at *Hajj Creiem*, also in Libya. In Algeria the widespread Aterian tool industry (about 80,000 to 35,000 BC) takes it name from *Bir el-Ater*, while the later Iberomaurusian (Oranian) (after about 12,500 BC) extended from Morocco to Algeria, where ochre-decorated burials have been found at *Columnata*.

The Capsian people, named after the *Gafsa* oasis in Tunisia, bring us into the Neolithic, after about 8000 BC with, eventually, the making of pottery and possible herding and food production. The earliest Capsians are noted for their huge shell mounds, for they loved snails. Finally, the glory of North Africa is the extensive, largely Neolithic, rock art of the Sahara, once enjoying a tropical climate. This is centered on the famous Algerian *Tassili N'Ajjer*, with extensions from the Atlas Mountains in the west into Libya (see *The Fezzan*). Also in Libya, some 400 miles south of Tripoli, a great mound and huge cemetery in an oasis marks the site of Gerama (*Germa*), capital of the warlike Garamantes, described by Herodotus, who submitted to Rome in 19 BC. They may well have been the descendants of the people whose rock art, in one of its late phases here and in Algeria, pictured warriors in light chariots careening headlong behind teams of horses. It is thought that this Saharan warrior caste with their chariots may well represent the amalgamation of the Sea Peoples, of Aegean origin, driven from Egypt, with the native peoples. Another site, *Ghirza*, about 150 miles southeast of Tripoli in Libya, a Romanized Berber settlement with its houses, a native temple, altars with Libyan inscriptions and mausoleums in a necropolis (some as late as the 4th cent. AD) shows the persistence of the native Berber culture in the back country of Libya.

Greeks and Carthaginians

When we move back to the coast of Cyrenaica in Libya we find a very different world, a Greek world. *Cyrene*, with its extensive ruins and huge necropolis, offers evocative remains, patiently excavated, ranging from the Archaic Greek (7th cent. BC) to the Byzantine—but somehow always Greek in feeling throughout. In the Ptolemaic (Hellenistic) period Cyrene was the leading city of the so-called Pentapolis of daughter cities spread out along the coast westward. These included *Apollonia*, its port, Euesperides (now *Benghazi*), Taucheria (now *Tocra*)—with a sanctuary dating back to the 620s BC—and Ptolemaïs (now *Tolmeita*), the latter a huge site distinguished by the ruins of its luxurious two-storied Palace of the Columns, an imposing building probably originally the residence of the Ptolemaic governor. Incredibly, the building was in use into late Roman times.

The Carthaginians or Punic people, being maritime folk, generally hugged the coasts, founding ports of call along the length of this vast littoral from the Atlantic to the eastern borders of Tripolitania in Libya. Included among these ports of call (and there were many more) were, in Libya *Leptis Magna*, with Oea (now *Tripoli*) and *Sabratha* strung out along the coast to the west; in Tunisia *Mahdia*, *Sousse*, *Carthage* itself, *Utica* (by tradition even older than Carthage); in Algeria *Hippo Regius*, *Algiers*, *Tipasa*, *Les Andalouse*; and in Morocco Lixus (*Larache*), the oldest site in Morocco, and Mogador (*Essaouira*), an outpost way down the Atlantic coast.

Persistent archaeological digging has uncovered more remains of this great Punic empire than one would think possible, considering the heavy overlay everywhere of the later Roman and Byzantine. In *Carthage* in particular, where the shapes of the two Punic harbors can still be discerned, many years of sporadic excavation and a concerted international effort from the 1970s have helped to fill in many details of its long history. The most interesting—and gruesome—of the Punic discoveries has been the *tophet*, a sanctuary where for most of Carthage's early history small children were sacrificed to the gods in times of stress. Other *tophets* have been excavated at *Acholla* and *Sousse* (Hadrumetum) in Tunisia.

The most interesting Punic excavation has been that of a complete walled town at *Kerkouane* in Tunisia, destroyed in 150 BC and thus preserved, with its house foundations now on view. A much simpler Punic settlement has also been excavated at Tamuda, near *Tetuan* in Morocco, with poorly built adobe houses. Not all Punic towns were on the coasts. Indeed many a Romanized interior city had its beginnings in the Punic period, like the great city of *Volubilis* in Morocco, though little from the period may have survived. A few other towns in the interior are also worth noting: *Maktar* in Tunisia, for instance, was a Numidian town with a strong Punic flavor reinforced by refugees from Carthage after that city was destroyed by the Romans in 146 BC. Maktar also yielded a *tophet* and many crude Punic stelae as well as the longest Punic inscription so far found, from one of the early Punic temples there (2nd cent. BC). Another Punic temple has also been excavated and preserved at *Constantine* in Algeria. Near *Les Andalouse* in the far west of Algeria a small Punic-Berber settlement has been excavated, dating back to the 6th cent. BC. More light has been thrown on

Punic religion, still quite Phoenician in its character, with the excavations of a sanctuary of Baal and Tanit at *Thinissut* (45 BC), an open air High Place dedicated to "Saturn" at *Bou Kourneïn*, in use as late as 215 AD, another center of Saturn worship at Aïn *Tonga*, and a High Place at *El-Kenissia*—all in Tunisia.

The Roman Period

Roman penetration of North Africa was a slow and somewhat haphazard process. It began with the defeat and destruction of *Carthage* in 146 BC. The rich hinterland of that ruined city became the new province of Africa with its capital at *Utica*. Carthage itself lay fallow for 100 years until Caesar decreed its resettlement in 46 BC, and its colonization under Augustus in 29 BC. Eventually, in the golden imperial years that followed, it became once again a huge and opulent city, third largest in the empire after Rome and Alexandria. Like Carthage, many of the Romanized cities of North Africa also had native origins—sometimes betrayed by the irregular streets, as at *Dougga* and *Thuburbo Maius* in Tunisia, instead of the usual Roman grid plan. Such native towns were in contrast to that supreme example of Roman grid planning found in *Timgad*, the "Pompeii of North Africa," the famous planned veterans' colony in Algeria. But whether native, a Roman colony or a veterans' town, all the cities eventually gained the usual Roman amenities.

The process of expansion continued after Numidia (roughly eastern Algeria) became a puppet state after Caesar's victory over Pompey (and Juba I of Numidia) at Thapsus in 46 BC. In 27 BC Augustus combined Numidia with Africa to create the larger province of Africa Proconsularis. He also established a string of colonies near or along the coast of Mauretanian Numidia; however, western Algeria did not become a Roman province until the reign of Claudius. Meanwhile Morocco to the west had become a province in 40 AD; but Morocco was never heavily Romanized, and only the northern part at that. In the east Cyrenaica (Libya) was established in 74 BC (Cyrene had been willed to Rome by the Ptolemies in 96 BC). Finally, Tripolitania (Libya) had been set up as a province by the late 1st cent. BC. Roman Africa was complete.

Thus by the 2nd and 3rd cents. AD, the golden age of the Roman Empire, hundreds of these Romanized towns and cities, strung out all along the fertile littoral of North Africa had become splendid exemplars of the Roman urban ideal, each with its baths, its temples and public buildings of marble, its luxurious houses equipped often with central heating and profusely decorated with colorful mosaic floors and frescoed walls. Today of course much of this splendor has disappeared or is buried beneath modern settlements. A few of the more complete and evocative ruined cities, however, stand out as major tourist attractions.

Cyrene, for example, amidst its abundant ruins boasts a magnificent Roman forum, built over the site of a Greek gymnasium, enclosing a spacious meeting ground comparable in size to Venice's famous Piazza San Marco. In Tripolitania the opulent ruins of *Leptis Magna* are dominated by another imposing forum, donated by the emperor Septimius Severus, a native son, with an impressive two-storied basilica at one end. In Tunisia the charming small city of *Dougga* (ancient Thugga) on its hillside offers the best-preserved Roman ruins in the country, in great contrast to the fragmentary remains of Roman *Carthage*, once a far larger city, whose most visible monument is the vast Antonine Baths behind the waterfront. Also well-preserved are the attractive ruins of *Djemila* (ancient Cuicul) in Algeria's Atlas Mountains. They illustrate how even a small provincial market town could boast an astonishing range of Roman amenities—three baths, triumphal arches, covered sidewalks along the main street, basilicas, markets, temples, a large theater, and splendid mosaics everywhere. The ruins of *Tipasa*, a coastal town west of Algiers, also evoke the prosperity of Roman North Africa, the remains tastefully displayed in a park. Finally *Volubilis*, in far western Morocco, was once an important Libyo-Punic center, enlarged by the cultivated Juba II of Mauretania. It became the seat of Roman Mauretania Tingitana, adorned, as the partial excavations reveal, with the public buildings and elegant houses, including a probable governor's mansion with 74 rooms, of a Roman provincial capital.

A number of other Roman sites are worth mentioning for their special features—*Tiddis* in Algeria, for instance, for its size. It is a miniature Roman-Punic town climbing up a steep hillside with a tiny forum on an artificial platform, only 20 by 30 yds. in size, flanked by a tiny curia and two diminutive triumphal arches. Yet a native son of this backwoods town, Q. Lollius Urbicus, was the experienced Roman general who invaded Scotland and was responsible for the Antonine Wall. He came home to die. Such was the Roman Empire. The extensive ruins of *Bulla Regia* in Tunisia are known for their air-conditioned villas: open-air atriums with living rooms off them, all excavated below ground to escape the heat, with light shafts, rooftop pools and ventilation shafts to make all things comfortable.

There were many theaters in these cities. *Cyrene*, for instance, had four, and the most magnificent theater of them all, at *Sabratha* in Libya, displays its restored three-storied stage building intact. Other fine theaters are found at nearby *Leptis Magna*, and at *Cherchell*, *Khemissa* and *Djemila* in Algeria. One of the most impressive of amphitheaters, third largest in the Roman world and comparable to the Colosseum in Rome in size and preservation, rises incongruously above the small Arab town of *El-Djem* in Tunisia, while at *Gebel Oust*, also in Tunisia, one finds the ruins of a remarkable healing sanctuary, 219 mosaic-floored rooms for the patients arranged around a large central hall and pool. Finally one might mention *Ammaedara*, far to the south in the Tunisian mountains. Though little excavated it is an interesting example of a frontier town, once a military post, then a veterans' colony. It too of course had a forum, temples, triumphal arches and even a theater.

Not only were there luxurious mansions in every town but there were numerous villas in the countryside, some very grand indeed. The villas, as was usual in the Roman world, were both dwellings for the prosperous owner and working establishments surrounded by fields, orchards, vineyards and farm buildings or workshops for the pressing of oil or making of wine and for the many crafts that often made these villas self-sufficient. What impresses us today is the sophistication and opulence of the living quarters of these villas. Many were seaside establishments such as a group along the coast of Libya. Reflecting the overflowing prosperity of Tripolitania, these often had terraced seafronts for the owner's pleasure, private bath suites, separate summer and winter quarters as at *Silin*, frescoed walls and magnificent figured mosaics, including a well-known sequence of gladiatorial scenes at *Zliten*. There were 45 rooms at *Taguira*, floored with mosaics, many with maritime motifs. (Another mosaic in the dining and reception rooms of a villa at *Acholla* in Tunisia depicted in realistic detail the gourmet foods consumed there).

Further west, at *Hippo Regius* in Algeria, the town villas boasted spacious pillared courtyards, fountains and, again, fine mosaic floors, illustrating the sophisticated background of St. Augustine's youth. One hillside villa had several stories. At *Tipasa*, also in Algeria, another two-storied seaside villa had not only its own bath suite but a private dock. Most of these villas were in use, with alterations, over an astonishingly long period, often from the 1st or 2nd cent. AD into the 5th. On an island off *Essaouira* (ancient Mogador) in Morocco, one 20-room villa had been occupied from pre-Roman times into the 5th cent. AD.

Indeed the wealth of Roman North Africa, as attested by continuing building, did not seem to diminish very much until late in the period. For example, after the empire had turned Christian under Constantine in the 4th century a great many Christian basilicas were built—and continued to be built into the Byzantine period that followed the Vandal occupation. To mention a few, Sufetula (*Sbeïtla*) possessed numerous basilicas, both late empire and Byzantine; so did *Carthage*. Some of the late empire basilicas were grandiose, for instance the Great Basilica at *Tipasa* (late 4th cent.), the largest in Algeria, with nine aisles and mosaic floors. Another Great Basilica at *Tébessa* (ancient Theveste) in Algeria —a pilgrimage center dedicated to St. Crispin—was two-storied with mosaic floors, and stood within a walled precinct that included many cells for the devout, a baptistery, library, a refectory and kitchen, a garden and an inn. At *Timgad* in Algeria the Christian complex of bishop Optatus, a schismatic Donatist and foe of St. Augustine, included many buildings around his great cathedral. Finally, the foundations of what is assumed to be St. Augustine's Basilica of Peace have been laid bare at *Hippo Regius* in Algeria. St. Augustine, 76 years old, died at Hippo in 430 AD while Gaiseric and his Vandals were besieging the town.

It was of course the frontier forts and the *limes* defense line that kept these villas and cities safe and prosperous. The purpose of this military establishment was to keep the nomads in check and if possible to induce them to settle down. During the Roman golden period life was relatively safe behind this military screen; Cuicul (*Djemila*) in Algeria actually tore down its walls in 211 AD to allow for expansion; Sufetula (*Sbeïtla*) in Tunisia never had a wall, nor did Teucheria (*Tocra*) in Libya until Byzantine times. Along the frontier a varying line of forts, earthworks, walls, blockhouses and watch towers were connected by a road system that also ran north into the settled area. The main links in this system were the larger forts along the *limes*, for example Ad Maiores (*Henchir Besseriani*), *Gemellae*, *Castellum Dimmidi* and Rapidum (*Sour Djouab*) in Algeria. Castellum Dimmidi, deep in the Sahara, was for a time the most southerly of the Algerian forts. In southern Tripolitania (Libya) were two oasis forts intended to guard the caravan routes to the south, *Bu Njem* and *Gheria el-Garbia*, (the largest, standing in Roman times in a fertile, irrigated area of Berber farmsteads).

The nerve center of this military network was *Lambaesis* in Algeria, headquarters of the Third Augustan Legion from 81 AD, once in a fertile area now a barren waste. Nevertheless the extant excavated ruins make it possible to visualize the entire layout of the 50-acre camp, as well as parts of the civilian settlement that grew up alongside it. Equally striking in its excavated ruins is the famous military town of *Timgad* nearby in Algeria, built originally by the Third Augustan in 100 AD for its veterans. It is one of the finest examples of a planned Roman military colony in the empire. One might also mention, in Morocco, a more modest example of an army town, also settled by veterans, *Thamusida*. It was walled, and next to it was an exceptionally large fort inside a circuit of walls with 18 towers.

Vandals and Byzantines

The Vandals, despite their reputation, seems to have done comparatively little vandalizing during the century they dominated North Africa. They freely used the existing buildings and left little behind to mark their presence—for instance, a crudely built chapel, one of the five churches in the frontier Tunisian town of *Ammaedara*. Life went on, though inflation grew dangerously and the Saharan nomads and mountain Berbers, left alone by the Vandals, waxed in strength, boding no good for the dying empire. Nevertheless there was over a century more of precarious revival of Romanized life under Byzantium until the Arabs swept over the country in the mid-7th cent. AD.

The eunuch commander Solomon under Belisarius, Justinian's great general, easily drove out the Vandals with only a few thousand men in 533–34 AD. The first order of business was to secure the conquest and preserve what was left of Classical civilization, hence numerous massive fortresses were built in Tunisia and Algeria. One of the finest and best preserved of these, with eight towers, was built by Solomon outside *Timgad* in Algeria in 539 AD. Also attributed to Solomon were the forts at *Ammaedara*, *Sbeïtla* (Sufetula), *Gigthis* and *Qsar Lemsa*, all in Tunisia, the latter very well preserved also. Other massive forts can still be seen at *Baghai* in Algeria, and at *Madaurus* in Algeria, where the huge fortress backs on to the older theater and covers part of the forum—the amenities giving way to the needs of security. There are also forts in *Thelepte* and *Younga* in Tunisia, and at *Maktar*, where a triumphal arch was also actually fortified, while outside *Cyrene* in Libya the Byzantines built a fortified church. Several cities also received Byzantine walls, *Le Kef* in Tunisia and notably *Tébessa* in Algeria where the walls are truly massive, with 14 towers.

In the east, where few forts are found or perhaps were needed, *Cyrene* and its dependencies, *Tolmeita* and *Tocra* in Cyrenaica in Libya, also received walls under Justinian, as well as *Leptis Magna* in Tripolitania. The Byzantine presence is also shown in *Apollonia* in Cyrenaica where a new bath complex was added to the existing ones, several churches built and a sprawling palace of the Dux on a hill above the port; for Apollonia was now the chief city of the Pentapolis. Notable too is the great basilica of Justinian in *Sabratha* in Tripolitania with its magnificent mosaic floor of birds entwined in vines (now in the Archaeological Museum, Tripoli). Byzantine basilicas are also found in *Le Kef* and *Younga* in Tunisia and elsewhere, and of course many earlier basilicas survived in use.

The Arabs

The initial wave of conquering Arabs, spurred on by a fanatical religion, moved both east and west from Arabia with incredible speed, reaching the borders of China, and crossing over into Spain in 711 AD. To the Arabs their religion and their culture were all the same; they brought with them not only Islam but a fast maturing and distinctive culture of their own to replace, in North Africa, that of Rome and Byzantium—though they had learned something, especially in building techniques, from their early contacts with Classical civilization in the Levant. By the 10th cent. the enormous Muslim empire began to break up into separate ethnic and political units, though all still Islamic of various sects. The Berbers of western North Africa began to take an increasingly important part in the welter of contending sects and dynasties that characterized the history of North Africa at this time. Their participation culminated in the conquests of the Almoravids and Almohads, the one dynasty soon succeeding the other. These were puritanical Muslim Berber tribesmen who swept out of the Atlas Mountains to conquer, eventually, Morocco, Algeria and Tunisia and extend their power into Spain. The Almohads, succeeding the Almoravids, finally lost Spain in 1235 AD and Morocco to the Merinids in 1269.

The entries in this guide for the Islamic period touch upon this tangled early Muslim history at many points, but necessarily in a most haphazard manner, depending upon which ruins or buildings have survived or have been excavated. For the earliest period of the conquest, *Kairouan* in Tunisia, founded in 670 AD, takes pride of place. Also in Tunisia *Monastir*, noted for its early Islamic monuments, served as a base in the 8th and 9th cent. for the initial Muslim conquests in North Africa. The first entry into Spain in 711 AD, supported by Berber tribesmen, was led by the famous slave Tarik, who defeated Roderick, ending the Visigothic occupation of Spain. *Qasr es Segir* on the Moroccan coast, the Muslim base for the conquest, has been excavated with interesting results.

The first dynasty we run across is that of the Aghlabids, whose capital after 801 was *Kairouan* in Tunisia, with their principal port at *Sousse*. Kairouan was taken from the Aghlabids in 909 by a dynasty that was to become one of the most important in the Arab world, the Fatimids, Arabs from the east who conquered North Africa, supported by Berber tribesmen. Establishing their capital at *Mahdia* in Tunisia about 912 AD, they moved east to conquer Egypt in 968, founding Cairo as their new capital the next year. Eventually the Fatimids ruled all of North Africa, Sicily, Calabria in Italy and much of the Arab east.

On their way to power the Fatimids destroyed Tahert, capital of the fanatical Ibadites near *Tiaret* in Algeria, who then fled south to *Sedrata*, only to have this new home destroyed by the Hammadids in 1072. (Incidentally, the Hammadid capital, *Kalaâ des Beni Hammad* in Algeria, founded in 1007, has been excavated). Another Berber dynasty, that of the Zirids, who at first ruled under the Fatimids and then became independent, dominated Tunisia, Algeria and Granada in Spain. Their capital in Algeria was at *Achir*, also excavated.

And so we come to the Berber Almoravids (1056–1147). Their first ruler, founder of *Marrakesh* in Morocco, captured *Tlemcen* in Algeria in the late 11th cent. and founded a new city there. But the rising Almohads took over Tlemcen in 1145 and also destroyed the Algerian capitals of the Hammadids, *Kalaâ des Beni Hammad*, and *Achir* of the Zirids, both in 1152. It was in this time of confusion, as the Almoravids were giving way to the Almohads, that the Normans of Sicily occupied most of the ports of the North African coast while the Christians advanced into Islamic Spain. However this resurgence of the west was temporary, for the conquering Almohads regained all that had been lost.

As Almohad power in turn waned, yet another Berber dynasty, the Zianids (1235–1339 AD) took over *Tlemcen* and by the 14th cent. had made of it a great Islamic center, until they yielded to the Merinids of Morocco. In Morocco itself, the powerful Islamic city of *Fez*, capital of the north, founded in 790, was successively ruled by the Almoravids, Almohads and Merinids. The southern capital of *Marrakesh*, founded in 1062 by Almoravids, grew into a large city in 1130, but was soon captured by the Almohads (1147) and eventually by the Merinids in 1269.

The numerous early mosques and other buildings, often austerely beautiful, and the ruins of lost Islamic capitals that survive from this complex early history of Muslim North Africa are described in the appropriate entries as above, chronologically bringing this archaeological survey of North Africa to a fitting conclusion.

LIBYA

AGEDABIA

Ancient town on the E. side of the Gulf of Sirte in western Cyrenaica, called Ajdabiyah in Arabic. It held a Roman garrison in the 1st cent. AD. The remains of an aqueduct, rock-cut cisterns and of a Roman fort nearby may be seen. As a caravan town at the junction of the coastal route and desert route south to the Sudan, it became an important Islamic center after capture by the Fatimids in 912 AD on their way towards Egypt. The ruins of an early Fatimid mosque—built soon after this date and one of the earliest known—were excavated here in the 1970s, revealing a rectangular building with arcaded courtyard and a sanctuary. A so-called *qasr* or fort of the same period—rectangular, with corner towers—was probably a resthouse for important travelers rather than a fort.

APOLLONIA

Coastal city in Cyrenaica, one of the Libyan Pentapolis (see *Cyrene*), founded well before 600 BC by inland Cyrene as its port. A road some 12 mi. long links the two. The large site, sporadically excavated in the 1950s and 1960s, lies close along the shore outside modern Marsa Susa. Most of the ruins date from the Byzantine period when Apollonia, known then as Sozusa, was the chief city of the province. Not much is known of the Greek period, whose levels have been little excavated. The Hellenistic city walls (about 310–280 BC), with round and square towers, curtain walls and gate, are best preserved around the acropolis and have been excavated. There is also a picturesque rock-cut Hellenistic theater outside the walls close to the water, and the former inner and outer harbor facilities, with part of the wall and well-preserved slipways (now mostly submerged) have been investigated by a British underwater team. A Doric temple of about 300 BC outside the walls has been excavated and a stadium has been located about half a mile to the west.

Within the walls are two baths, one Byzantine one Roman (2nd cent. AD), the latter with a large adjoining palaestra or exercise ground bordered by Corinthian columns, and a small plunge pool. Three churches (a fourth lies outside the walls) and typical houses have been excavated here. The Eastern Church (5th–6th cent. AD) near the main street, the largest—with columns, mosaic floor and baptistery—is quite imposing; the Central Church, partly restored, has a small atrium and marble fittings of fine quality; the Western Church, its rows of columns dividing its aisles and naves, also has a small atrium, mosaics and a

Apollonia, the courtyard of the Byzantine governor's palace (above) on a hill overlooking the city center and the sea. The notorious Theodora, later consort of Justinian the Great, lived here as the governor's favorite. Apollonia's long history stretched from before 600 BC, when it was the port of nearby Greek Cyrene, until Byzantine times when it was the main city in Cyrenaica. The attractive Greek theater (below) with the waves of the Mediterranean lapping at its foundations, must have been an entrancing spot for outdoor theatricals. (Courtesy: Donald White; Arcadia Kocybala.)

baptistery. On a hill above the city center, with a splendid view over the plain, hills and sea, lies a large array of ruins belonging to the Byzantine governor's palace (about 500 AD)—the palace of the Dux, head of the Byzantine Pentapolis. Its chambers were clustered around a colonnaded courtyard. On the west side was the official audience hall, on the north the council chamber, and on the south the chapel. The east wing was less imposing. The cemeteries lie east and west of the town. There is a small on-site museum.

ARSINOË

See *Tocra*.

ASABA'A, EL

In Tripolitania; the ruins of a Christian basilica (6th cent. AD) are located near here, about 50 mi. S. of Tripoli. With three naves, it is reported to be the best preserved of the nine churches so far found in Tripolitania.

BALAGRAE	See *Beida.*
BARCE	Modern Al Marj: See *Cyrene.*
BEIDA	In Cyrenaica, about 10 mi. SW of *Cyrene.* The town is thought to be the ancient Balagrae, a cult center of Aesculapius. Near it a sanctuary of the god has been excavated, close to the remains of a small Roman theater, half demolished in recent years. Excavations in 1966 71 uncovered a Byzantine settlement on the northern edge of Beida, including a monastery with small basilica (now largely restored) and a villa-farm with an olive oil factory.
BENGHAZI	The principal city of eastern Libya, in Cyrenaica on the E. of the Gulf of Sirte. Its major growth has been since World War II. There have been three towns on this ancient site. The original Greek colony of Euesperides (Hesperides) was probably founded in the early 500s BC by settlers from nearby *Cyrene.* The site was on a low hill between two lagoons, now salt marshes. Only traces of the settlement have been found. It may have been destroyed in 322 BC. Later the Ptolemies from Egypt conquered the area and built a new city in 247 BC, a mile or two southwest of the old site called Berenice in honor of Ptolemy III's wife. It became one of the Ptolemaic Pentapolis (see *Cyrene*). Roman by 75 BC, it was restored by Justinian in the 6th cent. AD, was devastated by Persians and Arabs, and had disappeared by 1000 AD. The present Benghazi was founded only by the 15th cent. Excavations in 1971–75 in an old Turkish cemetery have found remains of Hellenistic houses, of public buildings, of Justinian's wall and of a Christian basilica of the same period. Ancient tradition places the Garden of Hesperides and the river Lethe in the area. There is an archaeological museum at Benghazi.
BERENICE	See *Benghazi.*
BU CHEMMASC	The ancient Pisida, near the Tunisian border in Tripolitania, 25 mi. WNW of Zuara. Pisida was a Roman municipium with a strong Punic flavor. The ruins include baths with traces of mosaics, and Punic-Roman underground chamber tombs, marked above ground by conical pillars with three steps.
BU NJEM	Roman military camp, excavated by the French, in a back country oasis of Tripolitania, about 150 mi. SE of *Leptis Magna.* Conventionally rectangular, it held 10 barrack blocks, a headquarters building and a shrine for imperial worship on the back side of a court, with baths outside the perimeter. Built in 201 AD, it was abandoned in 273. The camp spawned a walled settlement that outlasted it. See also *Gheria el-Garbia.*
CYDAMAE	See *Ghadames.*
CYRENE	Leading Greek colony of Cyrenaica, on a lovely site high on a plateau in a well-watered area, about 5 mi. inland and some 12 mi. from its ancient port of *Apollonia.* Only part of the large site has been excavated, largely by the Italians, and some of the principal monuments have been reconstructed. Cyrene, the earliest Greek colony in Libya, was founded in 632 BC by settlers from Thera in Greece, driven from their island by drought. According to Herodotus, after two years in Crete they moved under their leader, Battus, to a site on the Libyan shore (which

has been identified), but were soon led by friendly natives to the present site where they settled around a spring, dedicated to Apollo but associated with the nymph Cyrene. Ruled for some 200 years by the descendants of Battus, the colony, in an exceedingly fertile region, grew prosperous, exporting horses, hides and a much-valued medicinal herb, silphium. After an interval of oligarchy, Cyrene came under the Ptolemies of Egypt in 322 BC and was bequeathed to Rome in 96 BC by its last king, becoming part of the Roman province of Crete and Cyrene in 75–74 BC. Soon after its founding Cyrene gave rise to other Greek colonies in the area. In the Ptolemaic era five of these became known as the Pentapolis (Cyrene, Apollonia, and the modern cities of Benghazi, Tocra and Tolmeita). Another colony, Barce, founded by dissidents from Cyrene in the mid-6th cent. BC, was destroyed in 322 BC. Barce has been lightly excavated. Cyrene, prospering under the Ptolemies and the early Roman Empire, was the birthplace of the Hellenistic scientist Eratosthenes and the poet Callimachus. Devastated by the violent Jewish revolt of 115 AD and rebuilt by Hadrian, it was again devastated by a massive earthquake in 365 AD. Thereafter it slowly declined until conquered by the Arabs in 647 AD, and was eventually deserted.

Although the visible remains are mostly Roman, or Roman rebuilding of earlier structures, Cyrene never lost its Greek character. The city lay in a valley between two hills with the Sacred Way running from the Sanctuary of Apollo on the west towards the agora and acropolis—the latter (little excavated) with Hellenistic/Roman walls, towers and a gateway. Within the precinct of the Sanctuary of Apollo are the foundations of an early shrine of Apollo (early 6 cent. BC) and near it the extant columns of the slightly later Doric Temple of Apollo, flanked by a Temple of Artemis of the same period. The semicircular fountain of Apollo lies on a terrace above. Added to the sanctuary area in later periods were Greek and Roman propylaeas or entrance-gates, a Greek strategeion (military headquarters), several small temples, and squeezed between the precinct and a hill, the Roman baths, built by Trajan in 98 AD and rebuilt by Hadrian after the Jewish revolt, with Byzantine additions. Here in 1913 was found the elegant marble Venus of Cyrene, now in Rome.

Beyond the sanctuary to the west the Greek theater, converted to an amphitheater by the Romans, overlooks the verdant plain to the sea. Cyrene boasted no less than four theaters—including a Roman theater and odeon and a later Market Theater, in the city center. The most interesting relics of the Hellenistic period are the rock-cut Greek baths along the Sacred Way, provided with rows of "sitz-baths," and the huge Temple of Zeus on a hill at the far northeast end of the city, larger than the Parthenon, an Archaic Doric structure, originally late 6th cent. BC and rebuilt by the Romans in the same form. Destroyed by the Jews, it has now been reconstructed by the Italians. It once held a marble copy of Pheidias's Zeus at Olympia in Greece.

The city center is dominated by the Greek agora (west) and vast porticoed Roman forum, the Caesareum or Forum of Prochus (east), along the north side of the (originally) Archaic-period Street of Battus. The forum, now reconstructed, is the most imposing monument at Cyrene. It had a temple at its center and was built on the site of a Greek gymnasium. The Street of Battus, leading east from the acropolis, is also flanked by public buildings and the partly reconstructed stoa of Hermes and Hercules; and along its south side, amidst public buildings and the Roman theater, is the palatial house of Jason Magnus. Covering two blocks, with courtyards, halls, mosaics, it attests to the wealth of these

The Sanctuary of Apollo at Cyrene: the reerected Doric columns of Apollo's temple look out over the fertile plain below. Close to the temple was the spring of the nymph Cyrene, beloved of Apollo and patroness of the city. This was the religious center of the ancient city, with the Greek theater beyond it turned into an arena by the Romans. At the other end of the widespread city ruins the Archaic Temple of Zeus (below) stands on a prominent hill. Destroyed in a violent Jewish revolt in 115 AD, the ancient temple, larger than the Parthenon, was reconstructed in the same form in Roman times and its huge columns have once more been reerected by the Italians. In ancient times a colossal statue of Zeus, modeled on that of Pheidias in Olympia in Greece, stood in the temple. (Courtesy: John Boardman; Arcadia Kocybala.)

The south wall of the Caesareum (above), the vast Roman forum of Cyrene, now reconstructed. It was built over a Hellenistic gymnasium. It contained a spacious open plaza, comparable in size to the famous Piazza San Marco in Venice, bordered by a colonnade and with a temple in the middle. In Cyrene's huge necropolis surrounding the city, some 1,300 tombs survive, some surmounted by curious faceless mourning statues. Many are rock-cut, with Classical facades, like the tomb pictured below. (Courtesy: Donald White; Arcadia Kocybala.)

Cyrenean provincials. The Greek agora, once embraced by stoas, has two round monuments within it, the larger one the Tomb of Battus, a cult center probably marking the tomb of the founder. Here, too, is a Temple of Demeter and a Hellenistic monument, a battered victory on a ship's prow, possibly commemorating Augustus' naval victory of Actium in 31 BC. Moving east into the later Roman civic center, there are remains of houses, temples, a fountain, a small church and to the north a larger 5th-cent. Christian basilica, both with fine mosaics. Beyond the southwest gate are Roman cisterns, and traces of a hippodrome to the north near the Temple of Zeus.

Outside the city to the south, across a wadi, is the very early Sanctuary of Demeter and Persephone (in use from about 600 BC), built on terraces. Excavated by an American team, it has yielded remarkably fine elements of sculpture and other rich finds. All the sculpture from Cyrene is of top quality, and some of it is shown in museums on the site. The extensive necropolis of Cyrene, with some 1,200 tombs still visible, covers several sq. mi. around the city, rock-cut to the north and west with Doric and Ionic facades (some lining the road to Apollonia); and above-ground structures on the plain south and east. All were robbed. Marshal Graziani used a few of the tombs as headquarters in World War II. Cyrene's principal museum is north of the site.

EUESPERIDES   See *Benghazi*.

FEZZAN, THE   A long sequence of prehistoric rock art, mostly Neolithic, in the Fezzan in SW Libya, has ben intensively studied by Italian-Libyan expeditions since 1955. Nearly 60,000 paintings and engravings have so far been registered, making the Fezzan, and particularly the Tadrart Acacus massif, an area almost as rich in this art as the better-known *Tassili N' Ajjer* in ALGERIA to the west. Indeed the same long sequence of art styles, reflecting the gradual drying-up of the Sahara as a whole, is found here as in the Tassili area. The dating in both regions is still controversial, but if, as claimed, the dates in the Fezzan are uniformly earlier than those for Tassili, the rock art impulse may well have begun here and spread westwards.

At the earliest rock art in Libya, all engraved, is dated at 6690 BC, the product of an early pottery-making people, as excavations at the sites have shown. The later, painted art follows the same sequence as at Tassili: big-game hunters shown tracking and killing giraffes, antelopes, elephants, hippos, buffaloes and lions in a still tropical environment; next, the period of the round-headed people followed by the pastoral period of massive herding of cattle; the introduction of the camel as the climate grew drier; and finally the period of the warriors, and of lively charioteers careening along behind teams of horses. In the end the paintings become stylized and derivative. The whole area of Saharan rock art, stretching from close to the Nile valley to the Atlas Mountains, offers one of the richest depositories of often superb rock art in the world. See also *In Habeter*, and in ALGERIA: *Aïn Sefra, El Bayadh, Hoggar Mountains*.

GARAMA   See *Germa*.

GARBIA   See *Gheria el-Garbia*.

GARGARESH   See *Tripoli*.

GERISA   See *Ghirza*.

GERMA   Oasis village over 400 mi. S. of Tripoli, about 15 mi. E. of Ubari. A huge mound here marks the site of ancient Garama, capital of the warlike tribe of the Garamantes. After a Roman campaign in 19 BC under General Balbus, for which he was given a triumph in Rome, the area became a client kingdom. A huge cemetery with an estimated 45,000 tombs extends 60 mi. east of Germa along the wadi Ajal. These are pit graves and chamber tombs, crudely decorated, marked by stelae, offering tables and basins. Most date from the Roman period (1st to 4th cent. AD) as some excavation has shown. A villa of the late Roman Empire has also been uncovered near Germa, and the restored "Mausoleum of Cecilia

Plautilla" south of the town dates from the 1st cent.—the southernmost Roman monument in Africa. There are also examples of Paleolithic and Neolithic rock art and other finds in the Germa region.

GHADAMES

An oasis town, 418 mi. S. of Tripoli near the Algerian border, once a center of the slave trade. It was the caravan town of Cydamae in antiquity and in the 3rd cent. AD was the site of a Roman fort. In the "Plain of Idols" southwest of the town, several large piers mark a former Roman necropolis.

GHERIA EL-GARBIA

Roman oasis fort, the largest in Tripolitania, over 125 mi. S. of Leptis Magna and 125 mi. W. of Bu Njem, built to protect the fertile areas of the wadis Sofeggin and Zem Zem, which in the Roman period, as recent surveys have shown, were occupied by many Berber-style fortified farms, valley settlements and hilltop villages. They were supported by a sophisticated agricultural system, long broken down. Of the fort's four gates, the main one had pentagonal towers. There was a necropolis to the southwest. See also *Ghirza*.

GHIRZA

The ancient Gerisa, a Romanized Berber settlement near the wadi Zem Zem (see *Gheria el-Garbia* above) about 150 mi. SE of Tripoli. The town, mostly 4th cent. AD, contained over 40 buildings including six three-story fortified farmhouses and a native temple, its numerous altars inscribed in Libyan script. Its two necropolises contained seven tall mausolea each, the largest 46 ft. high, of dressed stone with columns supporting architraves—some of temple type, others in pyramid or obelisk shape. The former had primitive friezes depicting local agricultural activities.

HAGFET ED-DABBA

Cave in the hills of Gebel Akhdar near *Cyrene*, Cyrenaica. An Upper Paleolithic stone industry, known as Dabban from its initial discovery in this cave, is found only here and at nearby *Haua Fteah*. An extremely early blade and burin industry, it is dated at about 38,000–13,000 BC and may have been introduced here from elsewhere, probably from the east end of the Mediterranean.

HAJJ CREIEM

Middle Paleolithic hunters' camp in Wadi Derna, about 50 mi. E. of *Beida*, Cyrenaica. About 40,000 years ago a group of about a dozen hunters stopped here for a few days at the most. They left behind them, to the astonishment of the excavators, over 1,000 flake knives and scrapers and the bones of up to 18 Barbary sheep, zebra, buffalo, and a gazelle!

HAUA FTEAH

Large and important prehistoric cave, close to the coast of Cyrenaica near *Apollonia*, which yielded the most complete sequence of prehistoric industries yet discovered in North Africa. Excavated in the 1950s, its 42 ft. of deposits ranged back to about 80,000 BC. An obscure Libyan pre-Aurignacian period was followed by Mousterian (two Neanderthal jaw fragments were found), the Dabban (see *Hagfet ed-Dabba*), Oranian (about 13,000–7000 BC), Capsian (see *Gafsa*, TUNISIA), Neolithic remains of pottery and domesticated animals (about 5000 BC), and finally Greek and Roman pottery.

IN HABETER

Neolithic rock carvings in the *Fezzan* near the Algerian border, about 500 mi. SW of Tripoli. Engravings on an escarpment above a wadi (In Habeter III) show naturalistic figures of giraffes and elephants, some in perspective, and hunters wearing jackal-headed masks. The masked hunters occur again at In Habeter II with other human figures suggesting Egyptian influence. More hunters, with bovids and a finely rendered buffalo (*Bubalus antiquus*), occur at a nearby site, Tel Issaghen.

LEPTIS MAGNA

Impressive ruins of a coastal Roman city in Tripolitania, 2 mi. E. of Homs and 65 E. of Tripoli. Ancient Leptis, with *Sabratha* and Oea (*Tripoli*) formed the "Tripolis" (three cities) of the fertile coastal area then called the Emporia. They also tapped the caravan trade from the interior. All were founded by the Phoenicians. In fact Leptis retained its Phoenician-Carthaginian character and language, mixed with Libyan elements, for many centuries after the Roman conquest. Septimius Severus, Roman emperor 193–211 AD was born here and greatly embellished his native city. Founded before 600 BC, Leptis was always a prosperous city, based on the olives and grain of the Emporia and the later export of slaves, semiprecious stones and wild animals from the interior for the Roman arenas. Very little has been found from the 600 years of Phoenician-Punic occupation— a few graves, statuary, inscriptions, remains of a warehouse. Leptis came under Rome in 46 BC and was made a colony in 110 AD by Trajan. A siege in the 4th cent. AD by the Visigothic Austurians and occupation by the Vandals in the 5th cent. began its decline. The recovered Byzantine city was far smaller. The Arabs (643 AD) ignored it and the sand gradually covered all, preserving the ruins for posterity. Excavations since 1920 have exposed much but far from all of the large site. The residential areas inland still lie buried.

The city lies along the wadi Lebda, running south from the harbor, now silted up. The earliest Roman area contained the Augustan Old Forum west of the harbor (built 5 BC–2 AD) with its temples to Liber Pater, Rome and Augustus (with an inscription in Neo-Punic), a smaller temple, a basilica, reconstructed under Constantine, and a Senate House. An intrusion is a later Christian basilica near the forum. The Augustan city extended southwards towards the market and theater, both donated, be it noted, by a wealthy Punic aristocrat, Annobal Rufus. The market, rebuilt in the Severan age, has two octagonal pavilions enclosed within porticos and market tables, one carved with standards of measure. A small elephant statue found here hints at one item of trade, ivory. Next to the market is the Chalcidicum (11–12 AD), another porticoed space with a small temple; it was probably another market; and west of both was the sumptuous small theater. Originally built 9–8 BC and one of the earliest in the Roman world, it was often rebuilt. It was decorated over the centuries with hundreds of statues, and there is a tiny temple of Augusta Ceres above the range of its seats. Behind its stage is a later porticoed courtyard enclosing a small temple of Di Augusti. Under Nero, about 56 AD, an amphitheater, one of the largest in the Roman world, was built on the shore east of the harbor. It had seating for some 25,000 spectators.

From early imperial times date two arches on the main street (*cardo*), one dedicated to Tiberius (37 AD), the other near the Chalcidicum and four-sided, dedicated to Trajan when Leptis became a colony in 110 AD. The Hadrianic baths (about 126 AD), flanked by a spacious exercise ground, are again as large as any in the Roman world, and were richly decorated and adorned with a wealth of statues. This already opulent city was further embellished in the 2nd cent. AD. A circus for horse-racing (161–62 AD) was built near the amphitheater; then its native son, Septimius Severus, added a magnificent complex between the

Leptis Magna, a Punic-Roman city,
was one of the most opulent in the
Roman Empire and its magnificent
ruins still reflect its ancient glory.
For example the small theater (above)
was adorned with a forest of statues.
Both it and the market were donated
by a wealthy Punic aristocrat of the
city. In the market were traded the
sources of the city's wealth—slaves,
ivory, semiprecious stones and much
else. A measuring table (below) is
carved with standards of measure.
(Courtesy: Donald White.)

The emperor Septimius Severus, a native of Leptis who ruled at the turn of the 2nd and 3rd cents., further adorned an already magnificent Leptis with a complex including a wide colonnaded main street and a huge new forum, also enclosed with colonnades. Along one side rose the incomparable basilica, shown here, with marbled walls and floors, an apse at either end, ranks of red granite columns. It was begun at the end of Septimius' life and finished by Caracalla. (Courtesy: Donald White.)

Hadrianic baths and the harbor—a long colonnaded street (250 columns) along the wadi, a florid three-story nymphaeum marking a bend in the street, a superb huge new forum with a basilica north of it; and a four-way arch at the southern end of the *cardo*—all faced with marble and exuberantly carved and sculpted by master craftsmen who may have come from Aphrodisias in Turkey, famous for its sculpture. Colonnades enclosed the forum, with a temple high on a podium at the southern end and the basilica (210–216 AD), one of the glories of the Roman Empire, flanking its north side. Its floor and walls were marbled, with two stories of red granite columns and an apse at either end. It was finished by Caracalla. Severus also enlarged the Augustan harbor with two moles embracing a new basin, a string of warehouses, a tall lighthouse, and two temples.

The Hunting Baths way to the west are probably also Severan or earlier. With vaults and domes remarkably preserved, the baths are noteworthy for their painted frescoes of the hunt, and a Nile mosaic. More fine mosaics have been found in numerous villas in the vicinity. An on-site museum at Leptis contains much of interest, though the finest objects are in the Archaeological Museum, *Tripoli.*

MARSA SUSA   See *Apollonia.*

OEA   See *Tripoli.*

OLBIA   See *Qasr Lebia.*

PISIDA   See *Bu Chemmasc.*

PTOLEMAÏS   See *Tolmeita.*

QASR LEBIA
(or ELBIA)

Probably the site of ancient Olbia, about 30 mi. WSW of *Cyrene*, in Cyrenaica. One of two Byzantine churches was excavated here in 1957 and a remarkable 35-ft. long mosaic was discovered in the nave. Made up of 50 small panels, it may depict the creation in a curious mixture of Christian and pagan symbolism. There are birds, fish, animals and monsters, a lighthouse (probably the Pharos at *Alexandria* in EGYPT), a shepherd, a satyr, the Castalian Spring at Delphi in Greece, traditional center of the pagan universe, a fort, the gate to a town (probably Olbia), and personifications of well-known rivers. Also depicted is a church, probably the church itself, with an inscription of a Bishop Makarios above it, dating it to about 539 AD. In an adjoining room there is a mosaic of a Nile scene.

SABRATHA

One of the three main Punic-Roman cities of Tripolitania (see also *Leptis Magna*, *Tripoli*), 42 mi. WSW of Tripoli. Its history was much the same as that of Leptis, though it was not as wealthy. However, we know that Sabratha had a trading office at Ostia, port of Rome. Established by the Phoenicians at least by the 5th cent. BC, it became Roman in 46 BC and a colony in the 2nd cent. AD when, like Leptis, it was at the height of its prosperity. It was sacked by the Austurians in the 360s and again by the Vandals in 450 AD. After 533 a brief revival by the Byzantines—the walls protected only the old city and forum—was terminated by the Arab invasion in 643. Then came the sand, again to cover all.

Sabratha was extensively excavated between the wars by the Italians, but is chiefly known for its magnificently restored theater. In lower levels of the forum area of the old city, close to the small harbor, a huddle of earlier shops, houses and streets and a Punic wall were uncovered. The forum whose ruins are now on view was colonnaded and was surrounded by structures from the 1st to 4th centuries AD, including five temples—dedicated to Jupiter Ammon (the Capitolium, on a high podium), to Liber Pater, to Serapis, to an unknown deity, and an Antonine temple (166–69 AD). A 4th-century curia lay to the north, and to the south the civil basilica, later rebuilt as a church. Between the forum and the sea lay the imposing Byzantine basilica of Justinian in which was found a remarkably fine colored mosaic floor, now in the museum.

In the 2nd cent. AD the city expanded to the south and east within the Roman walls, still traceable, which enclosed all but the amphitheater. Here in a new eastern quarter is the theater, begun in the late 2nd cent. and now thoroughly restored for modern use by the Italians. With its tall stage building and seating for 5,000 spectators, it is the best surviving example of its kind in the Roman world. The stage building rises 40 ft. high, in three stories, each with rows of Corinthian columns of variegated marble and black granite. Three doorways open onto the stage, and for the audience, entry tunnels and 11 staircases lead up to the seats. The front of the stage is embellished with 21 delightful reliefs picturing aspects of stage life.

Two more Christian basilicas (4th cent. AD) and private houses lie in the new quarter, and there are three bath complexes with fine mosaics, the Theater Baths, Oceanus Baths and Seaward Baths, the latter the largest, boasting a separate latrine with 30 marble seats. A number of elaborate villas have been found in Sabratha's residential quarters, some with Nile mosaics, and elsewhere Punic and Roman cemeteries. A half mile east of the theater, outside the site, was the amphitheater, built into and partly sunken into the former town quarry, with a

Sabratha, like Leptis Magna, both in Tripolitania, was an old Punic town which reached its apogee under the Romans in the 2nd cent. AD. It was late in that century that the superb theater (above) was built, probably the finest surviving example in the Roman world. Sited in a new quarter of the city, its stage building, lovingly restored by the Italians, rises 40 feet high with three stories of Corinthian columns of marble and black granite. Along the bottom of the building, facing the audience, are a series of delightful reliefs, one of which is shown below. (Courtesy: Donald White.)

maze of passageways beneath the arena floor; also, to its west, on the sea cliff, is the elaborate Temple of Isis. There is an on-site museum.

SILIN

A group of six seaside villas, some 12 mi. E. of the villa at *Zliten*, and about 34 mi. E. of *Leptis Magna*, in Tripolitania. Two of these, belonging to wealthy landowners, have been investigated. Built close to farm buildings with wine- and olive presses and warehouses for luxury goods brought across the desert, they

Crude carvings of heads, of phallic men and big-bosomed women are found in this curious Libyan open-air sanctuary at Slonta near Cyrene. It is obviously a native cult-place, but nothing more is known about it. The original Greek colonists of Cyrene married native women who must have worshipped in sanctuaries like this one. (Courtesy: Donald White.)

dramatize the overflowing wealth of Tripolitania in Roman times. The Villa of the Maritime Odeon is named for a kind of semicircular theater, its steps cut into the rock of the seashore in front of the villa for the owner's pleasure. The villa had a long portico, octagonal wings, baths and excellent mosaics. Similarly, the Villa of the Small Circus is named for a private perambulatory adjoining its baths. This luxurious villa had a terraced seafront, separate winter and summer quarters, the latter with belvedere tower, and rooms richly decorated with red porphyry, painted stucco and mosaic floors. See also *Tagiura*.

SLONTA

Mysterious Libyan grotto-sanctuary of uncertain date, on the hilly plateau 18 mi. SW of *Cyrene*. In the grotto are figures, rock-cut and sculptured, of nude phallic men and big-breasted women, and primitive heads.

SOZUSA

See *Apollonia*.

TAUCHEIRA

See *Tocra*.

TAGIURA

Another seaside Roman villa, about 12 mi. E. of *Tripoli*. Terraced like those at *Silin*, it had 45 rooms, baths, and an incredible wealth of mosaics, most with elaborate maritime themes. Built 157–61 AD, it lasted into the 4th cent. See also *Zliten*.

TARHUNA

Scattered Roman remains around an inland town on a plateau 40 mi. SE of *Tripoli*. These include remains of villas, farmhouses, numerous olive presses, a castle (possibly Roman). One villa to the northwest, at Scersciarra, was porticoed, with mosaic floors and a pottery kiln. North-northwest at Qasr Doga is a Roman necropolis with a mausoleum (2nd–3rd cents. AD).

TOCRA

Site of the ancient city of Taucheira, 40 mi. NE of *Benghazi* on the coast. One of the Pentapolis of Cyrenaica (see *Cyrene*) it was renamed Arsinoë under the Ptolemies, and came under Roman rule in the 1st cent. BC. Excavations in the 1960s, especially in the city's ancient sanctuary of Demeter and Kore, indicated that the town with its sanctuary was founded in the 620s BC, not long after the founding of Cyrene itself. Rich votive offerings were discovered in the sanctuary and quantities of imported Greek pottery, mostly of poor quality. Little is left above ground, but an agora, baths, temples, a gymnasium and houses have tentatively been identified. From a later period two Christian basilicas within the walls and two without have been uncovered. The limestone walls built by Justinian are the most prominent feature of the site, with 30 towers and several gates. Quarries nearby were later used for Roman rock-cut tombs. There is a small on-site museum.

TOLMEITA

The ancient Ptolemaïs, one of the Pentapolis (see *Cyrene*), about 60 mi. NE of *Benghazi*, in Cyrenaica. It was named by the Ptolemies of Egypt in their honor after they had taken over a small Greek coastal city whose name has been lost. Founded about 525 BC, it was the port for *Barce* some 15 mi. inland. The city began to prosper under the Ptolemies, and in the Roman period became one of the most flourishing cities in the region. Much of the huge site has been excavated, though not fully published. Of the 6th-cent. Byzantine walls, built by Justinian, the Taucheira (West) gate, defined by two square towers, is notable. There is the usual amphitheater, monumental street, two theaters (one in the upper and one in the lower town), an odeon, a porticoed forum built over 17 huge Roman cisterns supplied with aqueduct water, arches, late Roman and Byzantine baths (the former with garden hedges), an Ionic temple and several Christian basilicas, one fortified. Of a number of substantial houses, mostly Roman, the most impressive is the huge Palace of the Columns, in use from Ptolemaic to late Roman times—probably as the governor's residence and headquarters. It was, as an authority writes, grander than anything in Pompeii. It was two-storied, with a large peristyle, spacious columned hall, atrium, private suites of baths, mosaic floors and walls veneered in marble or painted plaster. Among the finds in the on-site museum are some outstanding Hellenistic reliefs of dancing maenads.

TRIPOLI

Capital and largest city of Libya, once ancient Oea, a lesser member of the Tripolis (see also *Leptis Magna, Sabratha*) in Tripolitania. A port founded by the Phoenicians, like the two others, it followed their history, reaching its greatest prosperity in the 2nd cent. AD when it also became a Roman colony. But unlike Leptis and Sabratha, Tripoli survived the Arab conquest to become a military and administrative center, which inevitably doomed its ancient monuments. Only one remains, a much-battered four-sided arch of marble, dedicated to Marcus Aurelius and Lucius Verus in 163 AD, which stood at the center of the ancient town. It was once capped by a cupola, and was decorated with reliefs, most of which have disappeared. Near it, traces of a temple of the 2nd cent. AD have been found. At Gargaresh outside Tripoli a 4th cent. AD Roman tomb contains a lovely painting of the deceased, a woman. The Archaeological Museum in Tripoli's Castle holds the most important archaeological collection in Libya.

Tolmeita, the ancient Ptolemaïs, was one of the Pentapolis of Cyrenaica—the five Greek cities that spread westward from the mother city of Cyrene. A small Greek port founded in the 6th cent. BC, Ptolemaïs was built into a grand city by the Ptolemies of Egypt, who renamed it for themselves. Again it reached its height under the Romans and was graced with two theaters, an amphitheater, forum, baths and temples. Under the colonnaded forum were 17 huge cisterns (above), fed by aqueducts. The Palace of the Columns (below) was a grandiose two-storied mansion, probably the governor's residence and headquarters. It had its own bath suite with latrines, shops, and many rooms around a series of courtyards, decorated with fine mosaics and painted and plastered walls. (Courtesy: Donald White.)

Sad remains of the once-splendid Arch of Marcus Aurelius in Tripoli, now capital of Libya. The arch is about all that remains of ancient Oea, one of the three coastal cities of Tripolitania with Leptis Magna and Sabratha. The arch, once surmounted by a cupola and with many more reliefs than now survive, marked the center of the ancient city. (Courtesy: Donald White).

ZLITEN

One of the largest of the luxurious Roman coastal villas of Tripolitania, less than 3 mi. W. of the modern town of Zliten, which lies 20 mi. E. of *Leptis Magna*. Excavated in 1914 and 1923, the villa yielded magnificent frescoes and mosaics, now in the museum at *Tripoli*. These include mosaics of the seasons, of Dionysus on a panther, a marine scene and the famous gladiatorial sequence, often reproduced. Two panels show gladiatorial combat in an amphitheater, the other two of the beast fights. All are quite graphic and unsparingly gruesome. Some scholars think the mosaics depict a particular event, the games held to celebrate another Roman victory over the Garamantes in 70 AD (see *Germa*). Like the other seaside villas at *Silin* and *Tagiura*, the villa at Zliten also had its own private bath suite.

TUNISIA

The pervasive presence of Rome in Tunisia and the rest of North Africa during the golden years of the empire is here symbolized by the strong face of Lucius Verus in a provincial bust from Tunisia. He was the colleague of Marcus Aurelius in the emperorship. He died in 169 AD; the emperor outlived him. (Courtesy: Embassy of Tunisia, Washington, D.C.)

ACHOLLA

An ancient town, now the modern Butria/Botria, in the Sahel region on the coast, in eastern Tunisia, 25 mi. N. of Sfax. Tradition has it founded by Punic settlers from Malta—a Punic *tophet*, a sacrificial precinct, was discovered here in 1937. Acholla was one of the seven free cities of the early Roman province of Africa and supported Caesar in the civil wars.

The site, excavated 1947–55, yielded two bath complexes and a number of opulent villas, all with fine mosaics (some are in the Bardo Museum in Tunis). Those in the Baths of Trajan (about 115 AD), adjoining the forum, included one that celebrated allegorically Trajan's victory over the Parthians. More baths (also 2nd cent. AD) on the south of the site were also adorned with mosaics. The House of Asinius Rufus, who was consul in 184 AD under Commodus, contains a mosaic of the labors of Hercules—and Hercules was the emperor's patron deity. The House of the Red Columns, east of the Baths of Trajan, had not only mosaics but frescoes. One room was decorated with what we would call still lifes. The Villa of the Head of Oceanus is named for a mosaic on that subject, and the Villa of the Triumph of Neptune (170–180 AD) sported that subject on its dining room floor; its peristyle was exceptionally large. Of the villa's nearly 30 rooms, 13 were paved with fine mosaics, including those in the small dining room and a reception room featuring gourmet food: mussels, artichokes, rabbits, cucumbers, eggplant, a lemon, a pomegranate—and a basket of roses. Acholla also had an amphitheater to the south, and several Christian tombs and a baptistery. Its port on the coast is said to include a breakwater, now submerged.

AGBIA

See *Musti*.

AGGAR

Unexcavated remains of an ancient town, now at Henchir Sidi Amara, at the end of a rocky pass and overlooking the Wadi Marouf, about 15 mi. E. of Maktar, central Tunisia. One sees the piers of a triumphal arch, which led to what must have been the forum, a colonnaded square faced by a temple, presumably the Capitolium. Another temple lies to the southeast, and a Byzantine citadel with corner towers overlooks all. On the plain at the foot of the mountain is the well-preserved mausoleum, called the Qsar Khima, of one C. Marius Romanius. At the far end of the pass, in the opposite direction, six arches of a Roman bridge out of the original 10 still stand.

AÏN TOUNGA

The ancient Thignica, a Romanized native center about 7 mi. NE of Teboursouk in north-central Tunisia. The ruins include an arch, theater, temple, cisterns and the usual Byzantine fortress. A center of the popular and long-lasting native Saturn cult (equated with a Punic god), the ruins yielded no less than 538 carved Saturn stelae.

ALTHIBUROS

See *Medeïna*.

AMMAEDARA

Interesting Roman frontier town on a wadi, near the village of Haïdra. It lies in the Tébessa Mountains at an altitude of 2950 ft. near the Algerian border, 33 mi. NW of Kasserine. In the 1st cent. AD it was the original garrison post of the Third Augustan Legion, responsible for guarding Roman North Africa. When the legion moved away, veterans were settled on the site, which became a flourishing town until, once again, it became a military post under the Byzantines in the 6th century, commanded by Solomon, Belisarius' lieutenant.

The site, its forum bisected by a new highway to Algeria, has been little excavated. Visible are the forum and the high podium of the Capitolium. To the east is an unidentified large structure with window openings, and on the wadi two arches, the larger one of Septimius Severus, later converted into a small fort by the Byzantines. A few seats and the paving of its stage mark the remains of the theater. The cemeteries contain a number of tall mausolea and one of the five churches dating from the 4th to 7th cents.—the Basilica of Candidus in the east cemetery. It contained chapels of the martyrs who died under Diocletian. The largest, the Basilica of Bishop Melleus, dated 568–69 AD, with marble columns, had a reliquary of St. Cyprian. Another was a Vandal chapel, crudely built (the Vandals were Arian Christians). Finally two more were near and also in the massive Byzantine citadel, with heavy square towers, built by Solomon to command the river and bridge. From early times the town was on a military road.

ASSURAS

See *Zanfour*.

BÉJA

Important market town, 55 mi. W. of Tunis, which overlies the ancient Vaga, or Vega, once a major Numidian town, later Rome's largest African wheat market. Nothing of the old city can be seen except traces of the Byzantine wall circuit. Tourists are directed 8 mi. south on a mediocre road to a well-preserved Roman bridge, 76 yds. long, spanning the Oued Béja. Called the Bridge of Trajan, it was actually built under Tiberius (29 AD) and renovated under Vespasian (69–79 AD). There are some excavations, started in 1960, about 5 mi. northeast of Béja in a remote spot at Henchir el-Faouar. Here the forum of ancient Belalis Minor, with some surrounding buildings, and baths, have been uncovered.

BELALIS MINOR

See *Béja*.

BOU KOURNEÏN

Native open-air sanctuary of the Saturn cult, on a high mountain above the plain of Mornag, about 12 mi. SE of Tunis. The sanctuary of the Punic-Berber deity, here worshipped on a High Place under the name of Balcaranensis, consisted of a walled precinct cut into the rock, enclosing an altar. Fragments of many Saturn stelae, dedicated between 139 and 215 AD by worshippers with Punic-Roman names, were found here. See also *Aïn Tounga*.

BULLA REGIA

Ancient Numidian-Roman town in the fertile Medjerda basin, a few mi. N. of Jendouba in NW Tunisia. Its luxurious underground living rooms, shielded against the intense summer heat, make it one of the most interesting sites in the Roman world. Bulla Regia, as its name implies, was a royal town of the Numidian kings. Punic-style chamber tombs and even earlier megalithic dolmens south of the town indicate early settlement. Under the Romans it grew prosperous from the grain of the Medjerda and became a colony under Hadrian.

The extensive site includes most of the amenities of a comfortable Roman city. The baths (late 2nd cent. AD), with vaults, two pools and traces of mosaics, still stand in various places two stories high. There is a forum (Hadrianic) and around it are grouped the Capitolium temple, a basilica, and the Temple of Apollo, where in 1906 was found the skeleton of a woman with an iron collar, inscribed: "Adulteress, prostitute, hold me, because I fled from Bulla Regia." The attractive theater, dating from Marcus Aurelius' time, is in good shape except for the back wall. Inset into the marble-paved orchestra is a mosaic of a bear. There is an amphitheater, unexcavated, a Temple of Isis, public and private cisterns, and from a later period a 6th-cent. Christian basilica with a bird and fish mosaic, marble columns and a baptistery, a Christian cemetery and a small Byzantine fortress.

Eight villas with underground rooms (3rd cent. AD) have been excavated (identified by the names of their mosaics) and 12 more are known. These are columned atriums in typical Roman style, placed underground with internal walls built in, and open to the sky. There were pools, and living rooms opening off the atrium on all sides, ingeniously ventilated and lit by shafts and light wells

Some of the eight sumptuous villas (3rd century AD) excavated in Bulla Regia (above), once a royal town of the Numidian kings. Many of these villas had entire suites underground, cooled by air shafts, to avoid the intense heat of the region—an astonishing example of ancient air-conditioning. Below is the atrium of one of these subterranean suites, with chambers leading off to the left. (Courtesy: Embassy of Tunisia, Washington, D.C.)

and further protected above by surface pools or shading. The largest and earliest is the House of the Fish with an elaborate series of shafts and six fountains in the atrium pool, fed from roof pools. The House of the Hunt had a ground-level atrium with a mosaic, and a complete suite below, reached by 22 steps—living room with Corinthian columns, bedrooms, vaulted dining room and a kitchen with a chimney shaft. Here indeed were "energy-efficient," air-conditioned houses worthy of our modern technology! Apparently the villas were owned by wealthy Romanized Africans with Punic origins.

BUTRIA/BOTRIA

See *Acholla*.

CAPSA

See *Gafsa*.

CARTHAGE
(Roman: Carthago)

Famous Phoenician city on the Bay of Tunis, NE across the Lake of Tunis from the capital city, of which it is now a suburb. Founded according to tradition by Dido (Elissa), a princess of Tyre in Lebanon in 814 BC, nothing archaeologically earlier than the mid-8th cent. BC has in fact been turned up, though it is now thought that the city was founded (as the Punic Kart-Hadasht) around 800 BC. By the 6th–5th cent. BC Carthage dominated the western Mediterranean and had become the most powerful maritime city-state in the west. Its colonies were planted on Sicily, Sardinia and the Spanish coast; it ruled all North Africa from Tripolitania (see LIBYA) to the Atlantic; and its navigators explored the Atlantic shores, from England to Africa. Indeed the explorer Hanno may have sailed south as far as Sierra Leone. Carthage challenged the western Greeks and Etruscans until checked by the Greeks of Syracuse at Himera in 480 BC, then during a series of bitter wars her great general Hannibal finally managed to bring proud Rome close to defeat. But Carthage eventually lost and its great city was destroyed and ploughed over in 146 BC. It lay deserted for 100 years. Colonized again under Caesar and Augustus (effectively 29 BC) the city revived, and over a period of more than 700 years became once again an opulent capital, this time of Roman Africa, a rival in size to Rome, and later a center of early Christianity. It still flourished during 100 years of Vandal rule and 165 more under the Byzantines, but was finally destroyed by the Arabs in 698 AD.

Considering that Carthage in the 5th cent. BC was a metropolis of well over 300,000 people, and was again as large under the Romans in the 2nd–3rd cents. AD, there is astonishingly little left of its 1,000 years of history at the site. True, the Romans did thoroughly destroy Punic Carthage, but even of their own great city (pillaged to build nearby Tunis) little survives above ground. In 1971–72 a rescue operation in advance of suburban development was launched in conjunction with UNESCO, and archaeological teams from over a dozen countries have been working at various sites in Carthage to salvage what is left.

Of the Punic period the most outstanding survival is the *tophet*, a sacrificial precinct behind the old harbors where from about 700 BC to 146 BC many thousands of firstborn infants and children were sacrificed to Tanit and Baal for the wellbeing of the city in times of stress, a gruesome burnt offering described in Flaubert's famous novel *Salammbo*. In the three successive levels excavated, the ashes were placed in urns under cairns or stelae—some 20,000 of them in only one period, roughly between 400 and 200 BC. The Punic interconnected harbors—the rectangular merchants' harbor and the round naval harbor to its north—may still be discerned. Out of the one Carthaginian trading vessels and

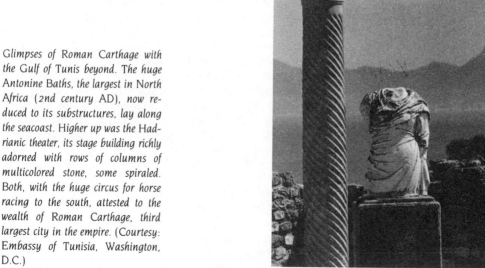

Glimpses of Roman Carthage with the Gulf of Tunis beyond. The huge Antonine Baths, the largest in North Africa (2nd century AD), now reduced to its substructures, lay along the seacoast. Higher up was the Hadrianic theater, its stage building richly adorned with rows of columns of multicolored stone, some spiraled. Both, with the huge circus for horse racing to the south, attested to the wealth of Roman Carthage, third largest city in the empire. (Courtesy: Embassy of Tunisia, Washington, D.C.)

out of the other war galleys sallied forth to dominate the seas. On an island in the middle of the naval harbor were 220 ship-sheds for the galleys, whose slip-ways have been unearthed. The Punic citadel was certainly on Byrsa hill above the town (and the Roman Capitolium too), but both are now covered by the Cathedral and a museum. On its slopes, and elsewhere in the city, Punic tombs and houses have been excavated in recent explorations, going back to the 5th cent. BC, the richest in grave goods before 480 BC; and an industrial and a residential quarter (3rd cent. BC) as well as part of the Punic city wall have been identified. Notably, on the east slope, a well-preserved Punic house of the 4th cent. BC has been laid bare.

Roman quays at the harbors may date back to the early Roman resettlement, and probably from the Augustan age an altar found on Byrsa hill, a poor imitation of Augustus' Altar of Peace in Rome. The most imposing Roman monuments are the ruins of the Antonine Baths (2nd cent. AD), once the largest in the Roman world outside Rome itself; but now only the substructures survive. It was a vast and sumptuously decorated building laid out facing the sea, with identical wings and huge octagonal halls. Its pools were fed by a splendid aqueduct whose source may be seen at *Zaghouan* and stretches of its arches at U*thina*.

Little of the elegant theater survived, though now somewhat restored. With its tiers of spiral and fluted columns of multicolored stone, as described by Apuleius in the 2nd cent. AD, it reflected the great wealth of the Roman city. Here Winston Churchill addressed the victorious Allied troops in 1943. Near it are the foundations of the Odeon (207 AD), for musical events, once the largest in the Roman world. The amphitheater and the circus (or hippodrome), for chariot racing, both greatly despoiled, lie behind the Byrsa hill. The circus, third largest in the Roman Empire and certainly the largest Roman structure in North Africa, has been completely stone-robbed. Nevertheless, from 1982 into 1986 American archaeologists managed to determine its ground plan and to uncover some of the massive substructures that supported the *cavea* or seating, as well as evidence (fragments of Corinthian columns and capitals) of a sumptuous marble colonnade that ran around the outside of the circus below the seats. The circus was in use from the 2nd through the 5th cents. AD, and it could seat from 60,000 to 75,000 spectators—for the Carthaginians were mad about chariot racing. As a bonus the archaeologists also excavated a huge dump piled behind the circus after it had gone out of use, a 7th-cent. Byzantine cemetery, and another buried section of the Theodosian wall of 425 AD—for the circus lay on the very edge of the ancient city. The excavation as a whole yielded countless small objects bearing on life in the late city—skeletons, pottery, curse tablets, objects of bone, vandal poems and much more. Near the amphitheater lie the great cisterns, part of Carthage's water supply, and others are near the baths, behind which is a pleasant archaeological park where Roman residences lie exposed.

Part of the restored House of the Aviary forms a small museum, the Antiquarium, outside of which a number of splendid late mosaics are on display. Indeed Carthage, with the other Roman cities of North Africa, has yielded an extraordinary quantity of mosaics from all periods. A fairly recent find is a large peristyle villa with mosaics, the House of the Greek Charioteer, built about 400 AD and completely refurbished in the early 5th cent. AD before the Vandal conquest (at a time, be it noted, when Britain was already slipping into the Dark Ages!). Under it were reused Punic cisterns in which was found a fine marble group of Ganymede and the Eagle belonging to its last owners, its pagan theme amazingly still cherished long after the introduction of Christianity. A recently found circular monument of the same period may have been an early Christian martyrium.

Detail from the "Horses" mosaic from Carthage, one of many excavated in the ruins of the Roman city. The art of the colored mosaic was highly developed in Roman North Africa and may even have originated there. (Courtesy: Embassy of Tunisia, Washington, D.C.)

Carthage, long a seminal Christian center, was the home of St. Augustine from 370 to 383 AD, and it had many Christian basilicas, most badly excavated and restored, like the Basilica of St. Cyprian (4th cent.), associated with Augustine's indomitable mother. Most were in use through the Byzantine period. The best preserved and largest in North Africa is the Damous el-Karita (*domus caritatis*) with a baptistery and subterranean rotunda. It was probably the seat of a bishop. Recent excavations have also uncovered an early Christian church with baptistery and an ecclesiastical establishment around it. A Jewish cemetery north of the city has also been excavated. The Carthage National Museum is on Byrsa Hill. There are also a number of small on-site museums and many finds from Carthage are in the Bardo Museum in Tunis.

CHEMTOU

The ancient Simitthu, 11 mi. SW of Bulla Regia in NW Tunisia. Once a native town (a Punic temple of the early centuries BC in Hellenistic style was found near the quarries), it was settled by Romans at the end of Augustus' reign and was known for its much-prized Simitthu marble of a yellow-orange color. Scattered here and there, the poorly-preserved ruins include a paved forum, baths, two temples, cisterns, an aqueduct, and the theater, built on vaults and richly decorated with local marble, including an orchestra pavement of multicolored marbles. There are also the remains of two Christian basilicas, also of bridges across the Medjerda River. Excavations are still taking place.

CILLIUM

See *Kasserine.*

CLUPEA

See *Kelibia.*

DJEM, EL-ORJEM

Or El Jem. The Roman Thysdrus, on a plateau of the Sahel, inland from the coast, 36 mi. S. of *Sousse.* Once one of the richest cities in Roman Africa, its wealth drawn from the export of olive oil, its immense amphitheater, third largest in the Roman world, still dwarfs the small Arab town of El-Djem around it. The remains of an earlier and much smaller amphitheater have been excavated, as well as those of baths, two temples, traces of a large circus that could seat 10,000, and a number of palatial villas with superb mosaics. The best of these are under protection in a small site museum; others are in Sousse and in the Bardo Museum, Tunis. The great amphitheater, its three tiers of arches still rising 120 ft. above the low Arab houses, is in good condition after a restoration in the 1970s, though its seats have gone. It could accommodate some 50,000 spectators—drawn of course from the entire region. Probably built under Gordian, proconsul from 230 AD, it was here that he was proclaimed emperor in 238, when 80 years old. There is an archaeological museum in the town.

DOUGGA

The ancient Thugga, the best-preserved small city in Tunisia, in a charming setting on the side of a hill, about 62 mi. SW of Tunis. A prehistoric settlement, then a leading Numidian center in the 2nd cent. BC under the remarkable King Masinissa, friend of Rome, it became a Roman market town of some 5,000 in the hills overlooking the fertile fields of the Medjerda River plain. Here Roman, Punic and native cultures mixed on equal terms, as attested by the number and religious variety of temples and shrines, while the city's antiquity is shown in its narrow winding seats, the survival of ancient walls and prehistoric dolmens at the top of the town, and its famous 2nd cent. BC Libyo-Punic Mausoleum.

The Roman buildings mostly date from the city's most prosperous period in the 2nd and 3rd cents. AD, when there were 10 other Roman towns in a radius of 30 mi. The public buildings were donated by wealthy Thuggan families. A small colonnaded forum, somewhat disfigured by the remains of a Byzantine fortress, ends in a plaza called the Square of the Wind Rose for a wind rose engraved on its pavement. The forum is flanked on the east by the remarkably preserved Capitolium temple (166 AD) facing out over the plain. Next to it, also facing south above the Square of the Wind Rose, is the Temple of Mercury with semicircular side rooms. It looks down over a market flanked on the east and west by arcades, each with 10 shops. South of the forum is the Temple of Tellus, again triple-roomed.

Well to the east of it is the interesting Hadrianic complex of three temples (128–138 AD), dedicated to Concord, to Liber Pater (the Punic war god) facing a large peristyle, and the small shrine of Frugifer, the town's local deity. The complex ends in the southeast in a theatral area of curving seats for some religious ritual. The great bulk of the Licinian baths (3rd cent. AD), symmetrically designed and now somewhat restored, lies across from the complex. There are smaller baths to the SE, with interesting latrines, and another large bath complex way to the south. Also 3rd-cent. are the arches of Septimius Severus to the

The small Roman market town of Dougga (ancient Thugga), its ruins the best preserved in Tunisia. The graceful façade of the Capitolium, a temple dedicated to the state gods of Rome: Juno, Jupiter and Minerva, is glimpsed through the entrance to the forum. This richly endowed town of only about 5,000 people boasted at least nine temples, some dedicated to native gods, three bath establishments, a market, a theater and a circus, as well as a number of luxurious villas. (Courtesy: Embassy of Tunisia, Washington, D.C.)

east (235 AD) and of Alexander Severus (205 AD) to the west of the city. The fine theater (168 AD), up the slope to the north and now restored and used for performances, faces out over the plain. Its seats, cut into the hillside, could hold 3,500 spectators.

On high ground north of the theater and outside the walls, a few columns mark the remains of the Temple of Saturn (late 2nd cent. AD) built over a temple to Saturn's Punic predecessor, Baal. It faces a large columned courtyard. Also outside the walls, west of the forum, is the lovely restored Temple of Tanit-Caelestis (about 230 AD) set inside a semicircular wall and portico. North of it are the ruins of a Temple of Minerva, cisterns marking the ends of two aqueducts and a large circus. Of the luxurious houses, some built on two levels down the slope, the so-called large House of El-Acheb was probably a market, the House of the Trifolium was probably a brothel, and the well-known House of Dionysus and Ulysses was built 250–275 AD. The mosaics are in the Bardo Museum, Tunis.

Outside the city to the south the restored Punic mausoleum, dating from the period of Masinissa and dedicated to one Ateban, rises 70 ft. in three stories, topped by a pyramid. It is the only important Libyo-Punic monument to survive in good condition. To the northeast of Dougga, at Teboursouk 3½ mi. away, are the unexcavated remains of a large city amidst olive groves, with a Byzantine fort.

GAFSA

Most northerly of the Tunisian oases, where the dry steppe meets the Sahara. This oasis of 100,000 palm trees was once the prosperous Roman settlement and Byzantine stronghold of Capsa, of which all that remains are several masonry-lined pools, possibly once a nymphaeum, into which children now dive to retrieve coins. Gafsa is better known for its prehistoric remains in the vicinity, identified as a series of cultures called the Capsian, dating from the Mesolithic (about 8000 BC) into the Neolithic period, characterized by large burins, backed blades and microliths, and later by bone tools. These are found in huge shell mounds extending into eastern Algeria, made up of snail shells; these early hunters ate snails in quantity. At Sidi Mansur near Gafsa excavations uncovered a long stratigraphic sequence extending from the hand axes of the Lower Paleolithic into the Capsian period.

GEBEL MLEZZA

On Cape Bon. Some years ago the French excavated 16 Punic tombs here of the late 4th cent. BC. There were wooden coffins, Egyptian amulets, and in one tomb wall paintings depicting a fortified town, a mausoleum, and an altar.

GEBEL OUST

Remarkable shrine and baths, dedicated to Hygieia, goddess of health, and Aesculapius, its ruins situated on the N. side of the Gebel Oust, about 15 mi. S. of Tunis—in use from Hadrian's time for five centuries into the Byzantine period. At its height it had over 219 rooms clustered around a large rectangular columned hall and a round room containing a pool, with 10 columns. The water issued from a grotto with a shrine to the two deities (later used as a church and baptistery). The rooms, many with individual tubs, had marbled or frescoed walls and mosaic floors, and many were bedrooms used by the ailing devotees, who were thought to be healed in dreams while sleeping near the god. Most of the mosaics were geometric, but one fine one depicted the seasons. Large reservoirs and cisterns completed the complex.

GIGTHIS

Provincial Roman town with Punic antecedents, on the Gulf of Bou Grara opposite the island of Jerba, in the south about 19 mi. NE of Medenine. The ruins, close to the fishing village of Bou Grara, were partly excavated in the early 20th cent. and are now much overgrown. Typically, this small town had an astonishing array of public buildings built in the prosperous Roman period, usually donated by wealthy citizens, and not always of the best materials. These centered on a porticoed forum with as many as nine temples and sanctuaries grouped around and near it. More porticoes bordered a street leading under an arch to the harbor and a jetty protecting it. There were two sets of baths, a market with a semicircular arrangement of shops, an inn, a civil basilica, curia and treasury. A Temple of Mercury lay outside the town, but, curiously, no theater, amphitheater or circus has been found. The neat suburban villas had central courtyards with peristyles, simple mosaic floors and frescoed walls. On a cliff over the sea to the north are the ruins of a fort built by Justinian's general Solomon.

HADRUMETUM

See *Sousse.*

HAÏDRA

See *Ammaedara.*

HAMMAM ZOUARKA	See *Maktar*.
HENCHIR EL-FAOUAR	See *Béja*.
HENCHIR SIDI AMARA	See *Aggar*.
IUNCI	See *Younga*.
JAMA	See *Zama*.
JEM, EL	See *Djem, El-*.
JUSTINIANOPOLIS	See *Sousse*.

KAIROUAN

Ancient Islamic city, the fourth most holy in Islam and a pilgrimage center, dominated by its Great Mosque and minaret, among the earliest in the Islamic world. Kairouan, in E. central Tunisia, 32 mi. SW of *Sousse*, was founded in 670 AD, even before the fall of Carthage in 698, by Oqba, or Okba (Uqbah ibn Nafi), a leader of the Arab invasion of North Africa. It was the first major Islamic city in the Maghreb, and after 800 AD became the capital of the Aghlabid dynasty.

Kairouan, a holy city of Islam and one of the earliest of Islamic cities in the Arab world (670 AD). It came under the Aghlabid dynasty in the 9th cent. that rebuilt the ancient Great Mosque, adding the severe minaret. Its buttressed outer walls are shown here (above). The Aghlabids also constructed the two huge cisterns (below) outside the town. The interior of the Great Mosque is adorned with ranks of Roman and Byzantine columns, some of colored marbles, granite and prophyry, all brought from nearby Roman cities. (Courtesy: Embassy of Tunisia, Washington, D.C.)

The Fatimids conquered it in 909 AD and their capital was then moved to *Mahdia* on the coast. Although Kairouan had lost its political independence, it was strengthened as a center of Islamic orthodoxy; and even after the Beni Hilal bedouins sacked it in 1057, leaving the city almost in ruins, its renown as a holy city survived even into the present. Because it is holy, and because of its semi-desert setting, Kairouan is an entrancing town, having escaped the growing urban sprawl of other Tunisian cities.

The old city is enclosed within brick walls originally built in 1052. The huge mosque dates back to the founding of the city in 670 AD. Several times enlarged, it was completely rebuilt under the Aghlabids after 836 and has since been four times restored. Nevertheless its early character, with its severely unadorned outer walls irregularly buttressed, its great courtyard paved in white marble and enclosed in serried arcades of Roman and Byzantine columns, has never been lost. The vast, many-aisled prayer hall is a forest of 114 antique columns, and the mihrab is flanked by even more splendid columns of colored marbles, granite and porphyry, all brought from Carthage, nearby Sousse and other ancient cities. The minbar, of intricately carved teak, was imported from Baghdad in the 9th cent., and the luster tiles around the mihrab, reused even here, are the earliest known. The massive square minaret, of the 9th cent., stands 115 ft. tall, and Roman inscriptions and reliefs are built into its masonry.

Just outside the town two enormous Aghlabid cisterns, of the 860s, have been restored, and at Reqqada a few miles to the south an Aghlabid royal suburb with palaces, fountains and mosques has been excavated. The museum of Kairouan, across from the Great Mosque, displays precious objects from the mosque and from Reqqada.

KANTARA, EL-   Modern village and Roman town on the SE shore of the island of Jerba where the modern causeway (on ancient foundations) leads to the mainland. The ancient Meninx was once a prosperous town. Trebonianus Gallus was proclaimed emperor here in 251 AD, but in a disturbed period lasted only two years. The site, under mounds of sand, has been only partially excavated, and erosion and tourism threaten its continued existence. Traces of a forum, baths, houses and mosaics and a Christian basilica have been found. The cemetery lay northwest of the town. There was once an amphitheater nearby.

KASSERINE   Strategic pass and town in a barren inland region 135 mi. SW of Tunis, much fought over in World War II. Part of the modern town overlies the ancient Roman Cillium, little excavated, whose abundant ruins extend over a plateau to the southwest. A three-storied Roman mausoleum in good condition rises in the modern town. A set of verses of 114 lines in tribute to the occupant, Flavius Secundus, is inscribed on either side of the doorway, and an epitaph to his family higher up on the second story. Another tower-mausoleum of the Petronii is in poor condition. A triumphal arch of the 3rd cent. AD dominates the ruins on the plateau, and the remains of an attractive small theater (probably 1st-cent.) are exposed on the edge. There are traces of a temple, of a Byzantine fort, a few arches of an aqueduct, and houses—whose mosaics are in the Bardo Museum, Tunis.

KELIBIA   Fishing port near Cape Bon's eastern tip, 50 mi. E. of Tunis. Its castle on a high rock embodies work of many periods, reflecting the antiquity of the settlement here, once called Clupea. From this Punic town, in the 4th cent. BC, the Syracusan tyrant Agathocles invaded the Carthaginian homeland with a large army, nearly captured Carthage, but was forced to retreat. After the Punic wars both Marius and Caesar settled veterans in Clupea. Ancient relics have been found here and there. Excavations have uncovered a Roman residential district along the side of a hill, notably a fine villa with peristyle court and mosaics, as well as a church containing 50 tomb mosaics of the 4th and 5th centuries AD. From this church also came a Byzantine masterpiece in mosaics, a clover-leaf-shaped baptismal font dedicated to St. Cyprian (6th cent.), now reconstructed in the Bardo Museum, Tunis. There is also a Byzantine chapel in the castle.

KENISSIA, EL-

About 4 mi. S. of *Sousse*. A Punic sanctuary, excavated here, showed the typical elements of a Punic High Place. There was a portico, an open court with a cistern, an altar on the highest point, reached by steps, chapels with statues, and a cemetery for the bones of sacred animals. See also *Bou Kourneïn*.

KERKOUANE

The only completely preserved Punic town known, on Cape Bon 5 mi. N. of Kelibia. Founded in the 7th century BC, it was laid waste in 310 BC by Agathocles of Syracuse (see *Kelibia*) and again by the Roman Regulus in 256 BC, before his defeat and capture in the First Punic War. It seems to have been finally destroyed about 150 BC—and its remains preserved for posterity. Continuing excavations have revealed a walled town, regularly laid out along the seashore (the sea is now rapidly eroding part of the site), with a temple and baths. The residential quarter, though not much to look at, has been restored. The houses, usually built around a court paved with a cement inset with bits of colored glass paste, had painted stucco walls, each courtyard featuring a sunken bath lined with mosaics. One of the larger houses, the House of the Sphinx, named for a terracotta altar in its chapel decorated with a sphinx, had 10 rooms, some used as glass and pottery workshops. The house was in use from 500 to 150 BC. The more important rooms were decorated with frescoes and mosaic floors, including a pebble mosaic of a griffin and stag. In its court was an oven, a grain mill and a hip bath.

The necropolis, a half mi. inland, dating from the 7th to 3rd cents. BC, was excavated in the 1960s and yielded grave goods showing Greek and Egyptian influences (4th–3rd centuries BC) and a red-painted wooden sarcophagus, "the Princess of Kerkouane," with a plastered cover in the shape of a goddess (Astarte?) painted in red, blue and yellow. It is now in the museum at the site of *Utica*. There is a local museum at the site.

LE KEF

An attractive town behind ancient ramparts on a hillside in the interior, about 90 mi. SW of Tunis. Here was Sicca Veneria, a Punic town, later an Augustan Roman foundation famous for its temple with religious prostitutes. Destroyed by the Vandals, the town's stones were freely used to build the medieval walls and the 17th-cent. Casbah. Several monuments of the ancient city are traceable, a small amphitheater and a theater near the Casbah, the baths with a hexagonal central hall, 12 large barrel-vaulted cisterns, some of the Byzantine town walls, the Christian basilica of Qsar el-Ghoula with its mosaic floors, and finally the grand Byzantine basilica of "Dar el-Qous," now restored, again with fine mosaics. Miscellaneous finds from the site are in the Bardo Museum, Tunis.

LIMISA

See *Qsar Lemsa*.

MACOMADES MINORES

See *Younga*.

MACTARIS

See *Maktar*.

MAHDIA

Or Al-Mahdiya, modern town on the coast, 32 mi. SE of Sousse. Of its earlier existence as a Punic and Roman port only vestiges remain. Mahdia was taken over as a fortress capital by the first Fatimid leader, Obeid Allah, called "El Mahdi," about 912 AD after the Fatimids had conquered the Aghlabids with their capital city of *Kerouane* in 909. From Mahdia El Mahdi hoped to conquer Egypt—finally achieved in 969 after his death. On the headland, site of the city named for him, he built a fort, and about 916 a mosque, which survives, somewhat altered but now restored. With its projecting portico, arcaded court and unadorned prayer hall it is a severe but interesting building. One gate of the Fatimid defenses, the Skifa al-Kahla, survives, and there are remains of a palace, either of Obeid Allah or his son.

Mahdia is also known for a fabulously rich ancient shipwreck, discovered in 1907 in shallow water some 3 mi. northeast of the headland. The capacious ship, which seems to have been on its way from Athens, probably to Rome, was loaded with an immense cargo of luxury goods, dated 2nd or 1st cent. BC. This included 64 heavy columns and many capital columns, separately stored, as well as an array of marble and bronze statues, reliefs, bowls, incense burners, bedsteads, lamps. A marble head of Aphrodite may have been a copy from Praxiteles. Heavy anchors, kitchen gear and a skeleton were also retrieved. The cargo may have belonged to an art entrepreneur catering to upper-class Roman tastes. The smaller finds are in the Bardo Museum, Tunis.

Maktar, the remains of the triumphal arch of ancient Mactaris (116 AD) at one end of the Trajanic forum, later fortified by the Byzantines. A very ancient city, Maktar maintained a strong Punic-Numidian culture well into the Roman period, when it lay in a once heavily populated, fertile area devoted to raising and exporting grain and olives. (Courtesy: Embassy of Tunisia, Washington, D.C.)

About 9 mi. north of Mahdia and 3 mi. inland on a side road lie the scanty ruins of Thapsus (Tapsus), once a Punic town at the site of Caesar's famous victory over the followers of Pompey and Juba, the Numidian king, during the civil wars that brought him to power.

MAKTAR

The ancient Mactaris, in central Tunisia 35 mi. SE of Le Kef, situated in the hilly region known as the Haut Tell. As a Numidian town, the site dates back to at least the 2nd cent. BC. Punic settlers, reinforced by refugees fleeing *Carthage* in 146 BC, mingled with the natives to give the town a distinct Punic-Numidian culture, which was maintained well into the Roman period, to about 180 AD, when it became a colony and Romanization was intensified. The ruins, excavated between 1944–56 and 1970–73, lie in and around the modern French-style town. Traces of the Numidian walls to the south, megalithic tombs intermingled with Roman and Christian, as well as crude Punic stelae now in the small museum by the gate, reflect the earlier phase. In a Punic sanctuary and *tophet*, excavated beside the Roman arch-gate, 85 more stelae were found (now in the Bardo Museum, Tunis). Many more were used in the substructure of the Roman gate, called the Bab el-Ain. Little is left of the recently excavated Temple of Hathor Miskar to the northeast (2nd cent. BC), which yielded the longest Punic inscription in Tunisia, while the Roman Temple of Bacchus in the middle of the town was built over a Numidian sanctuary. By the old Numidian forum, without a portico, which remained in use in the Roman period, there was a temple of the Roman-Punic god, Liber Pater.

To the south of the Bab el-Ain triumphal arch-cum-gate was the Roman forum of Trajan, paved and with a portico, with a triumphal arch of 116 AD at one end—later fortified by the Byzantines. North of the forum is a small amphitheater in good condition though unexcavated. To its south are the foundations of a Vandal basilica of Hildegundus (the Roman basilica has disappeared), and beyond that the remains of one of the two sets of baths, both late 2nd cent. AD. An east-west street, bordered by the old forum and other Numidian ruins, leads to all that is left of the Capitolium (169 AD). North of it lie the elegant West Baths (199 AD), the columns and graceful arcades of its court reerected. Like the baths at *Carthage* it had symmetrically identical wings. A ruined aqueduct appears behind the baths.

Outside the walls to the west lay the Hadrianic Temple of Apollo; to the south the most interesting building is the *schola*, or school for youths (dated 88 AD), a kind of clubhouse for a paramilitary group of young men of good Roman-Punic families, its rooms and meeting hall (later a church) grouped around a porticoed palaestra-courtyard. In a curious building nearby with interior troughs, the young men apparently supervised the storing of tax grain for export to Rome. The House of Venus, a large rich house with splendid mosaics, has recently come to light near the Hathor Miskar temple. There are several Roman tomb towers of Punic style like that of *Dougga*. These include the mausoleum of the Julii that rises near the arch-gate. Mactaris also had a Byzantine fort.

Roman ruins are plentiful in the once heavily populated olive and grain region around Maktar. At Hammam Zouarka are the remains of a large bath complex and the source of Maktar's aqueduct. A Latin inscription may be seen on one arch of the baths: "He who urinates here will incur the wrath of Mars." Two triumphal arches rise from the ruins of Uzappa near Ksour Abd el-Melek, some 15 mi. from Maktar.

MEDEÏNA

The ancient Althiburos, reached by a track from nearby Ebba Ksour, some 20 mi. NW of Maktar. Scattered ruins of this Numidian-Punic-Roman town, which became a colony under Septimius Severus, lie on a plateau in hilly country. They include in various degrees of dilapidation a forum with its Capitolium (185–91 AD), a Temple of Jupiter, and other buildings around it, including a *schola* (see *Maktar*) and a shrine of Aesculapius. There is also a well-preserved theater, a monumental fountain and a triumphal arch, and various mausolea. From the ruins of a number of private houses have come some notable mosaics, especially a ship mosaic of 289–90 AD, now in the Bardo, Tunis, picturing and usually naming 25 types of ships. One is a horse transport, and the horses in it are also given their names.

MENINX

See *Kantara, El-*.

MONASTIR

Modern coastal city 11 mi. ESE of Sousse, noted for its early Islamic monuments. It was a Punic-Roman town called Ruspina, Caesar's base for his African campaign, but nothing of this survives. In the 8th and 9th centuries it became an Arab base for the Islamic conquests in Africa. In a central square, bordered in part by the 8th-cent. walls and battlements, stands the massively austere

The 8th-cent. walls and the tower of the ribat (796 AD), a fortified monastery, in the old city of Monastir. Though once a Roman town, of which nothing is left, Monastir became a base for the initial Arab conquest of North Africa, and is known today for its fine early Islamic monuments. (Courtesy: Embassy of Tunisia, Washington, D.C.)

Ribat or fortified monastery, now restored, dating from 796 AD, though often altered. In its prayer hall is a fine museum of Islamic art, mostly Fatimid. Next to it stands the fortified Great Mosque, probably 9th cent., and the smaller oratory of Saïda from a few centuries later.

MUSTI

Roman town on a hillside in N. central Tunisia, 8 mi. SW of Dougga. A municipium probably founded by Caesar, its compact ruins include a paved forum, the columns of a portico, a temple, a street bordered by the remains of shops with a phallic sign indicating the site of one or more brothels, an oil press and a triumphal arch, now restored. The piers of an aqueduct are nearby. To the north a few miles stands a Byzantine fortress on the ruins of ancient Agbia.

OUDNA

The once prosperous Roman town of Uthina, 12 mi. S. of Tunis, probably founded as a colony in the early years of Augustus' reign. It lies on the line of the aqueduct from *Zaghouan* to *Carthage* and an impressive stretch of the aqueduct's arches may be seen near it. The remains, badly pillaged, date mostly from the High Empire in the 2nd and 3rd centuries AD, and include a temple, theater, amphitheater, triumphal arch, baths, which yielded some fine sculpture, and reservoirs and cisterns. Eleven luxurious houses, underlining the prosperity of this ancient agricultural region, have been excavated, revealing a total of 67 mosaics from all periods of the empire. The palatial house of the Laberii had 40 rooms, a large peristyle, and a famous mosaic in its atrium delightfully picturing the local farming and hunting life. There were also remains of several later churches and of two bridges over the wadi. The finds are in the Bardo Museum, Tunis.

QAIRAWAN

See *Kairouan.*

QSAR KHIMA

See *Aggar.*

QSAR LEMSA

The ancient Limisa; a massive Byzantine fortress at the foot of the Gebel Serj Mountains, about 30 mi. E. of Maktar. Standing on a plateau, it is square with projecting battlemented towers at the corners, equipped with "arrow slits," and is almost perfectly preserved, except to the southeast. Probably built after Justinian's reconquest of North Africa from the Vandals in 533 AD, it is similar to the contemporary fortress at *Ammaedara* and others in Tunisia. A large spring-fed Byzantine basin outside the fort supplied it with water. Inside are remnants of minor buildings, and about 500 yds. down the hill the remains of a small theater.

QSAR ZAMMEL

See *Zama.*

REQQADA

See *Kairouan*

RUSPINA

See *Monastir.*

SBEÏTLA

The extensive ruins of Roman Sufetula lie N. of this modern town in S. central Tunisia, 120 mi. SW of Tunis and 19 mi. E. of Kasserine. Sufetula was once a substantial city in the midst of a fertile grain and olive-producing region, important as part of Rome's "bread basket." Its irrigation is now being restored.

The magnificent forum of Sbeïtla (139 AD), once the Roman city of Sufetula. The triple-arched entrance leads into the large colonnaded forum. Behind are the three temples of the Capitolium complex, a most unusual arrangement—the central temple, remarkably well preserved, probably that of Jupiter. Sited in a once richly fertile area, the widespread ruins of Sufetula, except for the forum, are fragmentary and have been little investigated. It became an important Christian-Byzantine town with no less than seven churches of various denominations. (Courtesy: Embassy of Tunisia, Washington, D.C.)

Curiously, Sufetula never had a wall. Since the ruins have been little excavated, not much is known of its most prosperous period during the High Empire. Later it became an important Byzantine center, the home in the 7th cent. AD of patrician Gregory, who in 647 was defeated by the Arabs outside Sufetula, the beginning of the end for Roman North Africa.

The ruins center on the imposing forum (139 AD), remarkably well preserved, lined with arcades, a colonnade and shops and a curia, with a triple-arched entrance at one end and a most unusual group of three temples on high platforms at the other, forming a Capitolium complex. One temple (of Jupiter?) is well preserved, its sculptured decorations in good condition. The rest of the town is badly ruined, except for the fine arch of Diocletian, recently restored. A grid pattern of paved streets can be discerned, and baths, a theater, an amphitheater, fountains and house foundations, and the remains of an aqueduct-bridge over the wadi.

Apparently Sufetula survived the Vandal period unscathed. A tribute to its late blooming into the final Byzantine epoch are the ruins of no less than seven Christian structures, both Orthodox and Donatist (schismatics), as well as the Diocletian arch and the theater (restored). The original cathedral of Bellator (313–400 AD) has a chapel; the basilica of Vitalis became the cathedral under the Vandals. Its baptistery with a font displays fine mosaics. The basilica of Servus lasted into the Byzantine period, as did another church built alongside the forum. The 6th-cent. church of Saints Gervasius, Protasius and Tryphon was actually in use until the 10th cent. The chapel of Honorius dates from the 5th cent., and the basilica of Sylvanus and Fortunatus, a martyrium, is purely Byzantine in style and date. There are also remnants of several Byzantine fortresses.

SFAX

Second largest city of Tunisia, on the N. shore of the Gulf of Gabès, 150 mi. SSE of Tunis. It completely covers the remains of the ancient town of Taparura. Only a few sites are known from the city's outskirts—tombs, basilicas, a villa, the

The large Tunisian city of Sfax pretty well covers the remains of an ancient Roman city and an Aghlabid (Arab) port. Little is left of either except the Great Mosque and the massive Arab walls around the medina, shown here, dating in part to the 9th cent. and built out of reused Roman stone. (Courtesy: Embassy of Tunisia, Washington, D.C.)

House of the Poet. The city was also an early Islamic port under the Aghlabids. The mighty ramparts around the large medina, the central square of the old city, built of reused Roman stones, are in part 9th cent., as is some of the Great Mosque. The Sfax museum is in the City Hall, and some of the finds are also in the Bardo Museum, Tunis.

SICCA VENERIA   See Le Kef.

SIDI MANSUR   See Gafsa.

SIDI-ZIN   Paleolithic site in NW Tunisia, near Le Kef. Around an ancient waterhole here several levels were distinguished in 1950. The earliest, yielding limestone axes and pebble tools, belonged to the Lower Paleolithic—a rare find in North Africa as a whole and the only site in Tunisia (see also in ALGERIA: Aïn Hanech, Ternifine; and in MOROCCO: Sidi Abd er-Rahman). A middle Paleolithic stone industry was found in an upper level at Sidi-Zin.

SIMITTHU   See Chemtou.

SOUSSE   Tunisia's third largest city, the ancient Hadrumetum, located on the Gulf of Hammamet about 60 mi. SE of Tunis. It was an important Phoenician port of call long before the founding of Carthage, and like Carthage had a tophet, a sacrificial area, from which many interesting finds have come, now in the local museum. Its six levels date from the 7th cent. BC and extend, unlike Carthage's, into the 1st cent. AD long after the Roman occupation, though gradually the sacrifices became those of animals rather than children. Hadrumetum was attacked by Agathocles of Syracuse in 308 BC (see Kelibia, Kerkouane), and was the base for Hannibal's army before the final battle of Zama in 202 BC. His family had estates around the city. Caesar besieged it in 46 BC, and later as a Roman city it became one of the most prosperous in the province. It was made a colony under Trajan and reached its peak under the Severan emperors. It had the usual theater, amphitheater and circus and baths, though nothing is left of them, and luxurious villas inside and outside the city from which have come a wealth of over 250 mosaics graphically illustrating many aspects of life in the period. Many of these are in the Casbah Museum here, others in the Bardo Museum, Tunis. The Casbah also displays the best finds from the enormous catacombs of Sousse—some 240 capacious underground galleries lined with two to three tiers of tombs dating from pagan to early Christian times, about 15,000 altogether. The most interesting are the galleries of the Good Shepherd.

But Sousse today is an Islamic city, and was once a flourishing port under the Aghlabids (see *Kairouan*). From this period date the massive fortified monastery or *ribat* (821–22 AD) and the Great Mosque (850 AD) close by, both within the medina, the old city, whose walls were begun in the 9th cent. The Mosque of Bou Fatata (838–41) is one of the oldest in the Maghreb. The museum in the Casbah, the citadel built into the old walls, is most rewarding, containing not only the *tophet* and catacomb finds and fine Roman mosaics from the city, but also other discoveries from the region, including from *El-Djem*.

Sousse is again a large modern city overlaying an ancient Phoenician port of call with a tophet like that at Carthage, as well as the prosperous Roman city of Hadrumetum—once Hannibal's base before his final defeat at Zama in 202 BC—and an important Arab port of the 9th cent. AD. The latter is recalled by the massive Aghlabid ribat (821–22 AD), or fortified monastery, now used for concerts (right), and the Great Mosque of the same period close by.

Many rich Roman villas from Roman Hadrumetum have been excavated, yielding well over 200 fine mosaics. A detail from one of these, the "Triumph of Neptune" (now in Tunis) shows a Nereid (right). (Courtesy: Embassy of Tunisia, Washington, D.C.)

SUFETULA   See *Sbeïtla*.

TAPARURA   See *Sfax*.

TEBOURSOUK   See *Dougga*.

THAENAE   The modern Thina, ruins of a wealthy port town on the Gulf of Gabès, 7½ mi. S. of Sfax. Excavated 1947–55 and in 1961, the remains are chiefly notable for what is left of a number of baths, particularly the Baths of the Months, built under Diocletian. Named for a mosaic in it, the baths were well enough preserved to permit a reconstruction of the building with its roofing and its luxurious latrines. Thaenae was a Punic port, a colony under Hadrian and later an episcopal see. Also uncovered were the town's ramparts with semicircular towers and a monumental gateway. Two substantial houses yielded mosaics and a rare painting of Dionysus. Remains of an aqueduct, a circus, reservoirs and a pagan-Christian cemetery outside the walls were also found. The finds are in the Sfax museum and the Bardo in Tunis.

THAPSUS   See *Mahdia*.

THÉLEPTE   A village in arid steppe country, 17 mi. SW of Kasserine in western Tunisia. On its outskirts are the extensive ruins, covering about 200 acres, of a once-important military stronghold and city, little excavated and much stone-robbed. There was a theater, and large baths with mosaic floors whose brick arches still rise above the ruins. A heavy four-square Byzantine fortress with corner towers is comparable to those at *Ammaedara*, *Qsar Lemsa* and elsewhere. There are also the remains of six basilicas, including the Basilica of the Apostles, which housed an important council in 418 AD, and four chapels.

THIGNICA   See *Aïn Tounga*.

THINA   See *Thaenae*.

THINISSUT   About 3 mi. SE of Tunis, on the Bay of Hammamet near Siagu. Here was excavated a Punic sanctuary of Baal and Tanit, dated by a coin to 45 BC, consisting of a terrace fronting on three courts. In it was found a series of figures of the two gods, now in the Bardo Museum, Tunis.

THUBURBO MAIUS   Ancient market town with a long history, in a pleasant undulating landscape 32 mi. SSW of Tunis, in N. central Tunisia. Excavated between 1912 and 1936, the remains show irregularly laid out streets and even houses, which betray its origin as a Numidian and then Punic settlement. Veterans of Augustus were settled in the town in 27 BC and thereafter it became a collecting point for the grain that made the region important in supplying Rome. A colony under Commodus (161–180 AD), it entered a period of stagnation later in the 2nd cent. until the mid-4th cent. when new building and rebuilding of the old monuments took place. The ruins as usual center around the forum (161 AD), with porticoes and once paved, and the Capitolium (167–68) on a high podium, vaulted rooms beneath it holding the town's treasury and archives. Fragments of a colossal statue of Jupiter lie on the floor of the cella. The small curia with its council chamber stands on the forum's north side, richly decorated with a coffered ceiling, and the unusual round forecourt of a Temple of Mercury (211 AD) opens onto its south side. The colonnaded market with shops lies just off its southeast corner. To the southwest are the Summer Baths (late 2nd cent.), largest of two in the town, sumptuously decorated with marble and mosaics. A separate semicircular building held the elegant latrines. Near it the Portico of the Petronii, donated by a local worthy in 225 AD, consists of an open court, probably the bath's palaestra or exercise ground, enclosed by Corinthian columns of black marble, gold-veined. Opening onto it is a sanctuary of Aesculapius. The smaller Winter Baths lie in the northeast quarter (2nd cent., restored in the 4th).

Remains of four triumphal arches (three with a single arch, one triple-arched) may be seen and the foundations of comfortable houses—the House of the Waggoner, the House of the Labyrinth—whose mosaics are in the Bardo Museum, Tunis. There are also later, more modest houses from the Byzantine pe-

The forum of Thuburbo Maius (161 AD), another prosperous Roman town of some 7,000 inhabitants, grown wealthy as a collecting point for grain to be shipped to Rome. The Capitolium temple on its high podium can be seen beyond. The town's treasury and archives were kept in vaulted rooms under the temple and a colossal statue of Jupiter stood in the temple. From its fragmentary remains it is estimated to have been fully 21 ft. high. A colonnaded market with shops adjoined the forum. (Courtesy: Embassy of Tunisia, Washington, D.C.)

riod. The persistent Punic presence may be seen in a small temple of Baal-Saturn, another of Tanit-Ceres—the latter turned into a church in the 6th cent. and a font placed in its cella—and a Byzantine fort built over a temple of Saturn on a hill to the east. A sanctuary of Baalat has also been uncovered, and the foundations of a Byzantine basilica.

THUGGA   See *Dougga*.

THYSDRUS   See *El Djem*.

TUNIS   Capital of Tunisia, known for its famous Bardo National Museum, which contains comprehensive displays of art and artifacts from all over Tunisia. These date from the Stone Ages into the Islamic period. Especially notable are the many extraordinary Roman mosaics, mostly 3rd cent. AD, from Carthage as well as all over Tunisia. Many of these are figured mosaics with lively scenes throwing much light, for instance, on agricultural practices in Roman North Africa in the 3rd cent. In nearby *Carthage*, a suburb of Tunis, the Carthage National Museum houses finds from a century of excavation in the ancient city. There is also the National Museum of Byrsa and an on-site museum.

UTHINA   See *Oudna*.

UTICA   The modern Utique, 20 mi. NW of Carthage. According to tradition, Utica was founded by the Phoenicians as a port of call on the way west as early as 1100 BC—far earlier than Carthage, though nothing older than the 8th cent. BC has been found on the site. Once a shallow port on the Medjerda estuary, it is now 6 mi. inland. Utica, however, had its periods of glory; siding with Rome in the last Punic War, its reward, following the destruction of Carthage in 146 BC, was to be chosen capital and chief city of the new Roman province of Africa. After the Battle of Thapsus in 46 BC (see *Mahdia*) Cato, then governor of the province, who had opposed Caesar, committed suicide in Utica. The town was made a municipium in 36 BC, but as its harbor silted up and its old rival Carthage was restored and made the capital by Rome, it slowly went downhill all during the Roman period. At the site, periodically excavated since the 1940s, only two Punic cemeteries have been recovered from the early period. There is more of the Roman, though not impressive: a colonnaded street, a possible forum, a residential district with six houses and their mosaics, none apparently later than the 1st cent. AD, the remains of large baths, a temple, cisterns and a columbarium, partially restored. The best of the finds are in the local antiquarium on the site.

UTIQUE   See *Utica*.

UZAPPA   See *Maktar*.

VAGA   See *Béja*.
(VEGA)

YOUNGA   The ancient Macomades Minores, later called Iunci, 18 mi. S. of Sfax and 10½ S. of *Thaenae* (Thina). The sandy coastal site is dominated by the Byzantine citadel, later reused by the Arabs. Three Christian basilicas have been excavated here, one a small funerary chapel set amidst a 4th-cent. necropolis. Another, larger basilica with a baptistery, notable for its highly colored frescoes on stucco and later for its mosaics, apparently was in use from the time of Constantine into the 6th cent. AD. A third large basilica with mosaics is Byzantine. The finds are in the Bardo Museum, Tunis.

ZAGHOUAN   Charming modern town below the Gebel Zaghouan, 27 mi. S. of Tunis. A small triumphal arch or gate, restored, marks the site of a Roman town, possibly the ancient Ziqua. A mile beyond the town, set against the cliffs of the mountains, is the source of the great aqueduct built under Hadrian to supply *Carthage* with water. About 44 mi. long in its final version, it passed under hills in tunnels and across the plains on arches (see *Oudna*) and emptied into an immense reservoir at Carthage. The spring at Zaghouan, source of the water, is still enobled by the ruins of a once-lovely symmetrical nymphaeum (160–170 AD), built above a basin, with stairs leading up to a U-shaped court embraced by a portico. In the interior, behind the portico, were coffered ceilings, mosaic floors and a cella walled in multicolored marble.

ZAMA

Modern Jama, 18 mi. N. of Maktar, possibly the site of Hannibal's camp before his final defeat in the Battle of Zama in 202 BC. Other Zamas in Tunisia have been proposed for the site of the battle, but at this place there definitely was a Numidian-Roman town. Its remains include round megalithic monuments, and those of two aqueducts, baths, reservoirs and cisterns, a nymphaeum over a spring, and a Byzantine fortress. Six mi. from Jama, at Qsar Zammel, are the ruins of Vicus Maracitanus, including a temple, forum, a mausoleum and a Christian basilica.

ZANFOUR

The ancient Assuras, about 18 mi. SE of Le Kef in the Tell region of N. central Tunisia. The Roman town, an Augustan foundation, was prosperous enough to have no less than three monumental arches, an amphitheater, theater, a temple (its walls decorated with a garland and bull's head frieze in good condition), two mausolea, and two Byzantine fortresses.

ALGERIA

ABALESSA

See *Hoggar Mountains.*

ACHIR

Ruins of an early Islamic city, once capital of the Zirids (972–1152 AD), a Berber dynasty that ruled in Tunisia, Algeria and Granada, Spain—at first under the Fatamids and then independently. Achir, about 140 mi. southeast of Algiers in northern Algeria, was built by Ziri probably about 945 AD, a Berber warrior for the Fatimids whose son, Bologuin or Bulukhin, was put in charge of western North Africa in 972 by the first Fatimid ruler in Egypt. Bologuin rebuilt the city and renamed it Benia. Excavations have uncovered the foundations of Ziri's palace, a large structure with four smaller courts grouped around a larger colonnaded central courtyard, traces of the defensive walls built by father and son, and the foundations of a mosque.

AD MAIORES

See *Henchir Besseriani.*

AGADIR

See *Tlemcen.*

AÏN EL-BORD

See *Tigisis.*

AÏN EL-HAMMAM

See *Baghai.*

AÏN HANECH

Important Paleolithic site in northeast Algeria near Eulma (St. Arnaud), 15 mi. E. of Sétif. Here over 50 pebble tools were found near the site of an ancient lake, examples of the earliest types of tools so far known to have been used by man. Identified as belonging to the Oldowan culture, named after the Leakeys' site at Olduvai Gorge in Tanzania where they have been dated to about 2 million years ago, the examples from Aïn Hanech are polyhedral limestone balls from which flakes have been chipped. Some hand axes have also been found here. Associated with Villafranchian animal remains, the finds have been dated to 1 to 1.5 million years ago. They are displayed in Algier's Bardo Museum of Ethnography and Prehistory. See also *Casablanca* (MOROCCO) and *Sidi Zin* (TUNISIA).

AÏN SEFRA

An oasis and one of the centers for the numerous rock carvings and paintings to be seen in Algeria, dating from about 5000 to about 50 BC. Aïn Sefra lies in the Ksour Mountains, about 200 mi. S. of Oran in the W., close to the Moroccan border. About 6 mi. E., at Adhjra Mahisserat a herd of elephants and other beasts have been carved on a cliff, and some 6 mi. further on, at Tiout or Thyout, the rocks show men hunting ostriches with bows and spears and engaging in sexual intercourse; there are lions, elephants, rhinoceros, buffaloes, a cow. More carvings are to be found even further east in the Ksour hills and the Djebel Amour. See also *El-Bayadh, Hoggar Mountains, Tassili N'Ajjer.*

AÏN RAOUNA

See *Tigzirt.*

ALGIERS

Capital and largest city of Algeria, with a fine harbor. It was the Phoenician and Punic port of Ikosim, though no traces survive from the period, and very little from the Roman Icosium of the 1st cent. BC, which became a colony under Vespasian (69–79 AD). The Vandals dealt harshly with the city, which lay derelict until it was refounded by the Arabs around the mid-10th cent. AD as El-Djezaïr, named for its offshore islands (now gone). The town later passed under the Almoravids, when the Great Mosque (end of 11th cent. AD) was originally built, and then the Almohads. The Great Mosque as it now stands was drastically modified in the 16th cent. Algiers is important for us for its two principal museums: The Bardo Museum of Ethnography and Prehistory, with rich collections of Saharan art, and the Museum of Classical and Muslim Antiquities.

LES ANDALOUSE

Village and beach resort about 13 mi. along the coast W. of Oran. Near here excavations uncovered the remains of a Berber-Punic settlement on a seaside cliff. The rectangular houses, of adobe brick, had flat roofs. The lowest levels of one house, perched on its cliff, were dated to the 6th cent. BC. Nearby were five tomb mounds of the 5th cent. BC.

ANNABA

See *Hippo Regius.*

ANNOUNA

A large field of ruins of a Roman town on a plateau, little visited and only slightly excavated in 1903–09. Ancient Thibilis, which was strongly Berber-Punic in its culture until the end, yielded many inscriptions with Punic names, and Saturn-Baal stelae. A small Roman town, it only became a municipium in 305 AD. Standing above the fragmented ruins are three arches (3rd–4th cents. AD), one at each end of the main paved street, once bordered by colonnades, a third at the entrance to the forum. The forum, small, porticoed, with the usual basilica and curia, has been identified, as well as a market with shops and traces of temples. The elegant marble-paved house of the Antistii, a distinguished family in the days of Marcus Aurelius (2nd cent.), has been excavated. It had a formal garden. There is also a Byzantine fortress, and two Byzantine churches, one with its facade still intact. The finds are in the museum at *Guelma*.

AZEFFOUN

An out-of-the-way coastal village on the site of the Roman port of Rusazus, 24 mi. NE of Tizi-Ouzou in north central Algeria. Though unexcavated, it is one of Kabylia's most interesting sites. An early Phoenician port of call, it was an Augustan (Roman) foundation. The visible remains include a bath building, another large structure decorated with mosaics, bits of the town walls, and other unidentified remains.

BAGHAI

Or Qsar Baghai. Here, about 7 mi. N. of *Khenchela*, stand the ruins of a massive Byzantine fortress amidst dark cedar forests in the foothills of the Aurès Mountains. Its walls and towers are of masonry up to 8 ft. thick. It was near Baghai, in 689 or 690 AD, that the Berber queen Al Kahina defeated the invading Arabs under Hassan. About 1 mi. south at Aïn el-Hammam, there are traces of the ancient Roman hot baths of Aquae Flavianae. Their warm pools are still in use in a modern bathing establishment.

BAYADH, EL-

A town in the Djebel Amour (Saharan Atlas), 95 mi. SE of Saïda, NW central Algeria. The town centers a region, like many others rich in Neolithic rock carvings. At Hadjra Driess a 20-ft.-long panel depicts a herd of buffaloes; on the face of a high rocky crag at Merdoufa several large carvings may be seen; at Hadjara Berrik two-wheeled chariots from the late period are depicted. Lions, elephants, buffaloes, antelopes, ostriches and hunters appear near Qsar el-Hamra, Kreloua Sidi Cheik, and Gouiret ben-Saloul. Some 43 mi. to the south at Boualem there is a graphic depiction of a ram, its fleece carefully rendered, a disc of branches on its head. See also *Aïn Sefar*, *Hoggar Mountains*, *Tassili N'Ajjer*.

BEJAIA

Formerly Bougie, attractive city climbing a hill above the Mediterranean, 110 mi. E. of Algiers, now an oil port. Once a Phoenician port and the Roman Augustan foundation of Saldae, all that is left of either is in the small museum, with the exception of a Roman cistern. Of the later Hammadid period only two gates of the old city wall survive.

BIR EL-ATER

Paleolithic site in the Oued Djebanna, about 50 mi. S. of Tébessa in eastern Algeria, close to the Tunisian border. The Aterian stone industry, widespread in North Africa in mid-Paleolithic times (about 80,000 to 35,000 BC) from Egypt to the Atlantic, is named for the site. It apparently developed out of the Mousterian. The flaked stone tools are characterized by a distinct tang at the lower end, probably to help with the hafting. Since such a tool resembles an arrowhead, the Aterians have been credited with the invention of "man's first long-distance weapon," the bow and arrow.

BOUALEM

See *El-Bayadh*.

CAESAREA

See *Cherchell*.

CALAMA

See *Guelma*.

CALCEUS HERCULIS   See *El-Kantara*.

CAPE MATIFOU   The small coastal village of Tamentefoust on the Cape, on the E. side of the Bay of Algiers, may once have been a Punic port. It lies 9 mi. ENE of Algiers. Later it became the Augustan colony of Rusguniae with a late flowering as an episcopal see and as a Byzantine stronghold. Little is left of the ancient town. A mosaic from the baths (mid-4th cent. AD), cisterns, tombs, and some 100 votive Saturn stelae have been found. A large basilica, possibly from Vandal times and enlarged in the Byzantine period, yielded some interesting mosaics.

CARTENNAE   See *Ténès*.

CASTELLUM DIMMIDI   Roman fort, the most southerly in the Algerian Sahara, at Messaad about 80 mi. straight S. of Algiers. It was occupied as an outpost by the Third Augustan Legion (see *Lambaesis*) at least from 198 AD, the date of its headquarters building, to 238 when the legion was withdrawn after a disgrace. For a short time thereafter the post was held by auxiliary troops from Palmyra in Syria, used to desert warfare, who built a Palmyrene chapel for themselves, with frescoes very similar to those found at Dura Europus (also in Syria). It was then abandoned in a straightening of the lines of the frontier *limes* (see *Gemellae*).

CASTELLUM TIDDITANORUM   See *Tiddis*.

CHERCHELL   Modern port city of about 17,000, 50 mi. W. of Algiers. It covers the Roman city of Caesarea, which at its height in the 3rd cent. AD was a magnificent metropolis of about the same size, with all the Roman amenities and a double harbor, commercial and naval, like that of *Carthage* (TUNISIA). The city began as the Punic port of Iol and later became the capital of a king of Mauretania. In 25 BC Augustus gave it to Juba II as the Roman client king of Mauretania, who renamed it Caesarea in the emperor's honor. Juba II (52 BC–19 AD), who reigned for 48 years, was Greek-educated and a scholar and poet, who married the daughter of Cleopatra and Mark Antony and made his city into a center of Hellenism in North Africa. Caesarea came under Rome in 40 AD when Juba's son Ptolemy was murdered by Caligula, and was thereafter made the capital of Roman Mauretania Caesariensis by Claudius. It fell to the Vandals in 429 AD, became the capital of Mauretania Secunda under the Byzantines and finally fell to the Arabs in the 7th cent.

Naturally little is left of this once flourishing city. Excavations, however, have uncovered the large theater of 19 BC, with a stage building three stories high like that of *Sabratha* (LIBYA) next to the forum. Significantly, it was converted into an amphitheater in the 4th cent. AD. The huge West Baths (2nd cent.) have symmetrical wings like those of *Carthage* (TUNISIA), and was fed by two aqueducts, daringly if shakily engineered, whose arches, three stages high at one point, may be seen southeast of the city. An archaeological park preserves the remains of the Eastern Baths, with some mosaics, and the adjoining amphitheater, which witnessed the martyrdom, by wild beasts, of St. Marciana. The hippodrome site has been identified from aerial photographs. The best of ancient Caesarea is in the local museum, which has the finest collection of statues in North Africa, many from Juba II's famed group of Greek and Roman copies, others Hadrianic, as well as a fine array of mosaics. Other finds are in Algiers.

CIRTA

See *Constantine*.

COLUMNATA

Prehistoric site some 150 mi. SW of Algiers in the interior, in an area much more fertile in prehistoric times than now. Burials with actual tombstones over disarticulated bones, with red ochre and shell ornaments, date here from the Iberomaurusian period (after 12,500 BC). From the Neolithic period (after 8,000 BC) a local tool industry called the Columnatan was identified, and evidence of agricultural use of weighted digging sticks, bone sickles with flint teeth and handmills.

CONSTANTINE

Large modern city, about 200 mi. ESE of Algiers. Astonishingly, it sprawls over the top of a huge limestone cliff slashed by the incredibly deep and narrow gorges of the Rhummel River. It was also the important Roman city of Cirta, and before that a prehistoric site, a Phoenician settlement dating back at least to the 3rd cent. BC, and the capital city of the Numidian kings and then of Masinissa (3rd–2nd cent. BC), famous friend of Rome during the last Punic war. Masinissa, a cultivated and powerful king, encouraged Roman traders to settle in his town, but the Italian colony was wiped out by Jugurtha, his grandson, during his revolt against Rome in 112 BC, when he besieged his brother, Adherbal, ruler of the town. Cirta was refounded as a Roman colony under Julius Caesar in 46–44 BC and reached its greatest prosperity in the 2nd–3rd cents. AD. Damaged in the Roman civil wars in the early 4th cent. AD, it was rebuilt under Constantine as the capital again of Numidia and was renamed in his honor.

The ancient city is nowhere in evidence, except some Roman work in the citadel, traces of baths, of bridges across the Rhummel gorges, some reservoirs, and five arches of an aqueduct south of the city. A Punic temple, excavated in 1950 on a hillside at El-Hofra in the southern part of the city, yielded up to 1,000 stelae inscribed in Punic and a few in Greek, mentioning sacrifices, officials, priests, kings like Masinissa and his sons. Nine miles south of the city, at El-Khroub, is the imposing rectangular cut-stone mausoleum of Es-Souna, almost certainly that of Masinissa. Opened in 1915, the tomb chamber contained the ashes of the king in a silver dish, surrounded by his helmet, coat of mail, sword, spears and other objects, all of the 2nd cent. BC. The finds, with the stelae from El Hofra, and finds from neighboring sites such as *Tiddis*, are in the municipal museum.

CUICUL

See *Djemila*.

DIANA VETERANORUM

See *Zana*.

DJEBEL LAKHDAR

See *Tiaret*.

DJEDDARS

See *Tiaret*.

DJEMILA

"The beautiful," as the Arabs called the haunting ruins of ancient Cuicul, located in the Atlas Mountains 50 mi. W. of Constantine. The site itself, set high on a gently sloping ridge against blue mountains, is certainly beautiful—innumerable columns, wheel-rutted streets, high walls, an imposing temple, great baths, a lovely theater. Thoroughly excavated between 1909 and 1957 and remarkably well preserved, Cuicul was only a provincial market town, not large, founded as

The well-preserved ruins of ancient Cuicul are set on the high slope of the Atlas Mountains. Called Djemila, "the beautiful," by the Arabs, the site offers the tourist an entrancing glimpse into the life of a prosperous small market town of the Roman period. Among a number of temples is this lovely shrine of the Severan family (229 AD), which dominates the forum of the later, Severan quarter. (Courtesy: Direction de la Promotion, Algiers.)

a veterans' colony in 96 or 97 AD though probably of native origin. Yet at its height in the 2nd and 3rd cents. AD it had all the luxurious amenities of a city twice its size. Later, though torn by the Donatist controversy, it had a large Christian community, and it lasted as a market town, though much reduced, well into the Middle Ages.

The original colony, centering around a forum with shops sheltered under porticoes, lies to the north. Cuicul was walled, but in the peaceful 3rd cent. the walls were demolished, except the South Gate, which now opened into a new, Severan quarter to the south with another, larger forum. The old forum is bordered on the north by the high Capitolium temple (169 AD) with six columns still standing, and next to it an enclosed porticoed market and shops, donated by the wealthy Cosinus family. At its center is a hexagonal fountain. Across the forum to the south was a temple, to the east a curia, and on its west side the remains of a basilica (169 AD), separating the forum from the *cardo*, or main street, which once had roofed sidewalks. Two baths and a number of large houses lay near the forum.

The *cardo* led south through an arch and the old South Gate to the larger Severan forum, approached on the west by the restored arch of Caracalla (216 AD). Beside the arch are an apsed cloth market (4th cent.) and a nymphaeum. The forum is dominated on the south by the splendid well-preserved temple (229 AD) of the Severan family, its Corinthian columns set high behind a monumental double stairway. Beside it lay a 4th-cent. basilica. Southwest of the new forum are the remains of the Great Baths (183 AD) and southeast the restored

The Arch of Caracalla (216 AD), somewhat restored, marks the entrance to the Severan forum in Cuicul, a town that boasted several markets, baths, a theater, roofed sidewalks, fine mosaics in many of the buildings, fountains and comfortable villas. Though not large, Cuicul acted as the center for a populous and prosperous agricultural countryside. (Courtesy: Direction de la Promotion, Algiers.)

theater (161 AD), cut into the hillside with seating for 3,000, its stage building partly intact. There were eight major luxury houses in and around the older quarter and in the new quarter, in particular the grandiose House of Bacchus, two peristyle houses in one, lying next to the Great Baths. The Christian quarter (4th–5th cents. AD), which grew up in the southeast, contains three basilicas, a lovely (restored) round baptistery, and the bishop's house. The houses, churches and monuments were profusely decorated with mosaics, some very fine. Many of these are grouped, along with marble statuary and other finds, in the local museum.

GEMELLAE

Modern M'Lolli, Roman military camp and town (*vicus*) on the edge of the Sahara, about 21 mi. SW of the oasis of Biskra, well preserved under a blanket of sand. It was a station on the Hadrianic *limes*, the Roman in-depth defensive system, including camps, forts, blockhouses and watchtowers along a military road system in the desert that protected the wealthy towns to the north and indeed made them viable. Excavations at Gemellae revealed a major camp built in the 120s AD, holding 1,300 men. It was protected by a wall and ditch with towers and four gates. Inside there was a headquarters *praetorium*, an armory, a chapel. Remains of an amphitheater, three small temples, baths, an aqueduct and cemetery have also been found, while in the vicinity a number of civilian settlements, have been identified.

GOURAYA

Remains of a Punic-Roman port town, the ancient Gunugu, 16 mi. WSW of Cherchell, unexcavated except for the three cemeteries. These contained Punic chamber tombs that were used well into Roman times. They yielded amulets, Punic and Italian pottery, bottles, vases and painted ostrich eggs, as well as a Punic funeral mask of the 7th or 6th cent. BC. An Augustan Roman colony, the standing remains include ruins of baths, an aqueduct, a reservoir, and a Christian chapel.

GUELMA

Important modern road and rail junction and manufacturing town, inland 41 mi. SW from Annaba (*Hippo Regius*) on the coast. Under it lies ancient Calama, once a Punic town, then Roman, which achieved colony status by 238 AD. The ancient theater (3rd cent. AD), heavily restored in the 20th cent. and now used for performances, is about all that is left except for some walls of the large baths and traces of a Byzantine citadel built by General Solomon during the reign of Justinian. The museum, next to the theater, has finds from Calama and surrounding sites, including *Announa*, *Khemissa* and *Madaurus*.

GUNUGU

See *Gouraya*.

HENCHIR BESSERIANI

Desert ruins of the four-square Roman camp of Ad Maiores, which once held about 800 men, 3 mi. S. of the Négrine oasis on the southern slopes of the Saharan Atlas and some 100 mi. E. of *Gemellae*—both of them part of the *limes*, the southern defense line. Built in 105 AD under Trajan, it had four gates and square towers at each corner. The remains of a large civilian settlement can be traced just outside the camp. Just north of the Négrine oasis, a villa with an apsidal room, a hexagonal pool and a mosaic (now destroyed) has been discovered.

HIPPO REGIUS

Roman town, famous as the see of the great St. Augustine, who presided here as bishop from 395 AD until his death in 430, aged 76, while the Vandals under their king Gaiseric were besieging the town. Here he wrote his seminal *City of God*. Hippo was sited on the west side of a large bay about 260 mi. east of Algiers. Its ruins, overlooked by a modern French basilica which displays Augustine's arm in a wax image, lie about 1 mi. south of the large modern port of Annaba. Most noteworthy here are the foundations of Augustine's great Basilica of Peace with a clover-leaf baptistery, adorned with mosaics, near it.

The Roman town, though not large, was an important center for shipping grain to Rome, hence has the largest (and oldest) porticoed forum in the Maghreb, originally 1st-cent. AD, and a market from the same period enclosed in a colonnade, with a circular building at its center, perhaps a temple. It, too, is the largest market in the Maghreb, and also probably was the theater, Augustan in origin, cut into a hillside off the main site—though not much of it is left. There were several baths, of which the most impressive was the North Baths (3rd cent.), once adorned with statues, mosaics and frescoes. Its lower parts are well preserved. Since Hippo was a wealthy market center, it boasted quite a number of luxurious villas with pillared courtyards, fountains and especially fine mo-

Jumbled remains of the ancient forum of Hippo Regius, the earliest (77–78 AD) and largest in western North Africa—largest because Hippo was a major shipping point for grain to Rome. Its early date is indicated by the name of C. Paccius Africanus, the proconsul of the time, set into the forum in large bronze letters. Hippo is better known as the home of St. Augustine, whose great Basilica of Peace has been excavated, for he was bishop of Hippo and wrote his City of God here. He died in Hippo in 430 AD during the siege by the Vandals that virtually put an end to the city's prosperity. (Courtesy: Direction de la Promotion, Algiers.)

saics, dating from the 1st to the 5th cents. AD, some still in situ, others in the local museum. Many of these villas lay along what used to be the seafront. One large villa, built against a hill, had several stories.

Hippo, probably called Regius because it once was a residence of Numidian kings, was a very ancient city, possibly as early as the 12th cent. BC and with a Punic and Berber past. Punic was still spoken in Hippo in Augustine's times. A temple of Baal-Saturn, yielding many stelae, was discovered beneath the French basilica. The city never really recovered from the Vandal assault in 430–31. It was Gaiseric's capital until 439, was recovered by the Byzantines in the 6th cent., again suffered from the Arab raids and was finally abandoned in the 11th cent. AD. The museum, with a vast spread of stonework and inscriptions outside it and miscellaneous mosaics and other finds from the site inside it, including the famous marble Aphrodite of Hippo, is worth a visit. In nearby Annaba is the noteworthy 11th-cent. Zind mosaic of Sidi Bou Mérouane. Its prayer hall is adorned with antique columns from the forum of Hippo.

HOGGAR MOUNTAINS

Or Ahaggar, vast volcanic mountain range and upland area in the southern Sahara, a desert land of fantastic scenery peopled by nomadic Tuaregs. The Hoggar is a principal region of prehistoric rock paintings and carvings dating from the Neolithic and early historic periods, when the Sahara was more habitable than now (see also Aïn Sefra, El Bayadh, Tassili N'Agger). Though not for the timid, guides and guided tours are available. The rock art is concentrated in the southern part of the Tefedest range, with the village of Mertoutek as a center for excursions. Fine examples are to be seen at Hirafok in the north, at Idelès 20 mi. northeast and at Otoul. Finds and copies of some of the art are in the Bardo Museum, Algiers.

At Abalessa, 63 mi. W. of the local capital of Tamenghest (formerly Tamanrasset) an oasis is centered on the ruins of a fort that on excavation yielded Roman materials of the 2nd to 4th cents. AD, possibly indicating the southernmost Roman outpost in Africa. Also in the fort excavations in 1925 uncovered the rich Berber grave of a woman dating from the 4th cent. AD. She lay on an elaborate bier covered with red leather, accompanied by jewelry in gold, silver and gem stones. According to legend this was the tomb of Tin-Hinan, the first queen of the Saharan Tuaregs. Her skeleton and grave goods are on display in Algiers.

ICHOUKANE   See *Timgad*.

ICOSIUM   See *Algiers*.

IKOSIM   See *Algiers*.

IOL   See *Cherchell*.

IOMNIUM   See *Tigzirt*.

KALAÂ DES BENI HAMMAD   Excavations of the extensive site of the Islamic Hammadid capital, near the village of Bichara, 85 mi. SW of Sétif. Built from scratch in 1007 AD by Emir Hammad, son of Bologuin, founder of *Algiers*, it lasted only 146 years, until 1152 when it was destroyed by the conquering Almohads. Once a town of fabled luxury, with walls five miles around, little is left to impress the visitor. Attractively sited on terraces above a stream on the slopes of the Djebel Maâdid in the Hodna hills, the town contained many splendid, richly decorated palaces and a Great Mosque, whose plan, with a courtyard and 13 aisles in its prayer hall, has been revealed. Its minaret still stands 75 ft. high. The imposing Palace of the Emir had many reception rooms, private apartments, a harem, a garden and lake. Nearby was the elaborately ornamented Palace of Light, enclosed within a stone wall, with a massive square tower. The finds are in the Sétif museum and in the Museum of Classical and Muslim Antiquities in Algiers.

KANTARA, EL-   Arabic for "The Gate," appropriate name for a village at the southern entrance of a narrow defile in the orange cliffs of the Djebel Metlili, leading from Biskra 25 mi. S. through the Aurès Mountains to Batna near *Lambaesis* (Lambèse). The village, once called Calceus Herculis (because in mythology Hercules kicked open the canyon with his heel), held a garrison of Syrian archers from Palmyra in Roman times (see also *Castellum Dimmidi*). As aerial surveys show, the area during the High Empire of Rome was heavily irrigated, abounding in fields and settlements. Calceus has not been excavated, but the numerous architectural fragments, sculpture and inscriptions that have turned up are displayed in a small museum. The single arch of a Roman bridge is still visible in the defile.

KHEMISSA   The ancient town of Thubursicu Numidarum, on a hilly site high up near the source of Oued Mejerda, 18 mi. SW of Souk Ahras, in NE Algeria. Originally a Romanized Berber settlement, besieged by the guerrilla leader Tacfarinas early in the 1st cent. BC, it was in time thoroughly Romanized, became a municipium under Trajan (113 AD) and a colony before 270 AD. Later an episcopal see, it was also a Byzantine town. Excavations from 1900 to 1922 uncovered part of the ruins, including the old forum, paved and porticoed, cut into the hillside and approached by a stairway. It centered shops, a curia, a temple (later a church) and a basilica nearly as large as the forum itself. The new forum was flanked by a colonnaded market, baths, and a late triumphal arch (306–70 AD), triple-arched. The theater, Severan in date, one of the finest and best preserved in Roman Africa—though apparently never finished—had 18 rows of seats built on vaults against a hillside topped by the ruins of a Byzantine fort. A nymphaeum ("Aïn el-Youdi") with pools and built over a spring, and a temple of Saturn adjoined it. The finds are in the *Guelma* museum and in Algiers. Souk Ahras, 18 mi. NE, was Roman Thagaste, birthplace of St. Augustine. Only the Byzantine walls are left.

KHENCHELA

The ancient Mascula, halfway between *Tébessa* (Theveste) and Lambèse (*Lambaesis*) in NE Algeria. Mascula was a Berber-Roman town, later a municipium and important road junction, and briefly headquarters of the Third Augustan Legion, which later moved to Lambaesis. Khenchela has little to offer except the discovery of Saturn-Baal stelae, Christian catacombs, evidence of a shrine of Mithras, the soldiers' god, and a luxurious villa, discovered in 1960, with 15 rooms floored with fine mosaics.

KHROUB, EL-

See *Constantine*.

LAMBAESIS

Modern Lambessa, or Lambèse; magnificent Roman legionary camp, one of the finest extant, long the military capital of Africa and from the 3rd cent. AD capital of the province of Numidia. Situated now in a treeless waste, once fertile, 7 mi. SE of modern Batna and 16 mi. by road W. of Roman *Timgad*, it commanded the northern slopes of the Aurès Mountains and the El-*Kantara* gap leading south into the Sahara. From 81 AD Lambaesis was the headquarters of the Third Augustan Legion, the only legion permanently stationed in Roman Africa (much like the later French Foreign Legion). It had moved from *Ammaedara* in TUNISIA via Mascula (*Khenchela*) and Theveste (*Tébessa*) to Lambaesis, where it finally rested until its withdrawal in the late 3rd cent. AD. The presence of a Byzantine fortress nearby indicates a late extension of Lambaeses' life. Traces of the original camp, built under Emperor Titus, have been excavated southeast of the later camp. A larger camp was built in 128 AD expressly for a visit of the emperor Hadrian, whose welcoming address to the troops, on a stone inscription (now in the Bardo Museum, *Algiers*) was found in the camp. In 129, after Hadrian had left, the new and much larger camp (50 acres), now on view, was built.

The camp, laid out in the usual regular rectangle, centers on the imposing so-called "praetorium," still standing two stories high, which was actually an immense rectangular four-way arch (mid-3rd cent.) serving as a monumental entrance to the *principia*, the military headquarters area, behind it. This consisted of an ample paved courtyard, porticoed on three sides with a large basilica on the fourth, and with rooms opening off it—some workshops, others arsenals where piles of terracotta and stone missiles were found. At the back of the basilica were chapels, the military shrine of the standards and rooms for the *scholae* (late military guilds). Much of the southwest quarter of the camp lies under a 19th-cent. French prison, but elsewhere the walls, gates, streets, barracks and officers' quarters have been laid bare, as well as baths in the southeast. Outside the walls are the remains of another bath establishment and the amphitheater (169 AD), badly stone-robbed.

The larger of two civilian towns SE of the camp, inhabited by married veterans, traders, merchants and Romanized Berbers, lies partly under the modern

The so-called "praetorium" at Lambaesis, actually a huge four-way arch fronting the large principia, or headquarters, of the legionary camp. Lambaesis was the principal base of the Third Augustan Legion, sole legion in all of Roman Africa during the 2nd and 3rd cents. AD. Here was the actual center of the military power in Africa, linked to subsidiary camps and forts by the usual efficient Roman network of roads. The magnificent 50-acre camp, one of the finest examples in the Roman Empire, was laid out in the usual rigid rectangular pattern. It has been largely excavated for all to see, except for the southwestern quarter, covered by a modern prison. Outside the walls were an amphitheater, baths, and two irregularly planned civilian towns. (Courtesy: Direction de la Promotion, Algiers.)

village of Tazoult. Nevertheless much has been gleaned by excavations here. There was a forum, Capitolium temple on a high podium, an arch, baths and several other temples, including a mithraeum and a small temple of Aesculapius (162–210 AD), consisting of a porticoed semicircular entrance, a series of chapels leading to the main shrine, and health baths adjoining it. A septizonium masked the outlets of four aqueducts, and under the village were found a number of luxurious villas whose mosaics fill the local museum. An arch of Septimius Severus stood between the camp and the town, and east of the village are the ruins of the Byzantine fortress. About 2 mi. north of the camp, standing in a necropolis, is the mausoleum of Quintus Flavius, a prefect (leader) of the Third Augustan Legion in the 3rd cent. The small museum houses the mosaics, sculpture and other finds. More finds are in the Museum of Antiquities in Algiers.

MADAURUS

Modern M'Daourouch, ancient Roman-Berber town about 22 mi. S. of Souk Ahras. Apuleius, author of that racy novel *The Golden Ass*, was born here into a wealthy family around 125 AD, and young Augustine came here for part of his education before moving on to Carthage. The dominant monument in the rather fragmentary ruins, excavated 1905–23, is the theater, Severan in date, paid for again by another wealthy local family. Backing onto its stage building and partly covering the adjacent forum the Byzantines under Justinian constructed a massive fortress, still standing 30 or 40 ft. high—the arts giving way to military necessity. Madaurus, though yielding much evidence of its Libyan background and gods throughout its life, became a Roman colony in the 1st cent. AD, and its porticoed forum was built in the 2nd cent. Near or off it was a small curia, a basilica, a temple (of Mars?), and two baths, probably Severan, one for summer (large), one for winter (smaller). There were also remnants of arches, sanctuaries, and of two 5th-cent. Christian basilicas.

MANSOURA

See *Tlemcen*.

MASCULA

See *Khenchela*.

MEDRACEN

Berber funerary monument, rising 65 ft. high, about 200 ft. in diameter, in a necropolis 5 mi. S. of a village (Aïn Yagout), 20 mi. NE of Batna in NE Algeria. Its round base, encircled with 60 squat Doric columns, engaged, and three false doors, is surmounted by an impressive cone of 23 steps with a platform on top. There was an antechamber on the west, now in ruins, and a false entrance and vestibule on the east. Excavations in 1873 found the real entrance concealed inside the cone, leading down 23 steps to a tunnel into the tomb chamber, long ago robbed. The tunnel was supported and floored with cedar, which yielded a recent carbon-14 date of between 300 and 200 BC. So the tomb was too early for Masinissa or his son, but may have belonged to Masinissa's father, or to Syphax, the Berber king Masinissa displaced. See also *Tipasa*.

MESSAAD

See *Castellum Dimmidi*.

OUED ATHMÉNIA

Roman villa, about 30 mi. SW of *Constantine*, a large, wealthy working villa, excavated in the 19th cent., with 15 rooms floored with mosaics, its own baths, and very large stables. This, with mosaics of horses and hunting, indicates that the owner was horsemad and probably raised them. Built in Antonine-Severan times, the villa was destroyed in the early 4th cent. AD.

POMARIA

See *Tlemcen*.

PORTUS MAGNUS

Ancient town, 22 mi. E. of Oran, built high on a cliff back from the sea and partly covered by the village of Bettioua. It was once a Phoenician port of call, but during the minor excavations of 1950–63 little but pottery turned up for the

Punic period. The rest was Roman: a forum with a portico of cheaply stuccoed columns, large cisterns, a small curia, a Capitolium approached by monumental stairs. A street was also revealed, evidence of baths, and remains of houses built on different levels reached by steps, one house quite large, and a cemetery. Most of this was Severan, 2nd cent. AD. Portus Magnus then seems to have declined. The finds are in the Oran museum.

QASR BAGAI   See *Baghai*.

RAPIDUM   See *Sour Djouab*.

ROKNIA   Mysterious ancient necropolis of some 3,000 miniature megalithic dolmens, only two to three ft. high, scattered over more than a square mi, 7 mi. N. of the exceedingly hot sulfur springs of Hammam Meskoutine, the "Baths of the Accursed." The springs in turn are 9 mi. west of *Guelma*. Presumably Roknia was a native cemetery used over a long period during the 1st millennium BC.

RUSAZUS   See *Azeffoun*.

RUSGUNIAE   See *Cape Matifou*.

SALDAE   See *Bejaia*.

SEDRATA   Ruins of a 10th cent. AD town half buried beneath the shifting sands of the desert, 9 mi. SW of the oasis settlement of Ouargla. Founded about 908 AD by the fanatically puritanical Islamic sect of the Ibadites (or Rustamids), fleeing from Tahert (see *Tiaret*) after it was destroyed by the Fatimids, these industrious religionists worked hard and prospered in the difficult environment. But again the Orthodox, this time the Hammadids from *Bejaia*, descended on Sedrata and in 1072 destroyed it. The Ibadites fled once more, to the even more inhospitable M'Zab Valley where many still live. Excavations of the ruins, today again half-covered in sand, uncovered the remains of a complex of palaces from which some interesting sculptured slabs of gesso, now in the Bardo Museum, Algiers, were retrieved.

SÉFAR   See *Tassili N' Ajjer*.

SÉTIF   City in the High Plateau at 3,600 ft., 70 mi. WSW of *Constantine*. It covers the remains of ancient Sitifis, founded as a Roman veterans' colony under Nerva in the late 1st cent. AD, though it had a native past. Saturn-Baal worship was long established here. Under the Romans it was a strategic town on a military road, and was the base in 373–75 for the campaign against the rebel Firmus, and capital of Mauretania Sitifensis under Diocletian. Excavations have been carried out since 1959 revealing for its first two centuries a grid street plan, a temple and necropolis (now an archaeological park). Its high point was in the 4th cent. AD, from which remains of a circus, theater, amphitheater, baths, a temple, houses, and two Christian basilicas have been identified. Sitifis survived the Vandal occupation to gain a Byzantine fort built by General Solomon around 540 AD. There is a local museum.

SITIFIS   See *Sétif*.

SOUK AHRAS

See *Khemissa.*

SOUR DJOUAB

The Roman camp of Rapidum, founded by Hadrian in 122 AD. About 100 mi. S. of Algiers, it lay on the *limes* of Mauretania Caesariensis (see *Gemellae*) and had the usual rectangular plan, walls, towers and gates. Within the camp excavations in 1927 and 1948–53 identified the remains of the *praetorium*, small baths, the commander's residence, barracks, a granary and other structures. A town covering 37 acres grew up west and south of the camp, which was walled in 167 AD. Within were more walls dividing the town into three districts, probably to separate the tribal natives, resettled here, from the soldiers. There were comfortable houses along the grid of streets, a Capitolium, a temple of Ceres and a temple of Saturn-Baal outside to the northeast, stables, oil presses and mills. Some insurrection destroyed the town in the 3rd cent., but it was later restored under Diocletian. The necropolis has also been located.

TAGDEMT

See *Tiaret.*

TAGRART

See *Tlemcen.*

TAHERT

See *Tiaret.*

TAKSEBT

See *Tigzirt.*

TAMENTEFOUST

See *Cape Matifou.*

TASSILI N'AJJER

Vast sandstone plateau, some 50,000 square mi., in the southern Sahara, SE Algeria, running almost to the Libyan border. It is famous (with the *Hoggar* range to the southwest and an extension into LIBYA—see *Fezzan, The*) for its rich series of prehistoric rock paintings and carvings, many thousands of them scattered over a wide area. Tassili, which has been called the "largest open-air museum in the world," lies in a fantastic landscape of eroded rock formations, twisted and contorted, with deep fissures and seemingly bottomless canyons, forests of rocky needles and towering crags. Despite the distance and rough terrain, thousands of tourists, usually in guided tours, visit the sites each year by plane and auto and then on donkey-back and on foot, posing an increasing threat to the rock art.

This lively and often superlative art was first discovered in the 1920s, investigated in the 1930s, and intensively studied by Henri Lhote in the 1950s. Though the dating remains uncertain, most scholars divide the rock art into four periods: 1. the period of big-game hunters, then of round-headed men, little helmeted figures, apparently Negroid, carrying bows and arrows, and dated before 6000 BC; 2. the pastoral period of the cattle-herders, or Bovidian, about 5000–1500 BC, the cattle with lyre-shaped horns, the women wearing bulbous hairdos; 3. period of chariots and horses, after about 1200 BC, the charioteers armed with spears, shields and daggers, the light chariots of Hyksos type pulled by horses at full gallop; at this time, when the Sahara was drying up, Egyptian—and possibly Sea Peoples—influences are apparent; 4. Finally, at about 100 BC the camel begins to appear. Most of the art, however, is assigned to the Neolithic period when the area was well-watered and the art depicts a pastoral life and an abundance of animals—antelope, giraffes, elephants, wild asses, sheep and goats, cattle—and scenes of hunting and herding. The rock carvings are mostly in the northern Tassili, S. of Illizi, while the paintings—with bold colors: red, purple, yellow and brown on a whitish background—are to be found mostly in the region around Djanet in the south, a lovely oasis town and center for excursions. The paintings are often rendered in fine detail and with an invigorating sense of movement.

Selected sites included Tamrit with paintings of antelope, and near it Timenzouzine with its famous elephant, and the cave of Tan Zoumaïtik with early period, superimposed paintings of wild sheep, human figures, horned devils and other subjects. Northeast of Tamrit, at Séfar, are some of the finest paintings, including the enormous God Before Worshippers, masked figures, animals, archers, and a fine herding scene with cattle, two huts, and adults with three children. Near Séfar, too, are the rock carvings of In Itinen and the paintings of masked figures and cattle at Tin Tazarift, and of masked figures, an archer and chariots at Tin Aboteka.

At Jabbaren, about 12 mi. southwest of Séfar, some 5,000 figures include paintings of giant birds and humans, ostriches, human hands, scenes of hunting, herds of cattle, a procession of nude women holding hands, "The Abominable Sandman," a giant figure, and a female in red ochre, spotted in white. More paintings are found south of Jabbaren at Inaouanrhat, including a striking depiction on an isolated rock of a masked woman running. Finally, 6 to 7 mi. northeast of Jabbaren, at Ozanéare, many human figures are found, among them a family scene of seated and reclining people and children, a mother and child, cattle herders and archers, and a rhinoceros. See also Aïn Sefra, El Bayadh, Hoggar Mountains.

TÉBESSA

In the Tébessa Mountains, 110 mi. SE of Constantine near the Tunisian border. Although the modern town overlies the ancient city of Theveste, an unusual number of fine monuments survive—perhaps because most of them date from the late period of Theveste's flowering. Notable are the massive Byzantine walls, partly restored and best preserved on the north, with 14 towers, three gates and a walkway on top. They were built by Solomon, Justinian's general, in 539 AD after the reconquest of North Africa. Only six years later he was killed nearby in a battle with marauding Berbers. A four-sided Arch of Caracalla (214 AD) was incorporated into the walls as a gate and was thus preserved. Outstanding, too, is the elegant, beautifully preserved 3rd-cent. Temple of Minerva, now a museum, and the great Christian basilica. The amphitheater, later turned into a Byzantine fortress, was of unusual size. Its arena wall still stands to a height of 10 ft.; its gates are monumental, and 13 rows of seats survive.

Yet Theveste, despite its late flowering, was an ancient settlement, as attested by dolmens and Punic tombs in the area. The region also has many Paleolithic sites from a much earlier era—for instance, nearby Bir el-Ater. Theveste was a Berber settlement, captured by the Carthaginian general Hanno in the 3rd cent. BC, and in its earlier Roman period served briefly as headquarters of the Third Augustan Legion before it moved to Lambaesis. Shortly thereafter it became a municipium, then later a colony, and grew to become a flourishing market town on an important road junction. Here and there the remains of baths, houses and a temple have turned up, and the many fine mosaics retrieved may be seen in the museum.

The Great Basilica, presumably dedicated to St. Crispina, a woman aristocrat martyred under Diocletian in 304 AD, was one of the largest in all North Africa.

Its dating is uncertain—possibly in the early 6th cent. AD (oddly enough during the Vandal occupation), or earlier, in the late 4th cent. It stood within a large walled precinct, two stories high on a podium with vaults beneath—its foundations, with geometric mosaic floors, are well preserved. Within the precinct were also a formal garden, an inn with stables, and 89 small cells for monks and visitors, and other buildings; the basilica was obviously an important place of pilgrimage to the relics of St. Crispina, whose shrine may be the trefoil building to one side of the basilica. There was also a baptistery, library, refectory and kitchen, and an arched entrance to the precinct opening onto a wide main avenue within. The complex was destroyed by Berbers around 536 AD and rebuilt by Solomon, who used it as a prison.

A few mi. to the southwest is a complex of ruins of the 3rd to 4th cents. AD known as Tébessa Khalia (Old Tébessa), perhaps part of an imperial estate. These include several Christian basilicas, baths, a round temple, and a huge rectangular structure containing oil presses, a pond and other structures.

TÉNÈS

The ancient port town of Cartennae, on the coast W. of Algiers, 24 mi. N. of El-Asnam. A Punic port of call and Augustan colony (27–25 BC), it has scanty remains of town walls, mosaiced villas, cemeteries and cisterns. To the south of the town, over a mile away at Vieux (Old) Ténès, are the fragmentary walls, gates, bridge and a mosque of a 9th-cent. Berber town, said to have been founded by Andalusians from Spain. In the ruins of the mosque are Classical columns taken from Roman Cartennae.

TERNIFINE

Major North African Paleolithic site, excavated 1952–54 near this town, 11 mi. E. of Mascara in NW Algeria. Two jaw bones and part of a skull of *Homo erectus*, dated about 400–300,000 BC, were found here in deposits around an ancient lake or spring; also large numbers of Acheulian stone tools, including over 650 cleavers, hand axes and many worked pebble tools. The Villafranchian fauna remains included the giant ape and the sabre-toothed tiger. The finds are in the Bardo Museum, Algiers. See also *Aïn Hanech*; *Sidi Zin* (TUNISIA); and *Abd er-Rahman* and *Rabat* (MOROCCO).

THAGASTE

See *Khemissa*.

THAMUGADI

See *Timgad*.

THEVESTE

See *Tébessa*.

THIBILIS

See *Announa*.

THUBURSICU NUMIDARUM

See *Khemissa*.

TIARET

Town in the southern Tell region at the edge of the High Plateau, 110 mi. SE of Oran. About 4 mi. W., under the modern village of Tagdemt, are the meager remains of Tahert, capital of the puritanical Kharijite sect of the Ibadites (or Rustamids), founded in the 8th cent. AD by Ibn Rostem. When Tahert was destroyed by the Fatimids in 911, the Ibadites fled far south into the Sahara to *Sedrata*.

SW of the town on the road to Frenda are the famous Djeddars, the royal tombs of Berber kings, built in the Byzantine period—large square structures of dressed stone, sometimes huge, surmounted by stepped cones. The best of these rise on the hilltops of the Djebel Laghdar and near Ternaten. They owed something to Byzantine influence but belong to a long-standing type of Berber mausoleum dating from prehistoric times and including the earlier Berber mausoleums at *Medracen* and *Tipasa*. A large number of the more primitive dry-stone structures, of which the Djeddars seem to be a more developed form, are to be found again on the hills of Djebel Laghdar. The largest Djeddar on the crests of the Djebel Laghdar is called the Kèskès (for a native cooking pot). Its narrow passages open on 20 rooms, of which two were certainly tomb chambers.

TIDDIS

Charming small Roman town, a military dependency of Cirta (*Constantine*) about 18 mi. to the NW of that city. Rose-red Tiddis, the ancient Castellum Tidditanorum, unlike Cirta thoroughly excavated since 1941, climbs up a steep hill, all ups and downs, its main street, stepped and grooved here and there, winding in an S-curve from the bottom to the top, with stairways in between to reach the various levels. Even the tiny forum—only 10 by 30 yds., the smallest in Africa—is built on an artificial platform. Two small arches and a tiny curia open on to it. With no natural water supply, there are cisterns everywhere and a huge rainwater cistern at the top of the hill that fed the baths below. The Temple of Mithras, the soldiers' god, fronted by two pillars with winged phalluses, is built into a cave, and other grottoes were used as shops. A number of houses have been excavated and one luxurious villa (under a later potters' quarter), with its own baths, and traces of the Roman and Byzantine walls have been found, as well as a Christian chapel and two baptisteries.

The necropolis contains Roman and native tombs with inscriptions in Libyan and Neo-Punic as well as Latin. A Temple of Saturn-Baal, on terraces with a man-made cave, stood on the highest point of the hill. If one can believe the tomb inscriptions the hardy inhabitants, whether Roman or native, lived to a ripe old age in the healthy mountain air. Tiddis's most famous citizen was Q. Lollius Urbicus, who served as legate to Hadrian in the Jewish war of 132–35 AD, and also in Rome, Noricum, Lower Germany and Britain. He came back to die, for his large circular mausoleum can be seen a mile or so to the south of the town. The potters' quarter, crowded with kilns, apparently manufactured every kind of pottery artifact, from vases to kitchenware, tiles and toys. Tiddis seems to have slowly declined and had disappeared from the records by the 12th cent. AD.

TIGISIS

At Aïn el-Bordj, about 35 mi. SE of *Constantine*, aerial reconaissance discovered the remains of this minor Flavian settlement (83 AD) protected by a blockhouse. On the ground a Severan arch may still be seen. There is also a massive Byzantine fortress on the site with bastions all of 8 ft. thick.

TIGZIRT

Lovely coastal village and bathing resort, 13 mi. NNE of Tizi-Ouzou in the Greater Kabylia. Probably the site of a Punic port of call, it became the Roman provincial town of Iomnium. Some remains of a forum, a temple (2nd–3rd cent. AD), the walls (2nd cent.), baths, and houses have been identified. A 5th–6th cent. Christian basilica (probably Donatist) with three aisles and liberally decorated with crude Berber-style reliefs, is still standing in part, with a cloverleaf baptistery

next to it. On the hilltop of Taksebt, about 3 mi. east of Tigzirt, there are remnants of walls, baths, a large mausoleum and other structures, which may mark
the spot of an earlier Roman settlement before the inhabitants moved to Tigzirt.
At Aïn Raouna, over 10 mi. east, are some 10 large prehistoric chamber tombs,
built in Cyclopean stonework with heavy roof slabs, much like the dolmens of
western Europe.

TIMGAD

One of the finest surviving examples of a Roman planned town, called the
"Pompeii of Africa," built under Trajan in 100 AD by the legionnaires of the
Third Augustan Legion for their veterans stationed at *Lambaesis*, 16 mi. by road
to the west. Originally it also served the purpose of guarding the passes through
the Aurès Mountains that rise to the south of the high plateau on which Timgad
stands. The original town was built on a strict military plan, rigidly square, with
the north-south *cardo* intersecting the east-west *decumanus* at the central forum,
and lesser streets (with drains) enclosing 132 uniform insulae or blocks in between. Within a few generations, however, the original camp-like town had expanded to 125 acres, four times its original size—and in a much more haphazard manner. Yet it was still a small town—perhaps of 15,000 at most—but as
usual boasted superlative amenities, including 13 baths, two of the largest to
the north and south outside the original perimeter.

In the 4th and 5th cents. Timgad became a notorious center of the schismatic
Donatist Christians, particularly under Bishop Optatus, foe of St. Augustine. It
was sacked by natives in the early 6th cent., reclaimed by the Byzantines, and
fell to the Arabs in 647 AD and thereafter gradually disappeared beneath the
sands until it was rediscovered in the 18th cent. Excavations began as early as
1880. The ruins—the center largely laid bare and many of the outlying buildings
now visible—although cold in spirit have come to represent the most striking
example of the orderly Roman mind at work.

The original military colony, then called Thamugadi, was centered on the very
large forum, paved in blue stone and bordered by colonnades, shops and public
buildings, and a very public latrine with toilet arms carved in dolphin shapes.
An elegant curia clad in colored marbles, a small temple, and a well-appointed
small house, possibly reserved for the visits of the legion's legate, also faced
the forum, whose southeast side was taken up by a large Hadrianic civil basilica.
Often quoted is the inscription scratched on the forum's pavement: "Hunting,
bathing, gambling, laughing—that is to live." Just south of the forum is the
large, much-restored theater (160 AD), partly built on a low hill and seating
3,500 to 4,000 people, with a porticoed courtyard for "intermission" strolling
adjoining it. An international festival takes place here each May. Two blocks
north of the forum is an ornate library (late 3rd cent.), donated by a wealthy
citizen, with niches for 23,000 books (rolls), and east down the *decumanus* is a
double-apsed market. At its western end, at the edge of the original city and
tying it to a new quarter in the west, is Timgad's most famous monument, the
so-called "Arch of Trajan," actually built about 169 AD, a magnificent structure
with a central arch and two smaller arches for pedestrians.

The new quarter, probably for Romanized natives—its colonnaded streets
bending to the north—is dominated by the market of Sertius near the arch
(donated by a wealthy nabob of the 3rd cent. whose enormous house lies at the
southwest corner of the town) and the imposing Capitolium temple. The shops
and stalls of the market were enclosed within a porticoed rectangular courtyard

The famous ruins of Timgad, the "Pompeii of Africa," a planned town laid out on formal military lines by Trajan in 100 AD for the veterans of the Third Augustan Legion, whose base was at Lambaesis a few miles to the west. The so-called "Arch of Trajan" (below), actually built in 169 AD, separated the original four-square town, called Thamugadi, from a later extension that quadrupled the city's size. The straight colonnaded street leading up to the arch (above) is typical of the strict rectangular layout of the original city, centered on a large forum, which reflected the cold logical minds of the Roman planners. (Courtesy: Direction de la Promotion, Algiers.)

and a hemicycle facing on to it. The Capitolium (possibly 110 AD), most unusually far from the forum, was enclosed within a precinct with porticoes and raised on a high podium. Two of its tall Corinthian columns still stand. Across the road from the market is a small temple of the Genius of the Colony (169 AD). To the west of the Capitolium are the foundations of the grandiose Donatist Christian complex of Bishop Optatus—his huge cathedral, his residence, a chapel, baptistery and other buildings.

The new quarter of Timgad (above) with the Arch of Trajan just showing at the left and the two remaining pillars of the Capitolium temple in the background, whose ruins are seen in a closer view below. At its height Timgad possessed a remarkable range of amenities: 13 baths, a large theater, an ornate latrine in the forum, a library holding 23,000 books (rolls), two markets and a wealth of fine mosaic floors in numerous buildings, now gathered in the local museum. (Courtesy: Direction de la Promotion, Algiers.)

Another elaborate Christian complex—presumably the orthodox one—lay off the northeast corner of the town. Finally, well to the south of the town and of the large South Baths stood the massive Byzantine fort, built by General Solomon in 539 AD, the finest and best-preserved Byzantine structure in North Africa. Its walls, with eight square towers, enclosed streets, barracks, baths and a chapel. Probes under it revealed, surprisingly, that it had been built over a Severan healing sanctuary with a pool and spring, three temples, porticoes and a water garden. Possibly the sanctuary was built in honor of Septimius Severus himself. South of the fort is a vast Christian necropolis of some 10,000 burials, with a chapel. The small museum, to the north off the *cardo* before it enters the town, contains 500 years' worth of magnificent mosaics found in and around the town.

The remains of an ancient Berber village can be seen about 6 mi. southeast of Timgad, at Ichoukane. Of interest are several megalithic tombs, standing 7 to 9 ft. high, in its cemetery.

TIPASA

Modern seaside resort, highly extolled by Albert Camus, in a lovely setting 37 mi. W. of Algiers. The modern town covers half the site of an ancient town, also called Tipasa, but what is left is tastefully displayed, making the site one of the most interesting and evocative in Algeria. Tipasa was a very early native town and a Punic-Phoenician port of call. Embellished by the cultivated philhellene Juba II, king of Mauretania (about 52 BC–19 AD), one of whose capitals was at *Cherchell* 37 mi. to the west, it came under Roman rule and was made a colony in the 2nd cent. AD. In 146–47 AD, in anticipation of a Moorish attack, it was enclosed within massive walls, heavy enough for a walkway along the top, with 25 towers and three gates. Some of the wall survives. The Vandals took the town in about 470 AD and caused much destruction; but it was rescued by the Byzantines in 534, who left the remains of a small fort; then it fell to the Arabs, who robbed its stones to build Algiers.

Despite such depredations, the extensive excavations have revealed significant remains of ancient Tipasa, much of it now on view in an archaeological park behind the attractive villa-museum, holding fine mosaics and glassware, on the west of the small harbor. Here are the porticoed forum, Capitolium (foundations only), a curia and civil basilica on the western promontory, and the *decumanus* or main street leading southwest between two temples. One of these, the so-called New Temple had a paved courtyard, monumental staircase and portico. Among villas along the seashore was the elegant House of the Frescoes, west of the basilica, partly two-storied, with mosaic floors, frescoed walls, its own baths and dock. It was in use from Antonine to Byzantine times, and in its last phase housed a *garum*—a Roman fish delicacy—factory, with the fish kept in the peristyle pool before being pickled. Left of the *decumanus* was the amphitheater and the remains of a once-elegant nymphaeum built over the end of an aqueduct. It supplied water to the Great Baths, whose brick walls still arise amidst the modern town. Just before the West Gate is the theater, badly stone-robbed.

The Great Basilica (late 4th cent.), one of the largest Christian churches yet found in Algeria, stood on the western cliff of the sea, just inside the walls. Its foundations indicate it had nine aisles, with mosaic floors, a baptistery and ritual baths. Beyond it, outside the walls, the huge West Necropolis with its sarcophagi and catacombs contains the chapel of Bishop Alexander (around 400

Two of the 4th-cent. Christian basilicas in the lovely seaside resort of Tipasa, that of SS Peter and Paul (above), and the earlier basilica of the girl-martyr St. Salsa (below), both on the scenic eastern promontory of the city. Both basilicas are surrounded by many burials, especially that of St. Salsa, where over 500 tombs of the pilgrims crowd closely around the church. Tipasa also boasts extensive Roman ruins and Berber and Punic remains, the latter going back to the 7th cent. BC. (Courtesy: Direction de la Promotion, Algiers.)

AD) with burials that may be those of Tipasa's earliest bishops, a martyr's enclosure higher up, and a large circular martyrium containing 14 tomb niches. On the eastern promontory was another Christian necropolis with two basilicas. The earliest, that of St. Salsa, a girl martyred about 320 AD, whose bones lay in the basilica, was a major goal of pilgrims, and the sarcophagi of the faithful, over 500 of them, cluster closely around the church. More burials surround the mid-4th cent. basilica of SS Peter and Paul.

In the E., above the harbor, there is a Punic mausoleum and necropolis (and other tombs are found west of the harbor), whose excavated grave goods date back to the 6th and 7th cents. BC and include a strong native Berber element.

Interior of the Almoravid Great Mosque of Tlemcen (above). Tlemcen was an early center of Islamic culture in Algeria. Built in 1135 AD, the mosque, with its 13 aisles, bears a close resemblance to that of Cordoba in Spain. The stalactite work in the dome (top right) is the earliest known in the Islamic west. In the 14th cent. the Berber Merinids of Morocco three times occupied the city. Their besieging camp, now in the suburbs, grew into a settlement called Mansoura of which nothing is left but the imposing tall minaret and ruins of the mosque (below). (Courtesy: Direction de la Promotion, Algiers.)

A monumental Berber royal mausoleum, the "Tomb of the Christian Woman," stands on a hill about 6 mi. east of Tipasa. In diameter 203 ft. and 110 ft. high, it is circular like that of *Medracen*, built of dressed stone, with 60 Ionic columns and four false doors below a stepped cylinder. It dates from the 2nd or 1st cent. BC and has an elaborate series of corridors and chambers in its interior.

TLEMCEN

Attractive modern city in a lushly fertile region, once one of the great centers of early Islamic culture, 70 mi. SW of Oran near the Moroccan border. It began as the Roman military post of Pomaria on the *limes*, or frontier defenses. The site now lies about 2½ mi. out from the modern city. On it, in Abbasid times, the first Islamic settlement, called Agadir, was built in 771 AD by Idris I. Only the ruined minaret of his mosque (790) remains there now. In the late 11th cent. the Almoravid ruler Yusuf ibn-Tashfin, founder of *Marrakesh* (see MOROCCO) captured Agadir and founded a new city, Tagrart (now Tlemcen) nearby. In 1145 the Almohads took the city. In the next century, when Almohad power weakened, a Berber dynasty, the Abd el-Wahid of the Zianids, ruled Tlemcen and brought it to its apogee in the 14th cent. as a great Islamic center of 125,000 with a splendid court. Their rule, however, was contested by the Merinids, Berbers of *Fez* (see MOROCCO), who three times occupied the city.

The center of ancient Tlemcen was at the Place du Méchouar where the towers in the northeast corner and the minaret of the present military school date from the original Almoravid palace of Yusuf ibn-Tashfin. Off the central square of modern Tlemcen stands the Great Mosque, somewhat altered, built in 1135 AD by a later Almoravid ruler, its austere beauty and 13 naves bearing a close resemblance to the near contemporary Great Mosque of Cordoba in Spain. In the mihrab dome is the earliest known stalactite decoration in the Islamic west. The brick minaret dates from the 13th cent. On the square, too, is the ornate small mosque of Sidi Ben Hassan (1296 AD), a Zianid creation, which now houses the Museum of Antiquities with some Roman and fine Islamic collections. The besieging Merinids left much in the suburbs from the 14th cent. Of their fortified encampment, which grew into a settlement called Mansoura, only ruins of the mosque and minaret survive. The elegant shrine of Sidi Bou Mediène, with its great bronze-covered doors, has much to admire. The later mosque of Sidi al-Haloui, east, outside the city, is badly restored. In the Sidi Yakoub cemetery are many 11th- and 12th-cents. tombs, including the mausoleum of an Almoravid princess known as the "Sultana's Tomb."

ZANA

Modern town at the site of Roman Diana Veteranorum, 37 mi. NW of Batna in NE Algeria. A municipium and later a colony, it was settled by veterans of the Third Augustan Legion stationed at *Lambaesis* in the same region. The remains, centering around a spacious forum paved with flagstones (on which once stood a Byzantine church, now gone), include two arches, one single, the other triple-arched and well preserved. Dated 217 AD, the latter was dedicated to the emperor Macrinus. A small Byzantine fort was later built onto it. There is a temple of Diana, and a Byzantine fortress with square corner towers. An aqueduct brought water to the town, and several mausoleums can be seen west of the town.

MOROCCO

AÏN DJEMA

See *Volubilis*.

ASILAH

The site of ancient Zilis, on the coast about 20 mi. SE of Tangier and about 7 mi. NE of *Kouass*. It was possibly an Augustan foundation. A temple, baths, houses and traces of a theater have been identified, as well as a defensive wall.

BANASA

Located at Sidi Ali Bou Djenoun, a Roman colony on the left bank of the Sebou River in the interior, about 40 mi. NE of Kenitra. Originally a Mauro-Punic village, it was settled under Augustus (31–25 BC) by veterans of Spanish, Mauretanian and Syrian origin and named Colonia Augusta Valentia Banasa. It was sited on an important military road, part of the local *limes*, or defense line. Its later prosperity, however, came from agriculture and cattle raising. Twice destroyed during the 3rd cent. AD, it was finally abandoned in the second half of that century. Excavations have revealed a grid pattern of streets and insulae, a forum (an entrance arch survives), a market, several temples, including a possible Capitolium with five cellae, at least five bath buildings, shops, houses, and many olive presses and kilns. Its walls, with towers, were built in Severan times. A small military camp lay to the west of the town. Banasa has yielded an unusual number of interesting inscriptions.

BLED TAKOURART

See *Volubilis*.

CASABLANCA

Morocco's largest city and port, a major economic center of fairly recent origin. The only site of archaeological interest lies 6 mi. outside the city along the coast, at Sidi Abd er-Rahman, a quarry site where over half a mile of hillside over 60 ft. high, with caves, has been exposed to reveal an exceptional sequence of Paleolithic remains. In 1955 one cave yielded two fragments of the mandible of a *Homo erectus*, the so-called Casablanca Man, who lived about half a million years ago. These were associated with a working floor of Lower Paleolithic hand axes. The area yielded many such hand axes, some associated with the fossil remains of hippopotamus and rhinoceros, as well as cleavers, large flakes and polyhedral balls similar to those found at Aïn Hanech in ALGERIA. Some weighed as much as 19 pounds.

COTTA
  Or Jibila

See *Tangier*.

DAR ES SOLTAN CAVE

See *Rabat*.

ESSAOUIRA

Modern port city, once called Mogador, way down the Atlantic coast 60 mi. S. of Safi. It was a port of call for Phoenician traders (as well as the Punic explorer, Hanno) from the 7th cent. BC. Juba II, king of Mauretania in Augustan times, set up a factory on an offshore island opposite the town for the making of purple dye from the murex shellfish (huge shell mounds have been found on the mainland)—an old Phoenician specialty. Excavations in 1956–58 on the island, now deserted, turned up fragments of Punic, Attic, Cypriot and Ionian pottery, and

A madrasah, or religious school, in Fez. The ancient city, founded in the 8th cent. AD and known for its dazzling array of Islamic monuments—many of Hispano-Moorish design—has long been the cultural and religious center of Morocco with one of the oldest universities in the world. Fez reached its apogee in the 14th cent. under the Merinids. (Courtesy: Moroccan National Tourist Office.)

uncovered some 20 rooms of a long-lasting Roman villa, with baths and mosaics, that survived from pre-Roman times until the 5th cent. AD. Part of it has been washed into the sea.

FEZ

In French: Fès; ancient Islamic capital city, cupped in hills in a lovely situation on the banks of the Oued Fès, 40 mi. E. of Meknès. It has long been the cultural and religious center of Morocco, with one of the oldest universities in the world. Morocco's first Muslim capital, Fez was founded in 790 AD by Idris I from Baghdad, on the right bank of the river. His son, Idris II, established a new and larger city in 808 on the left bank, called the Andalusian Bank because refugees from Cordoba in Spain had settled there in the 9th cent. Other refugees from *Kairouan* in TUNISIA settled in the older city, called the Kairouan Bank. Under the Almoravids in the mid-11th cent. AD and their successors the Almohads, the two cities were united and Fez became a prosperous trading town and cultural center, in close relations with Moorish Spain. It reached its finest period under the Merinids in the 14th cent. as one of the most important and opulent cities in the Islamic world.

The glorious Islamic monuments of Fez, among them some of the finest surviving examples of Hispano-Moorish architecture and design, are too numerous to list. The vast royal palace, product of eight centuries of building, cannot be entered, and the Kairouan Mosque, dating from 859 and enlarged in the 10th and 12th cents., can only be glimpsed through its outer doorways. It is the oldest in Fez and largest in Morocco. With its attendant madrasahs, or religious schools (the earliest is the al-Seffarin of the 13th cent.), it forms the center of the ancient Kairouan University, still flourishing after 1,100 years. There are also the Merinid madrasahs and mosques, and on the other side of the river the Mosque of the Andalusians, founded in 861 and rebuilt in the 13th cent., with another madrasah. The northern section of the far-flung walls dates from the Almohad period, with the gates built under the Merinids. The best view of this most Muslim of cities can be obtained from the Merinid tombs on a hill above it. See also *Marrakesh*.

GOUR, EL-

In full, Souk el-Jemaa el-Gour; Berber mausoleum about 19 mi. SE of Meknès, dated to the 7th cent. AD. A somewhat Romanized mausoleum, undoubtedly of a Berber notable, it consists of a round cylinder of dressed stone standing on a platform and topped by a low cone. It seems to belong to the same traditional Berber monument style found in ALGERIA at *Medracen* and *Tipasa*, though these are earlier in date. See also *Tiaret*.

KOUASS

A port about 20 mi. SW of Tangier, once a Punic port that manufactured and exported amphorae to places such as Corinth in Greece and the Cadiz area in Spain. Many amphorae and 10 kilns dating from the 6th to 1st cents. BC have been found here. As the site of a later Roman town, Kouass is also known for the 40 surviving arches of its aqueduct, and a Roman blockhouse.

LARACHE

Modern port city 45 mi. SW of Tangier, NW Morocco. Some 2 mi. to the NE, on a hill above the marshy Loukkos River a few miles in from the coast, is the partially excavated site of Lixus, oldest dated town in Morocco, associated in mythology with Hercules and the Garden of the Hesperides. Like *Utica* in TUNISIA, its traditional date of founding was 1100 BC, but nothing earlier than the 6th or 7th cents. has been found. House foundations and a temple date from the 3rd and 2nd cents. BC and the town wall probably from the 1st cent. AD when it became a Roman colony under Claudius. A sacred precinct atop the acropolis contained no less than eight temples. There was a theater, later converted into a small amphitheater, with baths of Severan date adjoining it, and in the lower town a large *garum* factory (a fish delicacy) with 50 vats. This was in use from the 1st to the 4th cents. AD. Several large Roman houses have yielded mosaics (now in the *Tetuan* museum) and bronze statues.

LIXUS	See *Larache*.
MARRAKESH	Traditional capital of the south; a lively and fascinating Saharan city at the northern foot of the High Atlas, 130 mi. S. of Casablanca. Often in competition with *Fez*, the Islamic capital of the north, it began as a fortified kasbah set up in 1062 AD by Abu Bakr, who was soon replaced by the long-lived founder of the Berber Almoravid dynasty, Yusuf ibn-Tashfin. By the time of Tashfin's death in 1106 the Almoravids, heading a reforming militaristic group of desert tribes, ruled over an empire stretching from Senegal to Andalusia in Spain. Of this Almoravid period little is left in Marrakesh. The mosque built by ibn-Tashfin, excavated in the mid-20th cent., has disappeared. His son, Ali ibn-Yusuf (1107–43), first developed Marrakesh into a city. In 1130 he built the earliest version of the impressive ramparts, still mostly surviving—9 mi. in circuit, 15 ft. high, with gates and bastions. His mosque, too, has disappeared—all except a remarkable kiosk or pavilion attached to it, the Kouba al-Baroudiyin, a two-storied structure close to the later Ben Yusuf mosque and the huge 16th-cent. madrasah in the present medina. It was rediscovered in 1947 in clearing the area and now lies over 15 ft. below the present ground level.

The Almoravids were overthrown by the Almohads, a similar desert movement, whose leader, Abd al-Mumin, captured Marrakesh in 1147. Eventually the Almohads were to dominate most of North Africa and southern Spain. Outstanding among their monuments is the Koutoubia mosque with its great minaret. Originally built by al-Mumin in 1158, the mosque was completely rebuilt by his successor a few years later. It is not open to the public. The great minaret, dominating the city, is 40 ft. sq. and stands 220 ft. high, and is much like the Hassan Tower in *Rabat* and the Giralda in Seville, Spain. Built of sandstone and tastefully decorated with interlacing patterns, with a domed cupola on top, it was finished by al-Mumin's grandson, Yakub al-Mansur, in 1190. Al-Mansur also built a splendid kasbah containing 12 palaces with pleasure gardens. Of this only the monumental gateway, the Bab Agnaou, survives. Many other fine monuments, dating from later times and thus outside our period, are on view in Marrakesh, which suffered an eclipse when it was captured in 1269 by the Merinid Abu Yakub. It was to revive again in the 16th cent. for another golden period under the Saadians. The Dar Si Said palace houses the Museum of Moroccan Arts.

MOGADOR	See *Essaouira*.
QASR ES-SEGIR	Meaning "small castle," an interesting small fortified site on the Moroccan coast facing Spain, 27 mi. E. of Tangier. Here in the 8th cent. was the staging area for the Islamic conquest of Spain across the waters, and later it became a busy port, shipping supplies across the straits. The Portuguese, whose citadel dominates the site, took over in 1458 and held the town for nearly 100 years, when it was abandoned. Excavations in the walled town, begun in 1974, delved beneath the Portuguese levels to uncover much early Islamic work and many small finds from both periods, including defensive walls with two gate complexes. Inside the walls were the remains of a mosque (under the Portuguese church), a *hammam*, or public bath, marketplace, and narrow winding lanes bordered by houses with plastered or tiled courtyards, each with its own latrine.

The ancient Almohad walls of Rabat, now the capital of Morocco. The walls were originally 10 mi. long with five gates, and much is still standing. Rabat was originally two towns on opposite banks of the Regreg River, with Salé, a fortified port, across from Rabat proper. Both towns were built over the ruins of Roman Sala, much of which has been identified and excavated. (Courtesy: Moroccan National Tourist Office.)

RABAT

Modern capital of Morocco, at the mouth of the Bou Regreg on the Atlantic coast, 55 mi. NE of Casablanca. Briefly an important town in the 12th cent. under the early Almohads, it was not much more than a village thereafter until 1913, when it became the capital. In the intervening period its neighboring fortified town across the Regreg River, Salé, prospered as a commercial port and home of the Salé pirates (who captured Defoe's Robinson Crusoe!). Both towns covered parts of the site of Roman Sala, originally a Punic foundation and a prosperous town under the Mauretanian kings, then a Roman municipium and colony from the 1st cent. AD through the times of Constantine. The remains of Sala have been excavated (see below), but nothing remains above ground. Far earlier, the area, like *Casablanca*, was inhabited by prehistoric man.

The Rabat suburb of Chellah, which lies outside the Almohad walls. A Merinid cemetery with lovely gardens, ruined mosques and tombs, it covers the remains of the center of Roman Sala. Some Roman work can be seen here in front of and below the delapidated minaret tower. (Courtesy: Moroccan National Tourist Office.)

Rabat began with a 10th-cent. *ribat*, or monastic stronghold, on the river. This was seized from the Almoravids by Abd al-Mumin, the first Almohad, in 1146, and was used as a base for his Spanish wars against the Christians there. His grandson, Yakub al-Mansur, really founded the city, building the great walls, originally 10 mi. long, much still standing with five gates surviving, and a palace on the present Kasbah of the Oudaias, site of the original *ribat*. Only the magnificent fortified ceremonial entrance to the palace, comparable to his Bab Agnaou in *Marrakesh*, still stands. He also began an enormous mosque, left unfinished at his death in 1199 and now in ruins. Its huge tower-minaret, the Tour Hassan, with walls 8 ft. thick, now dominates Rabat. It is 53 ft. square and 144 ft. high and compares with his tall Koutoubia tower in Marrakesh. Salé, now part of Rabat, lies across the river. Once the port of Roman Sala, it is surrounded by 14th-cent. Merinid walls with several gates, notably the 13th-cent. watergate, the Bab Mrisa. Inside the walls is the Great Mosque, begun in the 12th cent. by the second Almohad, and near it the Madrasah el-Hassan, built in 1341 and now restored. Its arcaded courtyard resembles the famous Court of the Lions of the same period in the Alhambra in Granada, Spain.

The center of Roman Sala seems to have been in Chellah, to the SE outside the Almohad walls of Rabat, now a walled Merinid cemetery of the 14th cent. with lovely gardens, a ruined mosque, royal tombs and restored *hammam* or bath of the period. Excavations here and along the walls identified the agora and temples of Mauretanian Sala in Augustan times, and above the Mauretanian levels the Roman forum, Trajanic curia, basilica, a Capitolium, arch, baths, shops and a circuit wall—the appurtenances of a typical Roman town—as well as several necropolises.

Important finds of the Paleolithic period have also been found in the Rabat region. Fragments of the bones of a *Homo erectus* male from the upper Paleolithic levels—so-called Rabat Man—turned up in 1933 in a quarry south of the city, and excavations in the cave of Dar es Soltan, 4 mi. southwest on the coast, revealed Paleolithic tools of the Aterian type (see B*ir el-Ater*, ALGERIA), later tools of the Oranian period, and many tools and decorated impressed pottery fragments from the Neolithic—some of it resembling the Early Bronze Age bell-beakers of Spain. The small Archaeological Museum houses the Sala finds and a rich collection of bronzes from *Volubilis* and nearby sites.

SALA   See *Rabat*.

SIDI ABD ER RAHMAN   See *Casablanca*.

SOUK EL-JEMAA EL-GOUR   See *El-Gour*.

TAMUDA   See *Tetuan*.

TANGIER   Ancient city facing Gibraltar across the straits. Held by the English for 23 years (17th cent.), later an international territory until 1956, Tangier's crowded medieval medina, topped by the Kasbah, or citadel, rising over the small harbor, has given many a tourist his first glimpse of the true Orient. Unfortunately the once-important Roman provincial town of Tingis lies buried under both. The Petit Socco square in the heart of the medina was probably its forum, the main street now leading west its *Decumanus Maximus*, and the baths lie under the Kasbah. Tingis had a Punic background, became an Augustan foundation in 38 BC, a colony under Claudius and later the capital of Roman Mauretania Tingitana. Over 100 Roman sites have been reported in its territory, including working villas and necropolises. The town went through the usual Vandal and Byzantine periods, was captured by the Visigoths in 621 and by the Arabs in 682 AD, and was thereafter a Moorish town until the Portuguese occupied it in 1471.

Cape Sartel lies 9 mi. southwest of Tangier. Below its lighthouse, at Cotta (or Jibila) are the impressive remains of a large *garum* factory (the Roman fish delicacy) with deep vats for the salting of the fish, workshops, an oil press, a house, baths and a cemetery. A few miles south of the cape, important Paleolithic finds have been made at the Caves of Hercules (open to the public), facing a wide Atlantic beach. Here, among other finds, fragments of the maxilla (jaw bones) of a child of Neanderthal type were discovered in 1939.

TETUAN   Administrative capital of the Rif, a few mi. inland from the Mediterranean, 29 mi. SE of Tangier. The city, founded in 1310, was settled in the 16th cent. by Jewish and Muslim refugees from Spain, and with its gardens and foundations still retains a distinctly Andalusian character. The ruins of its predecessor, Tamuda, originally a Punic settlement, lie on the slopes of the Djebel Dersa 3 mi. southwest of the city. Excavations here from 1921 to 1958 investigated the pre-Roman town with poorly built houses of mud or adobe of the 2nd or 1st cents. BC, which were nevertheless built on a regular grid of streets in the Hellenistic manner. Around the 2nd cent. AD the Romans built a large camp here, walled, with 20 towers and four gates. A necropolis, with Roman tombs overlying Punic ones, has been excavated. The local museum contains finds from Tamuda, and from Lixus (see *Larache*).

THAMUSIDA

Roman town on the banks of the Sebou River 8 mi. N. of Kenitra, partially excavated since 1932. Its native name is Sidi Ali Ben Ahmed. There was a small native-Punic settlement on the site (2nd cent. BC), and the language was still Punic in Roman times when the town had been settled largely by Roman veterans. Most of the ruins were Antonine; the town was destroyed in the 3rd cent. AD. Outside it was an unusually large military camp, accommodating 1,000 men, constructed in the reign of Marcus Aurelius (161–180 AD). It had walls with 18 towers and the usual four gates, as well as a colonnaded main street. Inside it, barracks have been identified and the *praetorium*, or headquarters, excavated. Beside the *praetorium* and on part of its court a much later basilica was built in 250–270 AD. The town itself was enclosed within a circuit wall, slightly later than the camp, with semicircular towers. Within it 17 insulae or blocks have been excavated, revealing a temple and only one major house, with a peristyle and 22 rooms (about 150 AD). This modest army town, however, had its Great Baths outside the walls, with 59 rooms, also a quarter on the river front, only partially excavated, with a large warehouse and three temples. Thamusida also had a factory for the production of *garum*, a fish sauce popular throughout the Roman Empire.

TINGIS

See *Tangier*.

TOCOLOSIDA

See *Volubilis*.

VOLUBILIS

The finest Roman site in Morocco, situated on a fertile plateau at the foot of the Zerhoun Mountains, 12 mi. N. of Meknès. Volubilis was a flourishing Libyo-Punic town as early as the 3rd and 2nd cents. BC. A massive tumulus still lying in the center of the ruins today was probably the long-revered burial mound of an early native chief, and Punic-style temples, notably the impressively large so-called Temple of Saturn just inside the Roman walls, have been detected under later work. Many Punic-style stelae have been found. The town was enlarged under the long-reigning, Greek-educated Juba II—after 25 BC Augustus' client king of Mauretania (see *Cherchell*, ALGERIA), and may have been his western capital. Taken over by Rome in 40 AD, the town remained throughout this period and beyond it a small polyglot settlement of some 10 to 12,000 Libyo-Punic, Spanish, Syrian, and Jewish inhabitants with a distinct Hellenistic cast, probably imparted by Juba II. As the administrative seat of Roman Mauretania Tingitana, Volubilis saw much rebuilding and embellishment in the early 3rd cent. AD, the Severan period, when a new northeastern residential quarter was established within a new wide circuit of walls (2nd cent.) with eight gates and 34 towers. These replaced the earlier shorter Hellenistic walls, traces of which have been uncovered. Most of the extant ruins, excavated since 1915, belong to this period.

Part of the extensive ruins of Roman Volubilis, finest in Morocco, dating largely from the 2nd and 3rd cent. AD when it was the capital of Mauretania Tingitana. A very ancient city, Volubilis was earlier a small Libyo-Punic town dating back to the 3rd cent. BC, later Hellenized and enlarged by the cultivated monarch Juba II; but even in its most flourishing period under the empire, it still held a strong Punic flavor. (Courtesy: Moroccan National Tourist Office.)

Volubilis suffered severe attacks from native tribes in the 2nd and 3rd cents. AD and was finally abandoned by Rome between 274 and 280. However, Romanized Berbers long maintained a Roman life-style in the city, which was later occupied by Idris I in 788 and again by refugees from Spain in the 10th cent. Thereafter it disappeared from history.

The older, Hellenistic, town lay in the southern quarter, with Juba II's enlargement (mostly unexcavated) to the southwest. In the Severan period the quarter was rebuilt, with a new forum flanked by a magnificent civil basilica. Over the older forum and temples to the south, a large Capitolium temple was built on a high podium, and the forum baths. Volubilis had three baths, this, the Gallienus, and the North Baths, the largest. The new quarter to the northeast boasted a wide *Decumanus Maximus* with sidewalks, porticoes and arcades, leading from the new single Arch of Caracalla (217 AD)—of which little is left but the core and some columns—to the so-called Tangier Gate in the walls. Along it 23 luxurious houses have been excavated—Greek style, with courtyards, gardens and peristyles and many fine mosaics, some still in situ. The Roman-Berber owners made their wealth from the export of oil—10 of the houses include oil-pressing rooms—and did not disdain to include shops in front or behind their houses—121 shops have been found. A bakery lies beside the forum.

Near the top of the *decumanus* is the so-called Palace of Gordian—probably the governor's residence—two houses thrown together with 74 rooms and its own baths, oil presses and shops. Other large houses lie around the arch and in the older quarter, all named for their mosaics, statues or other features: House of the Columns, of the Ephebe, of the Horseman. The House of Orpheus in the old quarter had its own baths and a cypress-planted garden. The finest is the House of Venus, with mosaics in eight rooms and seven corridors and its

A fine mosaic in the House of Orpheus, one of 23 luxurious town villas excavated along the wide Decumanus Maximus or main street of Volubilis. Courtyards, peristyles and gardens graced these comfortable houses, and in the case of the House of Orpheus, central underfloor heating, its own baths and a garden adorned with cypresses—and a room for pressing olive oil, source of the Berber-Roman owner's wealth. In the mosaic Orpheus sits at the center with his lyre, trying to charm a set of very African, and rather indifferent, beasts. (Courtesy: Moroccan National Tourist Office.)

own large baths. In or near it were found two superb bronze busts, of Cato the Younger and the "Hellenistic Prince," possibly Juba II—for Volubilis was a noted center for bronzes. The House of the Labors of Hercules had 41 rooms and eight shops. The finds, mosaics and bronzes, are in a local museum and in *Rabat*.

In the fertile area around Volubilis 64 sites are known, including working villas, quarries and small forts. At Bled Takourart, ancient Tocolosida, 3 mi. south, is a large fort on the *limes* (2nd cent. AD), which held Syrian and Gallic cavalry. Remains of another fort of the same period are found at Aïn Djema, 12 mi. southwest of Volubilis, with traces of a civilian settlement around it.

ZILIS

See *Asilah*.

Index

Boldface numbers indicate main essay.